Rethinking Mexican Indigenismo

Rethinking Mexican Indigenismo

THE INI'S COORDINATING CENTER
IN HIGHLAND CHIAPAS AND
THE FATE OF A UTOPIAN PROJECT

Stephen E. Lewis

University of New Mexico Press Albuquerque

© 2018 by the University of New Mexico Press
All rights reserved. Published 2018
Printed in the United States of America

First paperback edition, 2020
Paperback ISBN: 978-0-8263-6151-6

Library of Congress Cataloging-in-Publication Data
Names: Lewis, Stephen E., 1967– author.
Title: Rethinking Mexican Indigenismo: The INI's Coordinating Center in Highland Chiapas and the Fate of a Utopian Project / Stephen E. Lewis.
Description: Albuquerque: University of New Mexico Press, 2018. | Includes bibliographical references and index. |
Identifiers: LCCN 2017015016 (print) | LCCN 2017050849 (e-book) | ISBN 9780826359032 (e-book) | ISBN 9780826359025 (printed case: alk. paper)
Subjects: LCSH: Centro Coordinador Indigenista Tzeltal—Tzotzil—History—20th century. | Tzeltal Indians—Mexico—Chiapas Highlands—Government relations. | Tzeltal Indians—Mexico—Chiapas Highlands—Politics and government—20th century. | Tzotzil Indians—Mexico—Chiapas Highlands—Government relations. | Tzotzil Indians—Mexico—Chiapas Highlands—Politics and government—20th century. | Instituto Nacional Indigenista (Mexico)—History—20th century. | Indians of Mexico—Politics and government—20th century. | Chiapas Highlands (Mexico)—Race relations. | Indians of Mexico—Government relations.
Classification: LCC F1221.T8 (e-book) | LCC F1221.T8 L49 2018 (print) | DDC 305.897/42807275—dc23
LC record available at https://lccn.loc.gov/2017015016

Cover photo: Indigenistas with ejidatarios in Chanal explaining the benefits of a plan to exploit their forest reserves. Photographer unknown.
Fototeca Nacho López, Comisión Nacional para el Desarrollo de los Pueblos Indígenas. 1963.
Designed by Felicia Cedillos
Cover designed by Catherine Leonardo

Composed in Minion Pro 10.25/13.5

*To the memory of my mom, Betty Lewis,
and to Owen, who might someday appreciate
his dad's fascination with Mexico and its people.*

Contents

List of Illustrations   ix

Acknowledgments   xiii

Introduction   1

Part 1 The Utopian Project

CHAPTER 1 **Dramatis Personae**
　　　　　The Indigenous, Ladinos, and Indigenistas   17

CHAPTER 2 **Negotiating Indigenismo**
　　　　　The Bilingual Cultural Promoter   41

CHAPTER 3 **Utopian Dreams and the *Mística Indigenista***   63

Part 2 Sober Realities

CHAPTER 4 **Winning the Battle, Losing the War**
　　　　　The INI versus the Pedrero Alcohol Monopoly   91

CHAPTER 5 **Take Two**
　　　　　The INI Charts a More Modest Course   113

CHAPTER 6 **Modernizing Message, Mystical Messenger**
　　　　　The Many Uses of the Teatro Petul   133

CHAPTER 7 **Medical Pluralism and the Limits of
　　　　　INI Health Programs**   155

CHAPTER 8 **From Innovation to Administration**
The Coordinating Center's Very Long Decade, 1958–1970   175

CHAPTER 9 **Did the INI Promote Caciquismo?**   205

Part 3 Crisis, Rekindled Populism, and
the Fate of Mexican Indigenismo

CHAPTER 10 **The Generation of 1968, the Critique of Mexican
Anthropology, and the INI's Response**   227

CHAPTER 11 **Indigenismo and the Populist Resurgence (1970–1976)**   245

Conclusion   265

Notes   279
References   319
Index   337

Illustrations

Maps
- I.1 Chiapas regions. 9
- 1.1 The Pan-American Highway in the early 1950s. 35
- 8.1 The INI's area of operations in the early 1960s. 177

Figures
- 1.1 CCI director Julio de la Fuente handing out diplomas in San Cristóbal, 1952. 32
- 1.2 CCI director Agustín Romano Delgado's identification card, 1963. 33
- 1.3 Marianna Slocum and Florence Gerdel in Oxchuc, circa 1955. 38
- 2.1 Bilingual mathematics lesson in an INI primer. 45
- 2.2 Making roofing tiles at La Cabaña, circa 1956. 48
- 2.3 CCI director Julio de la Fuente and education director Fidencio Montes Sánchez at a school event, 1952. 50
- 2.4 Two of the INI's first education promoters, 1951. 54
- 3.1 CCI director Ricardo Pozas promoting cooperatives, 1953. 71
- 3.2 Two men working at a consumer cooperative, circa 1960. 77
- 3.3 Dr. Roberto Robles Garnica chatting with men from Huixtán, circa 1956. 82
- 4.1 A woman speaking to her intoxicated husband, Tenejapa, 1956. 94
- 4.2 An INI employee working at the INI's bottling plant at La Cabaña, circa 1952. 112
- 5.1 Men clearing a road, circa 1960. 117
- 5.2 Applying pesticides or herbicides at one of the INI's experimental fields, circa 1965. 119
- 5.3 Man with pig, circa 1955. 120

x   Illustrations

5.4   Agapito Núñez Tom with students at La Libertad, circa 1960.   122
6.1   A Teatro Petul performance, late 1950s.   138
6.2   Women and children in El Roblar, Pantelhó, circa 1965.   144
6.3   Children enjoying the Teatro Petul in Romerillo, Chamula, on the Día del Niño, 1968.   149
6.4   A behind-the-scenes look at a puppet show in Belisario Domínguez, Chenalhó, 1958.   151
7.1   Boys in Tenejapa viewing the Teatro Petul during a DDT campaign against head lice, 1955.   161
7.2a & 7.2b   DDT powder being applied directly onto bodies and scalps, circa 1960.   162
7.3   Chamulan boys just vaccinated by INI nurses, circa 1955.   164
7.4   Men investigating a water tank, circa 1960.   167
8.1   Education promoters about to depart for Oaxaca City in summer 1963.   183
8.2   Girls dining at the INI's boarding school, late 1960s.   184
8.3a & 8.3b   Francisca Gómez López and Manuela Sánchez Gómez, two of the first *promotoras* to work for the Coordinating Center, 1963.   185
8.4   Alfonso Caso inaugurating the sawmill at Yashtinin (Las Casas), 1961.   194
8.5   Ejidatarios working at their sawmill in Yashtinin, 1961.   194
9.1   Oxchuc's transportation cooperative, 1963.   211
10.1   President Luis Echeverría listening to INI director Gonzalo Aguirre Beltrán at a meeting of the INI's Council of Directors, September 1971.   234
10.2   INI director Aguirre Beltrán and Salomón Nahmad Sittón, circa 1974.   239
11.1   The short-lived School of Regional Development, 1972.   252
C.1   Girls at an INI school, 1968.   271

Tables

2.1   INI anthropologists compare SEP and state schools with INI Literacy Centers, circa 1955.   53
3.1   Research questionnaire for the barrios of San Cristóbal de Las Casas.   66

4.1	The development of the aguardiente monopoly in Chiapas, 1948–1954. 97
6.1	Content for Teatro Petul performances. 140
7.1	The major campaigns of the CCI's health division. 165
7.2	The CCI's medical infrastructure in 1967. 173
8.1	Enrollment growth in INI schools in highland Chiapas. 182
8.2	Attendance by grade level at the start of the 1960 school year. 182
8.3	Students enrolled at the CCI's boarding school at La Cabaña. 184
8.4	Investment plans for forest ejidos in Chiapas, 1971. 197
9.1	Municipal presidents, 1968–1979. 210
10.1	The proliferation of INI Coordinating Centers. 243
C.1	Chiapas's poorest municipalities in 2011. 270

Acknowledgments

This book took a decade to research and write, and I gladly take this opportunity to recognize the many intellectual and personal debts that I have incurred along the way.

I begin by thanking Jan and Diane Rus for twenty years of support and friendship. Jan took me on as an unofficial "advisee" in the mid-1990s, long before he began advising his own doctoral students at the Centro de Estudios Superiores de México y Centroamérica (CESMECA) in San Cristóbal de Las Casas, Chiapas. His passion for the Chiapas highlands inspired me to write this monograph. Jan is extremely generous with his time and made extensive comments on the final draft of this manuscript. Diane also read and commented on the final draft and provided encouragement along the way. Naturally, I am responsible for any remaining errors and oversights.

In Mexico City, I am indebted to Margarita Sosa Suárez, who for years was the historian's most helpful advocate at the Biblioteca Juan Rulfo at the Instituto Nacional Indigenista/Comisión Nacional para el Desarrollo de Pueblos Indígenas (INI/CDI). As Subdirectora de Documentación y Catalogación, Margarita oversaw and improved the CDI's library, its document collection, and its incredible photo archive. In 2014, Margarita took her talents to the Fonoteca Nacional. I am grateful that she and Martín González Solano remain as interested in the history of Mexican indigenismo as I am. The conversation continues.

I also acknowledge the support and encouragement of Ángel Baltazar Caballero, who first introduced me to the INI back in 1993 and has taken great interest in my work ever since. He, Alfredo Ortíz Martínez, and Maura Tapia cheerfully fulfilled my countless requests for information at the Biblioteca Juan Rulfo. Silvia Gómez Díaz and Sergio Luis Contreras were instrumental in helping me find and reproduce the beautiful photogrhaphs in this volume. The Fototeca Nacho López at the Biblioteca Juan Rulfo is truly a national treasure.

Further afield, I thank my colleague Laura Giraudo of the Consejo Superior de Investigaciones Científicas (CSIC)'s Escuela de Estudios Hispano-Americanos in Seville, Spain. Laura has created a vibrant international network of indigenismo scholars and has encouraged me (and others) to participate in projects and publications. Laura and her husband, Juan Martín Sánchez, have hosted multiple conferences and continue to amaze with their devotion to their research and to the intellectual community that they have nurtured.

Archival research trips to Mexico City were made much more enjoyable thanks to my ex-*caseros*, Juan Manuel Maldonado and Alejandra Pons, and their two great kids, Vania and Baruch. Another loyal friend has been Mariam Yitani Baroudi, who for twenty years has been an insightful interlocutor about contemporary Mexico and life in general. Federico Morales Barragán has offered intellectual support and friendship for nearly as long. My semester in Puebla in 2009 became much more interesting and enjoyable after he introduced me to Cariño Paredes and José de Jesús Torres Sánchez. To these great lifelong friends, *un fuerte abrazo*.

In San Cristóbal de Las Casas, I owe a profound debt of gratitude to another friend of twenty years, Justus Fenner. Justus supervised the archival recovery project that opened the archive of the INI's first Coordinating Center to public consultation. I was fortunate enough to be among the first to use this archive. I also thank Juan Blasco López and Juan Pedro Viqueira for their support at key junctures. Just as important to my research in Chiapas is Vicky Jiménez Cruz, who for many years has offered me a room, a workspace, and steady friendship. At the INI archive at La Cabaña, Armando Ruiz helped me find documents and photos, and at the historical archive of the Secretaría de Pueblos Indios in San Cristóbal, Minerva Ramos Penagos cheerfully supported my requests for documents.

North of the US-Mexico border, Alec Dawson continues to set the standard with his innovative work on indigenismo and indigenous people. He read this manuscript for the University of New Mexico Press and made several comments that surely improved the final product. I have also benefited from my conversations with A. Shane Dillingham, who made several key observations on the book's conclusion. Tanalís Padilla, Susan Fitzpatrick-Behrens, and Mary Kay Vaughan also commented on chapters, and Jacob Rus customized the three maps in this book. I also thank friends and colleagues who have joined me on panels at American Historical Association (AHA), Latin American Studies Association (LASA), and Rocky Mountain Council for Latin American Studies (RMCLAS) conferences and offered insightful feedback.

At California State University, Chico, a David E. Lantis University Professorship in 2007–2008, a Summer Scholars grant in 2011, and a semester-long sabbatical in 2012 helped me research and write this book. Additional support was provided by the INTERINDI project "El indigenismo interamericano: instituciones, redes y proyectos para un continente, 1940–1960" (HAR2008-03099/HIST, 2009–2010) and the RE-INTERINDI project "Los reversos del indigenismo" (HAR2013-41596-P, 2014–2017), both projects coordinated by Laura Giraudo (Escuela de Estudios Hispano-Americanos at the CSIC) in Seville.

At the University of New Mexico Press, I thank editor Clark Whitehorn, a model of patience and good humor. His team at the University of New Mexico Press expertly guided the book to the finish line. I am also indebted to Norman Ware, who meticulously copyedited this manuscript.

My colleagues at Chico State have provided me with a welcoming and supportive work environment ever since my arrival in August 1998. I am also grateful to my history and Latin American studies students. Their spirited engagement and feedback have helped me clarify and hone my thoughts over the years. Last of all, Jessica Vandehoven read the entire manuscript and serves as my most immediate and trusted sounding board for my ideas. She and I are both relieved to see this project finally materialize!

Introduction

●◉◎ IN LATE 1994, months after the Zapatista Army of National Liberation (Ejército Zapatista de Liberación Nacional, or EZLN) rebelled against the Mexican government and drew attention to the plight of Mexico's indigenous peoples, roughly twenty allied indigenous peasant organizations seized the Tzeltal-Tzotzil Indigenista Coordinating Center (Centro Coordinador Indigenista Tzeltal-Tzotzil, or CCI) in San Cristóbal de Las Casas, Chiapas. This Coordinating Center had been opened by Mexico's National Indigenist Institute (Instituto Nacional Indigenista, or INI) in 1951, and its seizure and subsequent occupation were highly symbolic. It had been the INI's first and most important center, and its first directors included some of Mexico's most renowned *indigenistas*, as the practitioners of federal Indian policy were known. In spite of the opposition of Chiapas state governors, the state's alcohol monopoly, local ranchers, and many indigenous themselves, this particular Coordinating Center was hailed as a success at modernizing the indigenous and integrating them into the modern Mexican nation-state. The INI eventually built more than one hundred Coordinating Centers throughout the Mexican countryside. Despite the INI's work, however, most indigenous Mexicans in 1994 remained economically destitute and politically marginalized. By seizing this particular Coordinating Center at this time, the invaders made an emphatic statement—Mexico's postrevolutionary Indian policy, whatever its past merits, had failed.

The leaders who organized the take-over of this center issued a communiqué that spoke to the controversial trajectory of Indian policy in Mexico. "Rulers of the last five decades, we thank what some of you tried to preserve of our culture, and we very much lament the great failures of the development projects with our people," they wrote. "While you worked to integrate us into Western society, our roots dug deeper into the heart of our mother earth. Therefore, all attempts to disappear us or acculturate us failed." The occupiers also thanked "all of the indigenistas who sincerely wanted to work with us. For them, there will always be a place in our hearts." But they added: "We will also not forget the racist indigenistas, because their projects to crush the Indians never triumphed." The communiqué closed on a sarcastic note. It told the Coordinating Center's employees to begin packing their bags. The peasant organizations wished them a happy holiday season "and the longest vacations of their lives," because starting in January 1995 they would occupy all of the INI's buildings in Chiapas.[1] They relinquished control of the Coordinating Center's buildings several years later, but land-starved indigenous peasants still occupy and have built shacks on the compound's experimental fields.

Why was the INI's most celebrated Coordinating Center, the hallmark of Mexico's postrevolutionary indigenismo, seized and held by the very people that it was supposed to help? If the center had been such a "success," why were Tseltals and Tsotsils[2] still living in misery more than forty years after it first opened its doors? Lastly, who were the "good" indigenistas to whom the occupiers referred, and who were the "racists?"

This book evaluates the complex trajectory of Mexican indigenismo through a close examination of the INI's pilot Coordinating Center in highland Chiapas. Historically, remote Chiapas has often been on the margins of national trends, but when it comes to Indian policy, precisely the opposite is true. The CCI in Chiapas was the first to test the INI's often innovative development programs. It was also the first to confront ferocious local opposition, which prevented the INI from accomplishing broader structural changes in Chiapas and across Mexico. The malaise that struck the INI was first felt in Chiapas, and the deepening crisis in the 1960s slowly crippled operations in Chiapas before most of the other centers had even opened.

Chiapas briefly resumed its place at the vanguard of Mexican indigenismo in the early 1970s. After a new generation of anthropologists launched a devastating critique of Mexican anthropology and indigenismo, the INI responded by opening an innovative School of Regional Development (Escuela de Desarrollo Regional, or EDR) in 1971 on the grounds of the CCI in San Cristóbal. Viewed in hindsight, this school represented the INI's last great opportunity to reclaim bragging rights as the hemisphere-wide leader in indigenista policy. But the INI fired the school's director in late 1972 after she charted a new course that would have empowered indigenous leaders and encouraged ethnic self-determination. Ultimately, the INI was made irrelevant by the indigenous themselves, who advanced more radical agendas outside of the confines of Mexico's discredited corporatist state.

In 1994, the Chiapas highlands once again reshaped national Indian policy. When the Zapatistas briefly seized San Cristóbal and other towns and forced the federal government to negotiate autonomy and the role of indigenous cultures in contemporary Mexican society, they forced the final crisis of Mexican indigenismo. Embattled president Ernesto Zedillo (1994–2000) announced the dissolution of the INI in 1996, but the institute languished until 2003, when president Vicente Fox replaced it with the decentralized National Commission for the Development of Indigenous Peoples (Comisión Nacional para el Desarrollo de los Pueblos Indígenas, or CDI).[3]

Defining a Phenomenon

Indigenismo was a complex, often contradictory political and cultural movement. It typically celebrated an abstract notion of indigenous people and culture located securely in the past, but it also called for the modernization, assimilation, and "improvement" of living, breathing *indígenas*. Practitioners were typically non-Indians. The indigenista movement assumed its pan-American, institutional form in 1940 when delegates from nineteen countries met in Pátzcuaro, Mexico, and created the Interamerican Indigenist Institute (Instituto Indigenista Interamericano, or III). Each of the signatory countries pledged to create its own national indigenist institute and carry out the III's rather contradictory mission—to study and promote ways to improve the lives of the indigenous on the one hand, and to "uphold and defend their cultural particularities" on the other.[4] The III was formally constituted two years later and was based in Mexico City.

For the next thirty-plus years, there were nearly as many indigenismos as there were indigenistas. At one end of the spectrum, some indigenistas had no interest in indigenous languages and cultures and sought merely to "incorporate" Indians into the modern economic and political mainstream. At the other end, others not only sought to preserve indigenous languages, they also called for indigenous autonomy and self-determination. Indigenistas did not necessarily maintain fixed positions on this ideological spectrum. Mexico's Moisés Sáenz, who helped organize the Pátzcuaro conference, had been an assimilationist in the 1920s but became a pluralist in the 1930s and vigorously defended the value of indigenous languages and cultures.[5] Sáenz's vision of a politically and socially militant indigenismo failed to take root, however. For a variety of reasons, a gradualist, "apolitical," and "scientific" indigenismo took root throughout the Americas. The claim of being apolitical was initially useful to gain legitimacy and avoid confrontations, especially in a Cold War context. And the claim of being scientific—that is, using scientific tools to solve social problems—was associated with the rising importance of applied anthropology as a discipline and implied a certain degree of clinical detachment.[6]

In the best of times, indigenistas proposed and shaped policy. But more often than not, they lacked access to power and financial resources. Rarely did indigenistas offer radical solutions. And when they did, they confronted tenacious opposition and were usually forced to back down. Indigenismo's failure to overturn exploitative political and economic systems led to projects that attempted to induce cultural change in the indigenous themselves. These met with less opposition and were easier to implement.[7] What began as a radical, antiracist critique of the status quo in the 1920s and 1930s evolved into a tool and a discourse that equated progress with acculturation to European ways and legitimized new hierarchies.[8] Indigenismo went "from being oppositional and minoritarian to dominant and hegemonic," writes Estelle Tarica. Its legacy is contradictory, owing to indigenismo's "challenge to the status quo and its enduring presence within the status quo; its assertion of both Indian difference and of interethnic affinity and affiliation; [and] its framing of an Indian object and its search for a new kind of non-Indian subject."[9] History's verdict has not been kind.

INDIGENISMO IN MEXICO

For much of the twentieth century, the fate of Mexican indigenismo was tied to the state- and nation-building aims of Mexico's central government and the development of anthropology as a discipline. The popular upheaval of the Mexican Revolution and its immediate aftermath presented an opportunity for intellectuals, politicians, artists, educators, and social reformers to forge a new nation based on new cultural ideals. This resulted in what some scholars have called the "ethnicization" or "browning" of Mexican national identity.[10]

"Mexico developed one of the earliest and most successful and internationally influential national anthropologies," writes Claudio Lomnitz. "Its political centrality within the country has been remarkable."[11] The man who charted this course was Manuel Gamio, Mexico's first professional anthropologist. Gamio believed it "axiomatic" that "anthropology, in its truest, broadest sense, should provide the basic knowledge for the performance of good government." In 1916, Gamio proposed the creation of a Department of Anthropology that would study an entire territory and its people in order to facilitate what he called their "normal evolutionary development."[12] Anthropologists would serve as "the enlightened arm of government . . . best equipped to deal with the management of population, with forging social harmony and promoting civilization," writes Lomnitz. In fact, "the combined power of an integrative scientific method, embodied in anthropology, and its practical use by a revolutionary government was so dizzying that Gamio compared the mission of the Department of Anthropology with the Spanish conquest itself."[13]

During Mexico's immediate postrevolutionary period (1920–1940), indigenista social scientists, educators, and activists played an unprecedented role in crafting policy. As Alexander Dawson writes, "revolutionary indigenistas were united by their sympathy for the Indian and their desire to incorporate Indians into a reconstructed modern nation, in which living Indians were treated with respect and dignity, and their traditions accorded respect as the true national past."[14] They rejected the racial determinism that forever condemned the Indian to decadence. But most indigenistas were not content simply to celebrate indigenous Mexicans; they also wanted to study, modernize, educate, incorporate, and otherwise "improve" them. Rick López has commented on this glaring contradiction, concluding that "the tension between exaltation and denigration" of the indigenous was "irresolvable."[15]

Early postrevolutionary indigenismo was entrusted to Mexico's Ministry of Public Education (Secretaría de Educación Pública, or SEP). The SEP was Mexico's most important agent of social engineering at this time, but in states like Chiapas, its impact rarely lived up to the lofty rhetoric of its directors in Mexico City. The SEP's shortcomings were especially glaring in indigenous communities. SEP teachers in Chiapas were mestizos who generally spoke only Spanish and were usually steeped in anti-indigenous biases. They were unable and often unwilling to confront the structures and institutions that exploited the indigenous, like *enganche* (debt-labor contracting), recurrent epidemics, and what SEP inspector Eduardo Zarza described as "the participation of mestizos in governing indigenous pueblos, the former exploiting the latter due to their ignorance, to the point where parents pay them to keep their children out of school."[16]

SEP educators and social reformers had high hopes when Lázaro Cárdenas became president in December 1934. Cárdenas "believed that the Indian was a backward proletarian, possessed of a number of vices (alcoholism, fanaticism, isolation, etc.) and continually exploited by a variety of class enemies, but open to redemption."[17] Indigenismo became part of the president's populist political project; his administration created the Department of Indigenous Affairs (DAAI) in 1936. For Cárdenas, the keys to "incorporating" the indigenous into the Mexican mainstream were material assistance and federal paternalism. Late in his presidency, Cárdenas helped establish key institutions that would pay dividends once Mexico recommitted to indigenismo in the 1950s, like the National School of Anthropology and History (Escuela Nacional de Antropología e Historia, or ENAH) and the National Institute of Anthropology and History (Instituto Nacional de Antropología e Historia, or INAH).[18]

The zenith of Cardenista indigenismo came shortly before Cárdenas left office, in April 1940, when Moisés Sáenz and the DAAI hosted the First Inter-American Conference on Indian Life in Pátzcuaro.[19] Many delegates presented research that questioned the efficacy of the incorporationist paradigm. Some defended the right of indigenous people to preserve their own languages and cultures, to choose their representatives and forms of organization. The conference closed with a statement pledging "total respect" for "the dignity and the personality of the indigenous."[20] This pluralist moment was short lived, however. Cárdenas himself insisted on "Mexicanizing the Indian," and the man who succeeded him in the presidency, Manuel Ávila Camacho, called for "national unity" and had no interest in a culturally plural Mexico. When the III was formally constituted in 1942, its director—Manuel Gamio—soft-pedaled pluralism and kept the III studiously and intentionally apolitical.[21]

The 1940s were almost a lost decade for Mexican indigenistas. President Ávila Camacho (1940–1946) gave indigenistas neither the financial resources nor the political capital needed to shape federal policy. The DAAI was purged of leftists and pluralists. Its budget was slashed, and what little remained was spent on showy assimilationist projects.[22] One of the first acts of Ávila Camacho's successor, Miguel Alemán (1946–1952), was to dissolve the practically moribund DAAI and devolve its functions onto other federal agencies. Indigenistas, some indigenous communities, and foreigners with an interest in indigenista policy loudly criticized this move, which may have motivated the Alemán administration to create the INI in 1948.[23] Eight years after hosting the Pátzcuaro conference, Mexico finally fulfilled its pledge to create a national indigenist institute.

THE INSTITUTO NACIONAL INDIGENISTA

The law that created the INI outlined a tame, deeply paternalistic agenda. The INI would research the "Indian problem," study and promote ways to "improve" indigenous populations, and coordinate the action of relevant government agencies. The INI's director, renowned archaeologist Alfonso Caso, would report to and serve at the pleasure of the Mexican president; its council would include representatives from the Ministries of Education, Health and Welfare, the Interior (Gobernación), Agriculture, Hydraulic Resources, Communications and Public Works, and Agrarian Reform. After heated debate in the Chamber of Deputies, legislators added language that would include "representatives from the most important indigenous populations."[24]

Mexico's INI was clearly a product of its times. Its founding principles and mission drew from both Cardenista-era indigenismo and the developmentalist aims of the post-1940 Mexican state. Although indigenismo was no longer part of a populist project, the renewed commitment to indigenous people was certainly a throwback to the Cárdenas period. So too was the paternalist vision of the Indian as backward, isolated, and in need of protection. Like the SEP, the INI insisted tirelessly that the Indian "problem" was environmental and cultural, not racial. And, like the Cardenistas, the INI's founders believed that indigenous people required material and technical assistance, although the INI greatly expanded this idea and sought to promote and manage cultural change related to agriculture, education, health care, and the like.[25]

Mexican indigenismo was a nationalist project, and national integration was one of the INI's primary goals. At times, it seemed that Caso was channeling Lázaro Cárdenas:

> Our obligation is to make these millions of indigenous Mexicans feel like Mexicans; to integrate them by improving their economy, their health, and their education.... We need to bring to them everything that they have lacked during centuries so that they feel like ... members of a nation, of Mexico. The flag should symbolize not only political unity, but also the purpose of achieving the social and cultural unity of all Mexicans.[26]

Caso hoped to open two new Coordinating Centers every year; in 1956, he confidently declared that a total of forty centers should be sufficient. "We hope that the *indigenous problem*, as such, will disappear in twenty years." But "this doesn't imply that indigenous cultural values will have died. To the contrary, they will continue incorporating themselves into Mexican life ... so that Mexico becomes more Mexican."[27]

For Caso (and the INI), education in the Spanish language was essential to integrating four million indigenous Mexicans who had been "segregated from the country's progressive march."[28] Spanish-language skills were also a survival strategy. As Caso wrote in the first issue of *Acción Indigenista*, "It is not possible for an indigenous community to defend itself from those that attack it, nor can it develop itself like other communities in the country, if the men and women that form it cannot speak Spanish."[29] The INI's education program would employ a bilingual method to first teach literacy in the mother tongue, but only insofar as it facilitated literacy and writing skills in Spanish. This language policy was also a throwback to the Cárdenas period, for it had been endorsed at Pátzcuaro in 1940.

If the Cardenista imprint was unmistakable in the INI, so too were the priorities of a Mexican state that now privileged urban industrialization and capitalist growth. Indigenista policy would now be expected to contribute directly to Mexico's plans for industrialization, which required an expanded internal market, a larger labor force, and cheap and abundant food grown in the countryside (to feed the cities cheaply and allow for low urban wages). Mexico's political class also wanted the INI's help in relocating Indians when their homes and lands were affected by large hydroelectric projects. The INI's relatively tame approach is highlighted by Caso's pledge to address the "fundamentally *cultural* problems of the indigenous," such as the lack of communication with the outside world and the persistence of traditional farming and healing practices.[30] Rather than threaten the status quo, the INI was more likely to perpetuate it.

In short, the INI defies easy description because it reflected the commitments and ideologies of two distinct historical eras. Many prominent indigenistas were inspired by the Cardenista example. They were altruists and patriots who still believed that they could bring the Mexican Revolution to the indigenous countryside. Many felt that Mexico still owed a historical debt to this downtrodden population. This may have been what drove the oft-noted *mística* (mysticism) of 1950s-era indigenistas, "the ones who assumed and tried to wash away the shame of national society."[31] Once the mística ran up against the harsh realities of rural Mexico and once national priorities shifted, a more pragmatic indigenismo emerged that focused on assimilation, political control, and job security. The "mystics" gave way to the pragmatists; by 1970, the INI was a highly bureaucratized, rather ineffective branch of a discredited one-party state.

Why Highland Chiapas?

This book focuses on the rise and fall of the INI's work in highland Chiapas, but it also makes a more sweeping argument—that the fate of the INI's first and most important Coordinating Center had major implications for the

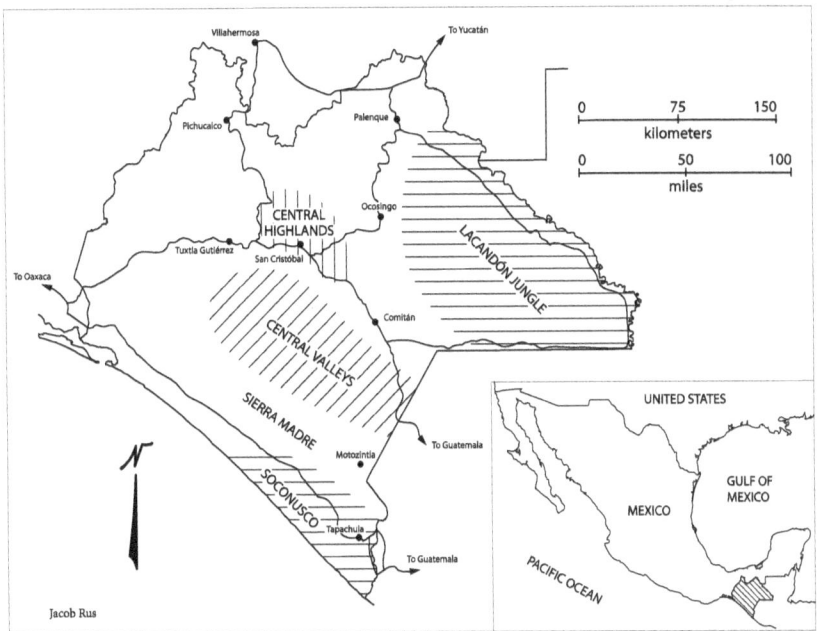

MAP I.1. Chiapas Regions. Courtesy of Jacob Rus.

indigenista project in the rest of Mexico. While the first nine chapters of the book zero in on the INI's programs in highland Chiapas, the last two chapters and the conclusion take a broader scope, insinuating the INI's Chiapas experience into the politics and upheavals of the late 1960s and 1970s, when Mexican indigenismo was challenged and changed forever.

On the face of it, given Chiapas's various idiosyncrasies, it was an unlikely place to hammer out national indigenista theory and practice. Chiapas is Mexico's southernmost state and was actually part of Guatemala during the colonial period. It only joined the Mexican federation in 1824. From that point forward, powerful ranchers and planters took advantage of the state's distance from Mexico City to defend the state's de facto autonomy from unwanted outside intervention. During the long dictatorship of Porfirio Díaz (1876–1880; 1884–1911), a time when peasants, factory workers, and miners across Mexico were routinely and piteously exploited, Chiapas drew special attention for the excesses of indigenous debt-labor contracting and earned national notoriety as a "slave" state.[32]

Chiapas's marginalization and isolation became especially clear during the

Mexican Revolution (1910–1920). During that violent decade, Chiapas was relatively calm for the first four years. When the revolution finally came to the state, it triggered little of the popular mobilization experienced elsewhere in Mexico. When the fighting began to die down in 1920, the victors in Chiapas were not the colorful rebels celebrated in corridos and mural art and film but precisely those forces that had *resisted* revolutionary reforms and reformers. In the ensuing years, Chiapas's political class managed to blunt the federal initiatives that we tend to associate with the Mexican Revolution, like land reform. Arguably, at midcentury, Chiapas was Mexico's most idiosyncratic and least typical state.

Once the INI was established in 1948, its top priority was not Chiapas but Oaxaca, where it found itself implicated in two very complicated projects. The first involved colonizing the fertile lowlands of coastal Oaxaca (near Jamiltepec) with tens of thousands of land-starved indigenous—"excess population," in Caso's words—from Oaxaca's Mixteca Alta. The second project, equally thankless, involved a collaboration with the National Papaloapan Commission to study and relocate tens of thousands of Chinantecs, Mazatecs, and Popolocs whose homes in the Papaloapan River basin (on the border of Veracruz and Oaxaca) were about to be flooded due to construction of the Miguel Alemán Dam. The INI would relocate these populations onto fertile, irrigated lands with schools, medical clinics, markets, and roads. Caso called this "improvement of the indigenous."[33]

Caso first mentioned Chiapas at the end of his 1950 annual report, when he noted the INI Council's decision to create a "center" in the highlands.[34] The region was not unknown to researchers; Sol Tax, his Mexican collaborator Alfonso Villa Rojas, and a team from ENAH had conducted fieldwork in the highlands in the mid-1940s and commented extensively on the region's fierce ethnic divide, the persistence of caciquismo (boss politics), the grinding poverty, and the pervasive use of alcohol. According to the CCI's three-time director, Agustín Romano Delgado, the INI Council chose the Chiapas highlands precisely because it wanted "to put to the test, under the most difficult conditions," its methodologies and policies. Chiapas would be the perfect laboratory: most of the highland municipalities were at least 95 percent indigenous; each municipality had its own customs and practices, which complicated the task of guided social change; the Tseltals and the Tsotsils were among the most populous indigenous groups in Mexico and were considered to be among the most culturally conservative and resistant to change; and the exploitation and discrimination that they suffered were exceptional.[35]

Once the INI Council had settled on highland Chiapas, it then had to decide exactly where to locate its first Coordinating Center. The eventual choice of the ladino (non-Indian) market town of San Cristóbal de Las Casas was quite accidental. Paula López Caballero has recently argued that the decision was "the result of circumstances, chance . . . errors, and improvisation."[36] All members of the INI Council initially *opposed* the choice of San Cristóbal, but budget constraints settled the matter in favor of the ladino market town. Quite simply, the INI could not afford to build a fifteen-kilometer road into the indigenous hinterland. Furthermore, local authorities had made available a parcel of land on the outskirts of San Cristóbal known as La Cabaña. Setting aside their initial misgivings, members of the INI Council agreed to a *provisional* Coordinating Center at La Cabaña until roads could be built.[37]

The INI's pilot Coordinating Center opened in March 1951 and soon became its flagship. As early as 1952, Caso was referring to it as a "training center." By the end of 1953, three of Mexico's most outstanding social scientists had each taken a turn at directing the CCI: Gonzalo Aguirre Beltrán, Julio de la Fuente, and Ricardo Pozas. Other high-caliber directors would soon follow. They took the reins of the CCI when they were still relatively young men, when the INI itself was in its formative, experimental stage. Their experiences in Chiapas in the 1950s informed their ways of thinking about indigenismo for the rest of their careers. This is especially evident in the writings of the INI's chief theoretician, Gonzalo Aguirre Beltrán. His *Formas de gobierno indígena*, published in 1953, drew heavily from his experience as director of the CCI in 1951; his best-known work, *Regiones de refugio*, published in 1967, argued that indigenous communities (like those in the Chiapas highlands) had retreated into self-defensive shells as a result of centuries of abuse at the hands of ladinos. Because merchants, businesspeople, and politicians residing in "centers of domination" (like San Cristóbal) were directly responsible for abusing the indigenous, Aguirre argued that INI Coordinating Centers should be established in ladino market towns so that indigenistas could work with both indigenous and ladino populations.

In short, the Chiapas highlands became critical to the development of INI theory and practice due to the vagaries of timing and circumstance. Once the INI decided to build its first Coordinating Center in the Tseltal-Tsotsil region, it could hardly admit Chiapas's unique historical trajectory, its very particular experience in the Mexican Revolution, or the extreme nature of ethnic relations in the state. The "success" of the INI's pilot Coordinating Center was probably a foregone conclusion. The indigenistas may have produced brutally honest reports and memos for internal consumption, but they took great pains to project a positive image of success to the Mexican public and beyond. Caso needed a successful indigenista project if the INI was to receive the additional funding that he began requesting in his very first reports to President Alemán. Already bogged down as a junior partner in complex colonization and relocation projects in Oaxaca, the INI was clearly pleased to be directing its own project. Failure in Chiapas was not an option; too much was as stake.

The Structure of the Book

The first three chapters of this book are grouped under the heading "The Utopian Project." Chapter 1 provides a brief historical overview of indigenous-ladino relations. It also introduces the high-profile indigenistas who took great pains to distinguish themselves from the local ladinos who lived off the exploitation of the indigenous. Chapter 2 discusses the linchpin of the INI's development programs, the bilingual indigenous cultural promoters, "change agents" who taught literacy and promoted the INI's development programs in their home communities. Chapter 3 chronicles the fate of the INI's first programs, when young social scientists imbued with the mística indigenista ran headlong into the stubborn realities of the Chiapas highlands.

The book's second section, titled "Sober Realities," begins by examining a dramatic clash between the INI and the illegal statewide alcohol monopoly controlled by Hernán and Moctezuma Pedrero. By the middle of 1955, the INI had successfully pressured the state government to curb the monopoly's most egregious abuses in indigenous communities. But these negotiations also placed limitations on INI programs and foretold a more modest indigenista agenda. Chapter 5 traces the INI's retreat on several fronts. The CCI was forced to jettison its most ambitious economic development schemes and focus instead on modernizing and assimilating indigenous populations. Key to promoting education, health care, and infrastructure was a bilingual hand-puppet troupe, the Teatro Petul. This remarkably innovative and effective tool of persuasion and negotiation is explored in chapter 6. Chapter 7 analyzes the CCI's recalibrated medical program, which generally recognized the reality of medical pluralism and emphasized preventive medicine. Chapter 8 describes the Coordinating Center's gradual decline during the "long sixties," when stagnant budgets and dwindling political support took their toll on INI programs and on the morale of its employees. Finally, chapter 9 considers the controversial question of whether the INI fostered caciquismo in the regions where it worked.

In the book's third section, titled "Crisis, Rekindled Populism, and the Fate of Mexican Indigenismo," the INI is no longer a major protagonist of indigenous development in Chiapas. Chapters 10 and 11 tack between national debates over Mexican anthropology and Indian policy and events on the ground in Chiapas. These very public debates were punctuated by the death in 1970 of the INI's founder and director, Alfonso Caso, and with the election of president Luis Echeverría (1970–1976), a populist who envisioned using indigenismo to calm and contain the Mexican countryside. Chapter 11 chronicles the rise and dramatic fall of the School of Regional Development, the INI's daring, even desperate attempt to answer its critics. Meanwhile, the INI's former charges squared off and fought for control of their municipalities.

Since the mid-1960s, scores of scholars have faulted the INI for its limited scope, its assimilationist aims, its bureaucratic inertia, its role in propping up an authoritarian regime, and its extremely modest returns. Its most vehement critics have accused it of practicing internal colonialism and even ethnocide—the extermination of indigenous cultures.[38] Today's critics focus on how INI discourse and practice patronized, feminized, and otherwise demobilized indigenous populations.[39]

Lost in this barrage of criticism is the fact that INI programs in the 1950s and 1960s were remarkably innovative for their time; in fact, for roughly two decades, the INI was unquestionably the Western Hemisphere's leader in indigenista policy. The critiques, which are repeated today in a variety of fields, fail to recognize the diversity of the indigenista experience and generally remove it from its historical context, ignore the extent of local opposition to indigenismo, and ascribe to Mexico's central government more capacity than it ever had. This is the first book-length history in English of Mexico's INI and its emblematic Coordinating Center in Chiapas. It is one of only a handful of books to treat indigenismo as a historical subject and to use archival sources to reveal its complexity. It explores how an indigenista project that initially contemplated major structural reforms, fought local exploiters, launched inventive education programs, and negotiated health programs ended up a widely criticized, largely ineffective bureaucracy that lost the support of the very people it purported to serve.

Part 1 The Utopian Project

CHAPTER 1
Dramatis Personae
The Indigenous, Ladinos, and Indigenistas

●●● THIS CHAPTER INTRODUCES the main protagonists of our indigenista drama. The first section explores the historical roots of Tseltal and Tsotsil communities in the highlands and introduces the institution that best epitomizes the exploitation of the indigenous by the nonindigenous in Chiapas—enganche. We then turn to the ladino. The term dates back to the colonial period, and while it is still commonly used in Guatemala, within Mexico it is unique to Chiapas. Unlike the term *mestizo*, which is a biological label used to refer to someone of mixed descent, *ladino* is a linguistic and cultural term. Although its meaning has changed over time, it generally refers to Spanish speakers who live in urban settings and adhere to mainstream Catholic cultural norms. As the stories and histories of the highland Maya make clear, the Indian's nemesis is nearly always a ladino.[1] Gonzalo Aguirre Beltrán wrote that the culturally isolated indigenous people of the highlands were locked in a "perpetual, mutually reinforcing embrace" with their ladino exploiters.[2] Only the intervention of our third major protagonist, the mestizo indigenista, could break this embrace.

The Indigenous

For nearly five hundred years, the indigenous people of highland Chiapas have captured the imagination of outsiders. Since the times of Bartolomé de Las Casas, the first bishop of Chiapas (1545–1546) and noted "defender of the Indians," observers have invested the indigenous with a wide, even schizophrenic spectrum of traits. "They have been the noble savage or the bloody barbarian, the perfect Christian or the irredeemable heathen, the model ecologist or the worst destructor of the environment, the inventor of the new democracy . . . or a being without individual will, manipulated by dark forces," writes Juan

Pedro Viquiera. "Angels or demons, but never or hardly ever human beings wrapped in contradictions, in internal conflicts, rich in their human diversity."[3] Today, the indigenous highlands attract tourists from Europe, North America, and—increasingly—other Mexican states. It may surprise some to learn that Chiapas is not the state with the largest indigenous population in Mexico—Oaxaca's is numerically greater. But Chiapas does have the greatest number of people who do not speak Spanish, both in absolute terms (371,315) and as a percentage of the population (32.5 percent), and nowhere in Mexico will outsiders find a denser concentration of indigenous people, or more municipalities where the vast majority of residents are indigenous.[4]

Indeed, what attracts outsiders to the Chiapas highlands today is the presence of apparently "traditional" indigenous communities and their inhabitants, many of whom still dress in colorful, distinctive garments and speak indigenous languages. To the untrained eye, their cultural practices, their *usos y costumbres* (usages and customs), seem rooted in the very distant past and show few signs of "contamination" from the modernizing influences of contemporary Mexican society.

Twentieth-century cultural anthropologists were among those captivated by the Tseltal and Tsotsil Maya. In 1957, Evon Vogt of Harvard University established the Harvard Chiapas Project because he believed that contemporary Tsotsils, especially those residing in Zinacantán, had religious and ritual practices, settlement and social patterns, and subsistence activities that could be projected back to the time of their ancestors in the Classic period more than a thousand years ago.[5] Vogt had been trained in the late 1940s at the University of Chicago by cultural anthropologists Robert Redfield and Sol Tax. The field of anthropology was still relatively young at that time, and it took pains to distinguish itself from other fields (like history) in order to legitimate itself as a discipline.[6] This may be what gave rise to a field of study within anthropology—the "community study"—that was purposely ahistorical, even as it made daring assumptions about the lives of people who lived over a thousand years ago. Vogt took this approach to Chiapas in the late 1950s. As he described it: "Our unique anthropological task was to describe, analyze, and understand the inner workings of the 'little communities' of Zinacantán and Chamula."[7] His team would then "project the contemporary data back in time."[8]

The Harvard Chiapas project was prolific and left a lasting impression on the way that academics and the general public think about the Chiapas highlands. Critics argue that this rich body of work created the impression that indigenous culture in Chiapas is timeless and static. According to Viqueira, cultural anthropologists applying the "community study" model "dedicated themselves to minimizing the transformations that took place during more than four centuries—ten, in the extreme case of Vogt—placing Indians at the margins of history."[9] Once the assumption was made that Zinacantán was a "closed corporate community," Harvard Project participants focused on the "inside" of Zinacantecan culture and showed little interest in *Zinacantecos*' political, economic, and historical connections to the outside world.[10]

In his 1994 memoir, Vogt defended his methodology while also making grudging concessions to his critics. "We considered it our task to go beyond the *easy work* of interviewing in Spanish the government officials and business proprietors . . . or of reading reports and documents in the provincial or state historical archives," he wrote.[11] In any event, he noted, such tasks were best left to other specialists. But given Vogt's narrowly focused, ahistorical methodology, the supposition that such communities were static and "closed" became a self-fulfilling prophecy. And the notion of timeless, traditional indigenous cultures has left a lasting impression on outsiders and even many specialists.[12]

Scholars working in historical archives have demonstrated that the cultural identities of the present-day Tseltal and Tsotsil Maya—indeed, of all people—reflect centuries of adaptation to outside forces. Archaeological evidence suggests that the highlands were probably populated by migrants from the Petén rainforest in what is today northeastern Guatemala. Sometime between the fifth and tenth centuries, Tseltal and Tsotsil developed into distinct branches of the Mayan linguistic family. At the time of the conquest, at least four powerful, plurilingual Mayan *señoríos* (lordships) in the highlands fought for control over land and trade routes. It is believed that the señorío of Zinacantán was struggling with the Aztec-led Triple Alliance of central Mexico for control over trade with the coastal territory of Soconusco. Each señorío occupied several ecological niches, from the hot, fertile lowlands of the Grijalva River valley up to the cool highlands at more than 2,200 meters.[13]

When the Spanish conquerors arrived in the 1520s, they broke apart the powerful indigenous señoríos and terminated pre-Hispanic political and territorial units in the highlands. They created instead a multitude of smaller, relatively autonomous and independent *pueblos de indios* (Indian towns), each with its own communal lands. The Spanish relocated natives from the fertile lowlands in the north and west to the highlands closer to the Spanish town of Ciudad Real (today San Cristóbal de Las Casas). Multiple sources describe Ciudad Real as a "parasitic city" that used its political, administrative, and religious powers to strip the indigenous of the fruits of their labors.[14] Spanish friars—especially the Dominicans—also resettled indigenous populations. The practice known as *congregación* concentrated dispersed (and sometimes rival) indigenous peasants into Spanish-style towns, which facilitated the process of evangelization. Iberian institutions like the Catholic Church, religious brotherhoods or confraternities known as *cofradías*, and patron saints became part of the landscape.[15]

It's hard to miss the irony of this quick overview of early colonial history. Contrary to those who claim that pre-Hispanic cultures, settlement patterns, and traditions had been largely preserved for roughly one thousand years, the region was, in fact, altered almost beyond recognition by the Spanish, who intentionally destroyed pre-Hispanic institutions and loyalties and relocated and "congregated" populations. Zinacantán, which Vogt used to extrapolate settlement patterns and social organization dating back centuries, was no exception to this general rule. To quote Viqueira, it—like many other Mayan towns in highland Chiapas—was "a colonial creation."[16]

Church policy toward the indigenous in colonial Chiapas failed in multiple ways, with important long-term consequences. In other parts of Mesoamerica, the clergy managed to instill some of the basic tenets of the Christian faith and—in the best tradition of Bishop Las Casas—often sided with the indigenous against rapacious Spanish colonials and served as social mediators whenever trouble broke out. But Las Casas himself had a tough time in Chiapas. During his brief tenure (1545–1546), he fought unsuccessfully against local encomenderos and settlers who routinely enslaved Indians in spite of a 1542 royal decree outlawing the practice. When Las Casas denied slaveholders the sacrament of confession and refused to absolve them of their sins, they rioted and twice drew their swords on him. Cooler heads soon suggested that Las Casas abandon his bishopric.[17]

The Dominicans, Franciscans, and others who came after Las Casas generally did not share the first bishop's concern for the plight of the indigenous. Chiapas was a colonial backwater, the indigenous were the region's only "natural resource," and all colonials, including the clergy, exploited them mercilessly. The friars spent relatively little time in indigenous towns, which allowed the indigenous to take great liberties with respect to Catholic doctrine and practices. The result was a deeply syncretic worldview, a mixture of Catholic and pre-Hispanic beliefs.[18]

Church policy during the colonial period, then, played a major role in the formation of the relatively autonomous, ethnically distinct indigenous municipalities that we see in the highlands today. As Viqueira notes, "with few exceptions, each present-day municipality corresponds with one of the *pueblos de indios* founded by the Dominicans who arrived in Chiapas in 1545, accompanied by Bishop Bartolomé de Las Casas."[19] The church's language policy also favored the formation of autonomous, ethnically distinct communities. To the extent that the regular clergy (again, mostly Dominicans) evangelized and administered to the indigenous, they did so in the native languages, not Spanish. This policy prevented the indigenous from learning Spanish and "passing" as ladinos, which would have freed them from the tribute rolls and allowed them to slip out of the control of the regular clergy.[20] The indigenous were neither linguistically nor spiritually integrated into broader colonial society. And because Spanish policy called for the spatial separation of the pueblos de indios from the rest of society and prohibited all non-Indians (except priests) from living in these towns, the end result was indigenous "homelands" similar to the apartheid structures that characterized South Africa for most of the twentieth century.

The early nineteenth-century independence movement brought an end to Spanish rule and weakened the church, but living and working conditions for the highland Maya did not improve. The capital of the province, Ciudad Real, was renamed San Cristóbal in 1829, then in 1848 it appropriated the name of the "defender of the Indians," Las Casas. Given San Cristóbal's historical and pitiless exploitation of the indigenous, Thomas Benjamin opines that this "lent honor to the city that was largely undeserved."[21] The provincial legislature launched an assault on indigenous lands, passing laws in 1826 and 1832 limiting the size of ejidos (village commons) and allowing private citizens to claim *terrenos baldíos*, the so-called vacant lands that the Crown had created as a buffer around indigenous communities.[22] In one particularly egregious case, that of Chamula, one well-connected ladino family—the Larráinzars—was able to claim three-quarters of the land not protected by its ejido—47,600 acres. The Chamulas who resided on that land were given the choice of moving off the land or remaining as serfs. "By 1850," writes Jan Rus, "virtually all of the state's Indian communities had been stripped of their 'excess' lands."[23]

As church resources declined after independence, so too did the number of priests in Chiapas. This afforded the indigenous even greater autonomy in their religious practices. The colonial-era indigenous cofradías gave way to the *cargo* system, a local civil-religious hierarchy. Individual cargo holders began to sponsor elaborate religious festivals formerly paid for by the collective cofradías. They often spent several years' savings to hold a prestigious post and to buy the meat, liquor, candles, and fireworks needed to honor an important saint.[24]

By the turn of the twentieth century, indigenous communities in highland Chiapas had been shaped by nearly four hundred years of colonial and postcolonial policy. The precontact señoríos were all but forgotten; the pueblos de indios had evolved into ethnically distinct municipalities, run by ladino municipal secretaries. Many of these municipalities had their own form of dress, their own patron saint and cargo system, and many had their own local dialect of Tseltal or Tsotsil.

If contemporary indigenous identities and communities are mostly rooted in policies of colonial exploitation, how do we explain contemporary attempts to preserve them? Wouldn't the indigenous be happy to see them swept into the dustbin of history?

It is important to think of the contemporary indigenous community as the collective and defensive response to the institutions and conditions imposed first by the Spanish Crown and the Catholic Church and later by the nineteenth-century Mexican state. While it's true that they served the political and economic interests of the colonial regime, and continued to serve the interests of postcolonial ranchers and planters, they also afforded the indigenous refuge from a system that intentionally marginalized, isolated, and humiliated them, compelled them to pay tribute, attacked their beliefs, and exploited their labor. Forced into such a precarious existence, the indigenous had no choice but to invest in and lean on social networks within their communities whenever they suffered a bad harvest, could not find outside work, or fell ill. After independence, indigenous communities led the defense of communal lands and attempted to fend off land-hungry ladinos. They were the only places where the indigenous found social gratification and prestige, which helps explain why indigenous men were willing to spend many years' savings on cargos.[25]

Today, it is common for well-meaning tourists, aspiring revolutionaries, and even naïve doctoral students to envision the indigenous community as an egalitarian, harmonious place that preserves practices that date back to the preconquest. But most scholars today would argue that this is a romanticized, ahistorical distortion. The reality is much more complex. Highland communities are "colonial creations," to be sure, but they have also become refuges for a brutally exploited people. The INI's challenge starting in 1951 was to persuade the indigenous of highland Chiapas to open their communities—their time-honored refuges from ladinos—to mostly nonindigenous indigenistas and to programs that aimed, among other things, to integrate them into broader Mexican society.

ENGANCHE

After 1880, Mexican and foreign entrepreneurs established coffee, sugar, cacao, rubber, and banana plantations in the sparsely populated lowlands in Pichucalco, to the north of the state, and in Soconusco, to the southwest. These commercial enterprises required seasonal laborers, a need that had profound implications for Tseltals and Tsotsils living in the highlands. Starting in 1891, Chiapas's modernizing governor, Emilio Rabasa, took steps to facilitate the flow of labor to the lowlands. He tried to force indigenous workers into the wage economy by abolishing the remaining communal landholdings and passing a vagrancy law. He also revived the head tax and added new police and school taxes and municipal fees.[26]

To further facilitate the flow of labor, ladinos developed a debt-labor institution called *enganche*. Ladino labor brokers known as *enganchadores* offered cash advances to indigenous workers who repaid the debts by working on steamy lowland plantations. Highland ladinos convinced themselves that the indigenous were naturally lazy, ignorant, and treacherous. They supported debt peonage not only for economic reasons but "because it played a role in maintaining the social and racial hierarchy and disciplined the indigenous population for its role in society."[27] And while lowland planters complained that indigenous workers often fled the plantations before they had paid off their wage advance, the arrangement suited them because they did not have to feed and house this workforce during the off-season.

For their part, some indigenous willingly availed themselves of this form of credit in order to pay off debts and buy candles and farm tools. But many others were victimized by enganchadores who used alcohol, guile, and even force to "hook" laborers. Workers walked unpaid for seven or eight days before reaching the plantations, where owners used demanding overseers, company stores (known as *tiendas de raya*), and private subterranean jails to maintain control over their labor force.[28] By 1910, ten thousand Tseltal and Tsotsil men were making the seasonal trek down to the coffee plantations of Soconusco.[29] So important was the rise of the fincas and their ancillary institutions, like enganche, that Jan Rus, in a volume dedicated to the centenary of the Mexican Revolution in Chiapas, concludes that the state's most important social phenomenon during the twentieth century was *not* the "fiesta of bullets" but rather the rise and fall of the plantation sector, beginning around 1880 and lasting nearly one century.[30]

Ladinos

The Mexican Revolution in Chiapas was a ladino affair. After giving themselves a scare in 1911, ladinos consciously avoided mobilizing the indigenous masses for the remainder of that tumultuous decade. In that year, just as the violence began to spread elsewhere in Mexico, ladinos in San Cristóbal turned to highland Mayan allies as part of their long-standing feud with lowland ladinos. The indigenous were led by a charismatic Chamula named Jacinto Pérez (El Pajarito), who opposed enganche and high taxes. Once Pajarito's movement got rolling, ladinos on both sides of the conflict (including the instigators) agreed that mobilized Indians represented a greater threat than their ladino foes. The ladinos closed ranks and crushed Pajarito's forces with the help of the federal army. For the next three years, while much of Mexico tore itself to pieces, there was no popular mobilization in Chiapas because the state's ladinos, whatever their differences, were united in their fear that renewed violence could unleash a race war that might sweep them away.[31]

Chiapas remained calm until 1914. In October of that year, a Constitutionalist army from central Mexico led by Jesús Agustín Castro entered the state and imposed a series of reforms at gunpoint. (His forces also executed Pajarito.) Most significant was his Workers' Law (Ley de Obreros). This law was the first of its kind in Mexico. It abolished debt peonage, enganche, and the tienda de raya.[32] Many of the state's ladino planters and ranchers responded by organizing a resistance movement. Led by a young law student named Tiburcio Fernández Ruiz and calling themselves Mapaches (raccoons), they fought the invading army to a draw over the course of the next six years. Actively discouraged from taking a more direct role in the conflict, the indigenous still suffered its consequences as the warring parties passed through their towns and fields, wreaking havoc and destruction. They were often pressed into service as guides, spies, load bearers, cooks, and servants, but only exceptionally as soldiers.[33]

The bloodletting abated somewhat in 1920, when Mexican president Venustiano Carranza was overthrown by his erstwhile ally, Álvaro Obregón. Since the Obregonistas had made common cause with the Mapache resistance in Chiapas, the Mapaches suddenly found themselves in control of the state. Their leader, Fernández Ruiz, became governor.

During the revolution's violent decade, much of Mexico experienced mass mobilizations that swept away or at least significantly altered the old political, economic, and social order. The popular character of the revolution left its mark on the 1917 Constitution. This document, which made provision for sweeping land reform, labor reform, and free, secular education, was arguably the most progressive in the world for its time. In Chiapas, however, local counterrevolutionaries prevailed over those who had tried to impose a reform agenda emanating from Mexico City. Governor Fernández Ruiz and those who immediately followed him were so successful at undermining the reforms built into the Constitution of 1917 that many historians and observers have argued—with some justification—that the revolution never arrived in Chiapas.[34]

Into the immediate postrevolutionary period, Chiapas was a state characterized more by Porfirian continuity than by revolutionary change. The state government effectively blocked land reform, and enganche continued to be practiced widely even though it had been banned by the Constitution. The tienda de raya had also been outlawed by the Constitution, but every major plantation in Chiapas had one. In 1927, a social worker with one of the SEP's itinerant Cultural Missions noted:

> I have found greater abuse by the "ladino" here than in any other state that we have visited. The enganchadors' houses are centers of exploitation. Each one is an aguardiente factory where the "Chamulas" leave the money that they were advanced by the enganchador. The indigenous arrive to the town where the placement agency is found and there, while the necessary arrangements are made for the trek down to the fincas, they are given all the aguardiente that they want. When that man returns to his senses, he finds that in his drunken state, he has been stripped of his last *centavo*. Now he is committed to paying back that which was already taken from him. Once they arrive at the fincas they are at the mercy of the *tiendas de raya*, which make sure that they remain in debt. Very often, that *peón* is never able to pay back the debt during his lifetime and his sons are the ones who stay in a kind of slavery, paying off what their parents owed.[35]

Needless to say, the ethnic divide in the highlands remained as sharp as it had been during the Porfiriato, and ladino abuse of the indigenous continued apace. According to two sources, during the 1920s and 1930s, young men from prominent ladino families in San Cristóbal were known to ride up to nearby Tsotsil villages when the men were away on the lowland plantations and rape defenseless indigenous women as they worked in the fields. In the early 1990s, a prominent ladino confessed on his deathbed to participating in these "rape brigades." Although remorseful at what he had done seventy years earlier, he rationalized his actions and those of his friends by saying: "Era cosa de chamacos" (it was something that kids did).[36] Indigenous servant girls were also frequently targeted as rape victims. According to Julio de la Fuente, ladinos rationalized and dismissed these rapes because, in the event that they resulted in pregnancy, they "improved" the indigenous race.[37]

Ladino treatment of the indigenous in the commercial center of San Cristóbal was still the stuff of fiction. Indigenous people could not enter the town on horseback, remain in town after 7:00 p.m., or even use the sidewalks without running the risk of being fined, arrested, and/or condemned to forced labor by the municipal police.[38] Drunks were especially targeted; after a night in jail, they cleaned the city streets, unpaid. At the market, ladino merchants had a particular set of weights and measures for Indians; when selling to them, a kilo weighed seven hundred or eight hundred grams and a meter measured just eighty centimeters. Diseased meat was set aside for sale to the indigenous, and they were routinely given incorrect change.[39] Ladino *acaparadores* (hoarders), operating with the blessing of the local authorities, installed themselves at the gates of San Cristóbal and commandeered indigenous goods at a fraction of their market value. Indian sellers who resisted were often beaten and thrown in jail by municipal police.[40] This practice, vividly described by Rosario Castellanos in her short story "Modesta Gómez," persisted into the 1960s.[41]

During the Cárdenas presidency, federal authorities launched a second major effort to bring the reforms of the Mexican Revolution to Chiapas. In 1936, after the president imposed his own candidate, Efraín Gutiérrez, in the state's gubernatorial election, the battle for political supremacy shifted to the ever-complicated highlands, where, as in Porfirian times, San Cristóbal de Las Casas (known as Ciudad Las Casas from 1934 to 1943) still exercised direct and indirect control over several indigenous municipalities, including Chamula, Zinacantán, Larráinzar, Huixtán, Tenejapa, and Oxchuc.[42]

LADINO INDIGENISMO

Shortly after he took office, Governor Gutiérrez appointed Erasto Urbina director of the euphemistically named Department of Indigenous Social Action, Culture, and Protection (Departamento de Acción Social, Cultura y Protección Indígena, or DPI).[43] The department had been created two years earlier as part of a state attempt to wrest control of Indian laborers from enganchadores. The department's claim to "protect" indigenous populations was laid bare by the fact that it made no attempt to bring Chiapas into compliance with federal labor laws. Rather, Urbina's predecessors set up "free placement offices" in densely populated indigenous regions, where its agents assigned seasonal laborers to lowland plantations. Federal education documents tell of the department's agents working together with enganchadores to convince entire communities to migrate to Soconusco for the coffee harvest.[44]

Urbina, on the other hand, used the department effectively to advocate for the indigenous, so much so that he was eventually targeted for assassination. A dark-skinned ladino who spoke fluent Tseltal and Tsotsil, he trained a corps of bilingual indigenous young men, aged sixteen to twenty-one, to serve as scribes and liaisons between their communities and his office. Urbina then used these literate young men to replace the traditional, monolingual scribes. Many of the men who controlled the highland municipalities after 1940—including the notorious caciques who dominated Chamula into the 1970s—got their start under Urbina.[45]

Urbina then took steps to create an indigenous coffee pickers' union under his control. The Indigenous Workers' Union (Sindicato de Trabajadores Indígenas, or STI) was Urbina's greatest contribution to state indigenismo. It negotiated a collective contract for its workers and curbed some of the worst abuses, at least initially. The contract required planters to pay the workers in national currency, not in tokens or certificates redeemable only at the company store. Planters were also required to hire only STI members. The contract further specified the amount of the cash advance and the daily salary. Planters had to provide hygienic lodging and medical care and medicine to its workers except in the case of venereal disease, in which case the workers were on their own. Workers' food and transportation costs were to be covered as they traveled to and from the finca zone. Lastly, planters were prohibited from keeping armed overseers in the work area.[46]

Most former workers recall Urbina and his legacy with great fondness. According to Tsotsils who were interviewed in the mid-1980s:

> The Sindicato brought the law. Even the finqueros began to respect us more. We started feeling a bit more human. The food improved on the finca, and the work, too. That's because the deceased Erasto was in charge. Don Erasto inspected the fincas, and told them to improve the food, so we wouldn't go hungry. . . . He said how many hours we could work. "Eight-hour days," he said. Before the Sindicato, the finqueros gave us more work, heavier work loads. Before, the enganchadores hit us, even the finqueros hit us—sometimes they even kicked us. But after the Sindicato, everything improved.[47]

In the 1990s, a Tsotsil and Tseltal writers' cooperative, Sna Jzt'ibajom (the House of the Writer), wrote and performed a play entitled ¡Vámanos al Paraíso! (Let's Go to Paradise!), which celebrated Urbina's work on behalf of indigenous coffee pickers.[48]

Urbina's legacy, however, is very mixed. By the late 1930s, his bilingual scribes were directing local agrarian committees and serving as representatives to official peasant organizations. In the early 1940s, they were coached to assume religious cargos and become *principales*, part of their communities' traditional hierarchies. In this way, Urbina's protégés combined "the secular power originally conferred on them by the ruling national party with the religious and cultural authority of native elders."[49] Mexico's one-party state learned that it could control entire indigenous communities by co-opting a relatively small number of "traditional" leaders who kept the peace and provided votes for the ruling party at election time.[50]

Urbina's enemies eventually got the upper hand. After the 1944 gubernatorial election, the new state government transferred him out of the state and fired all DPI officials who had been associated with him. Alberto Rojas, an enganchador, became director of the DPI and disbanded the STI in 1946. He also appointed fellow enganchadores to be highland municipal secretaries.[51] The DPI was so thoroughly in the thrall of ranchers, planters, and enganchadores that its director in 1950 ordered two of its mounted agents to spy on Urbina, who had returned to the state that year.[52]

By the middle of the twentieth century, the transportation infrastructure in Chiapas had improved to the point where peons no longer had to walk to the fincas. Some were being transported in *camiones de redilas*, medium-sized cargo trucks with metal railings around the bed. These trucks were usually used to transport livestock, but documents from the period indicate that up to forty workers could be transported at a time, standing, from San Cristóbal to the coastal city of Arriaga. Even though the STI's contract required plantation owners to pay the cost of workers' transportation, this was added to the workers' debts.[53]

Once they arrived in Arriaga, the indigenous peons often boarded southbound trains to the plantations of Soconusco. This practice, however, did not please the workers of Mexico's national railway company, and it placed the enganchadores in the novel position of defending the rights of the indigenous. In April 1951, enganchadores were told that, by presidential order, "the workers can only travel in special cars, separate from the ladinos." Since such cars were not available at the station, the workers had to wait four days until Arriaga's municipal president spoke with the station chief, who (after likely accepting a bribe) finally agreed to take the workers to their destination.

The scenario repeated itself days later in Tonalá, where the station chief refused to take the indigenous and refused to even speak with enganchadores Severo Villafuerte and Gildado Cordero. This prompted ten enganchadores to write a joint letter to the DPI stating that the unpleasant encounters at the railway stations "cause serious damage to the interests that we represent" and could harm the state and national economy. They doubted that such a presidential order existed, "because it would mean nothing less than the *discrimination against the indigenous race.*"[54] A solution was quickly found—any time a work gang of more than twenty-five was due to arrive at Arriaga, the enganchador was to telegraph the station chief so that he could make sure that a special train car was available. The crisis passed just as suddenly as it arose. The segregation of indigenous and ladinos continued in practice, and since the enganchadores were able to get peons to the fincas as requested, they quickly lost interest in fighting against the de facto "discrimination against the indigenous race."

The INI's preliminary reports from Chiapas were highly critical of the state's indigenista institutions. INI employees denounced the DPI's financial irregularities and referred to it in their internal memos as the Department of Indigenous *Exploitation*.[55] The DPI had neither the capacity nor the will to challenge deeply rooted ladino institutions that exploited the indigenous. In 1950, Tseltals and Tsotsils caught drunk in San Cristóbal were still compelled to clear the streets or pay a fine. Indians were still forced to sit at the back of the bus "and were cursed, slapped, and thrown bodily through the back door."[56] They were still used as load bearers because they were cheaper than mules and easier to replace. To the east, in Ocosingo, more than half of the indigenous population resided on fincas as resident debt peons. Carmen Legorreta Díaz posits that even those who managed to liberate themselves from this kind of servitude still believed that they were inferior to ladinos; in other words, the indigenous had internalized the region's brutal ethnic hierarchy.[57] Aguirre Beltrán noted in 1953 that in San Cristóbal, those ladinos who directly exploited Indians were not shunned; to the contrary, they were among the city's leading citizens. Enganchadores were given the more polite name of *habilitadores* (facilitators or providers). "Their profession, contrary to what one might assume, is not considered antisocial: the high status that they hold clearly shows that the city sanctions their activities; only the alcohol monopolists rival their prestige."[58]

Indigenistas

Federal indigenistas drew a sharp distinction between "modern" mestizos (like themselves) and "backward" ladinos who exploited the indigenous. In fact, after the INI had tangled with the ladinos in Chiapas for several years, the term *ladino*—which had been unique to Chiapas—became part of indigenista parlance throughout Mexico. As Emiko Saldívar Tanaka writes, "the INI's Coordinating Centers represented the national state—modernity and *mestizaje*—an external agent that could transform regions characterized by the ladino-indigenous dichotomy."[59] Gonzalo Aguirre Beltrán and others wrote that the exploitation and marginality found in the "regions of refuge" were holdovers from the colonial period. The indigenista symbolized the new, postrevolutionary Mexico that would rescue the ladino from a "retrograde," colonial way of life and the Indian from exploitation and marginalization.[60] Indigenistas saw themselves as guides and "big brothers" to the indigenous, "ready to help them achieve a better world."[61]

So, who exactly were the indigenistas who led the charge against backward ladinos? INI founder Alfonso Caso was one of the intellectual giants of postrevolutionary Mexico and the undisputed director of the INI until his death in 1970. A lawyer by training, Caso was one of the famous "Seven Sages" (Los Siete Sabios) who helped shape the political and cultural life of postrevolutionary Mexico.[62] When he became director of the INI in 1948, he had already directed the National Preparatory School, served as head of archaeology at the National Museum, founded and directed the INAH from 1939 to 1944, and served as president of the National University of Mexico (Universidad Nacional Autónoma de México, or UNAM). In 1951, he aspired to become the presidential candidate for the Institutional Revolutionary Party (Partido Revolucionario Institucional, or PRI) in the 1952 elections. But he was perhaps best known as the archaeologist who excavated the magnificent Tomb 7 at Monte Albán in Oaxaca. Today, his findings are on display at Oaxaca City's Regional Museum.[63]

Caso "absolutely" controlled Mexican anthropology, according to anthropologist Ángel Palerm. His intellectual and political stature gave him the confidence to assemble a team of highly qualified people who held a wide range of ideological and philosophical beliefs. In later years, Caso's mere presence—and his arrogance—may have had the effect of stifling self-criticism within the INI. Caso "routinely turned an intellectual discussion into a personal fight . . . which was very damaging," noted Palerm. "People like me who had some kind of intellectual disagreement with Caso paid the price."[64] But during the 1950s and early 1960s, a man of his stature and disposition was needed to negotiate with recalcitrant governors and dialogue directly with Mexico's presidents.

Caso's eventual successor was Gonzalo Aguirre Beltrán, a medical doctor by training. In 1942, Aguirre Beltrán worked briefly under Manuel Gamio, who headed the Demographic Department at the Ministry of the Interior (Secretaría de Gobernación); a few years later, he studied processes of acculturation under anthropologist Melville J. Herskovits at Northwestern University in Evanston, Illinois. Aguirre hailed from Veracruz and had attended the same high school as Mexican president Miguel Alemán, under whose watch the INI was created in 1948. Aguirre opened the INI's pilot Coordinating Center in Chiapas in 1951 and served as its first director. In 1952, he became subdirector of the INI and helped open the INI's next four Coordinating Centers in Huachochi, Sonora (1952) and three sites in Oaxaca: the Papaloapan Basin, Tlaxiaco, and Jamiltepec (all three opened in 1954). In 1956, he returned to his native Veracruz as rector of Universidad Veracruzana in Xalapa and served one term in Mexico's Chamber of Deputies (1961–1964). From 1966 to 1970, he directed the Instituto Indigenista Interamericano and was named director of the INI after Caso's death in late 1970. Aguirre Beltrán had acute political instincts and was ideologically promiscuous enough to avoid easy classification. As INI director, he briefly supported a period of critique within the INI while fiercely defending the institute and Mexican anthropology from its many external critics.[65]

To the left of Aguirre Beltrán politically were two men who immediately succeeded him as directors of the CCI in San Cristóbal, Julio de la Fuente and Ricardo Pozas. De la Fuente was born into humble circumstances in Veracruz. He became a rural schoolteacher, a social activist, and an accomplished artist. In 1940, de la Fuente was one of the radical delegates at the Pátzcuaro conference. Soon he was collaborating with Bronislaw Malinowski on Oaxacan markets as well as with cultural anthropologists Sol Tax and Robert Redfield. He also took courses at Yale. He accepted a post with the INI in 1951, directed the Coordinating Center in Chiapas in 1952, and then led the investigation into the Chiapas state alcohol monopoly in 1954–1955. De la Fuente was a man of great integrity and high standards who did not suffer fools. He was a passionate defender of the bilingual method of second-language instruction and criticized the notion of indigenous "incorporation" as inherently colonial long before it became fashionable to do so.[66]

Further to his left was Ricardo Pozas who, like de la Fuente, got his start as

FIGURE 1.1. CCI director Julio de la Fuente handing out diplomas in San Cristóbal. Photographer unknown. Fototeca Nacho López, Comisión Nacional para el Desarrollo de los Pueblos Indígenas. 1952.

a rural schoolteacher and worked with Tax and Redfield. Deeply influenced by Cardenista anthropology, Pozas conducted ethnographic research in Chamula in the 1940s that informed the INI's development program in the highlands. Pozas was a Marxist who came to believe that the INI's focus on ethnicity prevented Mexico's rural masses from forging a class identity. He was also an early proponent of turning indigenista practice over to the indigenous. Pozas left the INI in 1958 for professional and personal reasons and became professor of sociology at UNAM. In 1976, he published a blistering denunciation of the INI's burgeoning bureaucracy.[67]

Like de la Fuente and Pozas, Alfonso Villa Rojas was a rural schoolteacher and worked with University of Chicago professors Tax and Redfield. Born in Mérida, Yucatán, Villa Rojas began teaching in the Mayan town of Chan Kom in 1927, near the fabulous archeological ruins of Chichén Itzá. In 1930 he met Redfield, who was doing ethnographic research for the Carnegie Institution based out of Chichén. The two men began a long collaboration. Villa Rojas got his bachelor's and master's degrees in anthropology at the University of Chicago. He worked for the Carnegie Institution from 1935 to 1947 and conducted research in Yochib, Oxchuc, a Tseltal municipality in eastern Chiapas. From 1949 to 1952, he directed the Social Studies Department of the Papaloapan Commission and in 1954 opened the INI's Coordinating Center there. He returned in Chiapas in 1956 to direct the Coordinating Center at a time when it had to come to grips with its economic limitations. During those years, he helped Evon Vogt establish the Harvard Chiapas Project and assisted the University of Chicago's Norman A. McQuown, who led the Man-in-Nature project in Tseltal communities for several years. From 1967 to 1970, Villa Rojas served as research director of the Instituto Indigenista Interamericano and helped publish the III's journal, *América Indígena*. Villa Rojas followed Aguirre Beltrán back to the INI in 1970, when Aguirre became director and Villa Rojas served as undersecretary.[68]

FIGURE 1.2. CCI director Agustín Romano Delgado's identification card. Fototeca Nacho López, Comisión Nacional para el Desarrollo de los Pueblos Indígenas. 1963.

The last indigenista to be profiled here is Agustín Romano Delgado, who lacked the cosmopolitan ties and publishing heft of the other members of Caso's team but ended up becoming the prototype of the loyal career indigenista. Romano was part of the first generation of students to graduate from Mexico's National School of Anthropology and History and worked his way up the ladder at the INI. He eventually served three stints as director of the Coordinating Center in Chiapas and also directed INI Coordinating Centers at Papaloapan (1956–1958) and Huachochi (1959–1962). A political moderate and a steady hand, Romano was entrusted with managing the center in Chiapas during difficult times. His *Historia evaluativa del Centro Coordinador Indigenista Tzeltal-Tzotzil* is a detailed insider's account of the INI's pilot Coordinating Center.[69]

As these brief profiles indicate, the INI's leading indigenistas were learned, cosmopolitan men who had spent their lives outside of Chiapas. The Coordinating Center's first five directors—Aguirre Beltrán, de la Fuente, Pozas, Romano Delgado, and Villa Rojas—were charged with implementing the INI's ambitious agenda in a hostile region where ladinos considered them to be outside agitators and "communists." For many indigenistas, living and working at La Cabaña was difficult and stressful. In late 1956, Evon Vogt noted that San Cristóbal's ladinos and the indigenistas moved in entirely distinct social circles. After he and his wife attended a New Year's Eve party at the Lion's Club hosted by San Cristóbal's leading ladinos, he found it "illuminating to discover that the INI officials lived in a different social world and were unaware the Lion's Club dance had occurred and were surprised that we attended."[70] Indeed, the die was cast for conflict and misunderstanding within the Coordinating Center itself. The directors and technical staff came from Mexico City and other large cities, but the secretaries, drivers, mechanics, and field hands were generally ladinos from San Cristóbal, and many did not sympathize with the indigenista mission.

Setting the Stage

Having introduced the main actors in this indigenista drama—Indians, ladinos, and indigenistas—it is time now to set the ethnographic stage.

The INI began its work in seven Tsotsil municipalities, four Tseltal municipalities, and San Cristóbal de Las Casas. Given the dispersed settlement pattern of indigenous peasants, each municipality consisted of various, often dozens, of *parajes* (hamlets). In Chamula alone there were seventy-four hamlets, but in neighboring Zinacantán there were only fifteen. In 1951, each

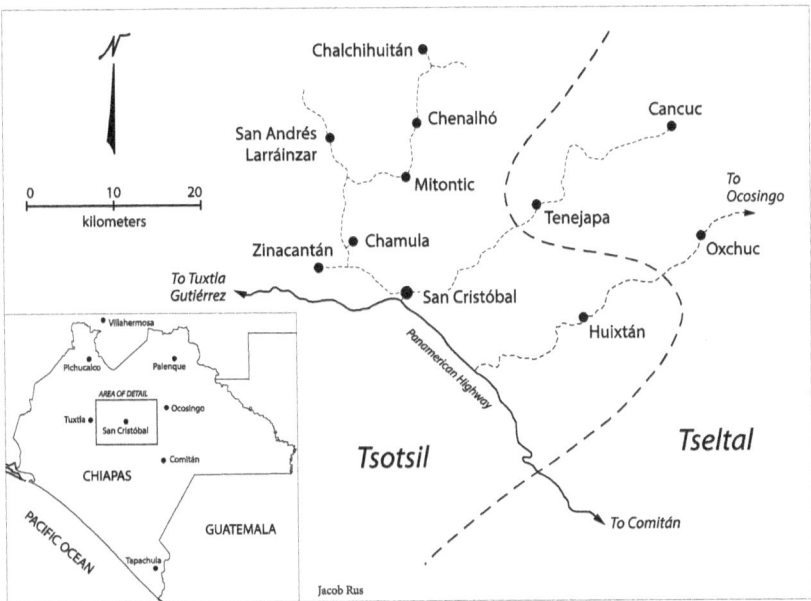

MAP 1.1. In the early 1950s, the recently completed Pan-American Highway was the only reliable all-season road in the Chiapas highlands. Courtesy of Jacob Rus.

municipality had a president (indigenous) and a secretary, who was invariably ladino. Real power was exercised by the municipal secretary, who was appointed by the director of the DPI in San Cristóbal, in violation of the constitutional guarantee of municipal autonomy. Over the years, the CCI's range of action expanded to eventually include some twenty municipalities, but for the sake of this study, we will focus our attention on the original twelve and especially on those municipalities where the INI had the longest trajectory and the greatest impact: the Tsotsil municipalities of Chamula, Chenalhó, and Zinacantán, and the Tseltal municipality of Oxchuc.

TSOTSILS

San Juan Chamula, located a few kilometers outside of San Cristóbal, was an obvious choice for the INI to begin its work. With more than 22,000 inhabitants in 1951, it was the most populous indigenous municipality in Chiapas, land starved and politically complicated. A census conducted by Chamula's first indigenous promoters showed that Chamulas were overwhelmingly illiterate and poor. Romerillo hamlet had 571 inhabitants (17 literate) grouped into 130 families, all of which practiced *unión libre*. Most of Romerillo's residents owned a few chickens, and maybe also a turkey. A few residents owned a cow or a horse. Among the other Chamula hamlets that were surveyed, Catixtic had 333 inhabitants, but only 7 were literate; and only 3 of Ichintón's 226 inhabitants could read.[71]

In a region of few roads, Chamula offered relatively easy access. But proximity to San Cristóbal also meant that Chamulas had borne the brunt of ladino exploitation over the centuries. As Robert Wasserstrom notes, Chamula "was not a region that had remained outside the mainstream of economic life, but rather a region that for nearly 300 years had been systematically pillaged and decapitalized."[72] This goes a long way toward explaining the municipality's closed, conservative nature. The only resident ladino allowed in the municipality was the municipal secretary. After 1951, indigenistas would have to tread lightly, if at all. Nowhere would the INI get less of a return for its investments of money and time. Little wonder that in a 1995 interview, Agustín Romano confessed that for the indigenistas, Chamula became an "obsession."[73]

In the late 1930s, Erasto Urbina recruited eight of his scribes from Chamula. The two most prominent were Salvador Gómez Osob and Salvador López Castellanos, better known as Tuxum. As boys, both Gómez Osob and Tuxum had studied at the Casa del Estudiante Indígena, a short-lived indigenous boarding school established in Mexico City in 1926.[74] The Casa was closed in 1932 in part because, in the words of SEP educator Rafael Molina Betancourt, some students displayed "a sick tendency to become exploiters and caciques by means of their superior cultural preparation."[75] Tuxum in particular would seem to embody this tendency. After several years of fighting with Chamula's traditional, monolingual religious authorities, Tuxum became municipal president (in 1943) after agreeing that he and other bilingual young men would serve a religious cargo within five years of holding office. Gómez Osob followed Tuxum in the municipal presidency, serving in 1945 and again in 1953. The power of Urbina's former scribes in Chamula and their self-serving use of "tradition" would create a powerful *cacicazgo* that would eventually slip out of the control of the indigenistas.

The INI would get better returns in nearby San Pedro Chenalhó. Unlike Chamula, which had expelled its ladino population, there were roughly three hundred ladinos residing in Chenalhó's municipal head town (*cabecera*) in 1950. Chenalhó did not suffer Chamula's land pressures, either. Many landless *pedranos* had received land during the Cárdenas years. In yet another contrast, a tradition of schooling was deeply rooted in Chenalhó, associated with a powerful, almost mythical leader and liberator.[76] Manuel Arias Sojob favored education as a means of self-improvement and self-defense. He helped the SEP establish schools in the municipality, and in 1936, an indigenous boarding school opened in Chenalhó. Arias became an Urbina scribe in the late 1930s, then municipal president in 1944. By the time the INI began operations in the region, there were already fourteen SEP and state schools operating in the municipality. The INI had no trouble finding bilingual young men willing to collaborate as cultural promoters, and INI programs were generally accepted.[77]

Zinacantán offers yet another kind of contrast. Most men received ejido grants in 1940 through the agrarian reform. But like Chamula, Zinacantán had an elaborate cargo system and a deeply traditional ritual culture. These features are what drew Evon Vogt to establish his Harvard Chiapas Project in Zinacantán. Because major trading routes had always passed through Zinacantecan hamlets—a situation that continued with the completion of the Pan-American Highway—many Zinacantecos were experienced traders. The indigenistas came to view the Zinacantecos as entrepreneurs who showed little interest in collaborating with the INI and becoming cultural promoters.

TSELTALS

Oxchuc was a small, densely populated municipality of sixty-four hamlets in the early 1940s. When the INI commenced operations, Oxchuc was just beginning to change in dramatic ways, thanks to Marianna Slocum, an American missionary linguist with the Summer Institute of Linguistics (SIL). This US-based organization trained missionaries to translate the Bible into indigenous languages and teach Indians to read. A native of Ohio, Slocum came to the hamlet of Yochib in 1944. Armed with nothing more than a flannelgraph board and a hand-wound Victrola, she taught literacy and Bible stories and started to translate the Bible into the local variant of Tseltal. In 1947, she was joined by nurse Florence Gerdel. Together, Slocum and Gerdel were a remarkably effective team. Both women offered spiritual guidance, and Gerdel literally healed the sick with modern antibiotics. Two years later, Slocum and Gerdel were invited to live with Protestant converts in El Corralito, another Oxchuc hamlet. Slocum helped them establish a relationship with Presbyterians in San Cristóbal. In 1950, El Corralito's "believers" built a church for its 420 parishioners.[78]

Slocum and the SIL were able to get a foothold in eastern Chiapas largely due to the institutional weakness and negligence of the Catholic Church. In the nineteenth century, the church battled with anticlerical Liberals and lost. Religious orders were expelled from the state, extensive church lands ended up in private hands, and many indigenous communities stopped paying religious dues and shunned priests altogether. The church's institutional woes carried well into the twentieth century. By 1940, the Catholic Church in Chiapas was

FIGURE 1.3. Marianna Slocum, right, and Florence Gerdel in Oxchuc. Photographer unknown. Fototeca Nacho López, Comisión Nacional para el Desarrollo de los Pueblos Indígenas. Circa 1955.

in no position to renew its evangelizing mission. Julio de la Fuente wrote that it held a "laissez-faire" attitude toward the indigenous and had been "careless, ignoring their social problems." Many priests "tolerated indigenous alcoholism" and permitted what he called "formidable alcoholic orgies" on saints' days. Nor did traditional spiritual beliefs and healing practices provide comfort to the people of Oxchuc. According to Villa Rojas and Slocum, traditional healers (*curanderos*) verbally abused and whipped patients to force them to admit to wrongdoing, and entire communities lived in dread fear of vengeful and jealous ancestral gods, witches, and their *naguales* (animal spirits). June Nash writes that the arrival of Slocum "provided an alternative . . . for a sanctioning system that had broken down."[79]

Slocum's converts were literate and sober, embraced a savings ethic, and were healthier and visibly better off than their neighbors. But the medicine that she and Gerdel dispensed was a direct threat to shamans; the missionaries' admonitions against alcohol consumption hurt the bottom line of ladino alcohol producers and vendors; and when converts refused to pay for the special Mass for Saint Thomas (Oxchuc's patron saint) and stopped buying candles and fireworks, religious leaders in Oxchuc's municipal center predicted a disastrous corn harvest.[80] In 1950, the missionaries' enemies launched a nasty rumor campaign against them. According to Oxchuc's municipal president, the indigenous were led to believe that Slocum was, in fact, a man dressed as a woman; that she fornicated with Indian girls who later claimed that "she has a big one—the size of a burro's"; and that she was also trying to corrupt married women.[81]

Things took a more dangerous turn later that year. Slocum's enemies summoned El Corralito's Protestants to the municipal seat, then informed Catholics that the Protestants had come to destroy the saints that were housed in Oxchuc's main Catholic church.[82] Hundreds of armed Catholics, both indigenous and ladinos, waited in ambush. The Protestants avoided a possible massacre by arriving the next day. Slocum and Gerdel were then summoned to the DPI in San Cristóbal—two days away by horseback—to face charges that they were disturbing the peace, fomenting opposition to local officials, and dividing the Tseltals into two warring camps. Oxchuc's alcohol merchants had brought the charges.[83]

The Protestants of El Corralito would suffer other setbacks, but their appeal spread so that, by late 1955, there were twelve parishes of "believers" within a one-day walk of El Corralito, each with its own chapel.[84] The Protestants also had footholds in the neighboring Tseltal municipalities of Tumbalá, Yajalón, and Salto de Agua. Protestantism was rapidly gaining new adherents just as the INI began working in the region. This represented an opportunity for the INI as well as a risk. Nobody was more qualified to prepare Tseltal language primers than Slocum, and her literate indigenous converts were logical candidates to become INI cultural promoters. But the INI did not want to be associated too closely with the *evangélicos* for fear of alienating indigenous Catholics, and Slocum's converts were often more inspired to preach than teach. Nevertheless, Slocum was the INI's most important ally in eastern Chiapas for several years, and the INI had little choice but to maintain a close if not entirely comfortable relationship with the SIL.

The Challenges Ahead

Despite thirty years of self-proclaimed "revolutionary" governments, highland Chiapas was truly a backwater when the CCI commenced operations. Outside of San Cristóbal de Las Casas, the region's commercial center, a modern transportation infrastructure hardly existed. Three seasonal dirt roads connected San Cristóbal with the nearby indigenous municipalities of Tenejapa, Chamula, and Zinacantán, and, according to Romano, each had been imposed "violently," against the will of the indigenous.[85] Other indigenous municipalities were roadless, connected to one another only by footpaths, and merchandise was transported on the backs of Indians. The health care infrastructure was even worse. Not a single public or private medical clinic existed in the indigenous municipalities. A poorly provisioned civil hospital operated in San Cristóbal, but indigenous patients reported suffering discrimination. And, as one of the CCI's first doctors noted, "the commonly held belief that the Civil Hospital is in fact an antechamber to the cemetery is not totally unfounded."[86]

The state of education in the highlands was only marginally better, if only because ineffective schools don't kill people. Thirty years after the SEP's founding, it had neither liberated nor "incorporated" the Tsotsil and Tseltal Maya; in fact, very few had even learned to read. Although the SEP sustained forty-two federal schools and the state of Chiapas another thirty-eight, these generally catered to the small ladino populations found in most cabeceras. A mere handful could be found in indigenous hamlets.[87] Only six of the federal schools offered grades one through three; the other federal schools offered just two grades. The offerings in the state schools were even bleaker; all but one of these schools offered only the "preparatory" grade where students were expected to learn Spanish literacy.[88] Especially distressing were the language and literacy figures in communities where the SEP had established rural schools *and* indigenous boarding schools. In Chamula and Huixtán, literacy rates in Spanish were only 2 percent and 15 percent, respectively; in Chenalhó, only 9 percent of the inhabitants spoke Spanish.[89]

In theory, the INI's Coordinating Center was to "coordinate" the various state and federal ministries charged with transportation and communication, health care, education, agriculture, and so on, but the INI soon learned that in highland Chiapas, it would have to go it alone. Simply put, apart from a few dozen poorly functioning schools, the Mexican state was invisible. The INI would be tasked with launching, funding, and supervising development programs that it had merely intended to coordinate. Moreover, it would do so in the face of opposition from ladinos and many distrustful indigenous communities. A lot was riding on the indigenistas' principal allies, the bilingual indigenous cultural promoters.

CHAPTER 2
Negotiating Indigenismo
The Bilingual Cultural Promoter

●●● EDUCATION AND SPANISH-LANGUAGE literacy were essential to the INI's programs of development and assimilation, but the indigenistas faced an uphill battle in the Chiapas highlands. SEP educators had learned several sobering lessons over the years. In 1935, Manuel Castellanos Castellanos became the SEP's education inspector for the Tseltal-Tsotsil region. He was tasked with implementing a mobilizing, popular pedagogy that included agrarian reform. The inspector struggled mightily against ladino alcohol merchants, enganchadores, municipal secretaries, and ranchers. The indigenous also presented obstacles and saw little point in sending their children (especially their daughters) to the SEP's poorly provisioned schools. Castellanos Castellanos used his monthly reports to the SEP to vent his frustration. He typically lambasted ladinos for obstructing the SEP's agenda, but he occasionally turned on the indigenous. In an October 1942 report, he called them "liars" who are "spiteful and obstinate in their passions" and feel "an innate hatred toward the mestizo." After declaring that "the ethical principles that guide their lives are distinct from those that constitute the base of our civilization," Castellanos Castellanos encouraged his teachers to "attend to the extremely important moral aspect of education, forming in said Indians feelings and habits that will make them more human."[1]

The SEP's inability to transform the Chiapas highlands had become manifest. Castellanos Castellanos—not to be confused with state indigenista Manuel Castellanos Cancino—began drawing up a blueprint for a new, more effective kind of education and social action that in many ways anticipated the INI. He called for more frequent school inspections, a greater emphasis on hygiene and vaccination campaigns, more teachers, and the use of the vernacular in the classroom. He stopped short of calling for an indigenous teaching corps. In 1944, the SEP's director of primary education in Mexico City, Lucas Ortiz, lauded Castellanos's "elevated vision" and then appeared to call for something akin to an INI Coordinating Center. The obstacles to SEP programs were "so profound and complex that the school by itself will not be able to resolve them in their entirety. What is needed is the coordination of a series of agencies, first to study these problems and then attack them jointly."[2]

The INI in Chiapas would draw liberally from the SEP's most forward-thinking programs and add two important innovations—indigenous *promotores culturales* and an "indirect" (i.e., bilingual) method of teaching Spanish literacy. The indirect method was not new; in fact, it had been endorsed at Pátzcuaro in 1940 after Maurice Swadesh's Tarasco Project (1939–1941) demonstrated that indigenous adults and children could learn to read and write in their native tongue in thirty to forty-five days.[3] Literacy in Spanish could then be introduced efficiently and successfully. Gonzalo Aguirre Beltrán drew liberally from the Tarasco Project experience when he opened the CCI in 1951. Indigenous cultural promoters and the "indirect" method of language instruction would become the linchpins of the INI's entire development strategy.[4]

This chapter discusses the selection and training of the INI's first indigenous cultural promoters. Many of these men were true pioneers who played critical roles in the political, economic, and social life of the highlands for decades to come. In addition to teaching basic literacy skills in both their native language and Spanish in the INI's Centros de Alfabetización (Literacy Centers), male promoters were expected to support infrastructure projects in their home communities and provide instruction in agricultural science and general hygiene. Starting in 1956, female promoters, although much fewer in number, introduced "modernity" to the girls and women of their communities in the form of Singer sewing machines, courses in hygiene and food preparation, and instruction in agriculture and animal husbandry. By 1954, fifty-three Literacy Centers had been established, and although many schools were fraught with problems such as low attendance (especially among girls) and ill-prepared instructors, the INI's program was firmly rooted.

First Steps

In March 1951, Gonzalo Aguirre Beltrán traveled to San Cristóbal de Las Casas to prepare the groundwork for the INI's first Coordinating Center. His principal task was to venture into nearby indigenous communities and find a few dozen literate Tseltals and Tsotsils willing to serve as cultural promoters. He traveled on horseback to hamlets that could not be reached by the INI's jeep. Helping Aguirre Beltrán identify potential promoters were Erasto Urbina and SIL missionary linguist Marianna Slocum. Urbina's role was perhaps inevitable. Even though his political fortunes were in decline, he still had plenty of pull in municipalities controlled by his former charges. Slocum's participation in Aguirre's search was also indispensable. When she received Aguirre's invitation to collaborate, she believed that "the Lord [had] opened another door to further implement the spread of His Word." Slocum, who declared that same year to the DPI in San Cristóbal that she was "not a Minister or agent of any religion" and had not "proselytized in order to increase the number of evangelical believers," was thrilled when Aguirre asked to use her Tseltal primers and requested that she train fifteen Tseltal promoters.[5] "Having the government undertake literacy campaigns in the Indian tongues was a giant step toward 'hastening God's Word' to every Indian tribe in Mexico," she wrote in her 1988 memoir.[6]

Aguirre's reliance on these two very different individuals would carry important long-term consequences. Some of Urbina's charges were already well on their way to becoming wealthy, powerful men; once the INI gave them more power and influence, it risked deepening the divisions already apparent in highland communities and fostering caciquismo. Slocum's converts were also problematic because they owed their loyalties to her, and some would not resist the temptation to proselytize in INI schools. The INI was a deeply secular federal institution that resented its unavoidable reliance on SIL missionary linguists.[7]

The INI's recruitment drive exposed the SEP's meager returns in the highlands. Aguirre searched high and low to find forty-seven indigenous men able and willing to collaborate with the INI. Some had studied three years or more at state and federal rural schools, or had attended the SEP's indigenous boarding schools in the highlands.[8] But only three of them had finished the sixth grade. Of this initial group of forty-seven, nine came from Chamula.[9] Aguirre noted that "most of them were [Urbina-trained] scribes, that is, they have a great ascendancy in the business of the community." In fact, in the selection process, prestige in the community weighed more heavily than educational achievement. Nine more came from Chenalhó, where schooling had been associated with indigenous self-determination since the 1910s. Most of Chenalhó's candidates had studied at the boarding school that the SEP established there in 1936 "and were, of course, the best prepared."[10] Aguirre and Urbina also recruited six men from Zinacantán and three from Huixtán. The only man they managed to recruit from Mitontic, a culturally conservative municipality just north of Chamula, was the municipal president, Diego Rodríguez López. His family would control teaching positions in Mitontic for the next few decades.

In spite of its dismal record in the highlands, the SEP's methodology, experience, and personnel served as a foundation for the INI's Literacy Centers. As Agustín Romano noted, the CCI's education program "represented, thirty years later, an extension of the rural schools, although with a methodology suited for application in indigenous regions." The CCI "took the community approach from prior SEP schools and changed the principal actor." The people who would direct the INI's schools would be "more than teachers," wrote Romano. "That is why these agents of change were instead called 'bilingual cultural promoters.'"[11]

Once the first generation of promoters had been selected, the INI began constructing its headquarters at La Cabaña in San Cristóbal. The indigenous were all too familiar with this particular site; the DPI's most important "free placement agency" had its office there, and thousands of seasonal workers passed through it every year on their way to the lowland fincas. In August 1951, the INI began training the Tsotsil men to impart the "preparatory grade" (pre-first grade) in their home communities in their native tongue. The CCI's initial training program at La Cabaña lasted about ten weeks and was taught almost exclusively by SEP employees and missionary linguists from the SIL. Subsequent training sessions for aspiring promoters lasted a mere thirty-five days. Dr. Kenneth Weathers, a missionary linguist with the SIL and author of a Tsotsil grammar, taught the Tsotsil language class and wrote the first primer (*cartilla*) in Tsotsil. Other classes were offered in Spanish grammar, mathematics, the natural sciences, medicine, and agriculture. Later that year, seventeen Tseltals were given similar instruction, with Marianna Slocum substituting for Weathers. Naturally, the INI's crash course provided the promoters with only a rudimentary foundation. The Coordinating Center's education inspector astutely predicted that "given their inadequate scholastic preparation, it will be difficult for the promoters to teach literacy skills in their native tongues and in Spanish in just one year."[12]

Weathers concurred. In December 1951, he wrote a very candid assessment of the INI's first generation of Tsotsil promoters. In his estimation, only a handful of the promoters were prepared to make an immediate impact in their communities. The best ones were former teachers from Chenalhó, but even they needed to be deprogrammed. "They need to forget some of the things that

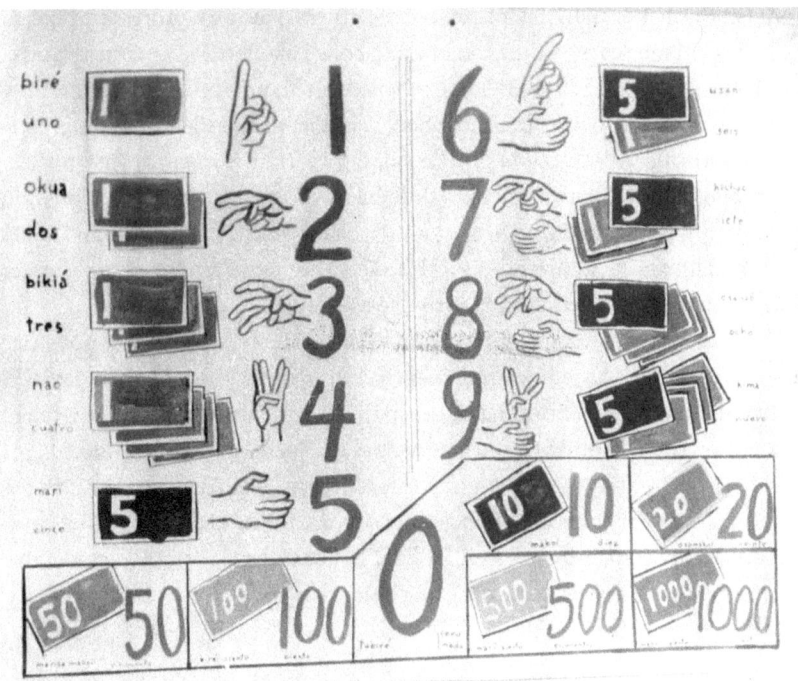

FIGURE 2.1. Bilingual mathematics lesson in an INI primer. Fototeca Nacho López, Comisión Nacional para el Desarrollo de los Pueblos Indígenas. Circa 1955.

they learned in their other schools so that they can be more useful for the present campaign," Weathers wrote, "but it shouldn't be difficult to convince them." The best teacher from Chenalhó was Antonio Arias Pérez, who wanted "to help the oppressed." Weathers characterized the two other former teachers, Diego Rodríguez López and Pedro Arias Pérez, as "slow."

Weathers's most critical remarks were reserved for the Tsotsils from Chamula. With the exception of Mariano Hernández Jiménez and Domingo Jiménez Centeno ("one of the best readers, with a decent command of spoken Spanish"), he found the Chamulan cadre lacking. Salvador Sánchez Gómez spent six years in the SEP's boarding school in San Cristóbal, became an Urbina scribe, and served as Chamula's municipal president in 1942. Weathers found him to be hardworking and serious, with a desire to help his pueblo, but felt that he needed additional preparation in Spanish and "[did] not demonstrate special intelligence." Pascual López Calixto also needed additional preparation, but his

Spanish was better than that of most of the other Chamulan promoters because he had spent ten years working on lowland coffee plantations. Domingo Gómez Osob, the brother of Salvador Gómez Osob (who became an INI nurse), seemed bright but probably never attended school as a child and needed substantial additional training. Weathers had little hope for other former Urbina scribes. Domingo Santis Diezmo "is very slow in reading and other work, possibly because his vision is failing him"; and Pascual Patixtán Likanchitom "seems lively and intelligent at times, but can also seem almost silly." Another promoter, José Santis Muñoz, "definitely has trouble reading."[13]

Weathers's other comments focused on the promoters' leadership potential. The indigenistas wasted no time identifying men who might someday take political control of their home municipalities. Of Salvador Sánchez Gómez, who would serve another term as municipal president of Chamula (1962–1964), Weathers accurately noted "a gift for leadership." Of Antonio Arias Pérez, Weathers wrote that his experience as a corporal in the army "gives him practice at commanding others."[14] Of Pascual López Calixto, Weathers noted that "with the necessary preparation" he could be a good promoter, "and could possibly do something additional."[15]

Negotiating Education in the Highlands

Introducing the INI's education program to the Tseltal and Tsotsil highlands involved negotiations at all levels. Cultural promoters had to begin by persuading their communities to set aside land for a new schoolhouse, a teacher's house, a basketball court, and a gardening plot. If local residents agreed to provide land and labor and agreed to make adobe bricks, the INI offered bricklayers as well as materials like windows, doors, cement, and wood, if none was available in the hamlet. Once the schoolhouse was built, the INI tried to provide it with a map, a flag, and a clock (for telling time and learning numbers), as well as language primers, pencils, notebooks, portraits of Miguel Hidalgo and Benito Juárez (a Zapotec from neighboring Oaxaca who became Mexico's most important nineteenth-century president), and some publicity about vaccinations.

Some communities balked at the prospect of an INI Literacy Center or conditioned their support for a school on other factors. At the Chamulan hamlet of Ichintón, some residents in early 1952 prevented the construction of the school, even though they had agreed on three separate occasions to support it. Ichintón was the first hamlet on the road that the INI was building to connect

San Cristóbal and Chamula with Chenalhó, and INI personnel often remarked that the community's resistance stemmed from its proximity to the ladinos of San Cristóbal. Although the INI's promoter at Ichintón, Domingo Jiménez Centeno, was respected by the community (and was one of the INI's most promising promoters), his work on behalf of the INI earned him death threats. The INI temporarily halted construction of the school. Two months later, Ichintón's elders again agreed to support the school after the INI promised to build a sewing room and provide two new sewing machines. The INI also vowed to hire only laborers from Ichintón for its local construction projects and promised to show movies in the hamlet.[16] Jiménez Centeno, who had feared for his life two months earlier, agreed to stay on the job.

Once a hamlet accepted a promoter and agreed to build a school, it generally accepted the INI's other development projects, like its hygiene campaigns, roads, and consumer cooperatives. In fact, some indigenistas were surprised at the speed with which many "traditional" communities embraced change. Most communities hedged their bets, selectively appropriating INI programs while holding fast to traditional beliefs. For example, at Chanal, a Tseltal community east of San Cristóbal, residents welcomed the INI school, a symbol of modernity, with a traditional gesture. One day before forty-two students dressed in white drill pants and shirts helped inaugurate the school, locals killed a sheep and buried its head in the center of the schoolhouse. The municipal president explained to the CCI's education director, Fidencio Montes Sánchez, that the sheep's soul would protect the building and prevent the students from getting sick. He then asked Montes to provide his community with a tailor and a Singer sewing machine.[17]

Even Chenalhó, with its prior tradition of schooling, required a careful blending of the modern school with local tradition. The hamlet of Polhó was among the first communities to build an INI Literacy Center and welcome a promoter.[18] Six years later, five students from Polhó were enrolled in the SEP indigenous boarding school in San Cristóbal. Yet this hamlet, which had apparently embraced the INI's message of school-based modernity, still had one foot planted very solidly in its ritual traditions. In June 1957, Polhó inaugurated a new, improved schoolhouse, with multiple classrooms, a tile roof, and a brick floor. This would become a "transition" school, offering grades one through three to bridge the gap between the *grado preparatorio* and the INI's boarding school at La Cabaña. The hamlet's Education Committee invited Montes to witness a ceremony meant to protect the schoolhouse and its users. Before the brick floor was laid, the blood of two slaughtered cattle was spilled

FIGURE 2.2. Making roofing tiles at La Cabaña. Photographer unknown. Fototeca Nacho López, Comisión Nacional para el Desarrollo de los Pueblos Indígenas. Circa 1956.

onto the soil to placate evil spirits that could do harm to the students. When Montes entered the main room of the schoolhouse, he noticed "fifty candles burning on an improvised altar, lots of pine needles spread across the floor and two of the town's oldest men praying on their knees with their heads touching the floor." The elders "asked that no force of nature damage the building, like lightening, hurricanes, floods, or earthquakes, and that the building provide shelter and protect the children from illness, fright, or other things." Montes wrote that "smoke from the incense burner filled the room, as did the music of two harps, a *violineta* and a small guitar, mixed with that of an oboe, a drum and two trumpets. Everyone present was very respectful and next to them were two jugs of *chicha*" (a traditional alcoholic drink made from fermented maize). After about one hour, the two elders joined Montes, Education Committee members, and an official from the municipal seat for dinner. Polhó's cultural promoter, Hilario Pérez Sánchez, enjoyed great prestige in the hamlet and was the one chosen to distribute cuts of beef to the roughly one hundred people who had witnessed the ceremony.[19]

At Polhó, the INI clearly built upon the success of prior educational projects in Chenalhó. But it is equally clear that the very capable Hilario Pérez Sánchez was the key agent of change in the hamlet. In 1955, Polhó's school was the first in Chenalhó to enroll girls, but it didn't come without a fight. Parents who opposed sending their daughters to school sent a gift (*bocado*) of chickens, eggs, plantains, and pineapples to Chenalhó's municipal president at the time, Tomás Pérez Arias. Had he accepted the gift, he would have been compelled to exempt the parents from sending their daughters to the school. After the promoter warned him not to accept the bribe, the municipal president refused the offering and the parents returned home. Several parents, egged on by a nearby federal teacher, later threatened to hang Pérez over his insistence that they send their daughters to school. The promoter held his ground. By 1957, seventy-five boys were enrolled at the CCI's Literacy Center in Polhó, alongside thirty-five girls. Girls began attending all of the INI's schools in Chenalhó, and even the state and federal schools in the municipality saw an uptick in girls' attendance.[20]

Hilario Pérez still faced opposition from local ladinos and Indians from Pantelhó and nearby ranches who were perhaps envious of Polhó's new schoolhouse and its tile roof, described as "majestic" by Fidencio Montes. Some skeptics predicted that the schoolhouse would collapse. The ladino owner of a nearby ranch advised Pérez not to educate the indigenous because later *se ponían muy alzados* (they became uppity). The SEP teacher at the nearby hamlet of Acteal told Montes that it would be pointless to build such a schoolhouse for "his" Indians because they were incapable of learning. When Montes responded that the people of Polhó had built the schoolhouse themselves with very little help from the INI, the teacher was incredulous.

For Montes and the INI, Polhó was like a shining beacon in the Tsotsil highlands, one of few bright spots. School attendance was satisfactory, and Hilario Pérez fought the right battles and was actively involved in basic agricultural and animal husbandry activities. Pérez also donated some of his harvest to less fortunate residents. Like the INI's other successful promoters, he understood the need for positive public relations and compassion. "That is when the people open their hearts to us and cooperate with the Institute so that together a transformation can take place," wrote Montes.[21]

The Debate over the "Indirect Method" to Literacy

It is difficult to overstate the importance of the INI's promoters in the early 1950s. Without them, the INI's entire development project would have failed;

FIGURE 2.3. CCI director Julio de la Fuente at a school event. To his right is education director Fidencio Montes Sánchez. Photographer unknown. Fototeca Nacho López, Comisión Nacional para el Desarrollo de los Pueblos Indígenas. 1952.

with them, it had a chance of succeeding, but only if they gained additional training. When the INI Council decided to move Aguirre Beltrán back to Mexico City in early 1952, it tapped rural educator and anthropologist Julio de la Fuente to replace him. Best known for his classic study of the Oaxacan town of Yalalag,[22] de la Fuente created the Dirección de Educación (Education Division) and invited three Zapotecs from Oaxaca to collaborate with him—Fidencio Montes Sánchez, Montes's nephew Onofre Montes Ríos, and Reynaldo Salvatierra. Of these, Fidencio Montes had the most lasting impact on indigenista policy.

Born in a Zapotec town in 1900, Fidencio Montes Sánchez grew up speaking both Zapotec and Spanish at home. An accomplished clarinet and violin player, he went to Oaxaca City as a young man and worked as a bricklayer, carpenter, and huarache maker. A Protestant missionary from the United States helped him with his early schooling. He then continued his studies at a Presbyterian school in Coyoacán, in southern Mexico City. The SEP's subdirector of education in 1926, Moisés Sáenz, had studied at the same school and saw to it that Montes got into the Escuela Nacional de Maestros (National Teachers School). Montes graduated in 1930 and eventually returned to teach in his hometown in Oaxaca. There, he "established the practice of speaking to [his students] in Zapotec for the first two years; for the remaining four years, the teaching was bilingual." As he told writer Fernando Benítez, "we built roads, combated alcoholism, opened a post office, and dominated the city hall."[23] In 1945, Montes became a federal education inspector based in Tuxtepec, Oaxaca, and six years later de la Fuente invited him to work for the INI. In 1952, Montes became director of education at the INI's Coordinating Center in Chiapas. He held the post for nine years and left an indelible mark on the INI's bilingual education method.[24]

Montes and de la Fuente believed that indigenous students could learn to read and write in their own language in three to four months and then acquire Spanish literacy within a year, but only if the teacher was skilled and the student body relatively homogeneous. Not all indigenistas embraced the "indirect method" of teaching Spanish literacy. In fact, de la Fuente's immediate successor in Chiapas, Ricardo Pozas, flatly rejected this pedagogical model. Within months of taking over the directorship, Pozas reported that the CCI's educators and linguists agreed that "oral instruction in Spanish should begin simultaneously with reading and writing instruction in the indigenous language since they are two completely distinct processes . . . and since one cannot serve as the foundation for learning the other."[25] Later in his career, Pozas expressed frustration that the "indirect method" had become practically institutionalized. For Pozas, who believed that indigenous languages were destined to disappear in Mexico, proponents of this method were "ideologues of social stability" who sought to keep indigenous peoples divided and separate from the Mexican mainstream. He cited his personal experience at Papaloapan, where he briefly directed the INI's Coordinating Center in the mid-1950s. There, the indigenistas worked with Mazatec settlers who spoke at least five different dialects and used Spanish as their lingua franca. According to Pozas, the Mazatecos wanted to be instructed in Spanish. Some of Pozas's other reasons for opposing the two-step, "indirect" method—for example, that proponents (like the SIL's missionary linguists) sought to advance the aims of

US imperialism—sound today like relics of past ideological battles.[26] Pozas's critiques are vivid reminders that Mexican indigenismo was always closely linked to Mexican nationalism. Despite their differences, both de la Fuente and Pozas sought the quickest route to a Spanish-literate Mexican citizenry, and both sought to use applied anthropology and indigenous cultural promoters as the means of achieving that end.

Fine-Tuning the Education Program

In 1952, de la Fuente's Oaxacan educators began supervising the first group of promoters and replacing those who, for one reason or another, could not meet the INI's expectations. They typically took fifteen-day inspection tours through the highlands on horseback, reporting on the schools' progress and promoting the INI's programs in health, sanitation, and local development. The fledgling schools faced serious obstacles. Many did not yet meet in classrooms. A total of 1,504 students were enrolled, but only 108 were female, and all but one of these came from Oxchuc, where Protestant missionaries had established a culture of schooling for both sexes.[27]

During de la Fuente's year at the helm, an average of four to six schools were closed down every month. Eight were closed in Chamula alone. Poor attendance and community resistance forced some closures, but others failed due to inadequate teacher preparation or teacher misbehavior (like drunkenness). In fact, thirteen of the original education promoters either abandoned their posts within a year or were relieved of their duties because of their limited Spanish skills or their resistance to the very changes that they were expected to embody. Fortunately for the INI, many young men were eager to fill the vacancies, and communities lacking schools began to request them. Increasingly, even where the federal or state government already provided a school, the indigenous asked that their teacher be replaced with a bilingual INI promoter who used the INI's method of language instruction.[28]

To correct anomalies among the existing corps of promoters, de la Fuente held monthly pedagogy sessions at La Cabaña. After promoters walked to the CCI to collect their pay (a journey on foot that lasted one to two days), de la Fuente asked them to remain at La Cabaña for two or three additional days to receive training. Most of the "lessons" had more to do with behavior than actual pedagogy. Promoters were told not to hit, fine, or threaten students (or their parents). As representatives of the INI in their communities, they were expected to act responsibly at all times, both inside and outside of the classroom. Adults, especially women, were to be treated with tact and respect;

TABLE 2.1. INI anthropologists compare SEP and state schools with INI Literacy Centers, circa 1955.

FEDERAL (SEP) AND STATE SCHOOLS	INI LITERACY CENTERS
Teachers	*Cultural promoters*
Local ladinos	Indigenous
Detached from the community where they work	Generally from the community where they work
Strictly teachers	Promoters of community development
Generally prejudiced against the indigenous	Identify with their community
Irregular attendance	Attendance monitored by supervisors and the community
Poorly paid (by ladino standards)	Well paid (by indigenous standards)
Morning classes	Morning and afternoon classes
Unprepared	Periodic training sessions
Lack of support	Support from other CCI sections, especially Visual Aids
Supervision	*Supervision*
Sporadic	Periodic
Lax	Strict
Superficial	Exhaustive with respect to both schoolwork and other development activities
Students	*Students*
Recruited by force	Voluntary enrollment
Required to perform tasks for the teacher	No required tasks outside of school
Corporal punishment on occasion	All types of punishment prohibited
Relative lack of recreation	Sports fields, balls, uniforms
Lack of services	Medical kit, barber shop, workshops

Source: adopted from Romano Delgado, *Historia evaluativa*, 2:28–29.

FIGURE 2.4 Two of the INI's first education promoters. The man on the right, Agapito Núñez Tom, helped landless Tseltals create the community La Libertad. Photographer unknown. Fototeca Nacho López, Comisión Nacional para el Desarrollo de los Pueblos Indígenas. 1951.

promoters were to use persuasion, not force, "or commit other acts that will distance them from the school." The INI's education inspectors also reminded promoters not to impart religious lessons. This admonishment was directed particularly at the Tseltals from Oxchuc.[29]

De la Fuente's monthly pedagogy sessions helped to correct some problems, but the task of rooting out underachievers (and training young men to replace them) was ongoing. Many of the INI's original promoters bowed out gracefully as the academic demands of the job intensified. In 1955, when the lack of SEP and state schools in the region forced the INI to begin offering the first and second grade, another round of older promoters resigned. Romano said that many who resigned "promised their wholehearted support to the promoters who were sent to their communities." By 1959, only twenty of the original forty-seven promoters remained at the head of INI Literacy Centers.[30]

Recruiting Women and Girls to the Classroom

In July 1953, Fidencio Montes reported forty-six schools in operation. While

1,507 boys and men were enrolled, only 207 girls and women were; that summer, 1,023 males and only 162 females attended school with any regularity because the scarcity of corn that year forced many to drop out of school and work as indebted laborers on lowland ranches and plantations.[31] Few girls or women attended INI schools, especially in certain Tsotsil communities. Many parents feared that their daughters could be seduced by the male promoter. Others feared that a woman who read and spoke Spanish might lose her indigenous identity, or might have difficulty finding a marriage partner out of fear that she would dominate her family or her husband. Others simply saw no point in sending their daughters to school and preferred giving them household tasks.

Although the INI's critics have accused the institute of not recruiting women into the ranks of promoters, nothing could be further from the truth.[32] The indigenistas' plans to develop the highlands and assimilate its indigenous population hinged, to a great extent, on their ability to get girls and women involved as students and as *promotoras*. The girls of today became the spouses and mothers of tomorrow, and as long as what the indigenistas called *lengua materna*—the mother tongue—remained indigenous, full assimilation would remain a distant goal. The CCI's director in 1953, Ricardo Pozas, attempted to address the matter by asking promoters to bring their wives to the monthly training sessions held at La Cabaña. At the July session, fourteen Tseltal and thirteen Tsotsil women accompanied their husbands. Several of them brought their children with them. INI social workers taught the women to operate sewing machines and cook balanced meals. They recommended the following dishes:

> Flour tortillas (salted and sweet), French fries, potatoes with egg . . . cheese enchiladas, guacamole, cabbage salad, radish salad, stew, mole, beef patties, *pescado en escabeche* [pickled fish] . . . squash, salsa picante, meatballs, *atole* with oats, rice, and flour, and desserts using apricots, apples, and bananas.

The CCI's social workers and nurses also instructed them in basic hygiene, such as the need to bathe their children, use outhouses, boil drinking water, use a comb, trim one's nails, and wash one's hands. Other tips were oriented toward "creating new needs" and forging modern indigenous housewives, including how to arrange one's house, how to prepare a bed, how to wash dishes and tables, the importance of sweeping one's house daily, and the advantages of cooking and grinding at waist level.[33] Most of this training was irrelevant to life in a Tseltal or Tsotsil hamlet. Many of the dishes prepared by INI social workers required ingredients that could not be easily obtained in the Chiapas highlands, required refrigeration, or were simply too expensive. (To the INI's credit, its cooking classes in subsequent years were more appropriate to the region and to the lifestyles of the highland Maya.) With respect to the hygiene and housekeeping tips, most were irrelevant in hamlets where freshwater sources were often distant, seasonal, or contaminated by livestock, and where most families were too poor to have beds, furniture, or cooking utensils or even the time to perform certain household tasks on a regular basis.

These shortcomings notwithstanding, Pozas forged ahead, and a second training session was held the following month at La Cabaña. Sixty women attended this session. Pozas hoped that if these women learned to read and write, he could eventually enlist them as INI promotoras, nurses, and social workers. As this session drew to a close, Pozas promised a prize to promoters who brought their wives back the following month able to read and write.[34]

In 1955, indigenistas noticed a disturbing trend that added fresh urgency to the campaign to educate girls and women. Several male promoters began aspiring to ladina wives or felt embarrassed by their monolingual indigenous spouses. Two promoters had actually left their indigenous wives and married ladinas. For the CCI's director at the time, Agustín Romano, this pattern represented a "grave danger. If this process of 'passing' accelerates and only involves indigenous men and ladinas, the indigenous woman will remain in a state of cultural backwardness," jeopardizing the overall stability of indigenous society. Despite this, Romano found a silver lining, for it "represented a step forward in the process of incorporating the indigenous with the mestizo," citing a "'permeability' between the two groups that would have been unthinkable three years earlier."[35] For the INI, however, the dangers represented by this emerging pattern clearly outweighed the opportunities. The CCI redoubled efforts to improve the attendance rates of girls and young women and recruited girls into its boarding school. Years later, the INI encouraged promoters and promotoras to marry one another; in 1960, four students from the INI's boarding school at La Cabaña married cultural promoters. For Romano, "this met one of our objectives: to form marriages where both spouses had similar training to avoid, to the extent possible, the abandonment of the wife for the above-mentioned causes."[36]

In 1954, a handful of Tsotsil girls began attending the INI's Literacy Center at Belisario Domínguez hamlet in Chenalhó. The INI quickly capitalized on this opportunity and sent María Rodríguez López, the first Tsotsil girl to study at the boarding school, to the hamlet's school. Rodríguez came from a relatively prosperous family in nearby Mitontic.[37] Initially, her title was *ayudante* (assistant), and she was only expected to teach sewing (on a Singer sewing machine), reading, and writing to girls. Soon, however, the promoter at Belisario Domínguez resigned, and Rodríguez was quickly promoted. She became a critical asset in the INI's campaign to boost female attendance in Tsotsil schools, especially in Chamulan hamlets. (Although Belisario Domínguez was technically part of Chenalhó, it was physically close to Chamula and populated by Chamulas who conducted most of their business in Chamula.) The INI's traveling puppet show performed skits that turned Rodríguez into a local celebrity, and Tsotsil women who attended the performances often agreed to send their daughters to school once it was staffed by a promotora like Rodríguez.[38]

By June 1957, Rodríguez's lack of academic preparation had caught up with her as her students began to surpass her Spanish-language ability. Rodríguez also had limited success with the women of Belisario Domínguez. Soon she resumed her studies at the boarding school.[39]

María Rodríguez López's brief stint at the head of the school in Belisario Domínguez may have ended in disappointment, but the INI could point to other small victories in the campaign to boost school attendance rates for Tsotsil girls. At Xunuch, another hamlet in Chenalhó, girls began attending school after the promoter's wife started helping him in the schoolroom. "The girls' parents seem reassured when there is an indigenous women in the classroom with their daughters," Fidencio Montes noted. "When the promoter's wife is present, the girls participate just as actively as the boys." At the Tsotsil municipality of Larráinzar, Montes reported that small numbers of girls attended each of the INI's four schools. The INI took heart in the fact that girls represented 20 percent of the students attending INI schools in 1957, 24 percent in 1960, and 29 percent in 1964. This figure slowly rose over time, but the indigenistas never fully overcame the opposition to schooling for girls.[40]

Preparing for the Future: The INI's Boarding School

The INI took an additional step to bolster its teaching corps when it opened a boarding school in 1953. This school accepted boys and girls who had completed the preparatory, first, and second grades. These students spent two or three years at the boarding school, then "graduated" and either established new Literacy Centers or replaced older promoters whose lack of academic preparation had become a hindrance. In 1953, the ratio of boys to girls at the boarding school was promising, if not entirely satisfactory—twenty-three boys were enrolled, alongside twelve girls.

Much was riding on the boarding school, and the INI made sure that not a minute was lost. Students received six hours of academic instruction daily ("national language," mathematics and geometry, natural science, social science, and drawing). They also received ninety additional minutes of instruction in agricultural work, as well as training in either physical education or military marching drills and an additional hour of music and singing. Finally, at the end of the day, students took two-hour-long workshops in either carpentry, sewing, printing, or puppetry.

The boarding school's official academic curriculum is easy enough to glean from the documents; the school's "hidden" curriculum, the less formal messages that students received, is harder to decipher. One way of gauging the "hidden" curriculum is in the students' choice of attire. Incoming students were given two sets of new clothes, and each student decided whether to continue wearing the clothes of his or her home municipality or to opt instead for "ladino" clothes. Romano reported in June 1954 that boys from Larráinzar and Chamula (Tsotsil) as well as students from Tenejapa (Tseltal) chose to continue wearing traditional clothes. The other boys were given two pairs of denim pants, two heavy shirts, four changes of underwear, four pairs of socks, a belt, and a pair of shoes. The female students were each given three huipiles, three skirts, two pairs of shoes, two ankle socks, three panties, two slips, and four meters of ribbons. One female student, who had already studied at the SEP's boarding school in Amatenango, preferred ladina clothes, but the rest chose to dress in the traditional way. All students were given combs, toothbrushes, toothpaste, soap, and Vaseline with DDT, and the female students were instructed to bathe daily. A few months later, Romano reported that all of the male students had chosen to dress like ladinos, which suggests the powerful attraction of assimilation at La Cabaña.[41]

Recruiting—and retaining—female boarding students was a permanent challenge. In 1955, partly in response to parents' complaints, the INI began sending girls to their home hamlets on a periodic basis. The girls were expected to demonstrate everything they had learned at the boarding school, including improved hygienic habits and new ways to prepare food. Ideally, these "working vacations" also reacquainted the student with her hamlet, since the INI planned to send them back home as promotoras once they had concluded their studies. These "vacations" also allowed the INI to weed out rebellious students; only those who showed promise were invited to return for further schooling.[42]

One year later, Fidencio Montes noted that the female students were making slow but steady progress. Winning over the confidence of the girls, their parents, and their communities was a difficult process "in which nothing less than the prestige of the Institute is at stake." He continued:

> Each one of our students bears all of the prejudices that the indigenous culture holds against the transformative innovations that we are trying to introduce. Many times the students themselves do not know what to do, and therefore we must watch them very closely, more closely than we watched the first promoters.[43]

Montes also noted that the girls had become more confident in themselves and were developing a desire to learn more and more. "We now see that they are making an effort to compete with the male students." Despite this, the INI boarding school would continue to have trouble recruiting and retaining Tsotsil girls and women. In February 1958, there were eight female students enrolled (out of a total of twenty-four), but only one girl was Tsotsil.[44]

Recruiting male students was much easier. In early 1957, education inspector Onofre Montes reported that more than fifty students from INI, SEP, and state schools applied for admittance to the boarding school in hopes of continuing their education. Only a handful could be admitted. "It was a real shame to see the rest of them leave so disappointed," he wrote.[45]

Conclusions

In late 1955, CCI director Agustín Romano took stock of the CCI's education program after its first four years. Through its schools, the CCI had gained a foothold in a very complicated region. "The battle has not yet been won," Romano noted, but the CCI had "exceeded expectations." Communities had begun to request promoters. They offered their labor and building supplies and promised to send their children to school. Most important of all, the CCI and its personnel had won their confidence. This was most clearly demonstrated in the case of the CCI's recently opened boarding school, where Tseltal girls were in attendance. "The fact that the girls' families gave them permission to leave their homes to live alone, in a 'ladino' setting, demonstrates their absolute confidence in the Center's personnel and is a very important step for the education of women."[46]

Other INI observers were not so convinced. In 1954, the INI's central offices in Mexico City sent Professor Ramón Hernández López to the Chiapas highlands for three months to assess the progress of the CCI. Although his overall report was quite positive, he found that many of the CCI's employees were either inadequately prepared or lacked a true indigenista spirit. Many of the promoters fell into this first category. He found them to be "deficient... due mainly to their hasty and incomplete preparation" and their inability to master the Spanish language. He seemed surprised that "many still do not realize that their training is geared toward converting them into true and capable leaders in their hamlets, communities, and even regions."[47]

In August 1956, Julio de la Fuente returned to highland Chiapas to evaluate the education program that he had helped to create. He toured some of the most difficult schools, those of the southern Tsotsil zone, mainly in Chamula and Zinacantán. "Our achievements are extremely precarious and do not reflect this Center's many years of work and experience in the region," he wrote. He was quick to note that his observations were not intended to be an indictment of the CCI's education system as a whole. "As we well know, this Center's most competent promoters are in the Tseltal and northern Tsotsil regions."[48]

De la Fuente's report caught the eye of the CCI's first director, Gonzalo Aguirre Beltrán. Two months later, Aguirre retraced de la Fuente's route and reported on the exact same schools. He too found conditions to be "generally rather negative: the teachers' houses are inadequate; the pedagogy is primitive and frequently wrong; rote memorization is predominate; student achievement is disappointing and slow; and frequently the promoter unintentionally prevents his students from advancing." He also noted that the CCI's inspectors "have not been critical enough." Aguirre also commented on the INI's boarding school, where he noted "a lack of adequate equipment and more rote memorization." He found student achievement there to be "a bit low in about half of the students and emphatically low in the case of four female students."[49]

Poorly trained teachers were clearly still a problem at the CCI's schools, but there were other factors that prevented student success. Education director Fidencio Montes compiled a daunting list that included "illnesses, poor attendance (both students and promoters) due to religious festivals, parental resistance, prolonged absences due to emigration to the lowland fincas, the temporary closure of schools, and the high turnover rate of promoters."[50] In some hamlets, especially in Chamula, village elders excused parents from sending their children to the INI's Literacy Center if they paid a ten-peso fine. During the dry season, water scarcity in parts of the highlands sometimes forced residents to abandon their homes (and schools) to reside elsewhere. Periodically, schools had to close because students had gone to the lowland plantations to work and eat. In July and August 1956, the lack of corn in parts of Tenejapa so greatly diminished the student body that schools were closed and the promoters were transferred to other schools where corn was more readily available. Students who remained in the highlands were too hungry to concentrate on their studies. As Montes noted, "before students read well or understand Spanish or write or perform calculations, there's one essential factor that can paralyze all scholastic activity—hunger."[51] The CCI needed to train better teachers, yes, but its education program also hinged on the outcome of its health and hygiene campaigns and its ability to improve local subsistence, increase agricultural output, and diversify the local economy.

Although problems remained, the INI's corps of bilingual cultural promoters put the institute at the vanguard of Pan-American indigenismo. Most researchers agree that the INI was the first government agency in the Americas to use indigenous promoters to teach reading and writing in the mother tongue before it was attempted in the second, national language.[52]

But these promoters did not emerge out of a vacuum. Whether originally trained by Erasto Urbina, Marianna Slocum, or the SEP, most of the original promoters were already immersed in larger agendas that sometimes conflicted with the INI's programs. At the very least, the INI reinforced and legitimized preexisting hierarchies when it chose former scribes to serve as promoters. In 1953, Aguirre Beltrán candidly discussed the need to work with former scribes, whom he labeled "indígenas ladinizados." He concluded that that there was no alternative to working with these proto-caciques.

> These people ... constitute the link between the indigenous community and the national community, particularly the ladino community of Las Casas.... They are not well viewed by their peers, because their behavior is unorthodox for the society that they live in—they charge their neighbors for their services, they receive salaries for the jobs that they perform for state or regional authorities, they are at the service of the national political machinery, and they have close and shameful business relationships with alcohol vendors, *enganchadores*, and urban merchants. But in exchange they fill an inescapable function—they facilitate the relationship between a closed and subordinate community with outsiders.

In a clear allusion to Chamula, Aguirre then noted that "it is precisely those communities that most resist acculturation that have the strongest group of ladinoized scribes, and they are the only ones that, for this reason, have been able to prevent the establishment of ladinos in their ceremonial centers and have limited, to the extent that it is possible, the bilious abuses of the ladino secretary."[53]

Placing education and development programs in the hands of such men risked the emergence of caciquismo. There were also dangers inherent in relying so heavily on Slocum's zealous converts. But these were problems that would manifest themselves down the road; for the time being, the indigenistas were most concerned with launching their integral development programs, even if it meant relying on people whose commitments and relationships might one day place them at odds with the overall indigenista mission.

CHAPTER 3
Utopian Dreams and the *Mística Indigenista*

🔴🔴🔴 OVER THE YEARS, the INI's many critics have faulted the institute's limited scope and its failure to notably improve the indigenous economy. Beginning in the 1960s, critical anthropologists accused the INI of practicing "internal colonialism" and aiding the national development effort at the expense of indigenous people and their natural resources. More recently, Alexander Dawson has called the INI "the neglected child of a conservative state that did not support radical agendas," one that did "little more than promote clinics, schools, the popular arts, and social welfare."[1] And Jan Rus has written that the INI's gradual approach appealed to a government that was "more concerned with industrial development and economic growth than equity [because] it turned the 'Indian question' into a technical problem that could be solved without sacrificing the investment climate."[2] There is a great deal of truth to these critiques, and there's no denying that in regions where Coordinating Centers were built, like highland Chiapas, most indigenous people even today still struggle to eke out a precarious existence.

But it wasn't for lack of trying. Between 1950 and 1955, indigenistas announced plans to dramatically restructure local economies, to the benefit of indigenous and nonindigenous alike. In one of his first reports to President Miguel Alemán, INI director Alfonso Caso noted that the INI Council was considering a proposal to create an "industrial center" in what he called the "Chamula region of Chiapas."[3] In 1953, Gonzalo Aguirre Beltrán boasted that the INI was elaborating a "vast plan" of regional, integral development in highland Chiapas that would improve indigenous standards of living, promote "harmonious" acculturation, and create a mutually beneficial "economic interdependence" with the ladino population. This would be done "without creating grave situations of interethnic tension that impede the process of biological and cultural mestizaje." This utopian plan would result in "the final integration of the country into a great community that is sufficiently homogeneous so that regional variations do not hinder the nation's progress."⁴

In more concrete terms, Aguirre Beltrán called for "strengthening the economy of the ladino city through its industrialization, and invigorating the economy of the indigenous countryside through its technological modernization." Acculturation, in other words, required major economic and technological change. Aguirre Beltrán noted that the INI in San Cristóbal was already working with the Federal Electrical Commission (Comisión Federal de Electricidad) to provide cheap and abundant electrical power "for the transformation of the craftsmen and colonial guilds into syndicates and modern factories that will cheapen production costs and create a working class that will break the prevailing caste system."⁵ This was an extraordinarily ambitious plan for San Cristóbal de Las Casas, a heretofore sleepy mountain town of some twenty-five thousand residents. Many of its residents were artisans; others, such as enganchadores, alcohol merchants, and acaparadores, participated in the timeworn tradition of directly exploiting (if not outright stealing) the labor and resources of the nearby indigenous population.

These were also bold projections for a fledging institution operating in a hostile environment. Still, the historical record shows that the INI tried to back these words with actions. In January 1954, Alfonso Villa Rojas proposed studying the social and economic interactions between ladinos and indigenous as a preliminary step.⁶ This proposal, which made non-Indians a subject of study, was almost unprecedented in the history of Mexican anthropology. Ever since Manuel Gamio had called for a Department of Anthropology in 1916, the target of the anthropologists' work had always been the Indian. What Villa Rojas's proposal makes clear is that the INI wanted to remake the ladino, too.

Indeed, if at any time in its history the INI "thought big," it was during its pilot Coordinating Center's first five years. This chapter begins with a description of the INI's remarkable, incomplete survey of the highlands' ladino population. It then turns to the road construction program, which facilitated all of the INI's development schemes. The chapter then looks at two utopian projects: one, an attempt to sink roots in and transform the Tseltal communities of eastern Chiapas; and the other, a program to establish consumer cooperatives. It concludes by looking at the first five years of the CCI's health division, when the indigenistas learned some hard lessons.

Marroquín's Surveys

In early 1955, a Marxist economist who hailed from El Salvador, Alejandro Marroquín, followed up on Villa Rojas's proposal and assembled a research team to conduct surveys of highland populations. The team started with San Cristóbal's eleven historic barrios. Marroquín's survey was exhaustive: among other things, it asked how ladinos lived, what their houses were like, whether they had access to water in their homes—many did not—whether they had toilets, how they made a living, what their tax obligations were, and what their relations with the indigenous were like. Marroquín also wanted to know about religious and political organizations, particularly whether there were anticommunist, Sinarquista,[7] or PRI-based organizations in the barrio. And how did these organizations get the word out to residents? Via posters, pamphlets, rallies, loudspeakers, or persuasion in the confessional? In short, the "anthropological gaze" was turned on *coletos*, the ladino residents of San Cristóbal.

Two months into his research, Marroquín was able to draw some preliminary conclusions. Although San Cristóbal still had many characteristics of a caste society, he was confident that "the economic factor is totally destroying the caste barriers that remain." People now married outside their barrio, and ladino girls in the center of town "made friends and flirted with students in secondary and preparatory school" even if they came from poor barrios on the outskirts. Marroquín came to view the peripheral barrios as spaces of integration; they brought the indigenous into town, and the people of these barrios shared common beliefs, superstitions, habits, foods, and even language with the indigenous. "What we need is mobility," wrote Marroquín, "the interpenetration of the marginal sectors: barrios and the center, barrios and the indigenous periphery."[8]

With the assistance of Tseltal and Tsotsil translators, Marroquín's team also interviewed people at the principal points of entry into San Cristóbal. Most people who entered the town were indigenous, and most came on foot. They sold charcoal, firewood, vegetables, avocados, eggs, lime powder, and pine needles, and they came to buy salt, chillies, candles, corn, and sugar. Once they approached the marketplace, however, they were besieged by the notorious *atajadoras* (interceptors who took indigenous goods at a fraction of their value). And once inside the market, the indigenous were still the victims of fraudulent weights and measures; at the meat counters, they were only sold giblets, intestines, and other undesirable cuts.[9]

TABLE 3.1. Research questionnaire for the barrios of San Cristóbal de Las Casas.

GENERAL TOPICS	SPECIFIC NOTES AND QUESTIONS
Boundaries of the barrio	Possible sources of information: the priest or the barrio committee.
Complete map of the barrio	
Historical background	When the barrio was founded, who were the first residents, details on growth, recent modifications, indigenous products and producers, ladino crafts.
Demographic information	Number of inhabitants, families, and literates; population by profession and trade.
Houses of the barrio	A description of the houses: bright or dark, what they are made of.
Religious organization of the barrio	Churches, meetings, celebrations, religious calendar; religious habits of the inhabitants; Masses, confessions, visits to and from the priest; offerings and donations; contributions to the church in the form of unremunerated work.
Economic organization of the barrio	The number of businesses, the number of clients; investments and municipal and state tax declarations; other economic establishments like cantinas, hotels and inns, banks, markets; salaries.
Political organization of the barrio	Political associations, anticommunist fronts, Sinarquistas, PRI organizations. The nature of political propaganda: posters, loose-leaf pamphlets, oral propaganda, rallies, use of loudspeakers, propaganda in the confessionals. The nature of political struggles in the barrio: are they vicious, open, violent, peaceful, etc. The number of important bureaucrats.
Social organization of the barrio	The barrio's societies or clubs, the class and ethnic structure of the barrio. Barrio schools: their role and quality. Institutions that give cohesion to the barrio. People who are away, unemployed, etc. Ethnic structure: whites, ladinos, or Indians.
Life of the barrio	Daily routines; alcoholism and delinquency; intrafamilial relations; barrio festivals and public services.
Rivalries between barrios	Conflicts and rivalries with other barrios. Is there collaboration? How many artisans work outside of the barrio? How many outsiders come to work in the barrio? What do they do?
Sanitary problems in the barrio	Are animals butchered at a slaughterhouse or at the home? Access to water, toilets, water tanks, sewage facilities, a river.

Source: CDI, BJR, Alejandro Marroquín, "Investigaciones de Chiapas," 1955.

Marroquín's team also began to survey the surrounding municipalities. The primary focus, once again, was on the ladino populations that resided in some of the cabeceras. At Larráinzar, for example, typical ladino occupations included shopkeeper, labor contractor (habilitador), finca employee, teacher, candlemaker, baker, driver, locksmith, mason, butcher, and marimba player. Last of all, Marroquín's team compiled information on the size of landholdings, property taxes, and the amount of sugar, coffee, corn, and beans produced in the region. It also compiled tax records from flour retailers, hotels, restaurants, bakeries, watchmakers, coffee dispensaries, candle factories and shops, aguardiente distributors, cantinas, pharmacies, public baths, billiard halls, enganchadores, and even ice-cream parlors.[10]

Underlying this rather frenetic collection of data was Marroquín's belief that economic development was the key to breaking down the caste system and integrating the region. Marroquín was especially interested in ladino poverty and the violence that seemed to permeate life in the Chiapas highlands. His team compiled an exhaustive list of all the crimes committed in San Cristóbal and the surrounding region from 1950 to 1954 and the first half of 1955. These included homicides, theft, sexual assaults, and "crimes against society." Marroquín's team took special care to note whether alcohol was involved and whether the perpetrator was literate. They also correlated escalating ladino crime (especially cantina violence) with economic distress, especially sugar, gasoline, and corn shortages.[11]

First Things First: "Penetration" Roads

Before the indigenistas could foster what Aguirre Beltrán described as "decorous and humane interdependence" between the indigenous and ladinos or help feed a rapidly industrializing country, they needed roads. Without them, the CCI could not feasibly provide supplies for school construction or stock its medical outposts or consumer cooperatives. A modern transportation network also served a less tangible goal—national integration. The INI's term for these roads—*caminos de penetración*—was an unfortunate one that nonetheless underscored the INI's concern with connecting modern Mexico with allegedly "self-isolated," culturally conservative indigenous groups.[12]

Aguirre Beltrán's goal in 1951 was not to find the quickest, most cost-effective route through the highlands but to connect as many communities as possible to one another and to San Cristóbal while steering clear of places deemed sacred by the principales (elders).[13] That summer, the INI, in collaboration with the federal Ministry of Communications (Secretaría de Comunicaciones), started work on the Las Casas–Chenalhó highway, which was to link five Tsotsil municipalities to San Cristóbal: Chamula, Zinacantán, Mitontic, Larráinzar, and Chenalhó. Aguirre Beltrán also prioritized road construction out to "population centers most resistant to acculturation, like Cancuc and Chanal, because that is where governmental intervention is most urgent."[14]

At this time, the CCI clearly needed roads more than the indigenous people needed or wanted them. This tested the indigenistas' negotiating skills. In the 1940s, Chamulas had opposed roads because they feared that improved communications between their municipality and San Cristóbal would simply make it easier for ladinos to exploit them. According to Ricardo Pozas and William Holland, many also believed that numerous *ik'al* (black gods of the underworld) roamed the region, capturing and selling Indians to ladino road crew chiefs, who used their bodies in construction projects or turned them into grease to lubricate their road-building machinery.[15] Many other indígenas were indifferent to roads. This attitude was also problematic, since the INI expected to tap into indigenous labor, both paid and voluntary. Roads were so important to the CCI's programs that the indigenistas sometimes violated their own commitment to negotiation and persuasion. In 1951 and 1952, construction commenced before some of the affected hamlets had agreed to support the project. Agustín Romano admits that the indigenistas applied "psychological pressure." They explained that resistance to the roads was "useless" and that they would be built whether the community's elders approved of them or not.[16]

The first conflict over road construction came in summer 1951, when the first fifteen kilometers of the road from Chamula to Chenalhó were being prepared. The road affected land under cultivation in densely populated Chamula, and the INI did not adequately compensate the landowners.[17] Soon, angry Chamulas from Ichintón, La Ventana, and Bechijtik refused to let the road pass near their fields. The INI had managed to convince the elders of the benefits that the roads would bring, but local residents were unmoved. They publicly upbraided their leaders in the marketplace and accused them of selling out to the "ladinos." The troublemakers were promptly apprehended and sent to the jail in San Cristóbal. When Aguirre learned of this, he ordered their immediate release and took measures to reestablish the peace in these hamlets. Construction of the road went forward.[18]

Another, more explosive conflict soon erupted. In August, residents of four different Chamulan hamlets stormed into the headquarters of the road-building contractor and threatened to take direct action if the road passed too close to their hamlets and affected land under cultivation. As in the previous case, local residents turned against their authorities and chased them out of town. The INI's indigenous staff at the Chamula medical clinic stopped showing up for work because they feared for their lives. The road contractor threatened to call in federal troops if order could not be restored, because inebriated Chamulas had been raiding the camp where his workers spent the night. Aguirre's assistant, Manuel Castellanos Cancino, turned to the nine Chamulan promoters that the INI was training at La Cabaña and took them to Chamula. These young men temporarily took charge of the local government until Erasto Urbina could intervene and restore the principales. Castellanos and Aguirre investigated the matter and learned that the "rebellious climate" was the result of an accumulation of factors. Among them, a Chamula woman had allegedly been raped by one of the ladino bosses of the road crew. The INI fired him and promised "total respect" for indigenous women.[19] Residents were also alarmed by the INI's vaccination program. Aguirre met with the principales, who agreed to allow the INI's medical staff back into Chamula and pledged to help the INI build its road. Aguirre also asked for their support in building a school in the "rebellious" hamlet of Yalichín and asked them to cooperate with the INI's incipient reforestation project. The principales agreed, but only after Aguirre made them a deal that they could not refuse. He promised the INI's help in acquiring additional land for Chamula, agreed to indemnify affected farmers with deliveries of corn, and offered to install a *molino de nixtamal* (corn grinder) in the ceremonial center of the municipality. INI largesse helped Chamula's principales restore their authority in these restless hamlets.[20]

After some initial resistance, most indigenous communities were quick to appreciate the economic advantages of roads, and soon each hamlet wanted to be connected to the growing transportation network. In 1954, the INI helped an indigenous transportation cooperative purchase vehicles and begin offering its services along the road linking Las Casas to Chenalhó. Shortly thereafter, a second cooperative began working the route that connected Las Casas to Larráinzar. But this did not turn indigenous men into reliable road construction workers, and traditional labor forms proved ineffective. As Henri Favre notes, "the case is interesting because it shows the limits of the types of traditional labor arrangements in which some indigenistas had placed such high hopes."[21] Absenteeism was chronic. In Romano's words, "many worked only long enough to gather the funds needed to cover some urgent need, or to pay the costs associated with holding a religious cargo to which they had been named." In 1954, the INI stopped employing large numbers of indigenous workers and opted instead to use heavy machinery acquired from the federal Ministry of Public Works (Secretaría de Obras Públicas).[22]

Oxchuc and Environs: The Promised Land?

The Tseltal region held great promise for the indigenistas. The INI's educators reported that the CCI's Tseltal materials—written by Marianna Slocum—were much better than their Tsotsil cartillas. The Tseltal promoters were generally more capable than the first Tsotsil promoters, whose "indolence" was noted by education director Fidencio Montes Sánchez. He reported that for the Chamulas, especially, "the school is simply a source of income to help them accumulate land or buy work animals." Tseltal promoters, on the other hand, "constitute the collective soul [of their communities], who advise, guide, promote, and organize under the direction of the Center."[23]

One other factor worked in the INI's favor in the Tseltal zone. Many of the Tseltals' ladino oppressors owned ranches in the area and employed the indigenous as *baldíos* who gave a few days of labor each week and other personal services in exchange for the right to reside on and work the land. When Erasto Urbina hastily executed land reform around 1940, he mainly targeted ladino ranches in the Tsotsil highlands. Ranches in the Tseltal region were left mostly untouched. This provided the INI with opportunities to promote land reform and turn desperate baldíos into landowners and grateful clients.

Given the ladinos' political and economic grip on the Tseltal region, however, the indigenistas had to work hard to gain entry. In Tenejapa, just east of San Cristóbal, the INI never truly sank its roots. It was a stronghold of alcohol monopolist Hernán Pedrero; his close associate Abraham Liévano served as municipal secretary. Montes described Liévano as "the most 'ladino' of all those found in the indigenous zone. He is always seen with a pistol in his belt, with dark glasses and a Texas sombrero. His completely severe attitude reminds one of a foreman." Tenejapa was a like a Wild West town, where murderers were sprung from jail after paying bribes to Liévano. SEP teachers in Tenejapa were also hostile to the INI and its cultural promoters. After several years of struggle, the INI shifted its attention to other municipalities.[24]

In Oxchuc, ladinos had ceded some political control to the indigenous, but they—especially Abraham Liévano's brother, former municipal secretary Juan Manuel Liévano—were still a force to be reckoned with and owned all of the

FIGURE 3.1. CCI director Ricardo Pozas promoting cooperatives. Photographer unknown. Fototeca Nacho López, Comisión Nacional para el Desarrollo de los Pueblos Indígenas. 1953.

surrounding land.[25] Religious differences also complicated the work of the indigenistas in Oxchuc. "Traditional" Catholics, abstemious Catholics, and Protestants lived in the municipality. In some hamlets, the religious issue was described as a friendly rivalry, but in others it was the source of tension and even violence. Most of the INI's initial successes came in hamlets where Protestants were the majority, like Mesbiljá, Cholol, and El Corralito, but if it hoped to have any success among Catholics it had to maintain a safe distance from the SIL.[26]

The INI had big plans for Oxchuc and the surrounding region. After a 1953 visit to several municipalities and hamlets, CCI director Ricardo Pozas wrote to Caso about a project that would use "surplus" population from Oxchuc to colonize parts of Ocosingo. Ejidos there would cultivate corn and other crops on a large scale, with modern machinery. Pozas noted that the project held the promise of "liquidating the system of servitude that exists in this part of the state. All of the resident *peones acasillados* [debt peons] who work on the fincas of Oxchuc are willing to move with their families to Ocosingo to colonize those lands."[27]

While Pozas and the INI waited for the governor's approval of this ambitious colonization scheme, they turned their attention to school construction. "Some of our schools here are models for the rest of the country," Pozas reported. In many Tseltal hamlets, the schoolroom (and the adjacent teacher's house) symbolized modernity and became a local point of pride. The school at Cholol, for example, featured a teacher's house "with its separate dining room, bedroom, and kitchen" as well as "a beautiful garden with white stepping stones, an orchard, a vegetable garden, henequen plants, a public washing place, a sports field, and a latrine."[28] Cholol's baldíos allowed the INI to encase their spring with cement, to protect their water source. They appreciated having allies "because they are constantly the victims of arbitrary behavior. They feel protected when the employees of the INI are in their presence."[29]

The indigenistas were also well received at Mesbiljá, and soon the hamlet became a showcase for the INI's work in the area. Mesbiljá was just four kilometers outside of El Corralito, which Pozas described as "a center of religious propaganda. We want to create lay institutions in a region where religion prevents the indigenous from recognizing the exploitation of which they are victims." In 1953, Pozas met with baldíos there to propose forming a new population center near the river. The INI then began building a central school that bridged the gap between eleven Literacy Centers, which offered very rudimentary instruction, and the boarding school at La Cabaña. Students who came from neighboring hamlets took their meals and the spent the night with local families. This provided a modest income to locals and exposed them to the modernizing impulses of the school. The INI also sent a social worker to the hamlet who taught women to sew on Singer sewing machines and to bathe three times a week using soap. She also urged residents to raise beds and cooking utensils off the floor and open windows to allow ventilation in the kitchen. Many Tsotsil communities had rejected this modernizing agenda, but the INI reported the residents of Mesbiljá to be receptive.[30]

Abasolo, a dependency (*agencia municipal*) of Ocosingo that borders on Oxchuc, became another bright spot for the INI. When education inspector Reynaldo Salvatierra approached residents to inquire whether they were interested in an INI school, he wisely brought several promoters from Oxchuc with him. One of the INI's standout promoters, Juan Sántiz Gómez, addressed the crowd in Tseltal, explaining the advantages of an INI school and its various programs. When he was done speaking, the municipal agent and four other ladinos began working the crowd, advising them not to invite the INI into their community. They claimed that the INI was a Protestant organization "that had used treachery to invade Oxchuc, the proof of which can be found at El Corralito." According to Salvatierra, the indigenous were "almost convinced. They were so agitated that at one point they threw themselves at us aggressively." Once the crowd settled down, Sántiz Gómez opened his shirt and revealed a religious medallion that identified him as a Catholic. He then said, "the people that advise you with false ideas are people who do not want Indians to lift themselves up." With that, the crowd abandoned the ladinos. Six indigenous men who could read and write signed up to begin training at La Cabaña. The INI subsequently opened a school in Abasolo.[31]

Abasolo soon sent one of the first female students to attend the INI's boarding school at La Cabaña. When students went back home for vacation, they were assigned various domestic tasks aimed at elevating the standard of living in their communities. In January 1955, one of the boarding school teachers, Lucía Morales, visited the students at their homes to monitor their progress. She reported that the student from Abasolo, named Marcela, enjoyed broad community support and had taught local women how to use a Singer sewing machine. When Morales conducted her home inspections, the women not only invited her in but gave her fruit and eggs as tokens of appreciation. "I explained to them that we had not come to cause problems and that I could not accept these things, because they need them, but they insisted," she wrote. "During my stay here they tended to my horse and when I tried to pay them for their work they refused to accept money and begged me not to insist because they would get mad." The people of Abasolo seemed genuinely grateful for the INI's support. "They explained to me that the pueblo is improving because there are no longer any ladinos. They love whoever visits them from the INI because they know that the INI loves them."[32]

By 1955, INI schools were in such demand in some Tseltal communities that people were willing to go to jail to have one. For example, Tseltal ejidatarios at Colonia Virginia in Ocosingo refused to accept the federal teacher sent by the SEP and demanded instead an INI cultural promoter. The SEP's education inspector and the local Indigenous Affairs delegate asked Ocosingo's municipal president to incarcerate twelve ejidatarios, including the president of the Education Committee, in order to "preserve the principle of authority." Once he learned of this, the INI's Fidencio Montes flew to Ocosingo and met with the federal education inspector. After explaining that he had no legal right to incarcerate the twelve men, Montes spoke with the prisoners. When asked why they refused to accept a SEP teacher, they complained that "they only show up one or two days a week." It had been years since the children had learned anything, and the schoolhouse was nearly in ruins because the previous teacher had used it to keep his animals. The ejidatarios "noticed that the INI's schools work well and that the students learn." After explaining that the INI could not place one of its promoters in a SEP school, Montes asked the SEP inspector and the newly appointed SEP teacher to work every day, even Saturdays and Sundays if necessary, and the ejidatarios pledged their support to the school and its *parcela escolar* (garden plot). Montes also offered to send an INI agronomist and a health brigade, and offered to split the cost of hair clippers and a basketball. Once this agreement had been reached, the ejidatarios were released from jail. But the municipal president had one final request—he asked Montes to explain to the ejidatarios that they still had to obey him.[33]

After a few years of work in the Tseltal region, indigenistas could claim some small victories. Although they had not yet "liberated" many baldíos, INI schools in this region were, on the whole, much more successful than those in the southern Tsotsil municipalities. Tseltal promoters were more skilled and dedicated, and their communities, by and large, had embraced the indigenista project. When the INI initiated a new training cycle at La Cabaña in February 1954, fifteen of the thirty-six aspiring promoters were from Oxchuc, and five more came from the small town of Abasolo.[34] In 1956, there were sixteen INI schools operating in Oxchuc; 581 children attended (including 132 girls), and remarkably, so too did 653 adults (including 277 women). Nowhere in the CCI's zone of operations did adults, and especially women, express so much interest in literacy. It may be no coincidence that Slocum finished her translation of the Oxchuc Tseltal New Testament in 1956. The impact of Protestant missionary linguists in the region—who taught the importance of reading scripture and having a direct relationship with God—cannot be overstated.[35]

In September 1956, shortly before Mexican Independence Day, Fidencio Montes toured schools in Oxchuc and was deeply moved by what he saw. At Mesbiljá, on the thirteenth of the month, "the altar to the *patria* was already prepared, with the austere images of [Miguel] Hidalgo and [Benito] Juárez signaling the road to redemption for these pariahs, victims for centuries in this hardscrabble region of the Chiapas highlands." After the school raised the Mexican flag, passersby "uncovered their heads in front of the national insignia, one of the biggest civics lessons that one could give." The next morning, INI promoters slaughtered a bull at 3:00 a.m. for the town fiesta, then raised the flag at 6:00 a.m. in the presence of authorities, children, and their parents, all of whom sang the national anthem and set off rockets. Later that day, schoolchildren recited poetry, sang, and performed skits about Mexican independence to a packed house, and one of the INI's promoters spoke in Tseltal of the debt that the Mexican nation owes to Hidalgo and Juárez. On the fifteenth, there was a basketball tournament, a market, a sumptuous meal for all participants, and a patriotic calisthenics demonstration featuring batons that were colored red, white, and green, the colors of the Mexican flag. That afternoon, Montes traveled to Oxchuc's municipal center. By the morning of September 16, Mexico's actual Independence Day, all sixteen INI schools in the municipality had arrived at Oxchuc's main plaza. There were dances, piñatas, more rockets, more basketball, more marching and calisthenics routines, and no alcohol. Montes estimated that at least three thousand people filled Oxchuc's plaza. "This made quite an impression on the ladinos." Montes also felt great satisfaction upon seeing "how the promoters carry out the instructions that we give them."[36] Given the INI's mounting frustrations with some of its low-performing promoters and schools in Chamula and elsewhere in the southern Tsotsil region, where half of the INI's schools still did not meet in a schoolhouse, this demonstration of patriotic sentiment brought hope. Perhaps national integration was within reach after all.

Not So Fast: The Problem with Consumer Cooperatives

The INI's first economic development program in indigenous communities involved the creation of consumer cooperatives. Cooperatives were a common feature of development plans in postrevolutionary Mexico. Proponents argued that egalitarian principles and collective forms of organization were innate to Mexicans, especially the indigenous. In the early 1950s, INI economist Alejandro Marroquín was one of several prominent indigenistas to express an almost blind faith in cooperatives, while Julio de la Fuente and others were skeptical that modern cooperatives could be grafted onto indigenous communities.[37] The INI's experience in Chiapas suggests that de la Fuente was right.

Consumer cooperatives were intended to stimulate and channel consumption and keep profits in indigenous hands. Ideally, they stocked products that Tseltals and Tsotsils were accustomed to buying from ladinos in San Cristóbal, like candles, matches, gasoline, batteries, salt, and even corn. Cooperatives could also influence consumer tastes. On the advice of INI doctors, cooperatives stocked hand soaps, detergents, evaporated milk, oatmeal, toothbrushes, and DDT soap and hair cream with DDT (to kill the lice that transmit typhus). The INI's forestry specialists urged cooperatives to stock kerosene lamps, which offered nighttime illumination, reduced the need for ocote (a very resinous pine tree native to the highlands), and slowed the rate of deforestation. The cooperatives also sold shoes and soft drinks, both produced at La Cabaña; the latter, called Yalel, was an alternative to aguardiente. For the INI, consumer cooperatives were intended to "defend the indigenous community from the repercussions of contact with the local capitalist economy" while also creating new needs, promoting the "right" kinds of products, and facilitating the community's socioeconomic development.[38]

In theory, then, indigenous consumer cooperatives met several important objectives for the INI. But in practice, they ran into a series of problems that were never fully resolved. In 1952, the CCI attempted to launch its first cooperative in Chamula. The first members were the INI's cultural promoters; each contributed what he could, and the CCI matched their contributions. This was a cooperative in its purest form; members did not earn dividends based on what they invested but on how much was consumed. Prices were kept below market price, and members paid even less for their purchases. But, to the surprise of some indigenistas, Chamula's promoters were not interested in lower prices at the cooperative store; they wanted a return on their investment. To prevent most of the members from leaving the cooperative, the CCI moved toward a system of yearly dividends based on each member's initial investment.[39]

In 1953, Pozas and the CCI were able to interest several other communities in forming consumer cooperatives, partly by touting the "success" of the cooperative in Chamula. But as the CCI's subdirector Raúl Rodríguez Ramos admitted, the Chamulan experience had been only "marginally successful. We still cannot say that our work has achieved the goal of establishing a cooperative system in an indigenous pueblo."[40] By 1954, most members of the Chamulan cooperative had given up on the entire enterprise and wanted to withdraw their money.

The cooperative at relatively distant Oxchuc held more promise. Merchandise could only be brought in by mule train, and Oxchuqueros appreciated the fact that the store provided goods that they could not otherwise find. INI anthropologist Carlos Incháustegui noted that "the store already forms part of the life of the community. It has been widely accepted, even by those who have their small stores, because they find items in the cooperative that they don't have." Both indigenous people and ladinos supported the cooperative, even if ladinos never shopped alongside Indians. On Sundays, an INI promoter set up a record player at the store, and it filled with indigenous people who listened to songs and requested favorites, all the while consuming cookies and candies.

FIGURE 3.2. Two men working at a consumer cooperative. Photographer unknown. Fototeca Nacho López, Comisión Nacional para el Desarrollo de los Pueblos Indígenas. Circa 1960.

Incháustegui ventured that "many of them did not get drunk on that day. We dream of having some records recorded in Tseltal, with jokes and propaganda and songs."[41]

One of the items stocked in Oxchuc's cooperative was the hand-operated corn grinder. According to Incháustegui, these saved women "two to three hours of work a day" and allowed for more hygienic preparation of the corn meal; metates, the traditional grinding stones, were placed on dirt floors. Spared the onerous task of grinding corn, women helped their husbands in the fields. This allowed the men to put more land under cultivation in those places where additional land was available.[42]

In 1955, four years after the INI opened its first cooperative, Marroquín continued to tout the positive dimensions of indigenous cooperatives. They facilitated the right kind of social change, they offered basic articles of consumption at a reduced price, they satisfied local demand, and they trained community members how to run small commercial operations. Ideally, they also stimulated group solidarity. But there were problems that even Marroquín could not ignore. In order to keep the cooperatives afloat, the CCI had allowed them to become small investment clubs. The cooperatives' founding members did not admit additional members because they wanted to protect their profits. This limited community interest in the cooperatives, which, Marroquín admitted, "serve the interests of the economically powerful more than they serve the communities themselves." Furthermore, the indigenous communities were, in Marroquín's words, "absolutely incapable" of doing the bookkeeping, so CCI staff had to periodically review their accounts. The shopkeepers themselves did not always "resist the temptation of committing small frauds that, over the long term, notably damage the cooperative." The only way to prevent theft, wrote Marroquín, was for the cooperative to actively manage and police itself. "All members of the community should denounce the abuses, the price alterations, the adulterations of merchandise, and the frauds that some shopkeepers commit when weighing items," he wrote. But, as he himself acknowledged, the shopkeepers and directors were almost always well-connected bilinguals who knew how to read and write and do simple math.[43] In Chamula, for example, the president of the cooperative's directorate was the municipal president; the secretary was an INI promoter; and the treasurer was Salvador López Castellanos (Tuxum), who also served as general secretary of the STI. Denouncing shady business practices in Chamula and elsewhere meant challenging powerful leaders who enjoyed close ties to the INI and, sometimes, the state government.[44]

To correct several of these anomalies, the CCI began to offer short courses in basic mathematics, accounting, weights and measures, and customer service. To drum up more support for the cooperatives, Marroquín urged a major publicity campaign using loudspeakers and print material in Tseltal and Tsotsil. The INI obliged him by setting up record players and speakers on plazas and playing amplified classical music in communities where such music had never before been heard. At Amatenango, the INI played Tchaikovsky, the first and third movements of Beethoven's Fifth Symphony, Fritz Kreisler's "Viennese Caprice," and Jules Massenet's "Meditation" before delivering a message promoting consumer cooperatives. As Montes wrote, "it was astonishing to see men and women leave their homes and enter the plaza, approach us silently and sit in a circle to listen, spellbound."[45] Elsewhere, the INI amplified classical music and music from other indigenous peoples in Mexico, like the Otomís, the Yaquis, the Huichols, the Coras, the Tonotonacs, and even music from Zinacantán and Chamula, with mixed results. Beginning in 1956, even the INI's hand-puppet troupe was deployed to promote cooperatives. But was this the best use of INI resources? The cooperatives did not truly function as such and had been commandeered by a handful of well-connected INI promoters. A program aimed at community development ended up reinforcing preexisting inequalities. The INI spent tens of thousands of pesos each year to keep nine cooperatives afloat, and it had to offer its vehicles to transport merchandise from San Cristóbal. And how long could the INI continue to incur the wrath of local ladinos, who argued that the indigenous cooperatives affected their bottom line?[46]

Modern Medicine in the Premodern Highlands

Perhaps the INI's most delicate task was that of introducing Western medicine to the highland communities. The situation was dire. Close to 80 percent of the indigenous population suffered from some form of parasitosis. Gastrointestinal and respiratory illnesses, including enteritis, bronchitis, whooping cough, typhus, and measles hit children particularly hard. Adults suffered from these and other ailments, including rheumatism and extreme malnutrition, as well as illnesses that they picked up during stints on lowland plantations such as malaria, onchocerciasis (river blindness), uncinariosis (hookworm), and amoebic dysentery.[47] The infant mortality rate hovered around 50 percent in many municipalities. Water sources in the highlands were often contaminated. The rate of lice infestation in nine municipalities was between 51 and 100 percent; in the three remaining municipalities, between 26 and 50 percent of the population was infected.[48] Tseltals and Tsotsils shared living quarters with pigs, dogs, and poultry; they slept on flea-infested blankets on dirt floors in poorly ventilated homes; they defecated outside, in the open air, but children (and animals) often defecated on the dirt floor.

Tackling these issues in a population that lacked a modern understanding of illness was no easy matter. Where indigenistas saw people suffering from preventable diseases, Tseltals and Tsotsils believed that illness was the work of witchcraft, an angry relative, or a divine curse. The indigenistas wanted to protect water sources by encasing them in cement, but the indigenous believed that springs were an opening to the underworld; encasing them would provoke the wrath of the gods. Indigenistas encouraged the indigenous to put cement floors in their houses, but where else would the indigenous bury their children's umbilical cords, which kept their homes *calientitos* (warm)? And when the INI built modern clinics in the highlands and staffed them with ladino doctors and nurses, the indigenous continued to prefer traditional healers, who spoke their language and treated them in their own homes where they were surrounded by family and loved ones. No dimension of the INI's development program more directly clashed with the spiritual underpinnings of Tseltal and Tsotsil culture.

The indigenistas' motivations were both altruistic and calculating. On the one hand, they believed that the postrevolutionary Mexican state had the obligation to introduce Western medicine to the people of this region, eradicate curable diseases, and improve living standards. On the other, modern medicine would help undermine what indigenistas considered "obsolete" aspects of native cultures. According to Gonzalo Aguirre Beltrán, indigenista practice was designed to "rationalize and secularize traditional concepts and medical practices" as well as "weaken the mechanisms of cohesion that are based on magic and religion." Once these goals had been achieved, Aguirre Beltrán wrote, the CCI "would lose its raison d'etre" and shift responsibilities to the federal Ministry of Public Health (Secretaría de Salud y Asistencia, or SSA).[49] For Aguirre, modern medicine would also diminish anxiety and criminality in the indigenous highlands. Traditional healers attributed certain symptoms to witchcraft, and the accused often were attacked; healers, too, often suffered fatal consequences if they failed to cure their patients.[50]

When the Coordinating Center opened its doors, its health program centered around four medical clinics that supervised a larger number of satellite medical outposts (*puestos médicos*). Each clinic was staffed by a doctor and a ladino nurse; the outposts were staffed by bilingual ladino nurses. Indigenous cultural promoters served as assistant nurses and translators. The CCI opened its central clinic at La Cabaña in 1951 and immediately began negotiating to open a clinic in Chamula. The Chamulas, however, were reluctant. Not only did Western medicine threaten traditional practice, but Chamulas allowed only one ladino to reside in their municipality—the municipal secretary. Once again, the CCI had to turn to Erasto Urbina, Manuel Castellanos Cancino, and Chamulan elders who had been hired to be bilingual health promoters in spite of the fact that they did not understand modern medicine.[51] One of these elders was Salvador Gómez Osob. After three rounds of negotiations, the elders allowed the CCI to build its clinic after it promised that the doctor and nurse would be the only additional ladinos allowed to reside in Chamula. In 1952, the CCI opened additional clinics in Chilil (Huixtán) and Yochib (Oxchuc).

The medical personnel who staffed the INI's clinics in Chamula and Yochib were likely the loneliest people in the Chiapas highlands. The supervising doctor at the Chamula clinic was Dr. Roberto Robles Garnica. "It drizzled all day long, the atmosphere humid, the central plaza deserted, the days windy, the clinic quiet," he wrote. "Since nobody came to the clinic, I decided that we should go to the homes of the indigenous families in search of the sick who were not interested in our services even though the consultations and medicines were free." But the indigenous were not interested in house calls, either. "Day after day we went from one hut to the next, and as soon as we got close, the people locked themselves inside their homes," wrote Robles Garnica. "From the outside, in a very soft and delicate voice, the indigenous nurse would give extremely long explanations, but the result was always the same: nobody opened their door."[52]

The first person to use the clinic was a woman who requested medicine "not for *cristianos* (people) but for some chickens who had diarrhea." Robles Garnica prescribed a sulfa drug "but was not sure whether it did any good." The first patient was a lamb that had been mauled by a coyote; Robles Garnica performed a skin graft. The first human patient may have fared worse than the animals. One day, when Robles Garnica and his Zinacantecan nurse were trying to round up patients, the nurse found a woman named María dying of starvation. The nurse figured out that she had mistakenly ingested a caustic that had caused esophageal stenosis. The INI took her to the clinic in Chamula. The medical team gave her an IV, and since she was covered with lice, the ladina nurse bathed her and covered her with talcum powder containing DDT. But after a few days, as soon as she was able, María fled the clinic. Robles Garnica later learned that she had found the clinic to be "cold"—not physically cold, because there were plenty of blankets available, but soulless, sterile, and completely alien. Robles Garnica never heard from María again but was certain that she had died without receiving additional medical care. "First failure and not the last," he wrote.[53]

Another failure at Chamula was the 1951 vaccination campaign against smallpox. Aguirre Beltrán again turned to Urbina and three of his former scribes to push this unpopular campaign against the will of the local population. The elders believed that smallpox was an illness sent by God. Their attitude was fatalistic; if God wanted to take away life, there was no point in trying to stop him. They also did not understand why preventive medicine was being applied to healthy people. Aguirre Beltrán eventually convinced them to cooperate, but other Chamulas resisted after some had mild reactions to the shot. Soon, even the elders withdrew their support from the campaign. The INI's medical team pressed on. When Chamulas threatened the INI's doctor with

FIGURE 3.3. Dr. Roberto Robles Garnica chatting with men from Huixtán. Nacho López, photographer. Fototeca Nacho López, Comisión Nacional para el Desarrollo de los Pueblos Indígenas. Circa 1956.

their homemade cap-and-ball pistols, he would show them his own. In time, the whole municipality was vaccinated.[54]

The CCI realized in retrospect that it was a mistake to carry out a smallpox vaccination campaign at a time when its very presence in Chamula was tenuous. Furthermore, smallpox was not the primary concern in Chamula, where typhus, typhoid fever, whooping cough, and measles exacted a greater human toll. Of these, typhus was the easiest to resolve, since it only required the application of DDT on clothing, not a shot. Experience taught the CCI to start with the relatively easy campaigns and later move on to the difficult ones.[55]

But even campaigns against typhus and typhoid presented difficulties. In late 1951, the INI learned that many residents of the Tsotsil hamlet of Chichihuistán (Teopisca) were suffering from high fevers, chronic diarrhea, and rashes, and that twenty-six had died. Dr. Ángel Torres, the INI's first director of medical services, took three nurses to the hamlet and surveyed the situation. Chichihuistán's inhabitants worked on nearby fincas and lived in huts "in great promiscuity." Most slept on the ground. Mosquitoes, rats, and fleas were everywhere, and "defecation [was] done in the open." The hamlet's water source was contaminated by animals that grazed upstream.[56]

Dr. Torres first described how the local curandero had been treating patients with symptoms of typhus and typhoid. "Residents kill a black rooster for him and give him a *garrafón* [seventeen to twenty liters] of aguardiente. They light candles in the room next to a cross made of pine branches. The curandero arrives daily or every other day and is paid money." He said prayers and spread ointments of unknown origin. "When the patient dies he says that the spirit took him/her away," wrote Torres.

Chichihuistán's initial response to the CCI's health workers was hostile. Most residents refused to allow them to take blood samples, fearing that it would take their spirits from them and kill them. "One family did not allow us to even use a thermometer on the patient," wrote Torres. "In view of the danger in which we found ourselves, I decided that five blood samples were sufficient."[57]

After two of the samples tested positive for typhus, Torres returned to Chichihuistán, accompanied this time by three indigenous nurses and armed with talcum power with 10 percent DDT and antibiotics. They learned that residents had turned against the curandero and killed him. Even more ominously, one of the patients whose blood sample had tested positive had died. This death caused "a grave state of anxiety," since it merely confirmed what locals already suspected about blood samples. The CCI's health brigade quickly retreated to La Cabaña. Aguirre Beltrán then summoned the elders of Chichihuistán and four nearby hamlets. Whatever Aguirre said, promised, or threatened produced a dramatic change in attitude, for when the *brigadistas* returned to Chichihuistán, they encountered no opposition. In the five hamlets, they spread DDT powder in 1,105 homes, doused 625 residents with the powder, and gave medical attention to 106 sick people. Although 6 died, the outbreak of typhus and typhoid fever was quickly contained, and most residents subsequently adopted a more positive attitude toward the INI's medical program.[58]

The hamlet of El Chivero was the last of the five to receive treatment from the CCI's medical staff. While they tended to the sick, a local curandero led a collective healing ceremony. Dr. Torres's description of the ceremony illustrates the potentially mortal consequences of traditional understandings of epidemic diseases.

> The *médico brujo* [witch doctor] arrived to plant a wooden cross in a hole dug by all those present. Four men and two women carried the cross. First, the women danced around the cross. Then the doctor placed a sheep's head and a little bit of blood in the hole while he prayed. The people lit candles and burned incense. Once the cross was in place they packed dirt around it. Each action was accompanied by ranchera music played on a guitar and mandolin.
>
> At this point, people had already drunk three liters of aguardiente. Some twenty people fired their shotguns into the air. Forty candles and pine branches were placed around the cross. An elderly couple, Domingo Hernández and Juana Pérez, came forward so that the doctor could take their pulse, since according to some residents they were the ones responsible for the sickness. The doctor indicated that the couple had fresh blood and that the sickness came from God. The doctor then collected 300 pesos from the people present.

The ceremony concluded with a feast. While the sheep cooked, "dancing and drinking built to a climax."[59]

Despite some isolated successes, the CCI's health division soon entered into a profound crisis. At Chamula, many regarded the INI's medical team the same way they regarded the fiscal police who entered their hamlets in search of clandestine aguardiente stills. They were seen as violating Chamula's autonomy and threatening traditional practices. Assassination rumors were rife, and the two indigenous promoters who worked with the ladino doctor and nurse essentially doubled as bodyguards.[60] Elsewhere in the INI's zone of operations, clinics were still virtually empty, doctors carried pistols for their own protection, and the medical outposts were in total disarray. At Chanal, force had been used to give the TAB vaccination (to protect against typhoid) to children at the INI's schools. Not only did this violate INI directives against coercion, but the result, naturally, was "counterproductive."[61]

The panorama was possibly worse at Amatenango. Dr. Robles visited the outpost there in October and found "not a single piece of medical furniture and no registry of consultations." The ladina nurse had vaccinated only a handful of people with TAB, and these vaccinations were spread out over the course of nearly a year, "which is useless, because no more than a month can pass between the first and second dose." Dr. Robles transferred the nurse to Aguacatenango because her relationship with the ladino schoolteacher at Amatenango, a declared enemy of the INI, prevented her from winning the confidence of the indigenous. Furthermore, the Catholic clergy in Amatenango believed that the INI was allied with local Protestants and further obstructed the INI's work.[62] Religious divisions also hampered the INI's work at Yochib, in Oxchuc, where Marianna Slocum and Florence Gerdel had introduced modern medicine in the late 1940s. The doctor at Yochib wrote that "the Catholic group hates the school and, unfortunately, there are still many people who think that our clinic is nothing more than a branch of the evangelists' activity."[63]

In January 1954, the INI announced in its official bulletin, *Acción Indigenista*, that the CCI's health division had been "reorganized." Several ladino nurses had been fired due to their poor performance; they were to be replaced by indigenous nurses.[64] Later that year, in his report to the INI's central offices, Ramón Hernández López blasted the ladino staff at the central clinic at La Cabaña for their apathy, their irresponsibility, "their dishonest conduct that damages the prestige of the INI, and the contemptuous and even rude treatment that they give the indigenous people. This constitutes an act of sabotage against the work of the Centro Coordinador." Weeks later, most of the remaining ladino staff was dismissed.[65]

The CCI's health division was still in crisis in early 1955. In February, Dr. Robles met with CCI director Romano and planned a fundamental reorientation of the division. Robles did not mince words; the medical outposts in particular were "bad institutions that feebly attempted to substitute traditional medicine." The nurses who staffed them were "notoriously ill prepared," and several of the bilingual health promoters had still not bought into Western medicine. This created a "vice-ridden work ethic that was anti-scientific and subject to the critiques of the communities for their notorious inefficiency." Robles believed that the INI should shift almost exclusively to preventive medicine, especially vaccinations, DDT campaigns, and the protection of water sources. He also proposed training *comadronas*, women (preferably bilinguals) who would work directly with pregnant women. Romano accepted Robles's recommendations, temporarily closing five medical outposts and moving their *promotores de salud* to the clinics, where they could pick up much-needed additional training. He also endorsed Robles's proposal to shift the emphasis of the health division to preventive medicine and education. The INI's health division would "relaunch" in 1956.

Conclusions

The years 1951 to 1955 were a time of utopian optimism and idealism at the INI's pilot Coordinating Center. As Carlos Navarrete Cáceres writes, "Anthropologists still believed it was possible to go to the countryside and rescue the ideals of the suspended Mexican Revolution." It was "the last time that they marched to 'Indian lands' in pursuit of a chimera."[66] Some of the country's most talented young social scientists were given the opportunity to craft programs that would be applied to dozens of additional Coordinating Centers in future years. It was a time when Caso could dream of industrializing "the Chamula region," when Aguirre Beltrán could write about a "vast plan" to dramatically transform the highlands and bring ladinos and Indians into a mutually beneficial economic interdependence, and when Alejandro Marroquín could undertake an ambitious survey of the ladino population. An equally audacious plan to resettle dispersed indigenous populations was launched by Ricardo Pozas in 1953. In what might be considered a reprise of colonial-era congregación, Pozas, the state's director of indigenous affairs Manuel Castellanos Cancino, and a translator met with indigenous populations across the region to propose their resettlement onto an urban grid that would have streets, piped water, stores, a school, and other services. Most Tsotsil communities balked at this proposition, but some communities of Tseltal baldíos consented.[67]

These were heady times for the indigenistas, a time when anything seemed possible. In the following passage, Dr. Robles attempts to capture the spirit at the Coordinating Center at the time of his hire, in 1953.

> [Director] Ricardo Pozas had a truly exceptional group of collaborators. They were Mexicans of diverse professions who considered their work on behalf of the Indians of the Chiapas highlands to be the most important of their lives. They were true apostles. The atmosphere at the Coordinating Center was contagious, and the most recent arrivals were quickly indoctrinated.... Everyone shared their experiences with them so that they could join this exceptional team. I have had the good fortune of working

with other well-prepared technical teams in other parts of the country, but I never found, nor do I think I will ever find, something similar to that excitement to elevate the Indians from the sad condition in which they found themselves.[68]

This, in short, is what became known as the *místíca indigenista*.

In terms of actual programmatic results, the indigenistas could celebrate some modest successes. By 1955, more than four dozen Literacy Centers had been established, and the CCI was taking steps to improve its corps of cultural promoters. The INI's efforts to build a network of roads had also paid dividends. But the indigenistas stumbled badly with their consumer cooperatives and medical programs. Given the anthropological research that predated the creation of the Coordinating Center, the INI's multiple miscalculations would seem to defy explanation. The inspiration for the cooperatives was largely ideological, based on naïve assumptions about indigenous culture rather than empirical observation. And since the indigenistas knew that the highland Maya did not grasp the principles behind modern medical practice, it is hard to understand why the INI built clinics and medical outposts, just as it is difficult to fathom why the INI's first doctors endorsed a disruptive vaccination campaign for a disease (smallpox) that was relatively rare in the highlands.

Looking ahead, indigenistas still had reason for optimism. School attendance was slowly on the rise; Marroquín's surveys were laying the groundwork for the economic transformation of the highlands; many Tseltals embraced the indigenista agenda; and roads were so popular in some communities that indigenous men were already forming transportation cooperatives. But the opposition of powerful ladinos in the highlands represented a gathering storm that threatened the entire indigenista project. The next chapter details the INI's fateful struggle with the Chiapas state government and the illegal statewide alcohol monopoly of Hernán and Moctezuma Pedrero.

Part 2 Sober Realities

CHAPTER 4
Winning the Battle, Losing the War
The INI versus the Pedrero Alcohol Monopoly

⦿⦿⦿ ONE OF THE proudest episodes in the history of Mexican indigenismo is told in this chapter. At precisely the moment when some of its development programs hung in the balance, the INI was forced to confront an illegal statewide alcohol monopoly controlled by two brothers who, as it turns out, had been named after key figures in the Spanish conquest of Mexico: Hernán and Moctezuma Pedrero Argüello. The Coordinating Center opened its doors just as the Pedrero alcohol monopoly was eliminating its last competitors. As the price of "official" monopoly alcohol in Chiapas rose and its quality fell, Tseltal and Tsotsil communities increasingly turned to the clandestine bootleg production of aguardiente. To suppress *clandestinaje*, the monopoly sent enforcers on abusive confiscation raids in the communities where the INI had begun its work. The INI opposed these occasionally fatal incursions, leading to accusations that it "sheltered" bootleggers. The "posh war," as it was known locally, was fought in the hamlets of highland Chiapas, in the offices of the state and federal government, and in the arena of public opinion.

This chapter is based largely on an exhaustive, formerly confidential report produced in 1954 at the height of the posh war. A series of confrontations between indigenistas, agents of the monopoly, and the monopoly's defenders in the state government led to the creation of the Commission to Study the Problem of Alcoholism in Chiapas. Alfonso Caso chose Julio de la Fuente, the CCI's second director, to coordinate the commission. Under the guise of studying indigenous alcoholism, de la Fuente's team researched and wrote a stinging indictment of the Pedrero alcohol monopoly and exposed the complicity of the Chiapas state government. So explosive was the final report, in fact, that the state government withdrew from the commission and blocked publication of the report. Shortly after de la Fuente's death in 1970, his personal secretary revealed in an interview that she had been under strict orders to keep the report under lock and key "because it dealt with secret things. It was confidential because it denounced the Pedreros."[1] In 2009, the INI's successor institution, the Comisión Nacional para el Desarrollo de los Pueblos Indígenas (CDI), published a slightly abridged version of the report.[2]

The INI's defense of Tseltals and Tsotsils from the depredations of the Pedrero alcohol monopoly and its allies was unquestionably heroic, but the outcome of this clash had ambivalent and ominous long-term consequences for indigenistas. The commission's report forced the state government to negotiate with the INI, and the protagonists agreed to a series of compromises that, among other things, brought an end to the indigenistas' more utopian schemes to restructure the regional economy. The INI's wings were clipped at its pilot Coordinating Center, with profound implications for the indigenista project in the rest of Mexico.

Alcohol and Its Meaning in Highland Chiapas

In the early 1950s, alcohol—especially aguardiente (literally "burning water," a rough cane liquor)—played an integral role in the secular and sacred lives of most non-Protestant Tseltals and Tsotsils. *Posh*, as it is known in the indigenous highlands, is made from *panela negra* (unrefined brown sugar). It has been produced in the region since the Spanish conquest and replaced chicha as the drink of ritual exchange for everything from *audiencias* (hearings) to marriage transactions. It was present at all of life's milestones, beginning with birth and baptism. Midwives were paid in food and aguardiente, and parents used it to celebrate the birth of a child. In most highland municipalities, posh played a crucial role in elaborate courtship rituals as a child reached adolescence. Once the girl's parents accepted aguardiente from the aspiring male or his representatives, they were expected to grant their daughter's hand in marriage. At the end of life, aguardiente (and chicha) was present at wakes, funeral processions, and burials. Bottles of alcoholic beverages were often buried with the deceased.[3]

Business transactions and legal matters also involved the exchange of aguardiente. People who aspired to a loan or a piece of land gave gifts of aguardiente in hopes of a favorable outcome. In a mostly preliterate society, a drink of *trago* had all of the binding qualities of a written contract.[4] In Chamula, aguardiente flowed copiously before, during, and after court hearings. Both litigants and defendants were expected to provide the authorities with aguardiente, who drank liberally during deliberations. Frequently, fines levied were payable in aguardiente; occasionally, the outcome of the hearing required both litigant and defendant to share a bottle together and part as friends.[5]

Aguardiente also played a major role in the civil-religious hierarchies of indigenous municipalities. Holding an office or cargo was very expensive, since it typically involved providing food and aguardiente for a major fiesta. Often, men had to be hunted down and thrown in jail before they would agree to serve, signaling their willingness by offering liquor to their captors. In order to defray the costs of holding a cargo, some municipalities like Chamula allowed only cargo holders to sell aguardiente.[6]

Posh also means "medicine" in Tsotsil, and it was used in the prevention, diagnosis, and treatment of illness. Shamans often poured aguardiente on their patients or onto hot rocks to expose patients to its vapors. They also used it to enter into trances to learn the cause of illness. Enterprising practitioners of Western medicine, such as ladino pharmacists in San Cristóbal, also made liberal use of aguardiente and denatured alcohol.[7] They induced its sale and consumption by preparing mixed drinks and attributing to them curative powers. For example, *aceite guapo* ("handsome oil") was "prescribed" as a painkiller; as an added bonus, it allegedly facilitated Spanish language acquisition.[8]

In short, aguardiente was an integral component of the sacred and secular lives of Tseltals and Tsotsils. It was ubiquitous in both work and play; in family and communal celebrations; in political and religious events; and in sickness and in health. It took the chill off bracing, high-altitude mornings, and it broke the monotony and eased the pain of a harsh life. The cultural and economic importance of aguardiente in highland Chiapas was such that any attempt to limit its production and distribution would have grave social consequences and foster clandestinaje.[9]

Excessive alcohol consumption, of course, had its downside. Anthropologists reported seeing children as young as seven scattered along roads or in plazas, drunk to the point of unconsciousness. Alcohol impacted school attendance, drained community resources, and often led to violence and familial dissolution. Women were often on the receiving end of their husbands' drunken rage. Aguardiente also played a pivotal role in enganche. As Aaron Bobrow-Strain has written: "Most ladinos categorically refuse to draw connections between the historic co-evolution of ladino prosperity and indigenous alcoholism, but the connections could not be more clear." Estates in highland Chiapas "combined sugar and coffee production into a seamless cane-coffee

FIGURE 4.1. A woman speaking to her intoxicated husband, Tenejapa. Photographer unknown. Fototeca Nacho López, Comisión Nacional para el Desarrollo de los Pueblos Indígenas. 1956.

complex in which aguardiente distilled from the first crop lubricated the production of the second."[10]

Many indigenous were aware of alcohol's dangers and its use as a tool of domination. According to one Tsotsil man who lived his entire life near Moctezuma Pedrero's former finca, Cucalvitz,

> they gave us lots of aguardiente. On Saturdays, the overseer gave everyone a drink, like a gift. Just a mouthful. But the workers wanted more because they had been working so much, and were so hungry. And soon each man had asked for his liter, which was added to his account at the finca. They had to pay it off with their work. It was very ugly.[11]

Not surprisingly, social reformers of all stripes have denounced alcohol consumption in the Chiapas highlands, including Protestant missionaries and, more recently, communities organized around Catholic liberation theology and the Zapatista Army of National Liberation.

The Emergence of the Alcohol Monopoly

The Pedreros' monopoly had humble beginnings. The brothers started out as itinerant peddlers and enganchadores based in Tapachula. By the mid-1920s, Moctezuma was making hats and producing soft drinks in Las Casas. Soon the brothers bought fincas. During the 1930s, the production of aguardiente in Chiapas was "free," and competition among producers was fierce. At one point there were ten distilleries in San Cristóbal alone. Three producers emerged to control production in the Chiapas highlands: Moctezuma Pedrero, former municipal president of San Cristóbal Mariano Bermúdez, and Jaime H. Coello. Competitors were eliminated through the use of "fraud, terror, tax evasion, and bribery."[12]

In the early 1940s, the state's remaining producers lobbied the state government to limit and eventually prohibit the sale of chicha. Jaime Coello and the Pedreros created regional alcohol monopolies through their work as alcohol tax collectors and regional producers and distributors of aguardiente. Each man had a network of distributors and vendors in the municipalities under his control; many of these subordinates also drew salaries as municipal secretaries. These men also pursued and punished clandestine producers to protect the interests of their bosses.[13]

According to popular lore, Moctezuma Pedrero got his big break when he won 10 million pesos in the national lottery in 1946.[14] By that time, Coello and the Pedreros owned four aguardiente factories, which they registered under the names of subordinates to avoid the appearance of an unconstitutional monopoly. Former employees testified that the Pedreros always kept two stills: one, registered and legal, operated eight hours daily and produced the legal amount of twenty-four *garrafones*;[15] the other, clandestine, operated day and night and produced seventy-two garrafones. State fiscal police, alcohol inspectors, and municipal authorities were paid to look the other way.[16]

The regional monopolies joined forces to become a statewide monopoly thanks to the notoriously venal Governor Francisco Grajales (1948–1952). Just days after he took office in January 1949, he suppressed the system of regional tax collection, paving the way for statewide fiscal control. Grajales also approved a restrictive alcohol law that granted near-monopoly conditions for select producers and distributors, in part by reversing previous legislation that had allowed indigenous cargo holders to sell alcohol. Days later, Coello and the Pedreros formed Aguardientes de Chiapas. At this point, for reasons unknown,

Coello and the Pedreros ended their working relationship, and the monopoly remained in the brothers' hands.[17]

In the early 1950s, the monopoly shifted into high gear and inaugurated its Ron Bonampak distillery in Comitán. The brothers took further steps to corner alcohol distribution networks both inside and outside of the state, controlling everything from aircraft to railway cars to even mule trains, and they were granted direct control over the federal treasury inspectors in Chiapas. Vertical integration became a reality in December 1952 when the Pedreros came to dominate a formerly independent sugar-growers cooperative called the Cooperative Society for Panela and Aguardiente Production (Sociedad Cooperativa de Productores de Panela y Elaboración de Aguardiente) and took over its distillery. By 1954, Aguardientes de Chiapas owned each of the five active, legal aguardiente distilleries in the state, controlled twenty-seven of the state's thirty-three alcohol and aguardiente distribution warehouses, had indirect control over the remaining six, and either owned or indirectly controlled each one of the state's 915 legal cantinas.[18]

Every step taken by the Pedreros' monopoly had far-reaching economic and social consequences. Over the span of just six years, the monopoly had forced the closure of sixteen distilleries and was keeping five of its own distilleries inactive. The number of municipalities producing sugarcane had dropped from eighty to fifty, and the number producing aguardiente fell from ten to three.[19] Since the Pedreros had become the only major buyer of panela and began to cultivate their own cane, they were able to dictate terms to the growers. In an ironic twist, the Pedreros' heavy-handed treatment of the state's sugar producers ended up threatening the monopoly's hold on the highlands. As George Collier notes, "the price of sugar dropped so low locally that a few Chamula families were able to afford an initial investment in sugar and build the first Indian distilleries. . . . By the early 1950s, clandestine Chamulan production began to dent the monopolists' market."[20]

Clandestinaje was so hard to suppress because it didn't take much to get started. Road construction in the highlands and the expansion of the transportation industry—two developments promoted by the INI—had the secondary effect of leaving behind big cans and barrels that the *clandestinos* used for their homemade stills. For their part, bootleggers were regarded as performing a useful public service. In some communities, they were considered heroes. They provided a socially necessary product at roughly half the price of monopoly aguardiente and risked retaliation from predatory producers who enjoyed access to the government's repressive apparatus. And when clandestinos

TABLE 4.1. The development of the aguardiente monopoly in Chiapas, 1948–1954.

YEAR	TOTAL PRODUCTION OF AGUARDIENTE		INDEPENDENT PRODUCERS		MONOPOLY	
	Distilleries	Liters	Distilleries	Liters	Distilleries	Liters
1948	19	1,092,088	15	929,295	4	162,793
1949	12	1,766,230	10	513,782	2	1,252,448
1950	7	1,985,156	4	487,250	2	1,497,906
1951	7	1,920,455	4	344,289	3	1,576,166
1952	10	1,552,262	5	391,749	5	1,160,513
1953	9	1,189,386	2	190,245	7	999,145
1954	5	940,126	0	0	5	940,126

Source: Lewis and Sosa Suárez, *Monopolio de aguardiente*, 177.

ambushed *fiscales* (officials from the state's Fiscal and Alcohol Inspection Board [Inspección Fiscal y de Alcoholes]), residents showed "great solidarity with the attackers. They do not reveal their identities to the authorities."[21]

Clandestinaje, Monopoly, and the INI

The INI's position on indigenous alcoholism was a sympathetic one informed by anthropological observation, pragmatism, and a dose of paternalism. Excessive alcohol consumption was a serious matter for the INI. It resulted in what indigenistas called "social disorganization." This included a "diminished life expectancy . . . extreme poverty, and the increased likelihood of sexual immorality, delinquency, and crime."[22] Alcoholics were less productive workers, led chaotic lives, and were harder to manage and control. INI schools and health campaigns preached temperance, and the INI's cultural promoters encouraged participation in sports and the consumption of other beverages. The indigenistas insisted on dry patriotic celebrations "so that the students learn the way to honor the national heroes." They did not want to give the impression that patriotic holidays were "run-of-the-mill celebrations indistinguishable from religious fiestas."[23] The INI's health clinics offered alternatives to healing rites that involved the exchange and consumption of alcohol. Its cooperatives tried to instill a new material culture so that indigenous salaries might be channeled away from alcohol.[24] Ever mindful of the cultural importance of alcohol among non-Protestant Tsotsils and Tseltals, and anxious to win their trust, the INI's anthropologists advised against a frontal assault against clandestine producers.

The indigenistas were forced to confront the alcohol monopoly within months of commencing operations. On November 8, 1951, Chamulas ambushed several state alcohol inspectors and fiscal policemen at the hamlet of Las Ollas. The state agents had just confiscated a clandestine distillery near the hamlets of Pajaltón and Tzontewitz. According to the official version, the agents were attacked when they stopped in Las Ollas to eat. Residents of both Pajaltón and Tzontewitz, brandishing sticks, machetes, and shotguns, killed two agents, wounded three others, and managed to recover the aguardiente still. At least two Chamulas were also killed in the fracas.[25] CCI director Gonzalo Aguirre Beltrán, a medical doctor by training, traveled to the scene of the violence and offered first aid. Many years later, he wrote that when he returned to San Cristóbal, he "presented a formal protest to the municipal president to demand the cessation of the abuses against the Indians who are harassed in the countryside and are prohibited from walking on the sidewalks in the city; if they do they are shoved into the gutter." Aguirre's protest earned him an audience with Governor Francisco Grajales.

> The governor summoned me to Tuxtla. After a long wait, he made me enter his office to tell me that if I continued stirring up the Indians, he would expel me from the state without warning by plane in the company of the *shalik* Erasto Urbina and Manuel Castellanos, my bad advisers.[26]

The timing of this clash could not have been worse for Aguirre Beltrán, who had spent the prior several months trying to win the trust of key indigenous leaders. Federal troops were deployed in the area, prompting most Chamulas to flee. State police, federal troopers, and other ladinos rampaged through Las Ollas and neighboring hamlets, beating men and women and stealing shotguns, blankets, horses, turkeys, and money. Sixteen bystanders were jailed, and a Chamula shot by an army sergeant was left behind to die. A week after the raid, Aguirre wrote Governor Grajales to report that "Las Ollas is deserted, as is Pajaltón, Tzontewitz, Chilinjoveltic and part of Romerillo. Women and children have fled to the mountains, leaving behind animals and crops." In case the governor did not get the message, Aguirre noted that "violence generates violence, and great tension has seized the indigenous zone. Using the federal army for police work only aggravates the situation."[27] In a separate letter to Alfonso Caso, Aguirre Beltrán wrote: "What's most unfortunate about all of this . . . is that a grave state of unrest has been created, and I don't think that it can be easily resolved. . . . the great confidence that the Chamulas had placed in us will not be recovered as quickly as we would like."[28]

The INI then conducted its own investigation into the incident at Las Ollas. Some of the fiscal agents who had seized the distillery and four unfortunate Chamulas were employed by the monopoly. Before forcing the four men to carry the dismantled distillery down to San Cristóbal, the agents tied them up and demanded 1,300 pesos. The Chamulas were freed when they agreed to pay the sum, but instead of procuring the money they convinced their neighbors to attack the officers. As the fiscales returned to San Cristóbal, they stopped in Las Ollas, where they sacked houses and stole poultry, blankets, and money. The attack came when the team sat down to eat.[29]

The conflict at Las Ollas set a precedent for future conflicts between the INI, the state government, and the alcohol monopoly. Aguirre Beltrán knew what he was up against. He wrote:

> I had a sharp altercation with the public prosecutor and told him that he was violating individual rights and provoking a state of unrest that could bring tragic consequences. I informed him that I would immediately name lawyers that would take charge of the defense of the Indians and make sure that the state courts abided by the constitutional procedures to which the indigenous are entitled as Mexicans.

Fifteen of the sixteen jailed Chamulas were immediately released. But Aguirre had little faith in the local criminal justice system. He believed that the only effective public defender would be an in-house (INI) lawyer, "disconnected from the vested interests in this state since these interests prevent the defense lawyers from acting with the energy and bravery that is required."[30] While Aguirre fumed, Governor Grajales issued a complaint to INI director Caso over the CCI's intervention at Las Ollas. He later journeyed to Mexico City to complain that his enemies were using the INI to attack him politically. Caso then wrote a letter to Aguirre urging him to "proceed with much caution" when dealing with the governor and other state officials.[31]

The violent confiscations continued into 1952. In August, state and federal officials from the Treasury Department approached the CCI asking for its cooperation in future confiscations. CCI personnel described these officials as "unfriendly, even aggressive." The agents then raised the stakes, claiming that the Coordinating Center sheltered bootleggers.[32] They left the CCI in a rage, and the confiscation raids continued at an accelerated pace.

Relations between the INI and the monopoly deteriorated further in 1953 when fiscal agents beat and arrested one of the CCI's cultural promoters, whom they accused of manufacturing aguardiente. The promoter, Lorenzo Díaz Hernández, was a man of great prestige in his home municipality of San Andrés Larráinzar. At thirty-nine years of age, he had served three times as scribe and another three times as municipal president. The indigenistas considered him an ideal candidate to promote change. Díaz received his training in April, returned to Larráinzar in May, and in no time had convinced the residents of Tres Puentes hamlet to build a school. According to CCI director Ricardo Pozas, Díaz taught thirty-eight children and twenty adults in his own home while the school was being built.

In late May 1953, as Díaz was reviewing the construction work on the schoolhouse, fiscales entered his house without a warrant, searching for aguardiente or a clandestine still. They found only corn, beans, and coffee. The frustrated fiscales then approached Díaz and asked him where he was hiding his still. When Díaz denied owning one, a fiscal agent hit him so hard in the mouth that he fell to the floor, bleeding profusely. As he lay there, the agents kicked him in the back. Díaz was then marched down to Bochil, where he was incarcerated for two days. On the third day he was forced to sign papers implicating himself in criminal acts and was then taken to Simojovel, where the fiscales offered him his freedom in exchange for 500 pesos. The INI asked the state attorney for indigenous affairs to get involved; soon, Díaz was released and returned to his school.

In subsequent conversations with Díaz, Pozas learned that the fiscales had initially raided the home of his brother-in-law, who had made two garrafones of aguardiente for his fiestas and healing rites. The fiscales beat the brother-in-law until he named Díaz the owner of the still. As Pozas wrote to Alfonso Caso, "Lorenzo's case is just one of many, but it is being used to impugn the work that we are doing. . . . Now the [new] governor [Efraín Aranda Osorio] is also convinced that a CCI promoter was engaged in the clandestine production of aguardiente, therefore defrauding the state treasury."[33]

In October 1953, residents of Las Ollas were again targeted by the monopoly's *pistoleros* and federal soldiers. Someone familiar with indigenista rhetoric wrote a letter to President Adolfo Ruiz Cortines on behalf of the raid's victims.

They lamented their "tormented condition as indigenous people" and suggested that the federal government's doctrine of social tranquility was a bitter, hollow promise for Indians in Chiapas. "Everything is opaque and cloudy when it comes to giving us the support and protection from our afflictions, as we are adolescents. We have absolute fear of the Monopoly and its *pistoleros*." The victims, who did not know how to write their names, used their thumbprints to sign the letter.[34]

In the December 1953 issue of *Acción Indigenista*, INI officials in Mexico City vented their frustration in a sharply worded commentary. Without specifically mentioning Chiapas by name, they explained that industrial alcohol monopolies had eliminated small-scale, artisanal production, driving up prices and forcing some indigenous groups into clandestinaje. Then, "rallying around the banner of a false anti-alcoholic Puritanism," the monopolies and local authorities resorted to violence and the legal system to suppress traditional production and defend their own interests.[35]

The Zinacantán Raid

If the INI needed one more incident to force a final showdown with the state alcohol monopoly and its defenders, it came during a confiscation raid in Zinacantán in January 1954. The state agents' version of the events was as follows: tax collector Gustavo Morales learned that clandestine alcohol was being sold at the festival of San Sebastián in Zinacantán. Seven state alcohol agents, one fiscal policeman, and soldiers from the Mexican army—brandishing a machine gun—went to Zinacantán and confiscated some one hundred liters of aguardiente when they were attacked by an estimated 1,500 Chamulas and Zinacantecos, who wounded and seized the agents' driver and the town's Catholic priest, Father Juan Bermúdez. After the agents took refuge in the town hall, the indígenas tried to break down its doors. The agents wrote that "some cartridges were fired from our guns" when the leader of the attack attempted to seize inspector Belisario Zepeda Morales. The leader fell wounded. The Chamulas and Zinacantecos then punctured the tires of the agents' vehicle and cut the town hall's telephone lines. Zinacantán's local government refused to help the besieged agents—only the municipal secretary intervened, "entertaining" the attackers until twenty federal soldiers arrived and restored calm. The state agents' declaration ended by saying that "the INI promotes clandestine production, because the [INI-sponsored] cooperative sells aguardiente."[36] A few days later, the treasury office in Tuxtla repeated this charge and went even further, asserting that INI employees told the attackers to cut the phone lines. The newspaper *El Universal* faithfully printed the agents' version of the story, calling it an "indigenous mutiny."[37]

The CCI did its own research and, not surprisingly, arrived at different conclusions. The incident began when state fiscal agent and finca owner Luis Franco Tovilla took four bottles of aguardiente from two inebriated Chamulas. One of the men, an important cargo holder named Mariano Pérez Hacienda, followed the agent and insisted on recovering his bottles. Franco pulled out his pistol and shot Pérez in the stomach at close range, perforating his bladder and intestines. Chaos ensued—outraged Chamulas and Zinacantecos threatened the agents, who shot their pistols into the air and took refuge in the town hall. Pérez was treated at INI clinics in Zinacantán and later Chamula because his family did not want him taken to San Cristóbal. When his condition worsened, his family relented, and he was operated on in San Cristóbal, where he later died.

Further INI investigations revealed more glaring discrepancies between the state's story and its own. Among them: Father Juan Bermúdez "emphatically denied twice that the Zinacantecos had attacked him," claiming instead that he had been injured earlier that day when his horse—spooked by a firework—had thrown him off.[38] Only two INI employees—a nurse and a supervisor of the local cooperative—were in Zinacantán at the time of the raid, and they both denied that the "mob" had tried to bust down the doors of the town hall. They also claimed that the fiscales never entered the cooperative store. How, then, could they know if the INI was allowing the sale of clandestine aguardiente?

The INI sought justice through legal channels, often working in coordination with Manuel Castellanos Cancino, who had been appointed director of the state's Department of Indigenous Affairs by new state governor Efraín Aranda Osorio (1952–1958). The indigenistas took depositions at La Cabaña against the ladino municipal secretary and replaced him with an indigenous man.[39] INI staff had become involved politically, legally, and emotionally in a situation that seemed to be worsening. When Pérez died, the INI paid half the cost of his coffin and transported the body to Chamula in an INI vehicle. Ladinos in San Cristóbal took note. An INI employee described the scene in Chamula when Pérez's mother approached the coffin. "The old woman fell to her knees in front of the casket crying inconsolably, blabbering incoherent words and hugging the casket frenetically," he wrote. "Such a spectacle puts a knot in one's throat."[40] Governor Aranda Osorio had been uncooperative, and if anything the monopoly and its agents in the state government had become more active, abusive, and belligerent toward the INI than ever before.

The Commission on the Problem of Indigenous Alcoholism

At this critical juncture, authorities in Mexico City likely prevailed upon INI director Alfonso Caso and Chiapas governor Efraín Aranda Osorio to put an end to the "posh war." In June 1954, they formed a joint INI/state commission, the first and last of its kind. Officially, the commission was to study how to reduce the consumption of alcohol by the indigenous population, how to improve the quality of the drinks, how to eliminate the "tensions" derived from the production and sale of alcohol, and how to improve the collection of state and federal alcohol taxes.[41] Led by the uncompromising Julio de la Fuente, the research team consisted of six members, four of them representing the federal government—an economist (from the Ministry of the National Economy), a fiscal economist (from the Treasury), a medical doctor (from the Ministry of Public Health), and de la Fuente himself, who represented the INI and served as commission president. The state government named two members, but neither played a role in elaborating the report. The commission's findings were to remain strictly confidential until both parties had had a chance to read the final document and evaluate its recommendations. At that point, if both parties gave their consent, the report would be published.

The scope and possible outcome of the commission clearly unnerved governor Aranda Osorio. At its first meeting, he implored the researchers to "constantly maintain an objective attitude in their research, discussions, and proposals." He even proposed that they call themselves the "Commission for the *Objective* Study of the Problem of Alcoholism Among the Indigenous of Chiapas."[42] The INI, anxious to put the governor at ease and win his cooperation, dropped the word "objective" but otherwise agreed to the title. As far as Aranda Osorio was concerned, indigenous alcoholics constituted the "problem," not the unconstitutional state alcohol monopoly that defrauded the state and federal treasuries, destroyed the livelihoods of thousands of cane growers and independent alcohol distillers and distributors, and routinely violated the rights of (and occasionally killed) indigenous Mexican citizens.

Between June and November 1954, the commission consulted state and federal documents, conducted interviews, and visited twenty-four municipalities, fifteen of which were largely or mostly indigenous. The final product was an exhaustive 319-page study with 82 charts, 25 pages of conclusions, and 694 pages of supporting material. In addition to reporting on indigenous alcohol consumption, it also told the history of the monopoly and exposed the

Pedreros' tremendous political and economic clout both in the highlands and in the state capital, Tuxtla Gutiérrez.

According to the commission's findings, the Pedreros enjoyed the support of the state government from top to bottom. State alcohol inspectors slapped a prohibitive tax on aguardiente and other alcoholic products introduced from other states, and fiscal agents used every possible pretext to confiscate imported alcohol like beer and tequila that competed indirectly with the products of the monopoly. The state revoked the licenses of independent producers and distributors of alcohol and opened and closed cantinas according to the whims of the Pedreros. State officials looked the other way when the monopoly's distilleries produced more than they were authorized, employed chemical additives to accelerate the fermentation process, and underdeclared its monthly production levels. The commission concluded that the monopoly daily produced five thousand undeclared liters of alcohol at its Ron Bonampak plant in Comitán.

The monopoly's skill at manipulating state politics and fiscal policy was matched by its ability to control alcohol inspectors and tax collectors, all of whom succumbed to the pressures and bribes of the monopoly to a greater or lesser degree. Many of them had been found guilty of filing false reports, and state and federal inspectors accused each other of the abuses that they meted out to indigenous bootleggers. (Federal agents attributed the state agents' brutality "to their illiteracy, their general ignorance, and their lack of preparation."[43]) Agents from the state's Fiscal and Alcohol Inspection Board received at least 500 pesos (over and above their regular salaries) from Aguardientes de Chiapas for each clandestine still that they destroyed. No fiscal police monitored the Pedreros' distilleries, which, of course, produced alcohol and aguardiente well in excess of the amount allowed by their licenses. As the commission concluded, "the delinquents are not the clandestine producers but rather those who suppress them."[44]

The commission then turned its attention to the quality of "official" alcohol. Since the Pedreros enjoyed monopoly status and controlled the state's alcohol inspectors, they had no incentive to produce a high-quality product at a competitive price. As part of its investigations, the commission ordered chemical analyses of each of the Pedreros' twenty-two products. The results were shocking and confirmed information obtained through interviews. The Pedreros diluted most of their products with contaminated water, then used alum to hide the dilution, sometimes in toxic quantities; they stored their products in dirty bottles and cans; they illegally transported aguardiente in gasoline tanker trucks; and neither state nor federal inspectors performed quality control or sanitation inspections on the monopoly. Thanks to the Pedreros' monopoly status, a liter of aguardiente "loaded with impurities (like rust and wax) so that it looks like mud" would sell in Chiapas for the same price as a liter of high-quality rum anywhere else.[45]

The high price of repugnant "legal" alcohol, of course, fomented clandestinaje, which had been on the rise since Aguardientes de Chiapas was formed in 1948. In that year, only 8 clandestine distilleries were discovered and dismantled; just five years later, 136 bootlegged stills were dismantled, most of them in relatively isolated indigenous communities. In the municipality of Huixtán, the high price of low-quality, "official" aguardiente led indigenous residents to contract a ladina woman to show them how to produce their own. By 1954, the municipality was home to at least 50 clandestine distillers, most of whom produced for their own ritual or familial use or for sale to a very limited market at half the price of the "official" product.[46]

The dire social consequences of the monopoly's activities extended far beyond those who drank toxic alcohol or were caught bootlegging. The monopoly created a climate of fear in the state. It was well known that the Pedreros paid twenty-five pesos to each informer who disclosed the existence of a clandestine distillery. In several indigenous communities, clandestine distillers turned in their competitors, triggering violence; in Chamula, alleged informers were lynched.[47] In several Tseltal communities, ladinos threatened to accuse Indians of clandestinaje if they did not sell their goods to them at fixed, low prices. According to one report, this sort of terror had the effect of partially depopulating the Tseltal town of Bachajón, where townspeople preferred life in the mountains to living in town, fearful of the next confiscation raid.[48]

After collecting a staggering amount of data about the monopoly and its abuses, the commission asked for—and received—an interview with Moctezuma Pedrero in his office. Pedrero's performance was masterful. Playing on the age-old charge that the federal government had neglected Chiapas, Pedrero clicked off his contributions to the state's development and infrastructure. He "made" the town of Bochil by building a mill, a store, and an electrical power plant; he introduced purebred cattle to the area; he installed an electrical power plant in Pichucalco; he built the road to his plantation at Cucalvitz; he sowed rice and built a rice mill at Los Custepequez "with magnificent results"; he built two coffee mills in Tuxtla; and the high prices of his aguardiente, he claimed, reduced alcoholism in the state. Last but not least was the hotel he built in Tuxtla, the Bonampak. "I could have built it in Acapulco or Europe," he claimed, but instead committed to the development of Chiapas. Yet he threatened in the same interview that if the business climate in the state turned against him, he would relocate to Oaxaca, where he already owned a sugar refinery. He played the role of the mortally wounded and misunderstood benefactor, calling the accusations against him "exasperating." "Before, it was different," he said.[49]

The Posh War and Public Opinion

For the indigenistas, this conflict was as risky as it was inevitable. The odds were certainly stacked against them. They were in hostile territory, far from Mexico City, and they could expect no help from the state government. San Cristóbal's Catholic church hierarchy had also turned against them. "They classified us as dangerous anarcho-communists," wrote Aguirre Beltrán, "to the point where we could not even hire an office secretary or a security guard until later, after we had proved that our conduct was inoffensive."[50]

The Pedreros, for their part, had been doing business in the state for more than three decades and had nurtured relationships with newspapers that were more dependent than ever on subsidies and handouts.[51] The Pedreros' sway over local media was evident on an almost daily basis. Newspaper headlines screamed "Another Magnificent Blow by the Fiscal Police Against Alcohol Bootleggers" and "Vigorous Hunting Party Against Clandestine Producers."[52] Other articles reported deaths provoked by the consumption of unofficial alcohol and advised readers to buy the official product. In July 1954, just as the commission began its research, the Tuxtla-based newspaper *El Heraldo* ran a four-part article titled "Collective Deaths from Alcohol" that accused INI promoters of operating clandestine distilleries and teaching students how to bootleg. Two weeks later, the same paper published a letter from Moctezuma Pedrero entitled "The Mortal Effects of Denatured Alcohol." Pedrero congratulated the author of the four-part story, implored the commission to investigate the means to ending clandestine production, and displayed grisly photos of two men who had died from ingesting contraband alcohol.[53]

The risks were clear, but the INI also stood to gain from its principled stand against the monopoly. The Pedreros had made plenty of enemies over the years, and their recent takeover of the sugar industry in Chiapas was highly unpopular. If most of the major papers in the state were still favorable to the Pedreros, several papers, big and small, condemned the monopoly on their editorial pages. Sometimes the condemnations were rather timid requests for the authorities to crack down on "centers of vice" or to rein in the abuses of the fiscal police. But other papers were more courageous, their denunciations more direct.

The national political tide may also have been turning against the Pedreros. When Adolfo Ruíz Cortines became president of Mexico in December 1952, he promised to crack down on the various monopolies that had emerged during the *sexenio* of his baldly corrupt predecessor, Miguel Alemán. The new president's crusade against those who monopolized the distribution and sale of basic goods in violation of Article 28 of the Constitution emboldened some local journalists to openly attack the Pedreros' monopoly in aguardiente and sugar derivatives. In June 1953, the San Cristóbal paper *El Demócrata* criticized the monopoly "that produces the cursed liquid that wreaks such havoc on the indigenous class . . . and submerges them in a state of misery and deprivation."[54] The following month, *El Demócrata* issued a thinly veiled condemnation of a Teopisca-based monopoly that was hoarding basic staples like corn, beans, and meat, causing prices in San Cristóbal to soar. (Hernán Pedrero had various warehouses in Teopisca.)[55] In June 1954, a column in *El Coleto* reported on the creation of the commission. The columnist, who identified himself only as Raffles, remarked that the INI should ensure that those who legally manufactured and sold aguardiente not use or add substances or chemicals that would "make the damned drink even more harmful than it already is."[56]

Once the commission began conducting research in summer 1954, the state's fiscal police entered a period of frenetic activity. No doubt the monopoly sought to highlight the threat posed by bootleggers. In July and August, alongside articles telling of drunks fighting inside or outside cantinas with sometimes lethal consequences, *El Coleto* reported between two and three confiscations a week. In one case, a confiscated still was transported from Teopisca to San Cristóbal in one of Hernán Pedrero's trucks. The monopoly's victims struck back, right in the heart of Pedrero's Teopisca stronghold, by entering one of his warehouses and pilfering twenty-five sacks of panela. Later that month, in San Cristóbal's municipal cemetery, the mausoleum that held the remains of Hernán Pedrero's son, Francisco Pedrero Corzo, was smashed to pieces. Police activity was intensified, with fatal results; in late August, a drunk fiscal entered a Teopisca cantina at 2:30 a.m., got into an argument, and shot and killed the man who tried to act as peacemaker. According to *Más Allá*, the enraged bar patrons then tried to lynch the fiscal.[57]

Suddenly, in September 1954, while the commission was still conducting research, the rate of confiscations dropped dramatically. The Pedreros apparently chose a different course in their attempt to win over the local population and fend off the INI. As Mexico prepared to celebrate its independence, the monopoly placed an ad in *El Coleto* reminding readers to buy Ron Bonampak rum as an act of patriotism. "Consume a local product because it is the best and because you support the local economy," it read.[58] Then, in October, *El Coleto* reported that Hernán Pedrero had donated a 35-millimeter film projector to San Cristóbal's Preparatory and Law School (Escuela Preparatoria y de Derecho). Later that month, when much of San Cristóbal was without water, Pedrero stepped in and used one of his tanker trucks to distribute water to affected areas. This won don Hernán the effusive praise of *El Coleto*'s editorial board, which called him "a sincere and altruistic man who has always cooperated on innumerable occasions," high praise from a paper that in June had condemned the monopoly and its defenders in the state government.[59]

The Pedreros' charm offensive lasted into 1955. But it didn't fool everyone. In June, Héctor Guisa wrote in *La Voz del Sureste* that he had been almost convinced by press coverage of don Moctezuma's Hotel Bonampak and don Hernán's proposal to build a hospital for the poor. But Guisa concluded that this was all a distraction. "Señor [Moctezuma] Pedrero is right when he says he's cooperating with the federal government to resolve the problem of alcoholism and alcoholics," he wrote. "Aguardientes de Chiapas is certainly getting rid of alcoholics . . . by poisoning them."[60]

The Pedreros could not let this stand in a major regional newspaper, especially at a delicate moment when the INI was likely negotiating with the state government over the status of the monopoly. Later that month, they took out a full-page ad in *La Voz del Sureste*. Their target was not Guisa but the paper's publisher, Roberto Coello Lescieur. They accused him of targeting them because they no longer bought advertising in his paper. The real problem in Chiapas was not the editor's "worn-out specter of a monopoly" but rather the clandestinos, "defrauders of the treasury, mainly Indians who do not know the law, because nobody has bothered to instruct them because they are considered irresponsible." Then the Pedreros got personal.

> Who lacks the moral authority to declare themselves an enemy of alcoholism, don Moctezuma Pedrero Argüello, who has never been drunk in his life, and whose principle requirement to accept or retain a worker is that he not drink, and who strictly prohibits the sale of liquor in his industries and his fincas, where more than two thousand people work? Or the director of *La Voz del Sureste*, who often enjoys the poisons produced by "the Pedrero

monopoly," "Ron Bonampak" and "Comiteco Balún Canán," and despite ingesting considerable doses enjoys excellent health, which is proof of its good quality?

The ad then closed with a promise to sue Coello Lescieur for defamation of character. "There is freedom of the press in Mexico, but there are also laws against uncouth blackmail artists."[61]

Of course, the INI played the public relations game, too, and had become quite skilled at creating positive publicity for itself. Since opening its doors in 1951, it had treated ladinos in its main health clinic in La Cabaña and reminded coletos that they, too, stood to benefit from the INI's road construction program in the highlands. In summer 1953, when scarcity and hoarding drove up the price of corn in the highlands, the INI purchased corn through its own channels and sold it at reasonable prices to San Cristóbal's ladinos. The INI also gave financial support to infrastructure projects in San Cristóbal that directly benefited coletos. For example, in early December 1954, as the INI's commission prepared its report, the CCI donated 25,000 pesos to a project aimed at reducing flooding in San Cristóbal. In August 1955, after a tornado hit the Barrio de Mexicanos (a San Cristóbal neighborhood contiguous with La Cabaña) and destroyed fifty-three houses, the INI gave medical treatment to those who had been wounded. In a sharply written article entitled "Odious Official Municipal Indifference Toward the Collective Misfortune," coleto paper *Más Allá* praised the INI's generosity.[62] These gestures helped the Coordinating Center ride out its worst crisis since its opening.

In indigenous communities, the INI turned its clash with the Pedreros to its advantage. At the height of the conflict, in the summer of 1953, the indigenistas wrote a text stating that "INI employees oppose the illegal activities of the fiscal agents in Chamula." INI personnel translated the message into Tsotsil, recorded it onto a tape, took it to Chamula, and played it at various times during a three-day fiesta. It set the record straight concerning the monopoly. "Most people receive us as friends," the recording explained, "but others do not allow us into their houses because they think we are looking for aguardiente distilleries, to denounce them to the fiscales. We have nothing to do with the fiscales."

We know that they do not respect Chamulas. They enter their homes without a judicial warrant under the pretext of looking for aguardiente, and they destroy their things and beat people and imprison them. The Institute condemns the acts of the fiscales. . . . the law says that an indigenous is equal to a ladino, but the fiscales do not respect the law.

The recording ended with a plug for the INI's schools. "We are teaching children what the law says so that when they grow older, they can defend their rights and the rights of all Chamulas."[63]

According to an INI report, "municipal president Salvador Gómez Osob and his principales listened to the recording. They later held a meeting and surely came to an agreement." INI personnel later remarked that Chamulas had begun to warm up to the INI and its Literacy Centers.[64] By standing up to the Pedreros, the INI took an important step toward winning the confidence of people whose mistrust of outsiders was firmly rooted in more than four hundred years of history.

The Negotiated Settlement

The commission's final report made several recommendations calling for the effective dissolution of the alcohol-aguardiente monopoly and greater oversight of Pedrero interests. It proposed the overhaul and federalization of all taxes on the elaboration of aguardiente, alcohol, and alcoholic mixes, such as those sold in pharmacies, and the installation of devices that would measure the amount of alcohol produced at distilleries. The commission also called for a purge of state employees charged with inspecting and taxing the alcohol industry and their replacement with "honest personnel." It recommended modifying state law to once again allow the elaboration and sale of chicha, and proposed a five-year ban against opening new cantinas. Other commission recommendations were aimed at raising the abysmal hygienic standards in the industry.[65]

In March 1955, commission members traveled to Tuxtla Gutiérrez to formally present the finished study to the state government and discuss its findings. When they arrived, they could not find the state government's two representatives. When the INI's representatives finally tracked them down, they claimed that their appointments to the commission had expired in October 1954. Meanwhile, Governor Aranda Osorio was in Mexico City. Clearly, the Chiapas state government opted to duck out of this final, crucial meeting. It instructed the federal representatives to "deliver the report to a [state] commission that will review and decide the best and most feasible ways to resolve the problem of alcoholism." This evasion infuriated the INI's directors in Mexico City. They instructed the commission's federal representatives to discuss and approve the document.

Our painstakingly detailed paper trail ends here, but it is clear that the INI and the state government soon entered into negotiations and that both sides ceded ground.[66] The Pedreros lost their monopoly status over the production of aguardiente in the highlands. The state alcohol inspectors were disbanded, and responsibility for controlling the production and sale of alcohol passed to the federal government. Tseltals and Tsotsils won the right to apply for and receive permits to legally manufacture aguardiente in their communities. In fact, as early as May 1955, entrepreneurial Zinacantecos approached Aguirre Beltrán in Mexico City to ask the INI to help them build a major aguardiente distillery! Aguirre persuaded them to drop their plan after explaining that the INI opposed the production, distribution, and consumption of alcoholic beverages in indigenous communities. Not coincidentally, that same month, the CCI in San Cristóbal decided to expand production of its Yalel brand soft drink, hoping to encourage the consumption of nonalcoholic beverages.[67]

The Pedreros themselves came out of the posh war unscathed. In 1953 and again in early 1954, at the height of the conflict, the brothers wrote President Ruiz Cortines to request a 7 million peso loan to build a sugar mill. Without a hint of irony, Chiapas's most notorious monopoly capitalists wrote the president that "we have corn, wheat, sugar, rice, and coffee plantations, and orchards dedicated to cooperating with your program of lowering the price of subsistence goods."[68] Nor did the posh war prevent the brothers from seeking higher office. Moctezuma Pedrero competed in the 1958 primary elections to become the PRI's candidate for governor of Chiapas. Although he and others were edged out by Samuel León Brindis, who appears to have been the preferred candidate of Governor Aranda Osorio and the local PRI establishment, he claimed in a letter to President Ruiz Cortines that he had sent nine thousand thank-you letters to his campaign supporters. In a thinly veiled attempt to curry favor with Mexico's probable president for the upcoming sexenio (1958–1964), Moctezuma carbon-copied this letter to the PRI's presidential candidate, Adolfo López Mateos. When López Mateos took office in December 1958, Moctezuma published a congratulatory message on the pages of *Novedades*, then followed up a few weeks later by sending the new president a holiday greeting card.[69]

Relations between the INI, the state governor, and the private sector became much more amicable following the negotiated "truce." Shortly after the settlement, the INI even began lodging its distinguished visitors in Moctezuma Pedrero's Hotel Bonampak. Former Pedrero pistoleros ended up working for the INI. After 1955, the INI also agreed to help in the effort to crack down on clandestine aguardiente production, which was still illegal in the state.[70] In the

FIGURE 4.2. An INI employee working at the INI's bottling plant at La Cabaña. Indigenistas promoted Yalel, their soft drink, as an alternative to aguardiente. Nacho López, photographer. Fototeca Nacho López, Comisión Nacional para el Desarrollo de los Pueblos Indígenas. Circa 1952.

early 1970s, when Governor Manuel Velasco Suárez finally broke up Aguardientes de Chiapas, the INI believed that there were roughly 360 clandestine stills in Chamula alone. The clandestinos made payments to Chamula's well-connected scribes-principales to keep the state away.[71]

During the posh war, the INI held its ground and produced a damning report that forced the state government to bring an end to the monopoly's worst abuses. But it was a pyrrhic victory. Following negotiations with the Aranda Osorio government, the INI agreed not to extend its reach into Pedrero fincas, where indigenous resident debt peons labored into the 1970s. It also pacified the Pedreros and other ladinos by privatizing some of its operations. Over time, San Cristóbal's well-heeled ladinos would co-opt many of the INI's promoters and former scribes, thereby fostering a new type of bossism in the highlands.[72] Finally, and perhaps most importantly, the INI's protracted clashes with recalcitrant ladinos in Chiapas would have national implications for the indigenista blueprint, as the next chapter details.

CHAPTER 5
Take Two
The INI Charts a More Modest Course

●●● THE POSH WAR was a watershed moment for the INI's Coordinating Center in Chiapas. It was not the first time that the indigenistas had clashed with powerful ladino interests, nor would it be the last. But it was the most important because several INI programs hung in the balance in the mid-1950s. Indigenistas and their mística ran up against the hard realities of the Chiapas highlands. Their strategic retreat can be measured in several ways, perhaps none clearer than the fate of Alejandro Marroquín's survey team, which stopped dead in its tracks in summer 1955. By that point, the team had managed to survey just five of San Cristóbal's eleven historical barrios and had barely begun to survey the ladinos living in the predominately Tseltal municipalities of Bachajón, Chilil, and Oxchuc. Today, the incomplete surveys and reports can be found in a file at the CDI's Biblioteca Juan Rulfo entitled "Investigaciones de Chiapas, 1955."[1]

It isn't hard to surmise why the INI decided to terminate the project at precisely the moment that its negotiations with the Chiapas state government were coming to a close. When the governor was told to rein in the Pedreros and the abusive fiscales, he likely demanded in return that the INI end its development schemes involving ladinos in urban environments. But even if he did not state that demand explicitly, the indigenistas could assess the mounting evidence and conclude that they had neither the political nor the economic clout needed to compel the participation of recalcitrant ladinos. The indigenistas would be tolerated—barely—so long as they focused their efforts on the indigenous themselves.

Once dramatic economic restructuring and utopian industrialization projects were taken off the table, the INI was left with its faltering consumer cooperatives, a timid program in agriculture, and a medical program that was still finding its way. The INI's plans to revive the indigenous coffee pickers' union (STI) were thwarted, and enganche remained in the hands of the state's Department of Indigenous Affairs (DGAI). One persistent bright spot, however, were the INI's schools in the Oxchuc region, even if the indigenistas' relationship with Marianna Slocum soured dramatically.

The Consumer Cooperatives Play Out the String

The INI's consumer cooperatives fared no better after 1955 than they had before. The indigenistas themselves remained split on the purpose of the cooperatives. Some, like Agustín Romano, saw them as a means to an end,[2] while Marroquín, Ricardo Pozas, and others thought that cooperatives *were* the end. The support of this latter group explains why the cooperatives were allowed to limp along for several more years despite their many problems. In 1956, the CCI's new director, Alfonso Villa Rojas, announced that the consumer cooperative at Yalentay (Zinacantán) had decided to fold; internal divisions plagued Aguacatenango's cooperative; and robberies had been committed at the cooperatives in Zinacantán center and Oxchuc.[3] At Amatenango, the cooperative had fallen into the hands of a small but influential clique, "and it's certain that now practically none of the members wishes to denounce the faults of any of the storekeepers." The INI's nurse there reported that the storekeeper had also operated a small, suspiciously well-stocked store out of his house ever since he had taken control of the cooperative.[4] Even in the handful of communities where they seemed viable, the INI's constant support and supervision were needed. When the cooperatives were mismanaged, residents usually blamed the INI. To avoid losing support for its other projects, the indigenistas often found themselves covering losses.

Such was the case at Oxchuc, where the cooperative initially met with broad support. A series of robberies in 1957 and 1958, however, put members at risk of losing their initial investment. In May 1958, education director Fidencio Montes Sánchez was given the uncomfortable task of explaining to Oxchuqueros that two of the robberies had resulted from careless management and that the third was quite likely perpetrated by one of the cooperative's storekeepers. "The situation became extremely delicate," he reported. "There was a riot and everyone demanded the return of their initial investment." Montes repeatedly explained the INI's position to Oxchuc's promoter, who then translated the message to the angry crowd. "Some were still angry and incited the people to dismantle the INI's medical clinic, saying they would recoup their losses that way." Montes tried to explain that the clinic was federal property; destroying it would be a federal offense. Ultimately, the INI agreed to reimburse members for their initial investment. The cooperative was closed. But many of those who joined the cooperative in 1953 were bitter that, five years later, they had not made any return on their investment. Soon, Oxchuqueros were demanding that a federal or state teacher replace the INI's promoter, "because they don't make us work and they don't require our children to attend school."[5]

In his March 1958 report to Alfonso Caso, Villa Rojas aired his frustration over the failing cooperatives. He stated emphatically that "the progress of our cooperatives leaves much to be desired," that they are "NOT having any success." Villa Rojas toyed with the idea of hiring someone to supervise them, but his budget would not allow it, and the cooperatives could not be expected to cover that expense, either. "So the problem becomes a vicious cycle, because if we hire a supervisor, we lose, and if we do not, we also lose." There were no easy answers, short of allowing the cooperatives to slowly wither and die.[6]

In a 1975 interview, Ricardo Pozas commented extensively on the CCI's consumer cooperatives, many of which he helped establish in 1953. He largely blamed his successor, Agustín Romano, for their failure. Pozas claimed that in Chamula, Romano saw no point in supporting consumer cooperatives once two of the cooperative's members—proto-caciques Salvador Gómez Osob and Salvador López Tuxum—opened stores of their own.[7] Meanwhile, competition from privately owned stores forced additional closures. By 1963, only three consumer cooperatives were left, and they soon folded.[8]

Transportation cooperatives were more self-sustaining, if only because they fell even more quickly into the hands of the rising indigenous middle class. The first to form with INI support was in Chenalhó, in 1954, soon after the new highway opened. Most of its members were INI education, health, and agriculture promoters. Chamula's transportation cooperative opened shortly thereafter, but it was a cooperative in name only, since it was soon controlled by Tuxum, his family, and his associates. Oxchuc's formed in 1963, founded by INI education promoters. Over the years, several more cooperatives were created, but again, a program that the INI created for the public good and funded with public resources ended up in the hands of its privileged class of upwardly mobile promoters.[9]

Treading Lightly in Agriculture

Given the profoundly rural nature of the Chiapas highlands and the fact that the entire population was engaged in farming, one would expect to find some of the INI's best work in the realm of agriculture. But the indigenistas' efforts in this area were hamstrung by several factors beyond their control. As a result, during most of the 1950s, the CCI's agriculture section was quite timid; by the time budget cuts began eroding the indigenista effort, few programs had been established. The net result of the CCI's effort to increase agricultural yields was, in the words of the CCI's three-time director, Agustín Romano, "rather unspectacular."[10]

The Chiapas highlands have always been difficult to farm. Even today's casual tourists notice the steep, rocky hillsides. All along the forty-mile highway from Chiapa de Corzo in the lowlands to San Cristóbal de Las Casas (elevation 7,218 feet), Tsotsil farmers plant corn on steep, 45-degree slopes. Many of these slopes have been eroded, and where the soil has not been washed away, it is very thin. A 1971 study carried out by Mexico's Ministry of Hydraulic Resources (Secretaría de Recursos Hidráulicos) showed that 75.2 percent of the land in the Chiapas highlands was "not appropriate for agriculture and livestock."[11] Crops were subject to frost, drought, and insect plagues, and rodents devoured much of what was produced because storage facilities were so inadequate.

Other factors forestalled a major revival of agriculture in the highlands. It made little sense to try to pull the indigenous out of their subsistence economy until roads were built to facilitate the transport of goods to regional markets. And until meaningful land reform occurred on a large scale, a structural transformation in agriculture was simply out of the question. In fact, the term "subsistence farming" is a misnomer in highland Chiapas, since most indigenous people did not farm enough land on which to subsist. One constant throughout the 1950s, 1960s, and 1970s was the need for most heads of household to supplement their meager farming output with stints on the lowland plantations.[12]

Lack of credit was another factor hindering the transformation of agriculture in the highlands. In the 1950s, the federal rural and ejidal banks did not lend money to the indigenous, and neither did the private banks, thinking that they were not creditworthy. This left them at the mercy of the usual suspects: the finca owner, the enganchador, the merchant, the compadre, or the moneylender (often indigenous), who charged usurious rates, usually between 5 and 10 percent *a month*. Without access to easy credit on good terms, the indigenous could not invest in new tools, seeds, barbed wire, chemical fertilizers, fungicides, herbicides, or pesticides.[13]

As detailed in chapter 3, the INI helped build a network of highways and rough access roads that extended slowly but steadily across the highlands. The

FIGURE 5.1. Men clearing a road. Photographer unknown. Fototeca Nacho López, Comisión Nacional para el Desarrollo de los Pueblos Indígenas. Circa 1960.

land issue was much more problematic. In the 1950s, even before the demographic explosion that was to come, land was already scarce in many municipalities. Sixty percent of indigenous lands were in the form of communal land (*terrenos comunales*) that the indigenous held before postrevolutionary land reform took place. Tseltal *comuneros* in the 1950s averaged only 2.6 hectares each, and Tsotsil *comuneros* only 1.6 hectares. In some land-starved Tsotsil municipalities like Chamula, Mitontic, and Zinacantán, people farmed on even less.[14]

Unfortunately, by the late 1950s, the land reform effort was stalled on all fronts in Chiapas. This demoralized the INI and the people whom it served. The indigenistas assisted the indigenous as they applied for land, applied to expand existing ejidos, asked to have temporary holdings made permanent, tried to resolve boundary disputes, and defended themselves from land invaders. But the formal agrarian reform process was in the hands of a huge, slow, often corrupt bureaucracy. According to Alfonso Villa Rojas, the indigenous found the land issue "infuriating." They often paid elevated sums to agrarian reform bureaucrats without the slightest guarantee of favorable resolution. In some cases, the indigenous waited more than thirty years to have their temporary holdings made permanent.[15]

Meanwhile, the lack of good, arable land impacted the CCI's other programs. In 1957, INI education promoters identified land scarcity as the single most important factor in determining poor attendance rates; if more Tseltals and Tsotsils had more land, there would be less need to migrate down to the fincas. In 1958, average daily attendance figures continued to hover around 65 percent. Villa Rojas concluded that "as long as the land problem goes unresolved (which, in any case, is not very productive), this type of emigration is unavoidable at certain times of year."[16]

Structural constraints, therefore, permitted only modest programs. CCI agronomists and promoters introduced innovations in several experimental fields, the most important of which was at La Cabaña. They began by introducing improved seeds for crops that the indigenous already grew. The CCI also recommended diversified subsistence production over growing just one or two crops for commercial purposes. Given the precarious nature of indigenous subsistence, the CCI could not take risks; nothing less than the entire indigenista project was at stake. In time, INI agronomists and promoters showed indigenous farmers how to practice terraced agriculture to prevent erosion and how to use insecticides and fertilizers to protect their corn and beans and increase output, and they distributed tens of thousands of apple, pear, plum, apricot, and coffee trees. Indigenous farmers accepted fertilizers, insecticides, and fungicides almost immediately, and the CCI sold these products at reduced prices. These inputs became increasingly necessary over the years as the population boom forced people onto smaller and smaller plots. By 1970, it was estimated that the average family plot in Chamula was just a quarter of an acre.[17]

In that same year, 1970, the INI reported that after nearly twenty years of agricultural promotion, output had only increased about 25 percent. In Romano's words, technical agriculture was "complicated" for the indigenous. "It requires, at the very least, easy access to capital or credit, and constant, timely technical support, at least during a certain period. These were all elements that the Coordinating Center could not provide with its scarce economic and human resources." Over time, writes Romano, "the center's agricultural program began to decay and, as happened in other areas, it eventually ceded to other government programs."[18]

The center's livestock programs did not fare any better. There are few flat grazing areas in the highlands, and historically the indigenous have not been much interested in cattle. Sheep were a different story, as they were prized for their wool, especially in Chamula. When the CCI tried to introduce a special breed of sheep (Rambouillet) in 1953 to improve the "creole" sheep brought

FIGURE 5.2. Applying pesticides or herbicides at one of the INI's experimental fields. Photographer unknown. Fototeca Nacho López, Comisión Nacional para el Desarrollo de los Pueblos Indígenas. Circa 1965.

over by the Spaniards, most of them succumbed to parasites, and the males went sterile. After this failure, the CCI adopted a more passive livestock program. Instead of trying to improve the cattle and sheep that had already adapted to the region, they limited themselves to improving forage (pasture grasses) and vaccinating and curing sick animals.[19]

The CCI's pig- and chicken-breeding programs were more active. The center lent its purebred stud pigs to indigenous farmers and asked only for a pair of piglets in return. Chickens not only provided eggs and protein, they were also commonly used to pay traditional healers and were themselves used in healing rites. The CCI installed a chicken farm at La Cabaña and raised a rugged breed (New Hampshire) known for its eggs and meat. Sometimes, the indigenistas used chickens as prizes at sporting events or gave them to schools. The sheer number of chickens in the highlands increased considerably due largely to the CCI's successful vaccination programs.[20]

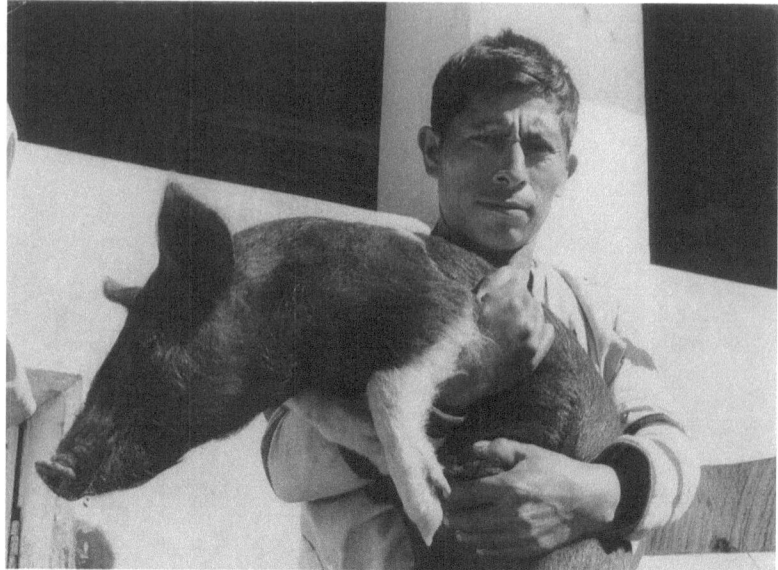

FIGURE 5.3. Man with pig, circa 1955. Photographer unknown. Fototeca Nacho López, Comisión Nacional para el Desarrollo de los Pueblos Indígenas. Circa 1955.

Back in 1952, when Aguirre Beltrán handed over the reins of the CCI to Julio de la Fuente, he advised him to "carry out the agricultural extension and experimentation programs with extreme prudence." In the short run, he advised against "introducing improved corn varieties and new techniques since we lack personnel to advise on the wisdom of these policies."[21] As Aguirre explained elsewhere, certain conditions had to be met before a transformation in agriculture could take place; agricultural innovation could only be part of a larger, integral development strategy.

> Agrarian reform is one of the prerequisites but there are others, generated internally by the indigenous communities or induced by development programs that motivate favorable attitudes toward change. Among those: the secularization and individualization of the [local governing] institutions, the weakening of the power of the traditional hierarchy, an increase in geographic and social mobility, exacerbating demographic pressure, an improvement in interethnic relations, and the construction of a transportation network and an educational system that combats illiteracy and monolingualism in the population; in sum, through the

implementation of an integral strategy that takes into account all aspects of the group's culture.

Until these prerequisites are met, agricultural work, defined as a process of disseminating a new technology, should be carried out with caution.[22]

Some of Aguirre's conditions were never met in highland Chiapas, like agrarian reform. Other prerequisites like secularization, individualism, increased mobility, population pressures, and an improved transportation and education infrastructure occurred in the late 1960s and 1970s, when the CCI in San Cristóbal was past its prime, suffering the effects of meager budgets, bureaucratization, and uninspired leadership.

In 1970, critical anthropologist Margarita Nolasco blasted the INI for advocating a slow, cautious approach in agriculture, which she dismissed as a "classic attitude of colonialist social anthropology."[23] June Nash, however, defends the INI's approach. INI projects "reaffirmed the collective strategies for the survival of small-plot semi-subsistence cultivation," she writes. The indigenistas "promoted existing agricultural techniques without highly capitalized innovation. Crop rotation, rather than expensive petrochemical fertilizers and other 'green revolution' techniques, was preferred." Elsewhere in Mexico, "large-scale dam projects and agroindustrial development were capitalized at the expense of the semi-subsistence sector."[24] In the Chiapas highlands, a modest approach to agricultural innovation was not only the most prudent approach, it was also the only option available to the INI.

Baldío Liberation and Other Victories in Tseltal Schools

The effects of the INI's pullback were not immediately felt in the Tseltal communities of eastern Chiapas. Although Ricardo Pozas's ambitious plan for a large-scale state farm in Ocosingo was never approved, the agrarian activity of the INI's cultural promoters in the early and mid-1950s began to reap tangible rewards. Cultural promoters were instrumental in organizing baldíos, who either solicited land through the formal agrarian reform process or purchased land outright with the help of an INI loan.

The INI's first agrarian success was in Tajpá, Huixtán, where baldíos had worked for a priest three days a week in exchange for the right to grow subsistence crops on his land. They tended to his goats, horses, and sheep, and they also worked as load bearers, carrying goods on their backs to San Cristóbal and Comitán, each about forty kilometers away. Promoter Agapito Núñez Tom

FIGURE 5.4. Agapito Núñez Tom with students at La Libertad. Photographer unknown. Fototeca Nacho López, Comisión Nacional para el Desarrollo de los Pueblos Indígenas. Circa 1960.

helped the baldíos buy five hundred hectares in nearby Oxchuc in 1952 and 1953. They called their settlement La Libertad (Liberty), and it soon boasted a medical outpost, a school, a road, and piped water. "La Libertad is where the integral development program has been most successfully applied and where each individual is conscious of being a free man after having lived in slavery," observed Fidencio Montes.[25] This modest victory paid several dividends for the INI. La Libertad produced two of the first three girls to graduate from the INI's boarding school with a sixth-grade diploma, and twenty-two of Núñez Tom's former students went on to become teachers.

Three other agrarian victories followed in rapid succession; baldíos at Onteal, Huixtán, also bought land in Oxchuc after their promoter, Marcelo Santiz López, narrowly avoided an assassination attempt. They created a new community near La Libertad and called it La Independencia (Independence). Campesinos at both La Libertad and La Independencia repaid their loans to the INI in four years after working various stints on Soconusco's coffee plantations. At Kistoljá, promoters managed to organize the baldíos and carve an ejido out of a large ranch on the border of Oxchuc and Tenejapa despite an assassination attempt against one promoter and a spurious rape allegation against another. The fourth case came from El Corralito, where baldíos from five ranches in Ocosingo created a community called Chulná. In 1958, Alfonso Caso personally handed out land titles to some 250 heads of household.²⁶

None of these modest victories came without a fight, and death threats against dedicated INI promoters were the order of the day. "We took great risks and there were times when we spent the night in the mountains and arrived to the school in the morning," wrote Núñez Tom. "And to go to the monthly pedagogy meeting at La Cabaña, we walked at night so that we would not run into people that threatened us at our schools."²⁷

The second half of the 1950s was a time of profound agrarian tension in Oxchuc and its vicinity. Once the INI's promoters had proven their ability to organize baldíos, ladinos came to believe that "under no circumstances should they permit an INI school on their land."²⁸ Tempers flared in several of Oxchuc's hamlets, and INI cultural promoters attempted to mediate conflicts and prevent violent clashes. More than once, the indigenous proposed expelling ladinos from their communities, "destroying the ladinos once and for all."²⁹

Meanwhile, Tseltal support for INI programs manifested itself in the flurry of school construction that began in the late 1950s. Most of the one-room schoolhouses erected in the early 1950s had been built using *bajareque* (wattle and daub, for the walls) and *zacate* (grass for thatch roofs). By 1957, these were in various states of disrepair, and some had even collapsed. In most hamlets, even in places that did not initially support the school, people offered their land, labor, and even construction materials to build new schoolhouses with brick floors and tile roofs. "They believe that tile roofs will bring them distinction and prestige," noted Villa Rojas. "Remember that until recently, the tile roof was used exclusively by the ladino class."³⁰ By 1959, Abasolo had the INI's largest school, with an enrollment of 121 boys and 60 girls. Four INI promoters taught first, second, and third grade, in addition to the *grado preparatorio*. "In 1953, Abasolo only had a church, a house that sometimes served as a school, the municipal building, and three huts," wrote Villa Rojas. "Now it is a great town with 252 houses," and each house had two rooms and a kitchen, along with sheds so that animals could be kept outside.³¹ INI anthropologist César Tejada Fonseca noted that "after years of observation, the people are convinced that the school is the key to their liberation."³²

The INI was even invited to begin working in Cancuc,³³ described by Sol Tax as "notoriously unacculturated and resistant . . . the most hostile village in a generally hostile area."³⁴ One night in 1957, a ladino vendor's market stall caught fire and accidentally set fire to the roof of the Catholic church. Indigenous Cancuqueros, many in a state of inebriation, retaliated by burning all of the ladino market stalls in the center of town along with the homes of sixteen Protestants. Cancuc's ladinos fled town, and one indigenous was killed in the melee. The INI offered to help Cancuc rebuild and donated money to the cause. INI employees distributed clothes to those who had lost everything. Cancuqueros then approached the INI for assistance in repairing the roof of the church and building a school and cooperative store. "This rapprochement is extremely important," noted Villa Rojas, "since Cancuc was the only pueblo that had shown no interest in the INI's work."³⁵

The INI and the SIL: Paradise Lost?

Ironically, these important victories came at a time when the CCI had a major falling-out with its principal ally in the region, Marianna Slocum. The relationship between the INI and the US-based Summer Institute of Linguistics/Wycliffe Bible Translators was always an unlikely one. In 1935, SIL founder William Townsend received permission from President Lázaro Cárdenas to begin working in Nahuatl-speaking Tetelcingo, Morelos. Cárdenas later visited Tetelcingo and was impressed to find the inhabitants reading in their own language. The two men began a long friendship. Given the overtly nationalist tenor of the Cárdenas administration, the president's support for US-based Protestant missionaries might seem improbable. Yet Cárdenas was no friend of the Catholic Church, especially in 1935, and his commitment to rural Mexico predisposed him to working with an organization that taught literacy to indigenous people. Cárdenas defended the SIL from charges that it represented an imperialist threat; Townsend, for his part, vigorously lobbied US authorities in defense of Cárdenas's 1938 decision to expropriate foreign-held oil fields. He later wrote a flattering biography of Cárdenas.³⁶

At first blush, it would seem that the INI and the SIL shared common goals. The missionary linguists preached sobriety and self-improvement and began introducing Western medicine to the Chiapas highlands a decade before the arrival of the INI. Both organizations promoted modernization and literacy, and both wanted to break down traditional hierarchies of illiterate older men and shamans, placing political and social control in the hands of young, progressive literates.³⁷ However, the methods and objectives of a secular nationalist institute of development and assimilation were bound to clash eventually with a foreign Protestant organization whose linguists believed that they were literally on a mission from God. In 1955, the INI's education supervisors informed CCI director Agustín Romano that Slocum was undermining the INI's attempts to educate girls at its boarding school at La Cabaña. The indigenistas had managed to recruit seven girls from the hamlets of Oxchuc, but when they returned to their home communities for winter break, Slocum apparently told their parents that the INI was corrupting their daughters and planned to take them all to Mexico City.

There was more bad news from what the INI referred to as the "evangelical zone." According to several sources, INI schools had become houses of worship, where promoters gave sermons and students sang religious hymns. When INI education supervisors tried to rein in this activity, two of its evangelical promoters promptly resigned. To make matters worse, Protestant converts refused to send their children to schools led by Catholic promoters. Romano vented his frustration to Slocum in a tersely worded letter, which was hand delivered by education inspector Reynaldo Salvatierra. "As you yourself realize, this center has been exclusively preoccupied with indigenous improvement and has not made distinctions concerning religious beliefs," Romano wrote. "The evangelical zone is one region where we have made the greatest effort, and we have always counted on your valuable collaboration." Romano warned that the INI could take "appropriate measures" to prevent the SIL from "disorienting" its inhabitants. According to Salvatierra, "once Slocum read the letter she looked completely nervous." Since the SIL's missionaries were US citizens operating with permission from the Mexican government, Romano's threat caught the attention of SIL directors in Mexico City.[38]

Salvatierra then tracked down and interviewed the seven female students and their guardians to determine whether they would return to San Cristóbal for another year of studies. Initially, the parents of five of the seven students refused. Salvatierra was able to convince the parents of two of them that the INI would never take the girls to Mexico City and had no interest in disconnecting the girls from their people. A third parent agreed to allow her daughter to return to the boarding school once Salvatierra also agreed to admit the girl's brother. Salvatierra promised parents that the INI would allow boarding school students to return to their home communities more frequently. Thanks to his lengthy conversations with each of the seven girls' parents, five of them resumed their studies the following year.[39]

Slocum was quick to respond to Romano's letter. She called his accusations "completely groundless" and suggested that he had been "misinformed." She then proceeded to remind Romano of the SIL's collaborations with the Coordinating Center. "For the last fifteen years we have dedicated our lives and efforts to the well-being of the indigenous people in this zone, following the precepts of our Savior, who 'came not to be served, but to serve,'" she wrote.[40] The two promoters who had resigned promptly reversed course and ask to be reappointed, probably following the indications of *la Gringa*.[41]

Romano's letter also caused a stir at the INI's central offices in Mexico City in a way that exposed the INI's continued dependence on the SIL. Aguirre Beltrán chided Romano for his letter's "harsh wording." "Reread your letters when you need to *reclamar* [complain], so that you can polish your prose and avoid hurting people," he wrote.[42] Romano responded days later. "You can rest assured that I always reread my letters and never say more than I want to say. Nevertheless, I will try to be a little more diplomatic."[43] Romano later wrote that the INI struggled to break its dependence on SIL missionaries; INI salaries were so low that it could not hire and retain Mexican linguists. The CCI had no new language primers to work with until 1975—and even those were written by an SIL linguist![44]

After Romano's dustup with Slocum, relations between the CCI and the missionary linguist remained frosty. The indigenistas came to believe that Slocum's control over her flock was so complete that with a word she could undermine INI projects and promoters. At Cholol, evangelicals withdrew their support from the school after they learned that their new promoter, a lapsed evangelical named Feliciano López Gómez, no longer attended the church at El Corralito. The INI was forced to close the school. At Pachtontijá, parents took their children out of school every Wednesday on pretext of illness in order to attend church in El Corralito. They also refused to allow their daughters to attend school with boys.[45] The promoter at Mesbiljá, one of Slocum's most promising converts named Francisco Gómez Sánchez, allegedly used his sway over residents to compel them to work for him for free. He warned that if they complained to the indigenistas, "God would punish them." The INI told him that he could either preach or teach, but he could not do both; and when he refused to give up preaching, he was fired.[46] In 1957, Slocum allegedly tried to have the promoter at El Corralito dismissed on rape allegations. The INI looked into the matter and determined that Slocum had probably advised the girl and the father to make the accusation; the promoter was admonished "to conduct himself in the best way possible and avoid discrediting the work of the INI."[47] In short, the INI was locked in a tense stalemate with the evangélicos of Oxchuc and western Ocosingo. The indigenistas defended a secular, nonsectarian approach to education and development, but they still relied on SIL linguists and evangelical promoters in evangelical communities. This dependence prevented the INI from taking a more aggressive stance against Slocum and others who sought to harness INI programs to a religious agenda.

In mid-1957, the INI commissioned anthropologist Alfonso Fabila to investigate the impact of Slocum and the evangelicals in the Oxchuc region. Fabila described El Corralito as the "Mecca of Protestantism," the center of Protestant activity in Mexico: "Every Sunday at 10:00 a.m., the roads fill with thousands of Tseltals from nearby hamlets drawn to El Corralito's temple." Fabila recognized that "not all is negative, because the converts no longer drink alcohol, they do not smoke, they do not fight among themselves, they don't hit their women, and they have a savings ethic, which are not small things." However, evangelism "is sowing division among our indigenous people, *who were always united*."[48] Slocum was expanding her range of action to include Yajalón, "and there is a constant ebb and flow of Americans in San Cristóbal traveling to the Usumacinta River Basin, on the border with Guatemala," where the SIL had established Jungle Camp, a training center for missionary linguists heading to South America. Fabila asked: "At what point in the future could this become a threat to Mexico?"[49] This was a serious concern for an institute that declared national integration to be its primary goal.

Fortunately for the INI, Slocum and Florence Gerdel soon left El Corralito to work in Bachajón, a Tseltal municipality where the INI had a minimal presence. In December 1957, the SIL's general director, William Townsend, and its director in Mexico, Benjamin Elson, met with INI director Alfonso Caso in Mexico City, undoubtedly to clear the air over what had happened in Oxchuc. Slocum presented Caso with a copy of her Spanish-language translation of Tseltal legends. A reporter from the national weekly publication *Tiempo* photographed the event and ran a lengthy and extremely flattering cover story about Slocum and her work among the Tseltals. Entitled "A Woman Civilized Them," it described the changes that had taken place in evangelical communities in Oxchuc. It certainly galled the indigenistas to read that "nobody in Chiapas—not the INI, nor the SEP, nor the SIL—ignores that she is the artifice of this change; that she, a weak, well-intentioned woman, full of faith, is the one who has civilized some of the Tseltal communities."[50] In 1963, Slocum finished her translation of the New Testament in Bachajón's dialect of Tseltal, and in 1964 she and Gerdel left Mexico and began working with the Páez Indians of Colombia.[51]

A Fortuitous Relationship: The Harvard Chiapas Project

The INI lost one valuable North American ally but it soon picked up another—the Harvard Chiapas Project, directed by cultural anthropologist Evon Vogt. Just as the SIL was an unlikely ally for the INI, so too was the Harvard Chiapas Project. After all, most Mexican indigenistas were fierce nationalists, and Mexican anthropology and indigenismo had a modernizing, assimilating mission. North American cultural anthropologists, on the other hand, were in search of exotic, unassimilated "primitives" whose lifeways they could record before they disappeared.[52]

Despite what would seem to be diametrically opposed agendas, the relationship between the INI and Evon Vogt was complementary and beneficial to both parties. One of Vogt's former students, Jan Rus, has written that the initial setbacks suffered at the INI's pilot CCI may have been what led the INI to invite Vogt to set up a long-range research center in the Chiapas highlands. It all began in 1955, at precisely the moment that the INI was negotiating with the Chiapas state government and was rethinking its medical and economic development programs. (The INI had also just had its first direct clash with Marianna Slocum.) That summer, INI director Caso invited Vogt to undertake research in Mexico. Vogt accompanied a high-level INI inspection team and visited Chiapas for the first time. One year later, on the advice of CCI director (and fellow University of Chicago graduate) Alfonso Villa Rojas, Vogt settled on Zinacantán as a research site. Villa Rojas introduced Vogt to Mariano Hernández Zarate, the INI cultural promoter, ejido commissioner, and most important elder at the hamlet of Pasté. In his memoir, Vogt expressed gratitude to Villa Rojas for placing him and his students "under the political protection of the leading caciques of Zinacantán and Huixtán." Apparently, both the INI and Vogt felt that the best way to enter "conservative" indigenous communities was to work through their caciques.[53]

Rus suggests that while the INI may have been genuinely interested in learning how the indigenous "closed themselves off and maintained their supposed isolation," it is more likely that "such investigations, undertaken just as [the] INI was being forced to back away from interfering in local elites' economic and political control of indigenous people, might draw attention away from the larger economic and political systems where intervention had caused such a reaction and refocus it on native communities themselves."[54] Cultural anthropologists trained in the community study tradition were likely to pay little heed to "outside" conditions and the overarching political and economic structures that the INI had shown itself incapable of altering.

The rest, as they say, is history. The Harvard Project (1957–1977) was exceptionally prolific, as Vogt and his more than 140 students published more than 40 books and 180 articles.[55] Rus suggests that the Harvard Project's visibility and prodigious output "helped confirm [the] INI's choice of the Tsotsil-Tseltal highlands as Mexico's emblematic indigenous region." This, despite glaring evidence that the Tseltal-Tsotsil highlands had been shaped by very particular historical circumstances and by a brutal, institutionalized ethnic hierarchy the likes of which were unmatched in the rest of Mexico. The Harvard Project's *representation* of Zinacantán became "the paradigmatic community. Forgotten was the fact that Vogt—guided by Villa Rojas—had chosen Zinacantán for study in the first place because it appeared to be more conservative and 'closed' than most of Chiapas's other Maya communities; that is, precisely because it was *atypical*."[56]

If the indigenistas wagered that the Harvard anthropologists' research would confirm their decision to focus on the inside of indigenous communities, they were right. The Harvard Project provided validation to a struggling institute that had just suffered a major blow to its original development plans. It lent the INI a much-needed international veneer of respectability and prestige at a time when it was struggling to receive political and economic support from Mexico City.

For as long as Villa Rojas directed the CCI, the INI and the Harvard Project worked together closely. Vogt and Villa Rojas enjoyed a good friendship. (Villa Rojas addressed his letters "My Dear Vogtie.") Both men had done graduate work at the University of Chicago (albeit at different times) under the same advisers, Robert Redfield and Sol Tax. In 1958 and again in 1960, the Harvard Project and its researchers were housed at La Cabaña. In time, as Vogt writes, the Harvard researchers "began detaching [themselves] more and more from [the] INI and other governmental programs and their technicians and identifying . . . more with the conservative segments of the Indian communities."[57] Given the INI's difficulties with local ladinos, this approach was politically astute.

At this juncture, the priorities of North American and Mexican anthropologists stood in stark contrast. Vogt claimed that while he "deeply sympathized with the pressing problems of illiteracy, poverty, and disease that plagued the Tsotsil," he "felt strongly that *basic* research on the culture needed to be done." Mexican anthropologists employed by the INI, on the other hand, spent their time "responding to the latest epidemic of disease or the most recent political crisis in the Indian communities and, as a result, were continually sidetracked from carrying out fundamental long-range research."[58] (Former Harvard Project participant Carter Wilson goes further, claiming that they were "taught to look down" on the INI's projects. "By our standards, their purpose was impure, and their efforts so far misguided failures."[59]) As Rus concludes, the Harvard Project's narrowly focused research on Tsotsil culture "appeared to justify the INI's fallback strategy from the mid-1950s on of treating the cycle of exploitation . . . principally from the indigenous side, as an 'indigenous' problem."[60]

Conclusions

The INI's retreat beginning in 1955 was undeniable, as grandiose schemes gave way to modest projects. Even its victories were tainted—in Oxchuc and western Ocosingo, where INI programs met with considerable grassroots support, the struggle with Marianna Slocum cast a pall and the window of opportunity for agrarian reform began to close. The INI also began suffering from inadequate budgets. The CCI's fourth director, Agustín Romano, was only supposed to spend one year in San Cristóbal (1954) before heading off to open a new Coordinating Center in the Cora-Huichol region. However, in February 1955, he was told to remain in Chiapas because the INI had not been allotted a budget sufficient to open the new center. (The CCI in Jesús María, Nayarit, finally opened in 1960). Romano noted that year that the CCI's budget was not keeping pace with the growth of INI programs. In order to keep projects afloat, the INI expected "a greater financial contribution from the indigenous for the construction of schools, roads, clean water projects, and the purchase of athletic equipment and breeding stock."[61]

Romano's replacement, Alfonso Villa Rojas, immediately had to contend with the INI's new budget reality. In February 1956, he learned that INI director Caso and a group of reporters from the *New York Times* wanted to visit the region in March. Villa Rojas, a cosmopolitan man, felt that the INI should maintain appearances at its pilot Coordinating Center. He wrote to the INI's directorate that the impending visit "forces us to do in just one month what you had planned to do in four." He reported that "the medical clinics and outposts are in an ABANDONED STATE." Doctors described the clinic at Chamula as a "white elephant," given its deterioration. "They would have said worse if they had seen the medical outpost at Amatenango," he added.

Significant material improvements were "UNAVOIDABLE to preserve the prestige of our Institute before the eyes of important visitors."[62] Of course, since the INI's health division had just made the decision to shift its focus away from clinics and medical outposts, Villa Rojas was hoping to present the reporters with a Potemkin fantasy of functional medical infrastructure. With help from nearby indigenous communities, the indigenistas hurriedly repaired and painted the clinics and outposts as well at La Cabaña itself, especially the guesthouse, which Villa Rojas sought "to leave in conditions similar to those of a good hotel." He even requested twelve towels "of the highest quality to use in those rooms when we have important visitors."[63]

Later in 1956, Villa Rojas issued another desperate call for better funding. In August, he wrote to the INI's treasurer in Mexico City to express "embarrassment for the trouble that I may have caused when I solicited more money via telegraph. When I ask for money by telegraph, *es porque el agua ya me pasó del cuello* [it's because I am about to drown]." In his letter, Villa Rojas also sounded exasperated by the political demands of the job:

> Directing this center is much more complex and overwhelming than one might imagine at first glance. There have even been times when I have wanted to quit, notwithstanding how much I like this kind of work and your valuable support. The part that's most frustrating and what takes the most time is the attention that one must give to all the problems and conflicts that arise between Indians, encomenderos, priests, missionaries, politicians, teachers, drivers, and others who make up this giant *olla de grillos* [madhouse] of 16,000 square kilometers and 125,000 inhabitants. One must maintain harmony with all of them, from the Governor to the last Chamula, and I can assure you that it is not easy.[64]

As the INI entered a prolonged period of waning political and financial support, the accolades of foreign visitors took on added importance. In late 1955, the indigenistas began to publish the eulogistic commentary of prestigious foreign observers in its official bulletin, *Acción Indigenista*. François Chevalier, the Latin American historian of French origin, called the INI's work "intelligent" and "humane," adding that "there is reason to believe that the indigenous problem will be resolved in the best social conditions. Such an institute lends honor to Mexico." George M. Foster, chair of the Anthropology Department at the University of California, Berkeley, wrote that he was "extremely impressed" by the work done in highland Chiapas. "You in Mexico have understood much better than we have in this country the importance and role of applied anthropology in economic and social development." More praise came from Evon Vogt, who had just made his first trip to Chiapas. "I consider the INI program to be the most extensive and most important program of applied anthropology that currently exists in the world," he wrote.[65] Finally, Sol Tax wrote in 1956 that his "extremely meaningful" visit to the Coordinating Center taught him "how quickly and how completely" the health, education, technology, and economic conditions of indigenous people can be improved by means of a "truly noncoercive and democratic program. In a short period of five years, Mexican indigenistas have carried out a revolution in the region."[66] These panegyrics, which were often repeated in subsequent issues of *Acción Indigenista*, came a time when the INI was reeling from its bruising fight with the Chiapas state government and the Pedrero alcohol monopoly. Now that its wings were clipped and its truly dire economic reality was becoming clearer, praise from prestigious foreigners helped the INI make the case for more political and economic support from Mexico City and no doubt boosted the flagging morale of indigenistas.

CHAPTER 6
Modernizing Message, Mystical Messenger
The Many Uses of the Teatro Petul

◉◉◉ AFTER THE INI was forced to abandon its ambitious plans to remake the Chiapas highlands, it turned its gaze inward to the only place where it would be allowed work—to the indigenous communities themselves. The INI's retreat coincided with a fortuitous innovation in the CCI's Department of Visual Aids, a bilingual hand-puppet theater called the Teatro Guiñol (later "Petul"). The CCI used the wildly popular puppets to promote all of its programs, particularly those related to education and public health. According to INI staff reports and publications, the indigenous talked and even argued with the puppets as if they were human. Children asked questions about the afterlife, and adults queried Petul, the lead puppet, about birth control and marriage strategies. In other words, while the CCI used the Teatro Petul to promote its modernizing agenda, Tseltals and Tsotsils assimilated the puppets into their lives and—to a certain extent—they appropriated them.

The Unlikely Emergence of the Teatro Petul

The Teatro Petul had a largely accidental birth. It was a product of the many limitations that hampered the CCI's Department of Visual Aids in the early 1950s. The department produced educational films, but showing them required traveling by horseback on slippery footpaths with a projector and an electric generator in tow. Meager budgets placed additional restrictions on film production. The department then settled on fixed filmstrips, which were cheaper to make and easier to project onto a screen using gas lamps. The cultural promoter would narrate the presentation in the local dialect of Tseltal or Tsotsil, illustrating the main points with concrete examples taken from the local community. The projections were such a novelty that in numerous cases the promoter had to prepare the public for what was about to occur. "In spite of this," reported *Acción Indigenista*, "the appearance of the first image was typically received with great astonishment and applause, which required the promoter to wait a little before beginning the oral explanation."[1]

By July 1954, the department had created several full-color fixed-image presentations, including titles like *Our Friends the Trees* and a presentation on microbes entitled *Animals That Are Seen and Not Seen*. During the INI's ongoing battle with the statewide alcohol monopoly, the department presented *Aguardiente* and *The Rights of Man*. Yet filmstrip presentations were also problematic. The indigenistas learned, to their dismay, that the indigenous were indifferent to the presentations unless they portrayed people of their own particular ethnic group or municipality. Custom tailoring each presentation was simply not feasible. The search for a low-cost, highly mobile, flexible tool of education and persuasion continued.

CCI officials first created the Teatro Guiñol in early 1954 with the simple aim of providing alcohol-free entertainment to highland communities. As William Beezley has noted, puppet troupes have a long history in Mexico. Hernán Cortés brought small marionettes to Mexico in 1519, and missionaries later used puppet theater to evangelize the indigenous.[2] Elena Jackson Albarrán has studied the SEP's use of the Teatro Guiñol in the 1930s, during the height of socialist pedagogy in Mexico. The architects of this puppet troupe were radical artists, intellectuals, and bohemians who had spent time abroad and been inspired by the Bolsheviks' socialist school puppet theater. They wrote scripts designed to foment class consciousness and combat superstition. But Jackson Albarrán notes that the puppeteers themselves felt stifled by the SEP's censorship board, which purged the plays of frivolous content and prohibited improvisation.[3] After 1940, it appears that the Teatro Guiñol fell out of favor as the SEP adopted a more conservative orientation and urban audiences gained access to more sophisticated forms of entertainment.

Hand puppets offered key advantages to the CCI in Chiapas. They were easy to make and operate, and the puppet stage could be quickly assembled and easily transported. Director José Núñez, of the National Institute of Fine Arts (Instituto Nacional de Bellas Artes, or INBA), instructed two Tsotsil men and two Tsotsil women[4] in how to manufacture simple hand puppets in European dress and stage shows of European origin, such as *Little Red Riding Hood*. Animal puppets were fashioned to resemble Disney characters. The troupe was well received by San Cristóbal's ladinos, but indigenous communities had trouble relating to story plots and characters of such foreign origin.

According to Teodoro Sánchez, a Tsotsil promoter who would later direct the troupe, even the puppeteers were confused by these adaptations of European folklore.[5] He described the troupe's first (and only) performance in an indigenous community, the Chamulan hamlet of Ichintón, just a few kilometers up the new road from the CCI. Ichintón had posed resistance to several of the INI's development programs, and its inhabitants were a tough audience for the inexperienced puppeteers. Sánchez described the public's reaction after watching several skits of European origin.

> The people did not react at all. Everyone was apathetic and expressionless. There was silence, apart from the occasional sneeze or yawn. We observed the crowd through openings in the stage, and they all looked angry. My compañeros and I felt very bad, even worse than the spectators.[6]

After the failed presentation at Ichintón, Director Núñez asked for a leave of absence to visit his family in Mexico City. He never returned to Chiapas.

The CCI's anthropologists were quick to recognize the troupe's initial shortcomings as well as its potential as a tool to educate and persuade. Left temporarily without a director, the puppeteers took steps to transform the Teatro Guiñol into something more appropriate to the surroundings. "We gave the puppets indigenous features and clothes from the municipalities of Tenejapa, Oxchuc, Chenalhó, Huixtán, Chamula, and Zinacantán," wrote Sánchez. "We also improvised skits and dialogues."[7] In summer 1954, the INBA sent Guiñol specialist Marco Antonio Montero to San Cristóbal to help the troupe perfect its puppetry techniques, costumes, and skits. The newly configured troupe began giving performances in fall 1954. In September, Teodoro Sánchez directed his first show, entitled *The Teacher*, at the school at Ichintón, the scene of the previous troupe's disaster. This time the lead puppet, Petul, was dressed like a Chamula, with a black vest, a white shawl with woolen yarn tassels, and a straw hat decorated with differently colored ribbons. And this time, the puppet troupe's performance was well received. After hearing the puppets speak in their own tongue, several of the hamlet's more curious women "went so far as to raise the curtain to discover what was behind it. Young and old enjoyed chatting with the puppets," wrote education supervisor Andrés Santiago Montes. Much to the indigenistas' delight, Ichintón's men asked the troupe to return and give another performance.[8]

Buoyed by their success at Ichintón, the CCI's directors scheduled several performances in some of the most resistant Chamulan and Zinacantecan hamlets. These performances confirmed the utility of the Guiñol's new orientation among men and women, young and old, and demonstrated the puppeteers' ability to respond to unanticipated situations. At Belisario Domínguez, an ejido of Chamulas in the municipality of Chenalhó, children and adults alike came alive when the puppets spoke to them in Tsotsil. Although the INI's ultimate language policy called for the "castellanization" of the Chiapas highlands, use of the lengua materna (mother tongue) was integral to the puppets' promotion of key programs related to hygiene, agriculture, and education.[9]

The performance at Belisario Domínguez was also important because it represented the first time that the troupe experimented with improvisation. Troupe director Marco Antonio Montero observed that "the result was quite satisfactory, since men, women, children, and even the promoter and the hamlet authorities dialogued with the puppets." A few days later, Montero spoke with the promoter to inquire whether the show had left any lasting impressions. The promoter commented that "some children were convinced that the puppets were of flesh and blood and spoke on their own; others weren't sure whether they were made of flesh or some other material . . . still others were trying to sing the round that the puppets had taught them."[10]

In late November, the puppeteers gave another experimental presentation, this time at the ceremonial center of San Juan Chamula. Montero called this an experiment to evaluate "whether we could distract the Indians who meet on the plaza with the sole aim of getting drunk." He concluded that the performance had been partly successful. "The Indians moved away from the stalls where alcohol is sold for as long as the performance lasted, but once it ended, they returned to drinking aguardiente," he wrote. Nevertheless, many Chamulas were extremely enthused by the performance and asked the puppeteers to return the following Sunday so that they could invite their wives and children.[11]

The performance at Chamula was not entirely without incident. As Montero had noted at earlier performances, "some differences have emerged between the public and the puppets," but these conflicts had led to instructive dialogues concerning the INI's programs and objectives. But at Chamula, audience participation nearly led to blows. As Montero reported:

> An inebriated Chamula man began insulting one of the puppets who was dressed as a Zinacanteco and was being manipulated by a Zinacanteco. Knowing the rivalry that exists between Chamula and Zinacantán, José,

the puppeteer, got angry, so much so that he began answering with insults, since the Chamula's comments mainly referred to the Zinacantecos' way of dressing and using breeches. Tempers rose to the point where José was about to put down his puppet and go out and punch the Chamula. Eventually José calmed down. To keep this from happening again, José was told that he should never respond to insults in the way that he did, since our mission is not to fight with the public but rather to entertain. In addition, we should always be prepared for adverse situations and know instantly how to resolve them.[12]

José apparently learned his lesson. Knowing that the troupe would give a performance the next day in Larráinzar, he changed the outfit of his puppet to that used in Larráinzar. The next day, when a different inebriated man began insulting the puppet for other reasons, José's puppet explained that the troupe had come as friends to entertain, not to fight with anyone. "Since the man wanted to speak to the puppet in Spanish, we took out another puppet that knew *castilla*," wrote Montero. Teodoro Sánchez, the leader of the troupe, knew that the drunk man's name was Juan. When the puppet called him by his name, "he was so surprised that he changed his attitude completely. From that point forward he engaged in a decent and correct dialogue."[13] Not only did José avert a potentially violent confrontation but the troupe was adaptive enough to turn a conflictive situation into one that served the long-term language policy of the INI.

The performance at Larráinzar's ceremonial center further confirmed Petul's popularity. On that day, Larráinzar celebrated its patron saint, San Andrés. The puppeteers set up the theater in a prominent place on the central plaza where thousands of Tsotsils from neighboring hamlets had congregated. The performance began just as the church bells rang to signal the start of the procession whereby San Andrés was visited by all of the saints from neighboring hamlets. Montero noted that the INI's hand puppets managed to hold the attention of those who were watching the performance. "They were very entertained and did not budge. The procession was largely disregarded, which demonstrates the degree of interest that the indigenous have in the puppets."[14]

By December 1954, the Tsotsil puppet troupe had exceeded all expectations. The young puppeteers had shown themselves to be extremely capable and quick to adapt to the unexpected; they also "boldly and freely discussed and ridiculed the patterns of conduct and traditional community values that are dangerous to one's health." As told by *Acción Indigenista*, the interaction

FIGURE 6.1. Teatro Petul functions became wildly popular in the late 1950s. Photographer unknown. Fototeca Nacho López, Comisión Nacional para el Desarrollo de los Pueblos Indígenas. Late 1950s.

between the puppets and the public "quickly turns the spectators into actors themselves, and soon a lively debate ensues as they drop their inhibitions."

> The agile exchange of questions and responses, of confessions and public requests, of demands and concessions, produces an atmosphere of happiness, confidence, and intimacy that allows us to inform the community of our health programs . . . and quickly obtain their active participation in our activities.[15]

At this point, the CCI's Tsotsil puppet troupe was given a new name to reflect its new orientation. The French *guiñol* was dropped, substituted by the name Petul, or "Pedro" in both Tseltal and Tsotsil, after Pedro Díaz Cuscat, a visionary Chamula who helped organize an indigenous revolt in 1869.[16] In the new Teatro Petul, the standout puppeteer was Petul's marionette, Teodoro Sánchez. Sánchez grew up in the bilingual (Tsotsil and Spanish) municipality of Ixtapa, to the west of the INI's work area. He attended a federal school for two years on the ejido where he was born, then studied the third and fifth grades in the municipal center, where ladino students beat him repeatedly and made fun of his awkward Spanish and his tattered clothes. Sánchez excelled in school in spite of the abuse but had to drop out to help his father in the fields. After performing his year of military service in Mexico City at the age of eighteen, he returned to Chiapas and joined the work crew that built the road connecting San Cristóbal with Chenalhó. Julio de la Fuente spotted him and offered him work as a cultural promoter. Soon, he was invited to join the Teatro Guiñol. Sánchez had a great sense of humor and an uncanny ability to improvise dialogue. He also played the marimba and the guitar. He was a true believer in the mística indigenista and the power of education. Before long, he was directing both the Teatro Petul and the CCI's Department of Visual Aids. His reports and his short autobiography are central to the discussion that follows.[17]

Content of the Teatro Petul

While the Teatro Petul continued to give a limited number of purely entertaining shows aimed at winning the trust of the highland Maya, such as adaptations of local folklore, the "new" troupe most commonly promoted education and facilitated the INI's many public health campaigns. In late 1954, the indigenistas drew up a list of topics for the troupe. Over the next several years, the puppeteers would perform hundreds of plays on the themes summarized in table 6.1.

In most of the performances, the lead puppet, named Petul, served as spokesman for progress and modernity. He was usually challenged by his companion, a gloomy puppet named Xun (Juan), who opposed the INI's programs and vocalized the public's doubts and concerns.[18] Rosario Castellanos, a Chiapanecan who arguably became Mexico's most prominent twentieth-century woman of letters, joined the Teatro Petul in 1955 and directed it in 1956–1957. Raised on a ranch in Comitán, Chiapas, and the author of the classic *Balún Canán* (The Nine Guardians), Castellanos also wrote skits for the Teatro Petul and used the Xun character frequently. As she explained, Xun was "reluctant to accept the advice of others. He didn't want to attend the Institute's schools to learn to read or speak Spanish and disdained the advice of the agricultural technicians who tried to help him improve the output of his plot." Instead of going to INI doctors, Xun sought out *brujos* (witches); he refused to help build roads; and he drank heavily and distilled clandestine aguardiente.[19]

One of the troupe's first plays was simply titled *Petul Visits the INI*. It was

TABLE 6.1. Content for Teatro Petul performances.

EDUCATION	Literacy and learning Spanish
	Increasing school attendance, encouraging girls to attend
	School construction projects: school buildings, houses for teachers, latrines; establishing workshops
	The indigenous and the ladino: overcoming attitudes of inferiority, forming self-confidence, knowing national laws
	Integration into the Mexican nationality, the indigenous as Mexicans. What is Mexico? Who are its heroes (Morelos, Juárez, and Cárdenas)? What is the Constitution?
HEALTH	When to go to the doctor
	Sanitation campaigns: DDT, human vaccinations, animal vaccinations, isolating and caring for the sick
	Local sanitation: using latrines, protecting water (surface water and wells), ventilating houses, household cleaning (floors, clothing, beds, flatware, keeping animals out of the house)
	Personal hygiene: washing hands and face, preventing the spread of illness by washing before eating, after defecating, etc.
	Introducing new elements of hygiene: brushing teeth, using toilet paper
	Hygiene and food preparation (boiling water, etc.)
	Medical explanations for regional illnesses: shingles, typhoid, whooping cough, measles, typhus, conjunctivitis, tuberculosis
	Medical explanations for imported illnesses: measles, onchocerciasis (river blindness), etc.
	Caring for mother and child in pregnancy and childbirth; neonatal care
	Nutrition
	Anti-alcohol campaign: social, economic, and biological consequences of heavy alcohol use
ECONOMY	Cooperatives: presenting the concept, promoting the store and its articles, managing a cooperative, improving consumption of consumer goods
	The fight against hoarders (*acaparadores*) and people who confiscate goods (*atajadoras*): how the INI or the cooperative can help
	The problem of resident debt peons, acquiring land
	INI credit: how to get it, how to invest it, how to pay back the loan
	Forming credit cooperatives (credit unions)
	Selecting different seeds for different regions, how to get them

ECONOMY	Fertilizers
	Irrigation
	Pests that attack crops: macroscopic and microscopic, pesticides and crop rotation
	Domestic animals: advantages of improved poultry breeds, caring for poultry, preventive vaccinations, advantages of improved pig breeds, caring for pigs, vaccinations

Source: Castro, "Las metas del Teatro Petul"; and AHCCITT, 1954, Ser. Dirección, Sec. Educación, Exp. 19-1954/2, "Las prioridades del Teatro Petul."

often performed in hamlets where the INI had a negligible presence. In the play, Petul goes to the CCI, hidden, and reports what he sees to distrustful Tsotsil elders. When asked whether the people of the INI are good or bad, Petul responds: "They are people who work." An elder replies, "Well, Petul, we also work and among us there are good people and bad people." Petul responds: "The same applies to mestizos, brother." (Note that Petul did not call the indigenistas *ladinos*.)

Later on in the play, Petul reports on the CCI's boarding school, where he learned that "Mexico is a very big, pretty country." In order for Mexico to be stronger, prettier, and richer, however, "all Mexicans have to work together. Almost all of Mexico speaks Spanish and we need to learn it too so that we can speak with our brothers." Petul then explains that the INI requires collaboration. "If they open a road, we need to work with the engineers; if they open a clinic, we need to help build it; same if they open a school. We need to send our children so that they can live better than we do." At the end of the play, one elder asks if the INI will take away their churches, which was a legitimate question, since the anticlerical campaign launched by Governor Victórico Grajales (1932–1936) was still within living memory of many. Petul, of course, assured them that their land and their churches would be respected.[20]

Unfortunately, the surviving documentation says nothing about how the indigenous responded to this play's messages. If elders were reluctant to trust the INI, it's hard to imagine them accepting the broader message of national integration. This did not stop the Teatro Petul from trying to patch together the nation, however. It frequently gave performances in the highlands on the meaning of Mexico's flag. It also celebrated the life of Mexico's indigenous president, Benito Juárez. The puppet troupe also occasionally performed for ladinos with the aim of promoting cross-cultural understanding. In late 1956, the Teatro Petul gave a show in Tuxtla Gutiérrez to an estimated five thousand spectators. The dialogue was in Spanish, despite the fact that the indigenous puppeteers were not fluent in the language. By all accounts, the performance was a rousing success; Sánchez crowed, "we conquered the hearts of the multitude." The state capital's newspapers the next day praised the performance, and the INBA's Teatro Guiñol troupe in Tuxtla was put back into commission.[21]

The Teatro Petul's success as a negotiating tool led to the creation of a Tseltal troupe in 1956. The two troupes were kept extremely busy and became an integral part of all of the INI's campaigns in the highlands. During a sixteen-day stretch in May 1957, director Rosario Castellanos kept a log of the troupes' activities. On the seventh of that month, the Tsotsil puppeteers gave presentations in Yalcuc (Huixtán) and Yashtinin (Las Casas) "with the sole purpose of entertaining and announcing more serious presentations in the future." Two days later, they gave a performance in Navenchauc (Zinacantán) to promote better hygiene to prevent the propagation of rainy-season illnesses like typhoid and dysentery. The next day, they were back in Yalcuc and Yashtinin to recommend vaccination against whooping cough. The troupe then tried to give a performance in Milpoleta (Chamula) but never found the hamlet. Meanwhile, the Tseltal troupe gave a performance at La Cabaña to entertain some visitors from Cancuc, who were seeking INI assistance for the first time following a fire in their town square.

On May 18, the Tseltal group gave a well-received performance in Aguacatenango to support the introduction of piped water. Four days later, the Tsotsil troupe gave the same performance in Navenchauc, but the result was less than satisfactory, "possibly due to the obstructionist activity of the state teacher who works there." Finally, on May 24, the Tsotsil troupe traveled to the hamlet of Chilil, but nobody was there to receive them because there had been some confusion over exactly when the show was to take place.[22]

The lack of infrastructure in the highlands meant that troupes got lost and communication mix-ups were fairly common. The troupes also had to contend with the rain, especially in the summertime. Castellanos tells of near biblical downpours, of the indigenistas' horses slipping and falling on muddy footpaths (in part because they didn't have horseshoes), saddles coming apart, and the puppeteers (and Castellanos herself) walking from place to place, sloshing in the mud, shivering and feeling quite miserable. If they reached their destination before nightfall, they usually slept on the floor of the schoolroom, but they occasionally had to make camp along swollen creeks or in corrals, among sheep and goats. Castellanos later reflected that she had returned to Chiapas "to find myself." Some have observed that her encounter with the misery of the indigenous countryside—an encounter denied by her upbringing—helped her to "shed her inherited cultural baggage" and come to maturity as a writer.[23]

Indeed, the CCI's puppeteers had to be ready for anything—inclement weather, inadequate infrastructure, and unpredictable audience responses. Improvisation became one of their hallmarks. If a certain individual was posing resistance to an INI program, Petul or any of the other puppets might call him out during the performance, according to Agustín Romano, who was directing the CCI at the time that the Teatro Petul was established. "Before the puppeteers arrived in the community, they took note of who was opposing the program," Romano said. "Then, during the show, Petul would ask, 'Don Pedro, where are you?' Don Pedro would identify himself, and a dialogue would ensue."[24] The highly popular puppets often managed to convince "obstructers" to drop their resistance.

The Teatro Petul was particularly useful in reaching indigenous women, with whom other types of outreach had failed. The puppeteers never missed an opportunity to encourage women to attend the INI's schools and become teachers themselves. In the following passage, a female puppet from a popular prohygiene play improvises a dialogue with some timid, curious women from Tenejapa. According to Teodoro Sánchez,

> The women seemed embarrassed and rarely spoke with Petul. We decided to bring out Candelaria. . . . At that point the women responded warmly to the greetings that we sent on behalf of the director of the CCI and the other leaders. Some women commented that Petul's voice sounded very pretty. One wondered how he knew their names. Who knows, replied another, he must have a very strong soul. We can see in Candelaria's face that she's not a common woman, she is *galanota* [outspoken, smart] and is not ashamed to speak. Yes, said the first woman, she's galanota because perhaps she is not married or is a teacher's wife.

One of the women then asked Candelaria if she was married. Candelaria responded in the affirmative and added that her husband was maestro Petul and that she too was a teacher. Candelaria then delivered the INI's message

FIGURE 6.2. Women and children in El Roblar, Pantelhó. Photographer unknown. Fototeca Nacho López, Comisión Nacional para el Desarrollo de los Pueblos Indígenas. Circa 1965.

concerning the importance of educating girls and women and claimed that the INI had taught her to read and write.[25]

The Teatro Petul was also integral to the success of the Open School, an adult education program launched in 1956 on the insistence of former CCI director Julio de la Fuente. The Open School was to be held outdoors on market days, when hundreds of adults were found buying, selling, and socializing in the central plaza of their municipality's cabecera. INI personnel set up chalkboards on basketball courts or in front of the municipal palace and used the Teatro Petul to hold the public's attention. Once several dozen adults had congregated around the puppets, an INI promoter would begin a lesson in reading and writing.

Rosario Castellanos's play *Petul and the Open School* was one of many designed to encourage people to attend the Open School. The play opens with Petul's foil Xun announcing that he wants to sell a nice poncho in San Cristóbal. But Xun doesn't know the value of money and cannot speak Spanish. Petul advises him to go to school so that he can learn to add, subtract, and speak castilla. Xun responds that he has no time for that and soon finds himself in San Cristóbal, where a fat ladino vender offers him fifteen pesos (three bills of five) for the poncho, which he claims is of poor quality. A thin ladino vendor offers Xun twenty pesos (two bills of ten) for the same poncho. The fat vendor, however, convinces Xun that three bills of five are worth more than two bills of ten. The vendors begin fighting. When a policeman shows up, he blames Xun for the ruckus and threatens to throw him in jail. With that, Xun offers his poncho to the policeman and walks home, empty-handed.

Once back at his house, he explains to his angry wife that although he drinks lots of aceite guapo he still cannot understand Spanish and is therefore easily fooled. Petul appears again, telling Xun that he should go to the Open School, which is held at the municipal center every Sunday. Xun's wife is initially upset because she fears that once Xun learns to read, he'll leave her for a ladina. Petul, who has an answer for everything, tells her that she too should attend the Open School so that they can learn together. The last lines of the performance reflect the concern of Romano and others that indigenous promoters were taking ladina wives and leaving unassimilated indigenous women behind in the development process.[26]

The indigenistas gave the Open School a trial run in Oxchuc in July 1956. They imparted lessons to an estimated 260 people, including 90 women. After Oxchuc's promoter gave a quick lesson on Benito Juárez, several men in attendance came up to the chalkboards and wrote their names. They were given a notebook and a pencil and told to keep practicing at home. The class lasted nearly two hours, and only once did the Teatro Petul have to intervene to keep the people interested.

At the conclusion of the language lesson, a different promoter taught a math class. Nine men came up to the chalkboard and wrote and read numbers. Because people were less interested in this class, "the puppeteers had to intervene constantly to hold their attention." This class lasted only one hour. There were an estimated 190 people in attendance, but only 35 of them were women. Two weeks later, the INI tried to hold a second Open School in Oxchuc without the Teatro Petul because the troupe had been unable to arrange transportation. Although 90 people showed up, everyone left once the language lesson was over. A basketball game followed pitting the students of the INI's school at El Corralito against promoters. Despite the day's setbacks, education supervisor Librado Mendoza Jarquín wrote that the Open School had still promoted the INI's agenda because it distracted people "from the religious rituals that have them all so absorbed."[27]

The Teatro Petul was also the main attraction at an Open School event in Chamula later that year. Once they arrived at the municipal center, the indigenistas used amplified *ranchera* music to draw a crowd to the municipal palace. This prompted Carlo Antonio Castro to ask "whether it might be possible to find some Tsotsil recordings to present the indigenous with something more appropriate than songs about incongruous flings and mestizo shootouts." So important was Petul on that day that the troupe director later suggested that the puppet itself should begin imparting one of the classes. Unfortunately, just as Petul had gathered a crowd of more than one hundred Chamulas, the crowd was distracted by a raucous incarceration at the town hall. Fifteen minutes later, Petul bade farewell to twenty-five men and one woman.[28]

Over the course of the next few years, the content of the Teatro's presentations continued to evolve. After the INI made the decision to drop the Open School due to its costs and its ambiguous results, the troupe was increasingly used by the INI's Health Division in its campaigns against whooping cough and typhus. Petul was also deployed in the INI's ongoing campaign against alcohol consumption. Rosario Castellanos wrote *Petul in the Anti-Alcohol Campaign* in which Xun comes home from the lowland fincas drunk on a mixed drink known regionally as *chucho con rabia* (rabid dog). He has spent all the money that he earned. Just as he is about to hit his wife, Petul arrives and gives him an injection. As Xun regains consciousness, Petul lectures him on the dangers of excessive alcohol consumption and clandestine, locally produced aguardiente. "Think about it," Petul says. "The law punishes those who distill contraband aguardiente. That's why the fiscal police and troops enter the hamlets. And when they find a still, they take the owner to jail."[29]

Another Castellanos play prepared Tseltals and Tsotsils for the onslaught of foreign tourists that has become an inescapable feature of the Chiapas highlands. In *Petul and the Foreign Devil*, Xun encounters a redheaded foreigner who speaks an incomprehensible language. Suspecting that he may be the devil, Xun drinks aceite guapo so that he might be able to understand him. Petul tell Xun that the foreigner is a tourist who heard that Xun's hamlet is "pretty" and wants to take pictures and buy souvenirs.[30] This skit was written after a German-American painter, Arthur Silz, was killed while attempting to climb Tzontewitz, a local mountain believed to be sacred by many Tsotsils.[31]

A "Humble Servant of the Government?" Or a Saint?

The Teatro Petul was immensely popular, even when some of the programs that it endorsed were controversial and disliked. The troupes were so well received that local authorities often organized dances afterward in their honor.

In several communities, the puppet Petul was attributed human characteristics. As Castellanos noted, "more than one indigenous man has approached him to ask, very earnestly, that he agree to be the godfather of his recently born son."[32] For others, Petul was a shaman of modernity, an all-powerful troubleshooter who endorsed Western medicine instead of more traditional remedies. Teodoro Sánchez told of a couple in the hamlet of El Pozo (Cancuc) who asked Petul about birth control in 1962.

> A man started telling Petul of his pain and suffering and explained that his wife was pregnant . . . and that he already had three little children and couldn't afford another. He said that he knew of some herbs that work very well, but they sterilize the woman permanently, and his intention was only to cure her for a while until the youngest child grew up. He asked Petul what medicine would prevent his wife from having more children. Petul responded that he didn't know how to prescribe medicine and recommended that he see the doctor in San Cristóbal or Oxchuc.[33]

Petul also heard about the opposite problem—infertility. In a hamlet of Chenalhó, Manuel Gómez Corochoch told Petul that his wife had been treated by a *comadrona* (midwife) but that she still hadn't gotten pregnant. He asked Petul to tell a doctor to give her the appropriate medicine. The puppeteers used a puppet fashioned to look like an INI doctor to recommend diagnostic tests at Chenalhó's clinic to see whether Gómez or his wife might have a medical problem. According to Teodoro Sánchez, Gómez became very ashamed at the mere suggestion that he might be the infertile one.

> He was so upset that he said, "¡Ay! ¡hijo de la chingada! It can't be. *Me considero ser hombre muy hombre* [I consider myself a very manly man]." Petul explained the solution clearly and thoroughly. Gómez was dazed, saying to Petul, "If I am the sick one, I give you permission to sleep one night with my spouse. She will leave me if we cannot have a family." Gómez's wife was very upset and said nothing, perhaps out of embarrassment or shame. While the dialogue took place, she remained hunched over without lifting her eyes. The crowd did not speak either; everyone was silent.[34]

As Petul's marionette, Sánchez was privy to other kinds of intimate conversations. In the Tseltal hamlet of Bapus (Cancuc), a luckless widower asked Petul to play matchmaker for him. According to Sánchez's report:

A man named Diego López Guach, 45 years of age, told us that his wife died 16 years ago, and since that time he has raised his three sons himself doing all the housework before going to work in the fields. He has to get up very early to make the tortillas, cook the corn and beans, and grind everything to prepare the daily meals. Now he feels tired. He has tried to find another *compañera*, but he hasn't had any luck and the young women ignore him. Lately he had his eye on a widow but she won't listen to him either and runs away whenever she sees him. He approached the parents of this woman and asked for their consent but they declined, in spite of the fact that he offered them three liters of aguardiente, two kilos of chillies, and a corn grinder.

López asked Petul "about 50 times" if he or someone from the CCI could force her to marry him. Petul recommended that he speak to the parents again or find another woman. Teodoro Sánchez noted in his report that young women did not want to marry older widowers, and "they are the ones that choose the man that they like the best."[35] This commentary suggests the growing power and autonomy of younger women and widows in Bapus (and perhaps elsewhere in the highlands).

In his brief autobiography, Teodoro Sánchez makes repeated reference to the trust that the indigenous placed in Petul. Women complained to him that their husbands returned from three- to six-month stints on the lowland plantations with no money, either because they had been robbed on the return trip home or they had already spent it on trago. Women also complained of abusive treatment. "Petul listened to their complaints, sometimes responding as judge, municipal agent, or education committee, imparting justice for these women as if they were plaintiffs." If the woman was a victim of spousal abuse and the accused husband was nearby, Petul would tell the husband to rectify his behavior. In extreme cases the puppet went even further, "sternly warning that if it happened again he would have to go to jail."[36]

For some individuals in more isolated communities, the Petul puppet was more than an all-knowing problem solver. He was practically divine. Again, we return to the testimony of troupe leader Teodoro Sánchez. He reported that young and old alike at Chimix, a hamlet in Chenalhó, believed that Petul had supernatural powers.

They all commented that Petul has a soul and cures people simply by speaking to them; others said that they had seen him move his eyes and his mouth

FIGURE 6.3. Children enjoying the Teatro Petul in Romerillo, Chamula, on the Día del Niño. Photographer unknown. Fototeca Nacho López, Comisión Nacional para el Desarrollo de los Pueblos Indígenas. 1968.

when speaking, and some believe that Petul is more than a saint. At times Petul has called them by their names, and they immediately stop laughing and become very serious and respectful and ask him if he knows the date of judgment day (the end of the world). Others ask if he knows the location of their grandfather's soul or that of their brother who died twenty years ago at the age of ten, and whether he has continued growing in heaven. Some ask him whether he made the trees, the rocks, and the rivers. Petul answers the question saying that nature made them, and explains that he is not a saint but rather a humble friend and servant of the government.[37]

This report suggests that Petul, an official representative of modernity, had been appropriated by these Tsotsils and endowed with traditional spiritual attributes. For them, Petul had one foot in the modern world and one foot in the spiritual world, which may partly explain his success.

Did Petul become something that contradicted the overall philosophy of a secular institute that sought to modernize and develop indigenous communities? In the passage above, Petul explained that he was merely a "friend and servant of the government." But Rosario Castellanos told a different story. "Through the Teatro Guiñol, the Institute has enriched the mythology of the Indians with mysterious and fantastic beings," she wrote in 1957. Was this a desired outcome? Castellanos asked herself, rhetorically, if the Petul "experiment" was a failure, "because the Institute never intended to further confuse the already muddled mix of the natural and supernatural that exists in the spirit of the Indians."[38] Apparently, the CCI's directors believed that the benefits of the Teatro Petul outweighed its possible costs, and they exploited Petul's ascribed powers as a means of pursuing a modernizing, secular end.

The Teatro Petul in the 1960s

The Teatro Petul had its greatest impact in distant hamlets without modern infrastructure. There was much work to be done in these communities, and distrustful, suspicious villagers had to be won over. Isolated from other forms of media, these people tended to be impressionable. Where Tseltal and Tsotsil communities came to accept the INI and its projects, the Teatro Petul gradually lost its impact. As people learned to read and write and as roads linked their hamlets to San Cristóbal, where other forms of media were available, the puppets were regarded as simply puppets, purveyors of entertainment and instruction, but nothing more.

The same general pattern of acceptance applied at the INI's Coordinating Centers outside of Chiapas. At the INI's third site, at the Papaloapan Basin, the INI was given the unpopular task of resettling Mazatecos whose ancestral lands had been flooded by the Miguel Alemán Dam. An article in *Acción Indigenista* described the Mazatecos as "more haughty and civilized" than the Maya of highland Chiapas. At Papaloapan, the puppet shows had to be "carefully planned and rehearsed." "The Mazatecos do not accept systematic propaganda, because they have acquired a phobia against official suggestions. All instruction must be 'masked' in presentations where entertainment is the primary focus." In Chiapas, on the other hand, what the article called "the simple nature" of the people, the lack of diversions, the poverty of the region, and the lack of roads facilitated acceptance of the Teatro Petul.[39]

In the early 1960s, as the CCI extended its operations deeper into Tseltal and Tsotsil regions, the Teatro Petul was kept very busy. Teodoro Sánchez

FIGURE 6.4. A behind-the-scenes look at a puppet show in Belisario Domínguez, Chenalhó. From the INI's 1958 film *Todos somos mexicanos* (directed by José Arenas). Fototeca Nacho López, Comisión Nacional para el Desarrollo de los Pueblos Indígenas. 1958.

noted in 1963 that the puppets did not fool the public in some Tseltal hamlets, even when the puppeteers were visiting for the first time. Most audience members understood that puppeteers hid behind and under the stage, "but they did not know how Petul's voice was amplified, nor did they figure out how the puppets knew the names of people in the audience. They think that some magic apparatus is hidden under the shirt of the puppeteer."[40]

In less remote communities, the Tseltal and Tsotsil troupes presented skits that carried messages promoting a capitalist work ethic, entrepreneurial behavior, and modern consumerism. These skits tended to be longer, less frivolous, and (arguably) less clever than those penned by Montero and Castellanos. For example, Teodoro Sánchez's play titled *The Thief* addressed why some indigenous people were getting wealthy while others were being left behind. Presented frequently in the early 1960s, when a minority of indigenous was able to take advantage of improved transportation infrastructure and expanding market opportunities, its message seems to exalt individual accumulation. At one point, Petul states that some people were poor "because they want to be poor. Today we are free to work as hard as we can." At a performance in Tzanembolóm, Chenalhó, a man named Mariano Pérez Bak told Petul that he looked younger each time he visited the hamlet. Pérez asked the puppet if he could take medicine to counter aging. Petul responded by saying, "Staying vigorous is a matter of eating very well, eating different foods," to which Pérez replied, "You're right, Petul, but we can't eat well here because *el medio no lo permite* [we can't afford it]." Sensing an opening, Petul took the opportunity to pitch education as the way out of the cycle of poverty.[41]

By the late 1960s, the Teatro Petul was losing its touch. At the conclusion of a 1967 performance at Lelemechig, Oxchuc (a particularly resistant part of northern Oxchuc, near Cancuc), one of the hamlet's principal Catholic *catequistas* (laymen) said that the puppets were devils and tricksters and had come simply to scare people. A few weeks later, after the Tseltal troupe presented *The Thief* to several communities, the troupe director noted that "in some cases the audience jeered the puppets, claiming that Petul was a *mandón* [bossy person] when he told them that they needed to work harder." Petul allegedly "understood the psychology of these people, and scolded them."[42]

Conclusions

As a tool of persuasion, negotiation, and education, the Teatro Petul was clearly successful from late 1954 into the 1960s in highland Chiapas. The puppets' effectiveness was such that indigenous people occasionally appropriated them in unanticipated ways. The more dramatic vignettes in this chapter suggest that Petul came to be regarded as a shaman or even a saint in some cases. Perhaps these "mystical messengers" partly undermined the secular developmentalist goals of the INI. These vignettes also raise questions. Did adults actually believe that direct communication with a puppet could solve the very real matters of family planning and courtship? Were they sober? Or, could it be that the indigenous were "playing" the INI?

Unfortunately, existing documentation cannot provide us with definitive answers. Petul's supplicants were probably sober, since INI staff was usually quick to comment on inebriation and in fact cancelled performances when too many members of the audience appeared drunk. Petul may indeed have been perceived as something far greater than a hand puppet. We have reams of anthropological studies at our disposal that would suggest that the spiritual world of Tseltals and Tsotsils could accommodate such an unlikely "saint." Yet surely most of the adults in the communities saw Petul for what it was. If this was indeed the case, why did some indigenous people choose to "play along" with Petul as they did?

Two possible explanations come to mind. Petul may simply have been regarded as a nonthreatening, culturally acceptable conduit to the ladino world. As director Montero concluded, the mistrust of ladinos was so great that many villagers "preferred speaking, fighting, complaining, laughing, and negotiating with the puppets."[43] Miguel Sántiz, who had asked Petul about birth control, surely realized that he was seeking advice from a hand puppet, but he may have chosen to dialogue with Petul because the puppet understood Tseltal, he (and the puppeteer) seemed friendly enough, and besides, Petul had come through in the past. The thought of taking a personal problem directly to a ladino—who may not have spoken Tseltal—may have seemed too daunting.

The Teatro Petul was likely different things for different people. For indigenous children, it was a source of entertainment. Some may have also believed that Petul had unique powers and may have consciously or unconsciously received the educational message that Petul imparted. For most adults, Petul's "powers" probably had more to do with his role as a direct conduit to the mestizo jefes of the CCI in San Cristóbal. Originally envisioned as one-way transmitters of modern messages from the CCI to indigenous communities, the puppets also became important conveyors of information from the communities back to the CCI. Still other adults, especially the local leadership, probably considered the puppets an amusing but unalterable feature of the post-1951 landscape. Petul was therefore able to appeal to the community at different levels, for different reasons, and performed some of the INI's most sensitive work. Although it is easy today to dismiss Petul as an agent of acculturation and a spokesman for the dominant ideology, it is important to remember the historical context that created Petul.

In her essay "Incident at Yalentay," which is based on a true story, Rosario Castellanos tells of a Tsotsil girl approaching the puppet troupe after a performance at the Zinacantecan hamlet to announce that she wanted to attend the INI's boarding school in San Cristóbal. Castellanos and the puppeteers were elated; at that time (1956 or 1957), the indigenistas still struggled to interest Chamula girls in formal schooling. When they returned to La Cabaña, they told education director Fidencio Montes the good news. Days later, Montes, Castellanos, and the puppeteers returned to Yalentay to get her father's consent. The girl, who had dressed up for the occasion, seemed "surprised and somewhat bewildered" to see the puppeteers unburdened by the puppet theater and the gear required to give shows. Montes spoke to her father, who refused to turn his daughter over to strangers; they would likely pervert her or turn her into an "uppity" Spanish-speaking Indian. Montes was about to give up when the old man offered his daughter in exchange for money. Montes quickly cut off the discussion. Castellanos narrates the end of the essay with words that underscore Petul's remarkable powers of persuasion.

> We set out on our return journey. We could still hear at our backs the words of bartering, then the insults, and then the threats to punish the girl who ran after us, her hair coming unbraided and sobbing.

"Why didn't you bring Petul?" she reproached us. "He was the only one that could have convinced my father."[44]

CHAPTER 7
Medical Pluralism and the Limits of INI Health Programs

⊙⊙⊙ AS DISCUSSED IN chapter 3, the INI's initial attempts to introduce Western medicine to Tseltals and Tsotsils were bold and misplaced. Throwing caution to the wind, the indigenistas built clinics that stood practically empty and pushed vaccination campaigns that involved coercion and sometimes even force. The various setbacks suffered by the medical staff forced a recalibration that took into account the reality of medical pluralism in the highlands—the presence and availability of two or more distinct healing systems.[1]

The adjustments that Dr. Roberto Robles Garnica and others made after 1955 showcase the negotiating skills of savvy applied anthropologists. The fortuitous, simultaneous emergence of the Teatro Petul greatly facilitated their work. Thanks in large measure to the Teatro Petul, the CCI had almost completely eradicated typhus and whooping cough by the early 1960s, and Western medicine was considered by many indigenous people to be effective in treating a range of illnesses. It produced lower infant mortality rates, fewer deaths by preventable diseases, and a greater life expectancy. But it cannot be said that the CCI had successfully replaced traditional medical practice with modern medicine, because even twenty-five years after the CCI opened its doors, the Chiapas highlands remained a medically plural environment.

The Foundations of Traditional Medicine

Although deities and healing practices varied by municipality, the following generalizations can be made about Tsotsil spirituality and healing.[2] At birth, Tsotsils were given an animal spirit companion called a *ch'ulel*. Political and religious leaders and curanderos were believed to have strong animal spirit companions, like jaguars, ocelots, and coyotes. These wild animals were valued for their strength, agility, and wisdom. Less valued animal spirit companions included skunks, raccoons, and weasels. The animals were believed to reside in a sacred mountain, usually the tallest mountain in or near the municipality, where they were watered, fed, and cared for by the ancestral gods.[3] Tsotsils shared their ch'ulel—and their fate—with their animal spirit companion. If their animal companion left the sacred mountain and was injured or shot, they would suffer a similar injury.[4]

Individuals typically became curanderos after a series of dreams in which they were taken to the sacred mountain and taught the healing arts by the ancestral gods. They learned how to construct an altar, how to pray, how to diagnose illness, and how to use herbs, flowers, candles, and incense in healing rites. Not all ailments required the assistance of a curandero. For those ailments considered "natural," like eating too much food determined to be "hot" or "cold," herbal remedies were usually sufficient. But when someone fell seriously ill, a curandero typically made a diagnosis by taking the patient's pulse and studying his or her circulation. One's pulse was considered the most tangible representation of one's spirit. Curanderos "pulsed" in order to literally see into the sacred mountain and determine the condition of the patient's animal spirit companion and whether it had been injured or attacked by more powerful animals or by naguales, roaming auxiliary spirits (often malignant). Once the diagnosis was made, treatment could begin. This typically involved the construction of an altar, prayers to Christian saints and ancestral gods, and ritual drinking. Curanderos typically sacrificed one or two chickens, believing that if they offered up the spirit of the chicken, the gods would release the patient's animal companion. After the chicken was sacrificed, it was plucked, put in a pot of boiling water, and later eaten. If the patient's health did not improve after a couple of treatments, the patient's family would find a different curandero, one believed to have a stronger animal companion and naguales and a proven record as a healer.[5]

As intermediaries between the natural and supernatural worlds, curanderos were both respected and feared. Theirs was a risky profession—if a patient died under their care, they could be accused of witchcraft. Curanderos sometimes hedged their bets. If they were not sure of the patient's outcome, they would delay making a diagnosis and prognosis. If the patient suffered from a high fever and a high level of discomfort—common symptoms of whooping cough, smallpox, and dysentery—and showed no signs of improvement, the curer could decide that the illness had been sent by God or the gods as divine punishment. After such a diagnosis, which was akin to a death sentence, the curandero would hastily leave the house.[6]

As Evon Vogt noted in Zinacantán, the concepts of ch'ulel and the animal spirit companion "are clearly related to social control." Deviant behavior such as violating moral codes, flouting central values, feuding with kinsmen, refusing to hold a cargo, or failing to financially support fiestas could "lead quickly and directly to punishment by causing the person to experience some form of soul-loss, or, in more serious cases, by having his animal spirit companion turned outside its corral to wander alone and uncared for in the woods."[7] The indigenistas agreed that traditional medicine supported an essentially gloomy, conservative cultural outlook. As Alfonso Villa Rojas noted while researching in Oxchuc, the prevalence of illness in indigenous communities and the fear of incurring soul-loss or the wrath of a witch meant that those who shared traditional beliefs "live in constant misery[,] and their possibilities for economic and social development are limited."[8]

Charting a New Course

After 1955, the INI began to deal constructively with the reality of medical pluralism in the highlands. The indigenistas took several steps to make their clinics more accommodating to Tseltals and Tsotsils. They built rooms to lodge the families of the sick so that they could accompany and pray for their loved ones for several days if necessary, and equipped rooms with incense burners. INI doctors often invited traditional healers to accompany their patients to the clinics to perform ritual healing rites. The INI even attempted to recruit traditional healers into the ranks of bilingual health promoters, but this effort appears to have failed.[9]

The INI's more experienced doctors understood that the indigenous were more likely to accept modern medicine if it complemented traditional practices. They willingly invited traditional healers to work with them, knowing that they needed good relationships with midwives and curanderos if they were to receive sick patients before it was too late. When INI doctors made house calls, they often found the traditional healer already at work. The better doctors waited until the healing ritual was over before they started tending to the patient. At times, doctors engaged in activities that might be considered farcical from a clinical point of view. For example, since the indigenous tended not to understand the causes of infections, doctors who prescribed antibiotics to cure an infection would also inject the affected area with distilled water.[10]

Sometimes, operating in a medically plural environment meant playing the role of a curandero. William Holland told of a doctor at Oxchuc's clinic who realized that only traditional medicine would bring relief to a patient who had taken a hard fall. The doctor learned of the accident in a letter. Suspecting that the patient had probably fractured his ribs and perhaps had a collapsed lung, he immediately got on his horse and rode five hours to the man's hut. He tied up his horse and went in to examine the patient. The doctor quickly realized that, from a biomedical perspective, there was nothing wrong with the patient. But the patient and his family were convinced that he was at death's door because his spirit had left his body during the fall; it had escaped through a bruise on his chest. The doctor turned to the man's wife and asked for a live chicken. He passed the chicken over the man's body in the form of a cross. He then slit the chicken's throat, just like a curandero would, and announced that he had offered the spirit of the chicken in exchange for that of the man. The doctor then injected the man with distilled water, explaining that "it helps keep the spirit in its place." Family members were so happy that they offered the doctor another chicken as a token of gratitude.[11] Agustín Romano wrote that some doctors willingly engaged in these practices but that "many took the dignity of their profession too seriously and refused to participate in this kind of charlatanism."[12]

The INI made an additional, somewhat counterintuitive concession to the environment in which it was operating—its clinics and outposts began to charge for consultations and medicine. This decision might seem odd coming from an institute that wanted people to use its services. However, experience had taught the indigenistas that free services were not "valued." They began charging a symbolic fee, a *cuota simbólica*, for consultations and prescribed medicine. This fee varied by location and circumstance. The clinic at Chilil charged ladinos the full price for medicine if they hailed from a settlement that had refused to help build the clinic. If a patient was treated for wounds suffered in a fight, Chilil's clinic made the aggressor pay the medical bills. INI fees were always exceedingly modest, usually around two pesos. By comparison, Holland estimated that the average curing ritual cost between twenty and forty pesos. That cost included the fee paid to the curandero as well as the copal, candles, chickens, and various liters of aguardiente needed to conduct a traditional healing ritual.[13]

Was the INI's medical staff up to the challenge of working in a medically plural environment? The INI's first doctors, like Roberto Robles Garnica,[14] specialized in rural medicine and were committed professionals, recent graduates of what would become known as the School of Rural Medicine (Escuela Superior de Medicina Rural) at the National Polytechnic Institute (Instituto Politécnico Nacional). Other young doctors had trouble making the transition from the urban hospital setting to the realities of work in the Chiapas highlands. Language barriers were always an issue, making it difficult to establish constructive doctor-patient relationships. The indigenistas tried to teach basic vocabulary to the medical staff, but many doctors stayed on the job for only one or two years, and their commitment to learning about the people and their language was limited.[15] In time, budget constraints forced the Coordinating Center to begin to rely on unpaid *pasantes*, medical school students who came to perform their residencies. Teodoro Sánchez, who directed the Teatro Petul, disdainfully described the pasantes as uncommitted youngsters who could not wait to get back to the city. "They made sure that their shoes wouldn't get muddy," he wrote. "I called them 'sidewalk' doctors.... many of them lasted only a year."[16]

Campaigns against Typhus, Malaria, and Whooping Cough

The CCI's most important preventive medicine campaign targeted typhus, a disease transmitted by the human body louse. Historically, typhus has affected stressed, malnourished populations living in substandard conditions. The first reliable description of a severe typhus epidemic was in 1489, among Christian soldiers laying siege to Moorish Granada. Typhus decimated Napoleon's Grand Army during his 1812 Russian campaign and killed millions during and immediately after World War I. Typhus also took its toll in World War II, especially in Soviet POW and Nazi concentration camps; it killed Anne Frank at Bergen-Belsen.[17] The insecticide DDT was first used in 1944 to control typhus at the end of the war. It was then used against the *Anopheles* mosquito, which can carry the parasite protozoa of the genus *Plasmodium* that causes malaria.[18]

The INI's campaign against typhus involved using staggering amounts of DDT. The indigenistas applied a dry powder soap that contained 10 percent DDT directly onto clothing and bodies, and sold Vaseline and hair gel containing DDT in its cooperatives. Teodoro Sánchez wrote that the INI sent tons of DDT soap by truck as far as roads reached. Then, it was unloaded and transported either by animals or humans—usually puppeteers—to the designated sites. Each puppeteer carried twelve kilos of DDT soap, in addition to his or her food, sleeping bag, pots and pans, and whatever supplies were needed for the puppet show performance.[19]

The CCI launched its first preventive medicine campaign against typhus even though other diseases like whooping cough were also prevalent and were more likely to be fatal. Typhus was easily eradicated by applying powder to clothing and directly onto people. As Dr. Robles explained: "Once the campaign has been objectively successful and the population sees that the lice—which transmit the illness—have diminished or disappeared along with the typhus, it becomes possible to undertake a vaccination campaign against whooping cough, which is a bit more complicated due the reactions that the immunized children often suffer." The whooping cough vaccination also required the mother to take the child to the clinic for shots three times at one-month intervals followed by another booster shot one year later.[20] Typhus eradication therefore met several INI objectives—it was relatively noninvasive, it promised quick, visible results, and DDT rid communities of lice, fleas, and bedbugs, something everyone could appreciate since everyone had them.

It is hard to overstate the importance of the Teatro Petul to the CCI's ambitious campaign to eradicate typhus in the highlands. The troupe gave dozens of performances encouraging the indigenous to allow INI personnel to apply DDT to their homes, their clothes, and even their bodies, typically performing a day or two ahead of the arrival of the CCI's medical staff. The first step was getting people to admit that they had lice. "The mere suggestion that the kids had lice was questioned," wrote Fidencio Montes. "It caused them shame, until miraculously this little puppet appeared and in a little more than an hour, the community was usually on board."[21]

One of the most popular and frequently presented shows during this campaign was *La Familia Rasca Rasca* (The Scratch-Scratch Family). In this play, puppets named Señora Chinche (Mrs. Bedbug), Señora Pugla (Mrs. Flea), and Señor Piojo (Mr. Louse) feast voraciously on an unhygienic indigenous couple. Only the intervention of the "sanitation brigade" puts an end to their incessant scratching. This "brigade" consisted of appropriately configured puppets named Señora Agua (Mrs. Water), Señor Jabón (Mr. Soap), and Señor Peine (Mr. Comb).[22] At the end of the play, they march triumphantly, singing:

> We are the
> Health Brigade
> Death to microbes
> And filth.
> If you want to cure yourself
> of your itching
> You have to bathe yourself
> with soap and water.
> You should comb yourself
> and wash your hair
> Always be sure to
> apply DDT.[23]

Medical Pluralism and the Limits of INI Health Programs   161

FIGURE 7.1. Boys in Tenejapa viewing the Teatro Petul during a DDT campaign against head lice. Photographer unknown. Fototeca Nacho López, Comisión Nacional para el Desarrollo de los Pueblos Indígenas. 1955.

During the second half of 1955, the CCI's health brigade applied eight thousand kilos of talcum powder with 10 percent DDT directly onto 51,167 people and 413,082 articles of clothing. As a result of this Herculean effort, there was no typhus outbreak in the Chiapas highlands during the winter of 1955–1956. One year later, Dr. Robles reported that out of the ten municipalities subjected to DDT in 1955, only Chamula and Chenalhó still reported cases of typhus.[24]

Not everyone supported the INI's DDT campaign. In 1956, the recently formed Tseltal puppet troupe traveled to Yochib, Oxchuc, and learned that the

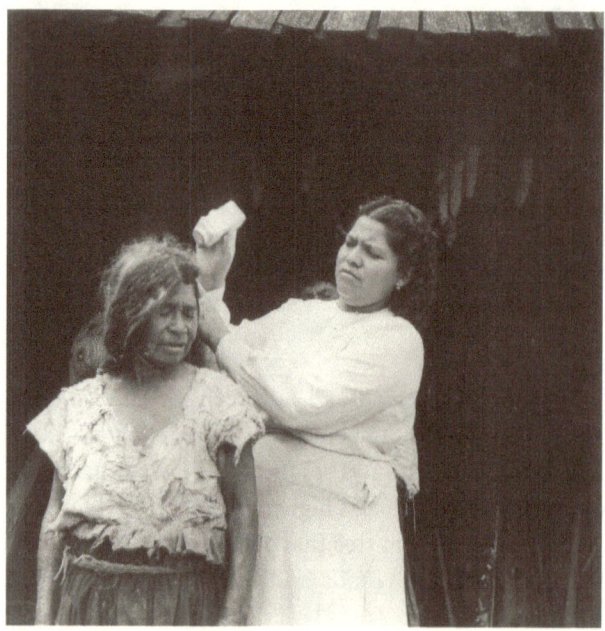

FIGURES 7.2A AND 7.2B. DDT powder was applied directly onto children's bodies... and directly onto scalps. Photographers unknown. Fototeca Nacho López, Comisión Nacional para el Desarrollo de los Pueblos Indígenas. Circa 1960.

rural schoolteacher's wife had given six lashes to each child who asked for DDT at the INI clinic. According to Rosario Castellanos, who accompanied the troupe, "she justified this punishment by saying that DDT is poison and that those who used it were dim-witted and would die just like the lice and the bedbugs."[25] Marcos Cueto writes that Mexican doctors in the late 1950s began to notice that the insecticide killed not only the *Anopheles* mosquito, body lice, and fleas but also bees, butterflies, mice, hens, and even cats. Rachel Carson's book *Silent Spring*, published in 1962, raised public awareness of the issue in the United States, and in 1972 DDT was the first pesticide banned by the recently created Environmental Protection Agency. This ban did not prevent US chemical corporations from continuing to export the insecticide to Mexico and other developing countries.[26]

On the heels of the apparently successful campaign against typhus, the CCI's health division had to respond quickly to an outbreak of whooping cough in Oxchuc, Larráinzar, and Chenalhó in 1957. The DPT vaccination (used against diphtheria, whooping cough, and tetanus) required three monthly shots, and since the first shot generally caused a mild reaction, the odds were high that the patient would not return for the second and third doses. The CCI hurried to treat the sick and vaccinate two thousand children, but because it had not been able to plan a comprehensive education campaign in advance, it encountered resistance to the shots.[27]

The following year, the CCI's health division launched a better-conceived DPT vaccination campaign. The Teatro Petul gave dozens of educational performances encouraging women to vaccinate themselves and their families. In *Petul, Health Promoter*, Petul explains to Xun and his wife that whooping cough is not caused by witches but by microbes, which can be controlled by vaccinations. He also explains that it takes three shots to be protected from whooping cough, and that even if kids have an adverse reaction to the first shot, it's necessary to go in for the second and third shots. In many performances, the doctor puppet injected the Petul puppet.[28] Many parents still hid their kids from the CCI's vaccination brigades despite the efforts of the puppeteers. One report suggests that the puppeteers and the INI's indigenous health promoters struggled to explain how the vaccination works. In spite of these and other problems, the INI was satisfied with the 1958 campaign; 71 percent of those who received the first dose of DPT received the second dose, and 58 percent received the third and final dose. These numbers

FIGURE 7.3. These Chamulan boys had just been vaccinated by INI nurses. Photographer unknown. Fototeca Nacho López, Comisión Nacional para el Desarrollo de los Pueblos Indígenas. Circa 1955.

compared very favorably to those obtained by the Ministry of Public Health in urban areas.[29]

After an outbreak of typhus in late 1958, the CCI resumed its campaigns against both typhus and whooping cough in 1959. The Teatro Petul gave eighty-five presentations promoting DDT application and another thirty-seven to support vaccination against whooping cough. The CCI visited 395 hamlets and applied DDT to 83,981 people and 646,150 articles of clothing; only 972 individuals refused treatment. In 1959–1960, there were no reported cases of typhus, and Villa Rojas declared that the five-year campaign had been a success.[30]

TABLE 7.1. The major campaigns of the CCI's health division.

ILLNESS	CAUSE	CCI TREATMENT	PREVENTATIVE MEASURES	CCI CAMPAIGNS
Smallpox	Either of two virus variants, *Variola major* and *Variola minor*.		Vaccination (the WHO certified the eradication of smallpox in 1979).	Sporadic; first vaccination campaign in Chamula in 1951.
Malaria	A bite from an infected *Anopheles* mosquito; generally contracted at lower elevations.		DDT applied in huts.	CCI joined a national campaign in 1955.
Typhus	A bacterium transmitted by lice and sometimes fleas.	Antibiotic (Chloramphenicol)	Vaccination; shaved heads; talcum power with 10% DDT on bodies and clothes and in homes.	Major four-year campaign started in 1955; ongoing.
Whooping cough	A bacterium spread by airborne discharges from the mucous membranes of infected people.	Antibiotic (Erythromycin)	DPT vaccination.	Case-by-case basis in 1957; major campaign started in 1958.
Typhoid fever	The ingestion of food or water contaminated with feces of an infected person; caused by *Salmonella typhi*.	Antibiotic (Chloromycetin)	Improved water source and food preparation; TAB vaccinations.	The INI responded to outbreaks as they occurred.
Onchocerciasis (river blindness)	A parasite (*Onchocerca volvulus*) transmitted by a blackfly of the genus *Simulium*; generally contracted on lowland plantations.	Antibiotics		As needed.

More Negotiations

Preventive medicine, of course, involved much more than DDT and vaccination campaigns. Contaminated food and water sources produced dysentery and typhoid fever, the latter caused by contaminated water carrying *Salmonella typhi*. Both were a common cause of death, especially among the very young. All indigenous homes had dirt floors, and animals entered, left, and occasionally defecated wherever they pleased. Babies crawled and occasionally defecated on these dirt floors, and everyone slept on the ground. The CCI responded with a sanitary outhouse campaign and encouraged the indigenous to raise their hearths so that cooking would no longer take place on the ground. They also encouraged the indigenous to ventilate their homes and sleep on raised beds. Perhaps the CCI's most difficult task was convincing the Tseltal and Tsotsil to encase their springs with cement to prevent contamination by animals and people.

The CCI's sanitary outhouse program was launched in the mid-1950s. Each INI school had a outhouse, and the CCI helped individuals install outhouses at their homes by offering concrete basins free of charge. Homeowners collaborated by digging the pits and providing the stalls. The Teatro Petul promoted this program by giving performances such as *Petul Has His Latrine*. However, as Villa Rojas wrote in 1956, "the process of convincing the families to accept this innovation is too slow." And in the few localities where there was demand for latrines, the CCI had difficulty transporting the heavy cement basins along rutted or nonexistent roads. The inescapable reality is that many indigenous saw little need for the outhouses. Ulrich Köhler suggests that communities built them to please the INI or to show gratitude for other INI projects, not because they saw any utility in them.[31]

In early 1958, the INI introduced cement and brick floors in select hamlets in Huixtán. The indigenistas also introduced the raised hearth, but Villa Rojas reported that this was a difficult concept to promote "due to the custom of burying a newborn's umbilical cord under the ancient three-stone hearth. The purpose is to keep the child's body warm and healthy."[32]

The CCI's health division also had to respond to occasional outbreaks of typhoid fever. Traditional healers typically attributed its symptoms to witchcraft. In 1957, the Teatro Petul was rushed to Navenchauc (Zinacantán), where residents had decided that the person responsible for an outbreak was the first person who had contracted the disease. In order to defuse this dangerous situation, the Teatro Petul gave a performance that tried to explain that the

Medical Pluralism and the Limits of INI Health Programs   167

FIGURE 7.4. Men investigating a water tank. Photographer unknown. Fototeca Nacho López, Comisión Nacional para el Desarrollo de los Pueblos Indígenas. Circa 1960.

symptoms were caused by microbes. After the performance, the CCI's health workers treated the sick and held a meeting with local authorities explaining the urgent need to protect the water supply by digging a well.[33]

The campaign to protect water sources required all of the INI's negotiating skills. Many springs were considered sacred sites, openings in the earth's crust that allowed communication with the Earth Lord. The indigenous periodically held elaborate ceremonies to clean and venerate certain watering holes, and used the water from these springs for ritual curing.[34] Many communities refused to encase their springs for fear of incurring the wrath of angry gods. Complicating matters for the INI was that encasement did not always work. Dr. Robles noted that the INI's technique was "very rudimentary" and "naïve." In some cases, the INI's work damaged the springs so that they no longer produced as much water.[35]

In April 1957, religious leaders in Chamula opposed efforts to protect a spring and introduce piped water to their municipal center. They feared that the spirits that protected the spring would feel "imprisoned" by the cement encasement (*caja de captación*) that was being built around it. The indigenistas used all the persuasive tools at their disposal, including the Teatro Petul. The INI decided to first encase a smaller spring that had no religious significance. It then piped the water to public pumps located near huts on the outskirts of the settlement. Villa Rojas hoped that the water pumps would "convince the people to change their attitude."[36]

Sixteen months later, after several conversations with Chamula's civil authorities, the Ministry of Hydraulic Resources, under INI supervision, was allowed to resume its work and bring piped water to Chamula's municipal seat. One more concession was necessary, however, because the pipe had to pass through some cornfields in Chamula's Barrio de San Juan. Residents had strenuously opposed the project, because the spring was located on their land. To facilitate this final step of the project, the INI announced in Chamula's market that it would pay for the corn that would be sacrificed in order to dig the trench.[37]

The INI went even further at Pasté, a Zinacantecan hamlet where the INI had initiated construction on a water tank. Residents asked the CCI to help fund a major religious ceremony that would be held in front of the tank. Residents had noted that their hamlet had been hit by a great many lightening strikes ever since construction began on the tank. They hoped that this ceremony would "calm the ire of the 'owners of the water.'" The INI promised to help finance the celebration, which was held on June 24, the day devoted to San Juan (Saint John), who himself had a special connection to water.[38]

One last testimony to the INI's effective negotiation strategies on water is related by June Nash, a prolific ethnographer who lived in Amatenango in 1957 and 1958 and again from 1962 to 1967. When piped water was introduced in 1962, "the curers who bathed their patients in the spring water objected since they were fearful of being cut off from the spring at its source," she writes. "INI promoters worked out an agreement with the town officials whereby a stream of the spring water was diverted into a pool at its source to provide access for curative bathing without contaminating the water carried in pipes to the town center." Nash cites this case to refute the common accusation that the INI was "an authoritarian and homogenizing scheme of ethnocide. In my experience in Amatenango, I found that there was a great deal of latitude for local communities to select programs on the basis of pragmatic assessment of what worked for them within their own cultural design." Nash paints a picture of a flexible institution that lacked the financial resources to be the ethnocidal Leviathan that some of its critics imagined; its promoters "showed a rare degree of cultural sensitivity even while adhering to male priority."[39]

INI Health Programs, Ten Years On

By 1961, the INI was working in sixteen municipalities, where more than seventy-six thousand Tsotsils and thirty-eight thousand Tseltals resided. Four main clinics (San Cristóbal, Chamula, Chilil, and Oxchuc) and eight medical outposts were in operation. That year, a doctoral student in anthropology from the University of Arizona, William Holland, researched the effectiveness of the INI's health programs. His findings shed light on the CCI's highly flexible responses to the resistance that it encountered to its programs, but they also suggest that the INI had made virtually no progress in its attempts to instill notions of scientific medicine in the highlands.

The heart of Holland's research was a survey that he conducted with the help of a Tsotsil assistant from Larráinzar named Pascual Hernández. Together, they interviewed 172 Tsotsil patients at three INI clinics and two INI medical outposts. At first blush, this sample group would seemed to be skewed, since presumably those who used INI clinics and outposts already believed in the efficacy of Western medicine. In fact, the interviews underscored the pervasiveness of traditional thinking about illness among even those who gave modern medicine a fighting chance. Even though 49 percent of the sample claimed to have come directly to the clinics and outposts without having first resorted to a traditional healer, 76 percent of the patients blamed their illnesses on magical or religious causes.[40] If over three-quarters of the patients in INI clinics and outposts attributed their illnesses to such causes, what of the indigenous people who did *not* visit INI clinics and outposts? What if Holland had interviewed Tsotsils on central plazas, or at markets?

And if 76 percent of the patients attributed their illnesses to magical or religious causes, what were they doing in a clinic or outpost of Western medicine? According to Holland, many indigenous considered INI doctors to be wizards who had their own particular ways of curing. This made them a reasonable, low-cost healing option; at the time, the INI was only charging a cuota simbólica of two pesos, and its medicine was highly subsidized. Some indigenous sought medicine to break a spell or a curse, or to protect themselves from bad airs or bad dreams, or to strengthen their animal companions. Some sought potions that would facilitate Spanish language acquisition. Aspirin, penicillin, and antibiotics were believed to be extremely effective in cases of soul-loss or witchcraft.[41] Vogt and Nash also noted that the indigenous readily took medicine to treat immediate symptoms. But because disease was usually understood to be punishment sent by the ancestral gods, addressing the root cause still meant resorting to the traditional healer, who could treat the soul-loss, the escape of the animal spirit companion, or the witchcraft that had caused the disease in the first place.[42] By no means did the Tsotsils in the clinics and outposts believe that modern medicine was a substitute for traditional folk medicine; at best, it was complementary.[43] On the other hand, Holland noted that indigenous beliefs about illnesses and cures were not that different from those of ladino peasants, who also believed that illness was caused by witchcraft, divine punishment, or the devil.[44]

Many of Holland's other findings suggest a population whose beliefs about medicine had changed little, in spite of the INI's efforts. Many Chamulas still refused to accept the INI clinic in their municipality, ten years after it first opened its doors. It is worth noting that communities farther from San Cristóbal, like Chichihuistán and Larráinzar, were generally more receptive to INI clinics, possibly because they had had fewer negative interactions with ladinos over the years. One indigenous health promoter at the Chamula clinic, who was also an elder, still believed after working for the INI for eight years that INI doctors could not cure cases of witchcraft or other "spiritual" illnesses. He told patients that if their animal companion was the prisoner of a witch, only an indigenous healer could liberate it.[45]

Holland noted that most Tsotsils still rejected surgery and could not understand how cutting open the body—thereby doing it additional, temporary harm—could produce a long-term improvement to the patient's health. They hated long stays in hospitals, because it meant time away from their familiar environment, where traditional healers spoke their language and family members prayed for their recovery. This made it hard to treat serious injuries or illnesses like tuberculosis, which often required long stays in a Mexico City hospital. Dr. Robles told of the case of Antonia, a girl whose tibia had been crushed by a falling tree. The doctor could see that she needed a tibial graft and that the cells of a good portion of her leg had necrotized. The INI made plans to fly the girl to Mexico City, accompanied by a social worker. Her parents seemed to consent to the trip until they suddenly disappeared. The INI's medical team found Antonia a few weeks later, in Majomut (Chamula). The girl's condition had worsened and the leg had atrophied. Robles learned through a translator that her parents feared that she might die in surgery and be buried in a Mexico City cemetery. "Her soul, surrounded by strangers, would suffer forever," they feared. If she died at home, she could be buried among her people and her soul could rest in peace. Robles wrote that when faced with such deep-seated beliefs, there was nothing that he could do. "Insisting was useless."[46]

If the clinics were unsuccessful at shaking the traditional beliefs of the

Tsotsils, what about the CCI's more successful preventive medicine campaigns? Holland suggests that just because the indigenous generally agreed to get vaccinated did not mean that their traditional notions of medicine had been dismantled. The belief that epidemics were a form of divine punishment "remained intact regardless of the activities carried out by the INI during the last ten years."[47] Tsotsils still resisted blood draws, still believing that they drained them of their spirits. This belief was reinforced by healers who took pulses to make diagnoses. However, the indigenous accepted injections—preferably, directly into the vein—so much so that traditional healers began incorporating injections into their curative rituals. Holland noted that the INI had better luck treating illnesses that were considered universal, divine punishment—like typhus, whooping cough, and smallpox—than those considered to be illnesses of the spirit, which were caused by witchcraft and could presumably be cured only by going to a traditional healer.[48]

Holland firmly believed that the successful introduction of modern medicine in a medically plural environment like highland Chiapas required a medically plural approach, with INI doctors working closely with traditional healers and indigenous health promoters. Modern medicine was more easily accepted and integrated when the doctor collaborated with those who enjoyed great prestige within the traditional social organization of the community. "If the INI is to realize its objectives," Holland wrote, "the modern doctor must complement the traditional healer instead of trying to exclude him, and the intercultural communication must be excellent." Nash tells of such a relationship between an indigenous father and son in Amatenango. The son, who was an INI health promoter, shared patients with his father, who was a highly respected curer. The father yielded to Western medicine in cases where its efficacy had been proven (for example, immunizations against contagious diseases and antibiotic injections), while the son called on his father to treat diseases caused by witchcraft.[49] Holland believed that INI doctors needed to be better educated in the ways of traditional medicine, and INI bilingual health promoters needed better training as to the theory and practice of modern medicine. Ultimately, wrote Holland, the indigenistas needed to train indigenous doctors.[50]

Conclusions

Of all the complicated outcomes of indigenista policy in highland Chiapas, none are more ambivalent than the INI's health programs. On the one hand, the indigenistas managed to almost completely eradicate typhus, malaria, and smallpox from the region, and deaths due to whooping cough, measles, and typhoid fever dropped considerably. Even the INI's long-forsaken clinics saw an uptick in activity. In 1957, Tsotsils from the ejido Yalcuc (Huixtán) actually requested a medical outpost and offered to feed and pay for the INI masons and provide them with lodging. Two years later, Villa Rojas wrote that the gravely ill throughout the highlands were less opposed to the idea of hospitalization than they had been in prior years. The number of consultations at INI clinics and outposts increased dramatically. In 1951, the medical staff performed 1,762 consultations (and a significant number of those patients were ladinos); in 1962, the CCI's medical staff performed 24,235 consultations at its clinics and outposts.[51]

The indigenistas had learned valuable lessons that would serve the INI at its other Coordinating Centers. After shifting their focus to preventive medicine, they learned to use the Teatro Petul, educational filmstrips, and explanatory talks in the local language before sending in the DDT or vaccination teams. Into the 1960s, the Tsotsil and Tseltal puppet troupes continued to be the CCI's most effective means of education and persuasion.

However, more than two decades after the CCI opened its doors, many indigenous still resorted to traditional healers before turning to CCI clinics and outposts, they shunned clinics for major medical care, and women still bore their children at home. In 1951, 3 women gave birth in INI clinics; in 1975, at a time of demographic explosion, only 129 women gave birth in a clinical setting. Indigenous women resisted clinical auscultations, especially when performed by single male doctors, and pregnancy and childbirth remained important ritual events.[52]

Publically, the INI claimed to be deeply respectful of indigenous healing rights and simply offered modern medicine as an alternative to traditional practices. This position was hammered home by INI publications like *Acción Indigenista*. In a 1959 issue, the INI told how its social anthropologists worked with its doctors and nurses to "avoid violence" to the indigenous culture. Medical professionals were instructed to not directly challenge indigenous patients who claimed that their ailments were caused by witchcraft; instead, they were to acknowledge witchcraft as a possible cause while simultaneously treating the ailment with the appropriate medicine. Successful treatment would ultimately win patients' confidence in the INI's clinics and outposts.[53]

Privately, however, the INI sought the disappearance of most indigenous healing practices, which it considered "obsolete." The indigenistas believed that nothing challenged the magical religious worldview of the highland Maya

TABLE 7.2. The CCI's medical infrastructure in 1967.

MEDICAL CLINICS	MEDICAL OUTPOSTS (*PUESTOS DE SALUD*, SUBORDINATE TO A CLINIC)
1. Central Clinic, San Cristóbal de Las Casas	Amatenango, Aguacatenango, and Romerillo
2. Chamula	Zinacantán
3. Chilil	San Gregorio and Yalcuc
4. Oxchuc	La Libertad, Abasolo, and Yochib
5. Chenalhó	Chalchihuitán and La Libertad
6. Larráinzar	None
7. Chanal	None

Source: AHCCITT, 1968/2, Dirección, from Nicolás T. Zavala to Dir. del CCITT Maurilio Muñoz.

like a vaccination or an antibiotic, and nothing threatened the foundation of traditional Tsotsil and Tseltal societies like a doctor of modern medicine. Western medicine, they believed, could serve as the catalyst that would upend traditional cultures and hierarchies. Holland also believed that Western medicine could provoke "revolutionary" changes. With the benefit of hindsight, we know that this did not happen. If anything, it was the other way around—Western medicine took root quickest in communities where traditional cultures and hierarchies were already in crisis, where—to return to Nash's language—"a sanctioning system . . . had broken down." This is how Marianna Slocum and Florence Gerdel used antibiotics to attract Tseltal converts in the 1950s. Medical pluralism is still a reality today in the Chiapas highlands, and most people resort to some combination of traditional healers and government clinics more than sixty-five years after the INI introduced Western medicine to the region. Revolutionary changes ultimately came to the region, but Western medicine was not the catalyst.

CHAPTER 8
From Innovation to Administration
The Coordinating Center's Very Long Decade, 1958–1970

◉◉◉ DURING THE QUARTER century of indigenista history under review in this book, Mexico changed dramatically, and so did its priorities. When the CCI first opened its doors in 1951, Mexico was still a predominately rural country, and many indigenistas were inspired by the Cardenista example of bringing the Mexican Revolution to the countryside. In 1960, however, census takers found more Mexicans living in urban areas for the first time in the country's history. Successive PRI presidents continued to emphasize industrialization and urban development and oversaw "a massive and systematic transfer of resources from country to city."[1] They struggled to provide the growing and increasingly assertive urban population with adequate housing, health care, education, and transportation infrastructure. Rural Mexico was placed on the back burner. As the violence of the revolution receded into the past, the campaign to stitch together a more unified nation lost its urgency. Advocates for the rural poor were increasingly ignored or were dismissed as "communists."

The INI's budget suffered as a result of this shift in national priorities. In 1958, a presidential election year in Mexico, its Coordinating Center in Chiapas ran a deficit of 172,000 pesos and largely financed its operations on credit. In early 1959, when the CCI was not given a budget sufficient to cover the previous year's deficit *and* finance its current operations, it literally ground to a halt and actually shuttered its doors for four weeks. "The complete lack of funding forced the paralysis of most of our vehicles for lack of fuel, lubricants, and parts, which we had been acquiring on credit," wrote CCI director Alfonso Villa Rojas. "Now we have reached our credit limits at the businesses and agencies that supply us." The Teatro Petul was grounded because there was no money to support its tours. When the INI temporarily laid off its puppeteers, one of them—Domingo de la Pérez Torre, also known by his Tsotsil name Romin Teratol—began working as an informant for the Harvard Chiapas Project and became its first Tsotsil employee.[2] The CCI's DDT campaign was interrupted several times because most sanitation brigade members were not being paid; the latrines program was also put on hold. "Salaried workers like the *peones* in our experimental agriculture fields, the *macheteros*, bricklayers, and road construction workers have also suffered a delay in the payment of their salaries," wrote Villa Rojas. "The workers will surely lose enthusiasm for their work because their families are experiencing an anguishing economic situation."[3]

Most distressing for Villa Rojas was the fact that communities continued to solicit the CCI's "collaboration for different projects for which the indigenous people contribute the greater part of the expenses. Even then, the CCI finds itself unable to satisfy their demands." For example, when the Oxchuc hamlets of Pachtontijá and Tuxaquiljá asked the INI to help defray the cost of the 30,000-peso schoolhouses that they were building, the INI could only offer each community nails worth 200 pesos. (In happier times, the INI offered a bricklayer, cement, windows, doors, and sometimes wood.) In short, it was becoming difficult for the CCI to maintain the confidence not only of its workers but also of the indigenous people who had come to believe in it.[4] Declining economic and political support from Mexico City also took a personal toll on the morale of the INI's employees in Chiapas.

The Indigenista Brain Drain

Indigenista work in highland Chiapas required working long hours for little pay in a hostile environment. As writer Fernando Benítez observed in 1961, "'La Cabaña' is a fortress surrounded by hatred."[5] Chiapas-born writer Rosario Castellanos noted that her coleto relatives were shunned once she began working for the INI. "In many cases the escape is bureaucracy, which we flee from as if it were a contagious disease," noted INI anthropologist Carlos Incháustegui. "The fact is that we are permanently on the verge of conflict."[6]

Throughout the 1950s, the indigenistas made repeated attempts to ingratiate themselves with San Cristóbal's ladino population, offering water in times of drought, subsidized corn in times of scarcity, and puppet shows and conferences to explain the INI's purpose and the need for greater national integration.[7] On patriotic holidays like Mexican Independence Day (September 16), indigenistas and the indigenous marched together through San Cristóbal's colonial streets, offering visual proof of a nation united. But these attempts appear to have done little to soften ladino attitudes about the indigenous—or

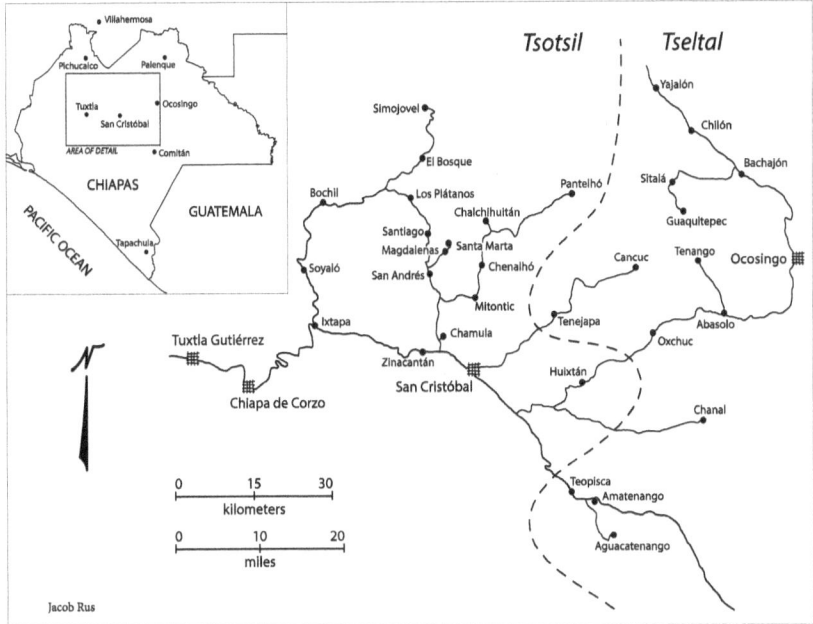

MAP 8.1. By the early 1960s, the indigenistas had expanded their range of operations to include most of the communities on this map. Courtesy of Jacob Rus.

the indigenistas. And once Fidel Castro's forces took Havana in 1959 and Cold War tensions rose in the region, Catholic priests and others in the region increasingly accused the indigenistas of being communists. Nearly ten years after the Coordinating Center opened its doors in the Chiapas highlands, they were still regarded as alien intruders.

The INI's financial woes added to the stresses of the job. Frustration mounted, morale suffered, and some of the CCI's most creative collaborators resigned from their positions. According to illustrator Alberto Beltrán, Carlos Jurado, Adolfo Mexiac, and other artists left largely because "the INI's budget did not grow. It remained the same for many years while the Mexican peso lost value; what you could do in 1950 was no longer possible seven or eight years later with the same amount of money." Beltrán, too, resigned after the strapped CCI abandoned most of its visual aid programs. For him, the problem went beyond inadequate funding. He also cited a feeling of impotence. "The indigenistas had to resign themselves to economic realities because of their weakness and the lack of support."[8]

Perhaps the most flamboyant manifestation of frustration came in October 1957, when Rosario Castellanos resigned from her post. After more than two years with the Teatro Petul, she wrote a devastating letter to Marco Antonio Montero, who was then serving as the INI's director of education in Mexico City. Although she did not identify the target or targets of her rage, she may have had a major falling-out with CCI director Villa Rojas.

> You're aware of the reasons I came to San Cristóbal, of how I enthusiastically tried to overcome my lack of technical preparation to carry out a position at this Coordinating Center. I've defended my hopes with all the tenacity that I could muster; I was willing to resist many disappointments. But what I've found here far exceeds my most pessimistic calculations. The situation gets worse every day, and those who dare to fight to defend the generous ideals that motivated the INI's founding are expelled, harassed, rendered impotent . . . or bought. . . . I don't know if the same thing happens in Mexico City. But here the worst have triumphed. It's impossible to describe the atmosphere here in a letter. . . . There are a thousand little details, repeated to the point of exasperation. It's authority transformed into injustice, awarding the profiteers. . . . It's the law, degenerated into an unhealthy whim. It's a handful of individuals defending their interests, superimposing themselves over those whom the INI promised to help.[9]

Her close collaborator, the linguist Carlo Antonio Castro, resigned at the same time, citing their quixotic struggle against "ignorance, improvisation, incomprehension, irresponsibility, bureaucratization, mediocrity, and greed."[10] Castellanos then accepted a post at the INI's Coordinating Center at the Papaloapan Basin just as her classic semiautobiographical novel of ladino privilege in Chiapas, *Balún Canán* (The Nine Guardians), was published.[11]

Castellanos's letter of resignation is a clear (if somewhat hyperbolic) indicator of the growing crisis in Mexican indigenismo that began in the late 1950s. The INI's early, experimental stage had ended; now it struggled to maintain programs that were already in place with diminishing resources. As Ulrich Köhler poignantly observed in 1963, "the enthusiasm of the first years seems to have been lost."[12]

The Coordinating Center's "brain drain" started at the top. The CCI's directors in the 1960s were, frankly, unremarkable. In no way did they measure up to the giants of Mexican social science who directed the project in the 1950s, men like Gonzalo Aguirre Beltrán, Julio de la Fuente, and Alfonso Villa Rojas.

Increasingly, CCI directors dedicated themselves to the mundane tasks of paper shuffling and supervision, although in their defense they lacked the personnel, the budget, and the political backing to do much else.

The Coordinating Center not only lost some of its top talent, it also had trouble replacing those who left. For example, in the late 1950s, it could not find qualified candidates to fill two social anthropologist vacancies. Villa Rojas wrote that successful applicants could help the INI navigate complex municipalities like Oxchuc, with its increasingly thorny political, ethnic, religious, and even generational rivalries. But he knew of "nobody who has both the academic preparation and the desire to fill the positions. The anthropologists who have passed through here have been more inclined to office work than field work, which is what is needed."[13] These vacancies became a major embarrassment for the INI, since it used the CCI in Chiapas as a national showcase for the merits of applied anthropology.

One of these positions was finally filled in 1960 by Ecuadorian anthropologist Armando Aguirre Torres, whose lengthy, dizzying monthly reports were so full of minutiae—and so devoid of synthesis and analysis—that they were of little use to the Coordinating Center or to INI administrators in Mexico City. Köhler, who spent time in 1963 observing the CCI's work, later commented that Aguirre "brilliantly performed his role as tourist guide. Nevertheless . . . he had not carried out any field research worth mentioning."[14] Several years later, after Aguirre submitted yet another superficial report to Mexico City detailing a trip to five Tseltal communities, assistant technical director Héctor Sánchez Calderón delivered a long-overdue rebuke. "The amount of time that you dedicated to this research—nine days—was too brief to cover such a broad and incommunicable area," Sánchez wrote. "Apart from the statistics that you took from preexisting studies of the region, the information is too superficial." And so on.

> You evidently did not formulate a research plan. . . . The information reads like a transcription of isolated facts that are not analyzed. It comes almost exclusively from teachers, government functionaries, and religious figures, and only rarely from the indigenous themselves because you devoted so little time to this project. Perhaps, for that same reason, the research does not explore extremely important aspects like the activities of the lumber companies and their relationship, in all its aspects, with the indigenous communities, or the repercussions of the work of Catholic organizations that operate in the region.[15]

This devastating critique notwithstanding, Aguirre held onto his post for nearly twenty years.

The CCI's hiring difficulties also forced it to retain employees whose personal conduct threatened to undermine the entire indigenista mission. In October 1967, nurse Rosenda Cruz Morales accompanied assistant doctor Miguel Muñoz Pavón on an inspection tour of Chilil's clinic and the medical outposts at Yalcuc and Chanal. At the end of the tour, Chanal's medical promoter invited the doctor to eat at his sister's house. According to the nurse, Dr. Muñoz began drinking with the medical promoter and, later, with Chanal's municipal authorities. A few hours later, Cruz and the INI driver grew impatient. When the driver tried to convince the doctor that it was time to return to San Cristóbal, "the doctor answered that he didn't give a #%"()$_/& who was waiting." By 8:00 p.m., the doctor was so drunk that he had to be carried to the jeep. He then insisted on driving. After four terrifying kilometers, the INI driver took the wheel, but the inebriated doctor kept falling onto him. According to nurse Cruz, when they finally arrived at the doctor's home in Chilil, he persisted in his belligerence, "directing the most obscene words at me, at his wife, and at the driver." Cruz and the driver finally made it back to San Cristóbal at midnight. She then wrote to the supervising doctor, Ricardo Romero Flores, requesting that she never again be sent on a supervisory trip with Dr. Muñoz.[16]

Remarkably, Dr. Muñoz held onto his job. After Cruz filed her complaint, he even tried to accuse *her* of insulting his wife. CCI director Alberto Jiménez Rodríguez found it "inexcusable and frankly immoral" to try to make her responsible for his "mistakes and offensive behavior." Two months and several incidents later, Jiménez finally sought to suspend—but not fire—the doctor.[17]

It's hard to imagine Julio de la Fuente—lead author of that masterful study of alcoholism and the alcohol industry in Chiapas—allowing Dr. Muñoz to keep his job in 1952. And would Ricardo Pozas have tolerated Armando Aguirre's mediocrity in 1953? Would Alfonso Villa Rojas have allowed either man to work at the center in the late 1950s? Apparently, in the wake of the indigenista "brain drain," the CCI could no longer be choosy. By the mid-1960s, the INI no longer attracted Mexico's best and brightest, and the Coordinating Center's directors seemed resigned to whomever they could find.

Education: The Tragedy of Success

The first immediate consequence of the INI's permanent budget crisis was that it forced a closer relationship with the Ministry of Public Education. In a sense, the Coordinating Center was a victim of its own success. In 1960, it sustained roughly seventy schools and employed about eighty cultural promoters. Attendance rates gradually rose, especially after the INI began providing school breakfasts. Support for INI schools continued to be strongest in Tseltal communities. "Very humble hamlets like Nabil, Tsopiljá, La Independencia, and La Libertad have magnificent schools made of *mampostería* [stone masonry] built by the children's parents. They have to be seen to be believed," gushed the CCI's new director in 1961, Raúl Rodríguez Ramos.[18] The CCI suddenly found itself unable to meet demand. Some students began requesting the opportunity to finish the entire primary school cycle (grades one through six) in INI schools. Of course, the INI never intended to teach anything beyond the pre-first grade, the *grado preparatorio*. Only after the indigenistas realized that SEP and state schools in the region were ineffective and generally hostile to indigenous students did the CCI begin offering grades one, two, and three at its Literacy Centers.[19]

Education director Fidencio Montes believed that the CCI's cultural promoters could meet this demand for grades four through six by finishing their own primary and secondary schooling. In 1959, thirty-two active promoters began taking coursework at the SEP boarding school in San Cristóbal to finish their primary school training. Those who had already completed the sixth grade began working on their secondary school degrees (grades seven, eight, and nine) through intensive summer and winter training programs at the SEP's Federal Institute of Teacher Training (Instituto Federal de Capacitación del Magisterio, or IFCM) in Oaxaca City. During summer 1960, forty-three promoters took classes in Oaxaca; thirty-two began the first year of secondary school, eight took the second year, and three entered their third year.[20]

The INI could also celebrate some modest successes at its boarding school. In December 1959, nine students finished the sixth grade, including the first three indigenous young women to ever finish primary school in the region. The following year, it enrolled more girls than boys for the first time.[21] However, budget woes forced the INI to dismiss a teacher and send twenty-one aspiring cultural promoters to attend schools with ladinos in San Cristóbal. This established a dangerous precedent, as the INI began "outsourcing" the training of its most important assets. Its boarding school became a place to teach vocational skills, not train future education promoters. In 1960, it accepted twenty-three students, including twelve future sewing instructors (all girls), five aspiring agriculture promoters, four carpenters, and two mechanics. Most aspiring education promoters studied at the SEP's Belisario Domínguez

TABLE 8.1. Enrollment growth in INI schools in highland Chiapas.

	MALES	FEMALES	TOTAL
1952	1,396	131	1,527
1953	1,524	295	1,819
1954	1,830	333	2,163
1955	1,917	375	2,292
1956	2,023	462	2,485
1957	2,396	574	2,970
1958	2,585	576	3,161
1959	2,879	660	3,539

Source: *Acción Indigenista*, no. 81 (March 1960).

TABLE 8.2. Attendance by grade level at the start of the 1960 school year.

	MALES	FEMALES	TOTAL
Grado preparatorio			
1st cartilla	1,350	504	1,854
2nd cartilla	327	70	397
3rd cartilla	9	3	12
First grade	520	99	619
Second grade	327	45	372
Third grade	229	16	245
Fourth grade	23	0	23

Source: ICCITT, 1960, "Informe de marzo," by Alfonso Villa Rojas.

boarding school in San Cristóbal, where the pressure to assimilate could be summed up in the school's letterhead, which read: "Mexicanizar al indio y no indigenizar a México" (Mexicanize the Indian and don't "indigenize" Mexico). The remaining students ended up at a SEP day school in San Cristóbal. Neither school taught integral development. The students were encouraged to return to their home communities during vacations, but this was not enough contact to prevent what Köhler described as "certain disagreeable forms of 'ladinization.'" Even the barely literate students "felt superior to the principales and

FIGURE 8.1. Education promoters about to depart for Oaxaca City in summer 1963. They took classes at the Federal Institute of Teacher Training. Photographer unknown. Fototeca Nacho López, Comisión Nacional para el Desarrollo de los Pueblos Indígenas. 1963.

ridiculed their opinions." Köhler felt that a certain degree of ladinization was unavoidable, "and this is absolutely what the INI pursues, since these indigenous should act as mediators between both cultures." Too much ladinization, however, "could render such promoters as ineffective as those teachers that were born ladinos."[22]

The budget crisis had yet another manifestation—salaries at La Cabaña were now so low that the INI could find no one to direct the boarding school and teach nursing, sewing, and the last three primary grades to its female students. The Coordinating Center made offers to seven female teachers, but none took the job. "Perhaps due to the good salaries that the SEP pays its teachers, it has been hugely difficult to hire a *maestra*," wrote Fidencio Montes in 1960. Months later, the girls still did not have a teacher, so the INI had to send five of them to the SEP boarding school in San Cristóbal for their fourth year of schooling.[23]

Meanwhile, the SEP's role grew. In 1960, the SEP covered the salaries of thirteen INI promoters; by 1963, that number had grown to twenty-three. Along with the savings, however, came headaches that would intensify as the SEP covered more and more positions. In yet another sign of the INI's

TABLE 8.3. Students enrolled at the CCI's boarding school at La Cabaña.

	MALES	FEMALES	TOTAL
1954	34	12	46
1955	33	14	47
1956	18	10	28
1957	12	9	21
1958	17	9	26
1959	13	9	22
1960	11	12	23
1963	12	18	30

Source: Acción Indigenista, no. 81 (March 1960); and ICCITT, 1963, "Informe mensual correspondiente al mes de marzo de 1963."

FIGURE 8.2. Girls dining at the INI's boarding school. Barros Martínez, photographer. Fototeca Nacho López, Comisión Nacional para el Desarrollo de los Pueblos Indígenas. Late 1960s.

FIGURES 8.3A AND 8.3B. Francisca Gómez López (top) and Manuela Sánchez Gómez (bottom) were among the first education *promotoras* to work for the Coordinating Center. Photographer unknown. Fototeca Nacho López, Comisión Nacional para el Desarrollo de los Pueblos Indígenas. 1963.

precarious budget situation, the salaries of eight additional promoters were split by the INI and the communities, and another seven promoters subsisted entirely on contributions from the communities where they worked and lived.[24]

From Promoter to Teacher; or, How the INI Lost Control over Its Agents of Change

Collaboration with the SEP was not without its dangers. In the early 1960s, it was a far cry from the institution that had tried to "bring the revolution" to Chiapas in the 1930s.[25] But by late 1963, the INI had no choice. Following negotiations, the SEP agreed to assume financial responsibility for the INI's schools in Chiapas and at the INI's other Coordinating Centers in Oaxaca (Huautla de Jiménez, Jamiltepec, Papaloapan, and Tlaxiaco), Chihuahua (Guachochi), and Guerrero (Tlapa). The SEP officially endorsed the grado preparatorio and allowed it and the bilingual first grade to be taught in its schools by bilingual cultural promoters, while the INI agreed to adopt the SEP curriculum in its schools beginning in the first grade.[26]

The SEP also created the National Service of Cultural Promoters and Bilingual Teachers (Servicio Nacional de Promotores Culturales y Maestros Bilingües). The service trained aspiring bilingual cultural promoters in just one year and gave entry-level teaching positions (Maestro A) to all INI promoters nationwide who had graduated from secondary schools. This was more than a change of nomenclature—once a cultural promoter became a federal teacher, he or she got a substantial raise, abided by the SEP's school calendar and its vacation schedule, joined the national teachers' union (the Sindicato Nacional de Trabajadores de la Educación, or SNTE), and no longer felt obliged to use the lengua materna or to lead projects of community development. This, in short, is how the INI began to lose control over its bilingual cultural promoters and how these teachers slowly came to embody ideas and agendas that had little to do with their previous indigenista mission.[27]

On paper, at least, the SEP's financial resources had a positive effect over education in highland Chiapas. In 1964, the SEP and the INI agreed to rationalize education supervision by dividing the highlands into eight zones. INI inspectors were given supervisory authority over all schools that operated in their four zones, including thirty-nine SEP schools; SEP inspectors, for their part, inherited thirty-five INI schools in their four zones. The SEP also agreed to fund an additional twenty-two schools in INI zones. After the administrative dust had settled, more than eight thousand Tseltals and Tsotsils attended 107 schools. Five years later, roughly twelve thousand attended slightly more than 200 schools in the highlands. The vast majority of these schools offered the grado preparatorio as well as grades one through three. Students who wished to finish primary school (through grade six) studied at one of eight "concentration schools" located in Chamula, Tenejapa, Oxchuc, and Chenalhó. These schools, also called *albergues*, offered basic meals and services to students who had to travel long distances.[28]

The teaching corps was also more robust, thanks to SEP resources. Five years after the merger, roughly 350 teachers and promoters offered their services in the Tseltal/Tsotsil highlands; 69 had earned their normal school degrees and had become federal teachers. Below them were 127 bilingual rural teachers, all of whom were taking classes at the IFCM in Oaxaca to get their normal school degrees and become federal teachers. They were followed by 165 SEP cultural promoters, who took classes to get their secondary school degrees (grades seven through nine), the requirement to become a bilingual rural teacher.[29]

However, what the INI gained in quantity it lost in quality. The effect was felt immediately in INI schools that now fell under SEP supervision. In summer 1964, residents in Huixtán, Chamula, and elsewhere threatened to withdraw support from their schools if they were not returned to INI supervision. Many teachers sent by the SEP to fill vacancies in Chiapas abandoned their posts after a couple of weeks and tried to return to their home states. Most of these teachers had been trained at urban normal schools and were therefore unprepared—pedagogically and otherwise—for the challenges of teaching in highland Chiapas. Education director Andrés Santiago Montes wrote that most of them "lacked initiative, turned in falsified [attendance] reports, failed to show up for work, and had a rebellious attitude toward complying with official orders." Others who had purchased their posts could barely sign their names; still others hoarded and later sold the food that was provided for school breakfasts.[30] The indigenistas also complained about the negative influence of the SNTE on their former employees. One indigenista called it a "false union education. It's to the point where more than one promoter has stated, 'We aren't the slaves of the inspectors.'"[31] Romano remarked that union membership "guaranteed the teachers almost total impunity to neglect their teaching duties and, of course, their work in the communities, because this was not the work of a 'true' teacher."[32]

When the SEP agreed to accept the bilingual grado preparatorio in its classrooms, it represented a moral victory of sorts for the INI. But this victory was short lived because collaboration with the SEP actually undermined bilingual education in highland Chiapas. The training that promoters and teachers received at the IFCM in Oaxaca City had nothing to do with bilingual education. As a federal teacher-training institute, it did not take into account regional, sociocultural, or linguistic factors. All instruction was in Spanish, and the students were never shown how to apply their new skills to a bilingual setting. The unspoken message at the IFCM was clear. Spanish meant progress; indigenous languages had no practical use in a school setting; and teachers who wanted to advance their careers were wise to leave their indigeneity at the door. This message was further reinforced by the SEP's salary structure—the best-paid teachers in this clearly bilingual region of Chiapas were those whose job title did not include the qualifier "bilingual."[33]

To make matters even worse, SEP officials at the highest level carried on as if the SEP had never endorsed the INI's bilingual method. In April 1965, the SEP's new director of federal education in Chiapas, Jorge Guillén Ortiz, summoned the INI's education inspectors to his office in Tuxtla to inform them that he was "not in agreement with the INI's method of teaching reading and writing in the native language." Guillén also reportedly believed that "the grado preparatorio should not exist" and wanted all INI schools to become SEP schools. The INI's education inspectors were stunned. Eventually, an official from the SEP in Mexico City told Guillén that he was required to abide by the SEP-INI agreement, but the encounter did nothing to calm the nerves of INI education inspectors who already rued the day when the INI agreed to work more closely with the SEP.[34]

Meanwhile, complaints against promoters and teachers began to mount. As the Teatro Petul toured the region to promote school attendance, the puppeteers increasingly heard about teachers who were incompetent, absentee, or worse. Some were accused of seducing and sometimes even raping girls, beating students who didn't learn their lessons, and fining parents of kids who deserted or got married early. Many indigenous teachers and promoters came to identify culturally with ladinos and adopted hostile attitudes toward indigenous people, refused to speak their mother tongue, and lived in urban centers.[35] Ricardo Pozas described them as "archetypes of ladinization. They do not farm nor do they teach the students to farm. The aspiration of every young indigenous male is to become a promoter, to dress like a ladino and use a wristwatch."[36]

The Cruelest Cuts

The INI's dire budget situation actually worsened in the mid-1960s. Mexico entered the third decade of its so-called economic miracle, and the country's ruling party continued to privilege urban, industrial interests over those of the countryside. During the presidency of the fiercely conservative Gustavo Díaz Ordaz (1964–1970), INI programs that had struggled to limp along in the late 1950s and early 1960s began to fold. It has been suggested that INI director Alfonso Caso had not supported Díaz Ordaz's 1964 presidential bid but had instead favored Donato Miranda Fonseca, who served as secretary of the presidency for President Adolfo López Mateos.[37] The vindictive Díaz Ordaz might have taken his revenge on Caso by financially strangling his institute.[38]

In 1967, the INI's budget was reduced by 257,000 pesos, and Caso imposed a hiring freeze at all Coordinating Centers. He also required that all of the money "recovered" by the centers from the indigenous population be remitted to the INI's central offices in Mexico City. This included payments for everything from fertilizer to medicine to loans and the cuotas simbólicas paid for consultations at medical clinics and outposts. Remitting this money to Mexico City had the effect of crippling these programs.[39] In Chiapas, the Coordinating Center was also prohibited from spending more than 10,000 pesos that had been collected the prior year for home improvements at the celebrated hamlet La Independencia (Oxchuc). In his appeal for that money, the director of the Health Division, Dr. Ricardo Romero Flores, reminded the Coordinating Center's director, Alberto Jiménez, that it wasn't easy to get the residents to agree to the program. "We promised to carry it out expeditiously . . . and we ask that you help us keep our word, since broken promises discredit people and government institutions and complicate future programs."[40] The decision to remit "recovered" funds to Mexico City meant that his division was completely out of needles, syringes, thread, and medicine with more than three months left in the year. He would be forced to close four medical clinics and outposts.[41]

The 1967 budget crisis dealt a crippling blow to the INI's health programs in Chiapas. At that time, the INI averaged more than twenty-one thousand indigenous consultations per year in its seven clinics and eleven medical outposts. Most of the consultations involved respiratory illnesses, arthritis, and rheumatism as well as maladies caused by poor nutrition—anemia and acute vitamin and protein deficiency. CCI doctors also performed some minor surgery (like tooth extractions) and gave lots of DPT and smallpox immunizations. But the federal Ministry of Public Health (SSA) had begun to "invade the CCI's work area."[42] The SSA took charge of the typhus and vaccination campaigns. In 1968, the CCI's health program dug just one well, encased just four springs, and installed only thirty latrines. When residents asked for help in obtaining piped water, they were told to refer their requests to the SSA.[43]

The indigenistas resented the SSA's "invasion," just as they came to resent their association with the SEP. Experience had taught them that the SSA's deeper pockets did not necessarily translate into any improvement in the provision of health services for Tseltals and Tsotsils. For example, the CCI was highly critical of the way that the SSA carried out its Rural Community Development Program (Programa Cooperativo para el Desarrollo de la Comunidad Rural) in 1967. Jiménez claimed that the SSA's staff in San Cristóbal "has always shown little or no willingness to allow this [INI] center to participate in the programs that it claims to execute."

> These programs, which are designed for the purposes of demagoguery, publicity, and exhibitionism, tend to be carried out preferably among the mestizo population adjacent to San Cristóbal de Las Casas. They hold little or no benefit for the rural community. The few works that they undertake lack planning and are left in hands of unscrupulous upstarts.

Jiménez felt it prudent to keep his distance from a relationship "that could damage the prestige of the Coordinating Center itself."[44]

Meanwhile, the CCI's health division faded into irrelevance. In late 1970, the CCI's chief physician, Gregorio Alapisco González, wrote to Director Maurilio Muñoz Basilio to complain that the CCI had not begun work on a single one of the health-related infrastructure improvements that had been budgeted for that year.[45] Four days later, he fired off a follow-up salvo to complain that too many of the CCI's medical clinics and outposts were staffed by unpaid pasantes. Gone were the days when the CCI trained bilingual indigenous nurses, men and women, to staff the medical outposts. The pasantes "know nothing about the cultural characteristics of the indigenous groups and the problems they face, nor are they interested in solving these problems," Alapisco wrote. Their principle concern "is to earn extra income for their return to the city, when they present their professional exam.... They don't bother themselves with knowing about the indigenous problem, because their work is transitory and rotational."[46] Experience had given way to expediency.

The Forestry Program

Even since its creation in 1948, the INI was part of a larger project to manage and exploit Mexico's natural resources, including its forest reserves. In the Sierra Tarahumara, the INI Coordinating Center at Huachochi managed the resources of roughly a dozen Tarahumara forest ejidos. The INI also had big plans for the Chiapas highlands, where some of the richest forests were held as ejidos by indigenous communities. Until roads were built, these forests were relatively safe from commercial exploitation. But because small-scale, illegal poaching by the communities themselves was a problem, the CCI deployed the Teatro Petul to persuade the indigenous to protect their most valuable natural resource. One presentation frequently given in the late 1950s was *The Dream of Petul*, in which Petul tries to cut down a tree, tires, takes a nap, and begins dreaming. The tree explains to him that trees bring rain for his cornfield, prevent erosion, and provide compost for planting. The tree tells Petul not to cut him down until he has planted young saplings available at the Coordinating Center.[47] Other CCI programs promoted tile roofs and discouraged the use of wood shingles. With less success, the indigenistas encouraged the use of oil instead of firewood and charcoal for cooking.[48]

As Villa Rojas sarcastically noted, nobody followed the work of the INI more assiduously than local *rapamontes* (clear-cutters). The INI's roads brought more forests within reach "at no cost to them," while its overall campaign to raise living standards and promote consumerism meant that some indigenous populations "were more inclined to extract some economic benefit from their forests."[49] By 1960, roads connected forest-rich hamlets to San Cristóbal de Las Casas, and local logging companies began pressuring indigenous ejidatarios for the right to harvest their trees. The indigenistas began to more explicitly counsel the indigenous to use their resources wisely. They cited studies showing that cutting forests indiscriminately to plant corn was not economically viable, nor did it allow indigenous families to sustain themselves without performing seasonal stints on lowland fincas.[50] But ladino logging companies exploited the distrust that many communities still felt toward the INI and often convinced them to sign away their forest reserves for a fraction of their market value. They even began extracting legal commitments from communities *before* roads were completed. Villa Rojas reported that at Matzam ejido in Tenejapa, their goal was to "seal off the community" from competitors—and the INI—"through offers that can be compared to those of the conquistadores who bartered trifles for indigenous gold." The loggers "gifted tennis shoes and basketballs as signs of future benefits" after the indigenous ejidal commissioner signed a contract "whose most elemental terms are unknown."[51]

Once again, the INI had to square off with powerful local interests—in this case, the logging companies, the local sawmill operators, the director of the ejido development office in San Cristóbal, and state and federal teachers who served as their agents. By June 1960, logging companies had already obtained signatures from the ejido commissioners at Yashtinin, Chigtón, Tzajalá, Fray Bartolomé de Las Casas, and elsewhere. The INI struggled to reverse the damage. For four years it had tried to establish a model forestry project at three ejidos. But, as Villa Rojas emphatically noted, the INI had not been able to demonstrate to the indigenous "the difference between A FORESTRY PLAN THAT BENEFITS THEIR FAMILIES compared to LOGGING THAT BENEFITS FAMILIES WHOSE NATIONALITY HAS BEEN SOAKING IN SO MANY BEACHES THAT IT HAS ALREADY LOST ITS COLORS."[52]

Time was not on the INI's side. The INI's forestry project moved slowly through official channels. By contrast, as Villa Rojas noted, "the rapamontes have achieved a true miracle in their race against the clock and against forestry legislation." In Chilil, between March and June 1960 "they took all the timber that their consciences would allow and then filed the necessary contract with the ejidal commissioner on June 28, just as the last trucks left, loaded with logs." To add insult to injury, the antiskid chains on the tires of the loggers' trucks damaged the recently opened road. Once the INI paid to fix the road, Villa Rojas mused, the loggers would be back for more.

Villa Rojas's outrage leaps from the pages of his lengthy report. Writing again in capital letters for emphasis, he argued that all INI employees "HAVE A MORAL OBLIGATION TO DEFEND THE INDIGENOUS COMMUNITIES' FOREST PATRIMONY AGAINST CONSTANT ATTACKS." In order to demonstrate the merits of the CCI's forestry programs, Villa Rojas felt it "extremely necessary to initiate as soon as possible one case of rational timber harvesting that will justify four years of paperwork and words." He also recommended that the INI find a legal way to directly control indigenous forest reserves and, if possible, annul contracts.[53]

Yashtinin (Las Casas), a hamlet of Spanish-speaking Tsotsils, became the Coordinating Center's model forest ejido. In 1958, an INI forestry engineer proposed a five-year timber harvest and a plan to reforest the land. One year later, federal authorities granted the ejido authorization to exploit its forest. At that point, ladinos Jesús Aguilar and Rodolfo Lobato became very interested in doing business with the ejidatarios. Aguilar owned a local sawmill, and Lobato wanted to purchase the cut lumber. Both men signed lopsided deals with Yashtinin and five other indigenous hamlets that had forest ejidos. "For a few thousand pesos, the ladino logging interests seized millions," lamented *Acción Indigenista*. Villa Rojas reportedly cautioned residents: "Think, reflect. You shouldn't give away what is yours just because someone comes here saying he's a general."[54]

In early 1961, the INI intervened legally to have the contract revoked. The affidavit gave INI director Alfonso Caso, CCI director Raúl Rodríguez Ramos, and Forestry Department director Eliseo Peralta Porras the power of attorney and the right to advise and intervene in the exploitation of Yashtinin's forest reserves. It also allowed the INI to rescind the contract signed with Lobato and granted indigenous ejido commissioners the right to enter into new contracts on better terms.[55]

By March 1961, on the Coordinating Center's ten-year anniversary, the INI had a victory to celebrate at Yashtinin. Caso traveled to the hamlet to celebrate its new contract with sawmill owner Aguilar, which would net the ejido 100,000 pesos a year for five years. This contract eliminated the Lobato family as middlemen, allowing the ejidatarios to sell their cut lumber directly to the highest bidder. The INI boasted that this new arrangement made Yashtinin the wealthiest ejido in Chiapas. Soon, other ejidos began requesting INI assistance. Later that year, the Coordinating Center optimistically created a Forestry Department and hired a forestry engineer.[56]

But the Lobatos didn't go down without a fight. Months later, CCI director Rodríguez complained that "the noble principles of the INI have been obstructed by vested interests" at Yashtinin. The Lobatos and the federal schoolteacher told the ejidatarios to withhold their support from the school that the INI wanted built in the hamlet. They also advised them to take their profits in the form of cash payments; the INI at the time was drawing up an investment plan that would benefit the entire community.[57]

Since Yashtinin had become the INI's model forest ejido in highland Chiapas, the indigenistas had no choice but to prevail over their local enemies. Ultimately they did, but the victory was costly and time consuming. Besides canceling the contract with the Lobatos, they pursued new sawmill and marketing contracts, they did the technical work with the trees, and they helped formulate the ejido's future investment plans.[58] At Huajam Yalcuc (Huixtán), the INI also canceled a contract with the Lobatos, then arranged a five-year harvest and community investment plan and installed a circular saw so that

FIGURE 8.4. Alfonso Caso inaugurating the sawmill at Yashtinin (Las Casas). Hermanos Mayo, photographer. Fototeca Nacho López, Comisión Nacional para el Desarrollo de los Pueblos Indígenas. April 1961.

FIGURE 8.5. Ejidatarios working at their sawmill in Yashtinin. Photographer unknown. Fototeca Nacho López, Comisión Nacional para el Desarrollo de los Pueblos Indígenas. 1961.

the ejidatarios could do their own sawing. Ejidatarios at Fray Bartolomé de Las Casas also agreed to allow the Coordinating Center a role in managing their forest reserves. But the INI's overtures to ejidatarios at Flores Magón, Chilil, Sajalá Baluitz, Chigtón, Chivero, and Francisco Serrano, located to the east of San Cristóbal, all fell on deaf ears.[59]

The INI would suffer a stinging defeat in 1969 at the Tseltal municipality of Chanal. In June, indigenistas learned that Chanal's ejidatarios were divided over whether to allow a Oaxaca-based lumber company called La Chixonse to harvest and mill their forest reserves or whether to do it themselves, with help from the INI. The indigenistas offered to take the ejidatarios to Cusárare in the Sierra Tarahumara, where the INI had helped the Tarahumaras build a sawmill and harvest their forest themselves. But La Chixonse had already worked hard to sway key members of the community. The lumber company's representative, Íñigo Banda Bernal, had bribed Chanal's elders to sign a contract that offered the community 3.5 million pesos over ten years, a considerable sum. But INI forestry personnel estimated that the company would make a profit during that period of 50 million pesos.[60]

Indigenistas scrambled to prevent the lopsided contract from being signed. Manuel Castellanos Cancino, director of state's Department of Indigenous Affairs (DGAI), asked the state governor, José Castillo Tielemans, to intervene. The CCI's director of agriculture, Antonio Vera Mora, suggested that the INI work with the DGAI to remove Chanal's municipal president and secretary; the CCI's new director, Maurilio Muñoz Basilio, wrote that "through teachers and promoters we could bring this population under control. This is absolutely urgent and necessary."[61]

In late August, Vera attended a meeting at Chanal where community members decided how to harvest their lumber. Chanal's municipal president and secretary "had their instructions," he reported. "Whenever we tried to address the community, they distracted the people and brought up problems that had nothing to do with the forestry question." Chanal's authorities argued that the INI had tricked the community on multiple occasions, citing the failed cooperative store and a couple of animal husbandry projects. Vera concluded that "it's extremely urgent that the INI's director [Caso] intervene to prevent the fraud that La Chixonse plans to commit on the community of Chanal, in which the interests of state government functionaries are surely at play."[62] But the indigenistas soon realized that La Chixonse had beaten them at their own game. Although the INI still had the right to revoke the contract, La Chixonse had successfully persuaded the people of Chanal that it, and not the

Coordinating Center, best represented their interests. The CCI would not be given another opportunity to work with a forest ejido in Chiapas.

By 1971, all three forest ejidos that had agreed to work with the Coordinating Center—Yashtinin, Huajam Yalcuc, and Fray Bartolomé de Las Casas—had completed their five-year logging contracts. The CCI's Forestry Department turned its attention to executing the ejidos' investment plans, which were aimed at purchasing good farmland at lower elevations, building schools, and creating jobs. Yashtinin's ejidatarios found a finca that they wanted to buy in La Trinitaria (near the Guatemalan border). With over 400,000 pesos in the bank, they had more than enough money to buy the property. But the purchase had to be approved by the INI's central offices in Mexico City as well as the Coordinating Center's Department of Economic Development, the state's sometimes hostile Ejidal Development Office, and two federal ministries. It took over a year to get these permissions and finalize the purchase.

Later in 1971, the Coordinating Center's forestry work was put on hold—permanently. The INI's central offices told its Coordinating Centers to halt their activities while the new presidential administration of Luis Echeverría contemplated changes to the forestry management law.[63] But in Chiapas, the game was already up. Juan Luis Sariego's work on the INI's much grander forestry program in the Sierra Tarahumara also points to disappointing outcomes. There, too, the indigenistas' dream of financing development through logging was thwarted by mestizo logging companies. Deforestation brought erosion and the disappearance of flora and fauna, as well as the negative social impacts of the monetization of the communities' economies, which brought violence and alcoholism. "In sum," writes Sariego, "what was conceived as a motor of development became its principal obstacle."[64] Although the INI's work in Chiapas was on a more modest scale and does not permit such thorough longitudinal analysis, its forestry program was certainly crippled by the same web of outside interests.

From Innovator to Junior Partner

As its programs were absorbed or disappeared altogether, the Coordinating Center was increasingly brought in as a junior partner or was asked to perform "mop-up" duties for larger, better-funded federal ministries. In the late 1960s, the Federal Electricity Commission (Comisión Federal de Electricidad, or CFE) began constructing the La Angostura Dam on the Grijalva River south

TABLE 8.4. Investment plans for forest ejidos in Chiapas, 1971.

YASHTININ (STILL WAITING TO BUY THEIR FINCA IN LA TRINITARIA)	HUAJAM YALCUC (PLANNED)	FRAY BARTOLOMÉ DE LAS CASAS
Purchase finca	Purchase a finca	Build a school and house for the teacher
Two prefabricated schools	Improved seeds	School furniture
Office for the ejidal commissioner	Work tools and fertilizers	Monument to the Mexican flag
Cash payments to 126 ejidatarios	Clear land, put up fences	Office for the ejidal commissioner
Basketball court	Build corrals and stables	Latrines
Monument to the Mexican flag		Carpentry workshop
Open-air theater		Barbed wire
Ejidal commissioner expenses		

Source: ICCITT, 1971, from Dir. del CCI Carlos Felipe Verduzco to Dir. del INI Gonzalo Aguirre Beltrán, May 10, 1971.

of the highlands. The INI was charged with relocating the people who lived in the river valley, in the municipality of Venustiano Carranza.

"Resettlement" projects were not new to the INI. Its Coordinating Center in the Papaloapan Basin administered to the tens of thousands of mestizo and indigenous farmers (most of them Mazatecos and Chinantecos) whose lands were flooded following the construction of the Miguel Alemán Dam. The Ministry of Hydraulic Resources (SRH) initially created the Papaloapan River Commission and named Alfonso Villa Rojas to direct the Office of Population Resettlement. Villa Rojas and his team had the unenviable task of convincing four thousand families to leave behind their ancestral lands, their sacred caves, and their ancestors' gravesites and relocate onto new land that was between 50 and 250 kilometers away. Some family heads agreed to resettle on plots of ten hectares. People less willing to relocate were taken to the dam site to watch the heavy machinery at work, with hopes that they would resign themselves to the circumstances. Some families refused to move and were forcibly escorted onto trucks and boats by police as the waters rose.[65]

The INI's Coordinating Center in Papaloapan was created to assist the Papaloapan River Commission. Its first director was Villa Rojas; he was followed in the post by Chiapas veterans Ricardo Pozas and Agustín Romano. Indigenistas believed that the resettlement presented an opportunity for Mazatecos and Chinantecos to become modern citizens integrated into a more developed and homogeneous Mexico. Rosario Castellanos, fresh off her blistering resignation in Chiapas, shared this view in a letter to American friends living in San Cristóbal.

> The situation of the indigenous here is very different from what you find in Chiapas . . . and very stimulating. Something as enormous as the construction of a dam is needed to shake the very foundations of a world rotted by injustice and misery. . . . All this movement, this contact between people of all cultural levels and backgrounds, this direct experience with technology, all this has influenced the mentality of the indigenous, opening them to a multitude of new ideas and placing them in new situations that must be resolved by new methods.

She seemed to call for something equally "enormous" for Chiapas, something akin to the ambitious economic restructuring plans that were ruled out in 1955 at the end of the posh war:

> In Chiapas we are using half measures; nothing will be resolved until radical economic steps are taken. As long as the indigenous do not have more resources than they currently have, as long as a social cataclysm does not push them into direct and massive contact with the ladinos, their transformation will be slow and ineffective.

If people got hurt in the process, Castellanos seemed unconcerned. "All this means violence, in most cases abuses of authority, indelicate treatment of human problems, suffering, etc." But the tradeoff was worthwhile, she wrote, because the Coordinating Center at Papaloapan "will not be needed in a few years because the indigenous will be a mestizo or will be so acculturated that it will not be necessary to treat him like a marginal man."[66]

In the end, INI anthropologists relocated 86 percent of the affected population in the Papaloapan Basin. The indigenistas also supported education and health programs, gave legal assistance, and offered help with agriculture and economic development. But the INI was highly critical of the commission, which failed to provide the housing, schools, and clinics that it promised and failed to provide prompt indemnification for lost property. In a bitter irony, the resettled Mazatecos received neither electricity nor irrigation for their crops.[67] Following the budget crisis of 1958, crucial road projects were abandoned, making it nearly impossible for the resettled population to get their goods to market. The commission also altered the terms by which the resettled people paid for their land, increasing prices tenfold. Nearly half of the colonists abandoned their plots.[68] Poverty and malnutrition were ubiquitous. Far from their sacred caves and burial sites, the Mazatecos' religious cycles were permanently disrupted. Mestizo merchants, money lenders, and employers ended up dominating the Mazatecos, just as they had before the resettlement. Critical anthropologists accused the SRH and the INI of committing "ethnocide" against the Mazatec people, forcibly disrupting their rural lifestyles and compelling them to join the rural proletariat on extremely vulnerable terms. Aguirre Beltrán vehemently denied these charges.[69]

The experience at Papaloapan was not lost on either the CFE or the INI. Both institutions proceeded with caution in Chiapas, at least initially. The CFE promised to compensate the resettled population with land of their choice. However, an INI report suggested that the resettlement of the people at Vega del Paso would be complicated—the population was split between mestizo ejidatarios and Tsotsil comuneros. As was the case at Papaloapan, the mestizos had long dominated the Tsotsils. The indigenistas were concerned that if the resettlement was not done right, the mestizos would reestablish themselves as the dominant group.[70]

The Tsotsil comuneros first asked to be settled on land that had once been theirs "according to our old titles dating back to King Charles III of Spain, during the Spanish colony." These lands had been lost "due to the turbid maneuvers of the wealthy in connivance with venal authorities."[71] After the CFE proved unwilling to expropriate this land, the comuneros found a suitable alternative called El Reparo. However, as they wrote to CCI director Muñoz, the CFE wanted to move them to another, smaller piece of land where it would be easier to provide them with electricity. "We will forego that service if they will allow us to move to the land that we all prefer," they wrote, noting that the CFE had become "cold" and indifferent to their plight.[72]

Three months later, in September 1970, they wrote again to Muñoz in a state of panic. "Time marches on, and in spite of our repeated letters they do not respond to us. . . . None of us can receive credit from the Ejidal Credit Bank, because we don't know where we will live, let alone where we will work and care for our cattle." They added, "The torrential waters of La Angostura now threaten us, and in very short time our old homes will be destroyed."[73] No doubt this scenario sounded familiar to Muñoz. An Otomí from the state of Hidalgo, Muñoz took his first job with the INI as an anthropologist at Papaloapan; between 1957 and 1959 he assisted in the resettlement of four Mazatec communities.[74]

Ultimately, the Tsotsils' pleas fell on deaf ears. Muñoz approved a decision to move them onto contested land near the municipal seat of Venustiano Carranza, where other comuneros were already working.[75] The INI, in partnership with the CFE, had once again ceded to expediency, and once again a resettlement project ended up disappointing indigenous people, whose livelihoods were disrupted for the sake of a major hydroelectric project. Once again, the INI had been used to "mop up" after a larger federal ministry. Unable to really shape the outcome of the resettlement, it was left to deal with its social consequences with greatly diminished resources.

The Making of a Perfect Storm

Maurilio Muñoz's annual report in 1970 highlights one of the great ironies of the INI's trajectory in Chiapas. "In contrast to previous periods, now the indigenous come to the INI when they need teachers, medical services, bricklayers, fruit trees, studs to improve their livestock, legal advice for their agrarian transactions and to defend themselves from injustices, technical advice to improve their crop yields, stipends so their kids can continue their studies, and cheap corn when their crops fail," he wrote. "Unfortunately, the INI does not have sufficient resources to attend to all of these demands."[76] Tragically, the Coordinating Center's hallmark programs were undermined at a time when seasonal work on lowland plantations began to dry up and the state's population grew at an annual rate of 3.35 percent.[77] This "perfect storm" set the conditions for the social conflicts that would erupt during the last three decades of the twentieth century.

Despite the Coordinating Center's modest efforts to stimulate the indigenous economy, thousands of Tsotsil and Tseltal men and boys continued to work at least part of the year on lowland plantations, availing themselves of the cash advances offered by enganchadores. In the 1950s, federal indigenistas tried to make this kind of work unnecessary by "liberating" baldíos in Tseltal communities. They also worked to raise the rural minimum wage and tried to restore Cardenista vigor to the STI. These efforts were stymied by the Chiapas state DGAI. The DGAI also reappointed Chamula's most important cacique, Salvador López Tuxum, to resume his post as general secretary of the STI following an eight-year hiatus. Tuxum could be counted on to keep the rank and file in line, especially in Chamula, which provided about one-fourth of the highlands' seasonal workforce. Through these measures, the state government outmaneuvered the INI and ensured that the STI remained a reliable and docile supplier of labor to lowland fincas.[78]

In the early 1960s, Guatemalans began to pour across the border looking for work. This upset the seasonal labor status quo, which, for all of its obvious abuses, at least provided some work each year for thousands of Tseltals and Tsotsils. Finqueros came to prefer Guatemalan workers because they worked for even less than local workers, they generally did not require *anticipos* (cash advances), and if they did take *anticipos* they were unlikely to flee because they had nowhere to go. And because they arrived at the plantations on their own, planters did not have to pay an enganchador or deal with the STI and its collective bargaining contract, which theoretically protected workers from the most egregious abuses.[79]

The Guatemalan influx could not have come at a worse time for Tseltal and Tsotsil men, who suddenly needed work on lowland plantations more than the planters needed them. Enganche and work on the lowland fincas, long a hated reality of life in highland indigenous communities, had become a necessary evil.

There is abundant evidence for the reduced demand for indigenous field workers, especially along the border with Guatemala. In 1966, the DGAI's free placement office in Motozintla reported that it had stopped contracting indigenous Mexicans. The delegate there, Ramiro Aranda Osorio, reported that at least 6,308 Mexican workers from border municipalities had found work on the fincas, but they were not paid cash advances because planters no longer needed to lure them to the fincas—they came on their own accord. He also reported that Mexican immigration officials allowed Guatemalans to freely enter the country and take jobs formerly given to indigenous Mexicans, even though this was in violation of federal labor law and the STI's collective bargaining agreement.[80]

Aranda Osorio found this new state of affairs deeply disturbing. Brother of the former governor of Chiapas Efraín Aranda Osorio, he had worked as a labor inspector for the state government in the 1930s, then served as Motozintla's municipal secretary and held a variety of posts in the state and federal government. He had absorbed plenty of revolutionary nationalist rhetoric during his lifetime and apparently was still a true believer. In one of his lengthy monthly reports, he told of clashes in the 1930s with foreign planters and administrators over the living conditions on their fincas, in particular a German named Tencher, "a Hitler, only less moderate and more impulsive than the Austrian with the swastika." Aranda concluded that "today, after so many struggles and thanks to the insistence of our revolutionary regimes, even the foreign owners (at least in this region) have at least partly understood the principles and justice of our revolution."[81] Yet his revolutionary nationalist vision clashed with the facts on the ground. On repeated occasions, he asked his superiors whether they still intended to protect the rights of Mexican coffee pickers.[82] Aranda never got a clear answer to his question.

In August 1969, the new general secretary of the STI, Agustín Méndez Gómez, decided to enforce the law. He wrote to Fernando Acosta Ruiz, manager of Soconusco's Coffee Growers Association, to remind him that hiring Guatemalans was "illegal since it displaces Mexican workers and violates the sovereignty of our country." It also violated federal labor law, which "only permits the entry of foreign workers when it has been determined that there are not sufficient workers to harvest the crop." Méndez sent a similar letter to three coffee growers in September. The growers were not amused. One night in October, while Méndez was enjoying beers with a fellow Oxchuquero at his home in San Cristóbal, municipal police forcibly entered the house, frisked him and his friend, and hit Méndez's wife when she tried to intervene. Both men were taken into custody; they were released the following day by order of San Cristóbal's municipal president.[83] As the detention of the STI's general secretary suggests, Soconusco's Coffee Growers Association was calling the shots; immigration authorities acquiesced to their requests; and neither the DGAI nor the STI was able or willing to force the growers to legally hire Mexican workers.

Trends in Mexican agriculture also conspired against seasonal laborers as the state and federal government began to favor the cattle industry with generous subsidies and protections. This policy shift, which Juan Pedro Viqueira describes as "truly criminal," encouraged many ranchers and planters to abandon labor-intensive crops like coffee, tobacco, corn, and sugarcane and turn their land over to cattle.[84] During the 1960s, the cattle herd in Chiapas grew at an annual average rate of 9.8 percent; by 1970, the state's cattle industry ranked third among Mexican states.[85]

Meanwhile, the Coordinating Center's rural development programs barely limped along. A 1968 report from agriculture section chief Antonio Vera Mora underscored the devastating effect of withering budgets and shifting national priorities on his work. He admitted that his section's output was "low," but he suggested that agricultural activities "did not have or take on the same importance as other activities at the CCI." Vera even ventured that administrators had been "a bit discriminatory" when allotting scarce resources. His section was so desperate for funds that agronomists at the experimental plot in Chanal had to use mud instead of wax when grafting crabapple trees. "Technically, this primitive method is shameful to register in our reports, because today, not even the poorest fruit farmer or arborist uses mud."[86]

In this context, the indigenistas' inability to facilitate major (or even minor) land reform in the 1960s became even more glaring. In 1970, they reported that they could find no fincas to target for agrarian reform in the municipalities of Las Casas, Huixtán, Larráinzar, Mitontic, Chenalhó, Teopisca, Chanal, Amatenango del Valle, Zinacantán, or Oxchuc—nine of the twelve municipalities in the INI's original area of operations. "This means that the communities that have solicited a *dotación* [ejidal grant] or *ampliación* [enlargement] will be disappointed," reported the director of the CCI's judicial department, Moisés Flores Rocha. "Not only is there a lack of parcels, but the parcels themselves are insufficient. . . . the lack of cultivable land on the ejidos leads to unprofitable small-scale farming." Many cattle ranchers had *concesiones de inafectabilidad ganadera* (certificates of inaffectability) that protected them from land reform. Flores Rocha suggested that the INI investigate the validity of these concessions as well as those granted to ranchers and lumber companies that operated in large swaths of the eastern municipalities of Ocosingo and Las Margaritas.[87] The CCI's predicament in 1970 recalls Peruvian socialist José Carlos Mariátegui's admonition forty years earlier that any attempt to resolve the "Indian question" through administrative or police measures, through education or transportation infrastructure, is doomed to fail if it does not address the land issue.[88]

In 1967, the INI proposed one last, highly ambitious project in Chiapas to somehow avert the gathering storm—it planned to resettle ten thousand families (fifty thousand people) from the crowded highlands to Las Margaritas, in eastern Chiapas, over the course of eleven years. According to INI calculations, the population density in the twelve municipalities where it initiated its work in 1951 was 81.4 inhabitants per square kilometer; the average in Chiapas was 16.4 per square kilometer. But in some municipalities, the crowding was truly dramatic; in Chamula, there were 326.9 inhabitants per square kilometer, and in Oxchuc, 174.7. Citing what it called the "demographic explosion," the INI proposed the purchase of 140,000 hectares in the area and the construction of a highway, a sawmill, and a Coordinating Center. The INI's Council of

Directors approved the proposal, but the Díaz Ordaz administration did not. Meanwhile, migrants from the highlands voted with their feet and began colonizing the Las Margaritas area on their own.[89]

Conclusion

Throughout the 1950s and 1960s, INI founder and director Alfonso Caso repeatedly stated that INI Coordinating Centers were never expected to be permanent fixtures on the rural landscape. The fact that larger, better-funded state and federal ministries were absorbing INI functions could be seen as a positive sign; it meant that the Mexican state was finally taking responsibility for providing basic services in indigenous zones. Viewed in this light, then, the fact that the CCI's roads section was replaced in 1968 by the Chiapas State Ministry of Public Works was a positive development, as were the agreements formalizing working relationships between the INI, the SEP, and the federal Ministry of Public Health. But it must have been supremely disappointing for the INI to see its programs and its experience give way to federal ministries like the SEP, which was hostile to the INI's proven bilingual method, and the Ministry of Public Health, which showed no interest in learning from the INI's experience of working in a medically plural environment. The INI's surrender to cattle ranchers and timber interests must have been even harder to swallow. Thousands of land-starved and desperate Tsotsils and Tseltals began the one-way trek to the jungle in eastern Chiapas, where they would try to eke out a living in a fragile ecosystem. In 1972, former INI economist Alejandro Marroquín would cite this exodus to eastern Chiapas as evidence of the INI's "visible decline."[90]

Without a doubt, the CCI in highland Chiapas entered the 1970s a weakened institution. But it was not yet irrelevant. CCI director Maurilio Muñoz's concluding remark in his sober year-end report for 1969 shows that even after a long decade of decline, the CCI in Chiapas still drew an international audience. He noted with evident pride that researchers from dozens of world-renowned universities had visited the CCI that year, and so had reporters from several countries; diplomats from the UN, France, Canada, and Great Britain; and development specialists from eighteen countries across Europe, Asia, and the Americas.[91] Still, it was clear that less than twenty years after its founding, the CCI in highland Chiapas was important more for what it had been than for what it had become.

CHAPTER 9
Did the INI Promote Caciquismo?

⦿⦿⦿ OF THE MANY charges levied by the INI's critics, the accusation that it fostered caciquismo (boss politics) is perhaps the most serious.[1] In the context of highland Chiapas, the charge is particularly grave because former INI promoters-turned-municipal-presidents used their clout to expel tens of thousands from their communities beginning in 1974.

Caciques are best thought of as brokers who operate in a hierarchical patron-client system in which individuals are linked through bonds of patronage and reciprocity. They control access to resources like land, jobs, loans, public works, and political power. Caciques are civilians; most are men, but a few are women, and while they can be found in urban, professional settings, they tend to operate in rural areas, among people who are relatively disenfranchised and disconnected from the state and who turn to caciques to provide them with needed resources. Alan Knight suggests that caciques "may be seen as products of the incongruous union of 'modern' politics with 'traditional' society."[2]

Thanks to the pioneering work of Luz Olivia Pineda, Jan Rus, and others, highland Chiapas may be the best-studied case of contemporary indigenous caciquismo in Mexico. Pineda has studied how INI promoters and SEP teachers assumed political power in their communities and became "cultural caciques." Rus argues that Chamula's scribes-principales manipulated "tradition" (local religion that mixes Mayan beliefs and folk Catholicism) to become power brokers in Chiapas's most populous indigenous municipality.[3] Pineda's work directly implicates the INI and especially the SEP; Rus's work emphasizes how powerful ladinos, the Chiapas state government, the INI, and the PRI all had reasons to nurture Chamula's caciques and look the other way when they committed abuses.[4]

The rise of the promoter-caciques coincided with other significant changes in highland Chiapas in the 1960s. Seasonal work on lowland fincas began to dry up, the population continued to grow, and the gap widened considerably between the relatively prosperous few (usually INI promoters and their families) and the deeply impoverished majority. As the highlands became more crowded and complicated, and as INI programs languished, other actors took the stage. The most important newcomer was Bishop Samuel Ruiz, whose philosophical and theological transformation over the course of the 1960s would have profound implications for indigenous people in Chiapas for the remainder of the twentieth century. In 1966, Bishop Ruiz sponsored an organization, Misión Chamula, that became the first major target of the INI's former charges in Chamula. The clash between Misión Chamula and Chamula's cacicazgo set the stage for the violence and expulsions that would forever change life in the Chiapas highlands.

Shaping the Political Arena

Even before the CCI opened its doors, the indigenistas were on the lookout for promising, literate young indigenous leaders. In some municipalities, like Chamula, power was in the hands of Erasto Urbina's former scribes-principales. Salvador Gómez Osob was the municipal judge, and Salvador López Tuxum was the municipal treasurer. The indigenistas felt that the only way they could work in Chamula was by going through Urbina's former scribes, especially Tuxum, and they were probably right. He had become practically the only conduit to a complex, vote-rich municipality.[5]

In other communities, the INI hoped to undermine the existing leadership, or at least bend it to its will. Such was the case at Cancuc, a Tseltal agencia municipal of Ocosingo and home to the cacicazgo of Miguel Ordóñez. Cuban American anthropologist Calixta Guiteras-Holmes described the near-legendary Tseltal strongman this way:

> He goes about armed with an old Smith and Wesson revolver and prefers American bullets to those of his own country. Always clean, almost always drunk, he serves at the bidding of the "boss" [the Chiapas delegate for Indigenous Affairs].... He attended school for some months, learning rudimentary reading and writing, which made him a scribe, "servant of the town," and attorney for his people and his own interests before the Ladino authorities in Tuxtla and San Cristóbal.... He is indispensable as a collaborator and dangerous as an enemy.[6]

Pedro Pitarch has called Ordóñez "the de facto and uninterrupted wielder of power in Cancuc from the early forties to the end of the sixties." His résumé might be compared to that of Chamula's Tuxum.

> He held various political and religious posts, but his real power had two bases: his band of armed followers (independent of kinship bonds), which he used to defend himself from his enemies, and, more importantly, the fact that he was considered by the authorities of the state of Chiapas and the Department of Indian Affairs as the perfect interlocutor in any matter relating to Cancuc.[7]

One of the first two INI cultural promoters to be sent to Cancuc reported that they were "openly entrusted with the mission of breaking . . . Ordóñez's hold on power." They were finally successful "after several years of political tug of war." Pitarch notes that "now, the bilingual teachers have come to monopolize the positions of political power" in the municipality.[8]

When the INI commenced operations, each indigenous municipality in the Chiapas highlands had a municipal president, who by law had to be indigenous, and a municipal secretary, who was invariably a ladino, chosen by the state's Department of Indigenous Affairs. Municipal presidents were elected, often by the outgoing members of the *ayuntamiento constitucional* (town government) and the principales. They handled the internal affairs of the municipality. Municipal secretaries served as liaisons to the state government. They collected taxes, recruited young men for military service, rounded up debt peons for the enganchadores, and often sold alcohol. Bilinguals, with some legal knowledge, they tended to be drawn from the lower strata of San Cristóbal's ladinos or from the municipalities where they were assigned.[9]

The INI had to tread lightly in its efforts to influence the internal politics of indigenous communities. In his book *Formas de gobierno indígena* (1953), Aguirre Beltrán described how the Coordinating Center planned a "fundamental modification of indigenous government." What he called "the integration of Tsotsils and Tseltals into national life" largely hinged on five goals, and whether and when they were attained. These were: "(1) diminishing the number of functionaries in a community; (2) secularizing power; (3) reinforcing the authority of the municipal president; (4) introducing monetary payment (not only prestige) for services rendered to the municipality; and (5) substituting the ladino municipal secretary with indigenous secretaries."[10] The INI could expect resistance from the Chiapas state government and from the indigenous themselves, since the overall plan involved a direct assault on traditional, age-based religious hierarchies.

The Coordinating Center's indigenistas—in conjunction with the state's director of indigenous affairs, Manuel Castellanos Cancino—tackled Aguirre's fifth point almost immediately. They attempted to substitute ladino secretaries with literate indigenous men who (it was presumed) would perform the functions of a municipal secretary without committing the abuses for which the ladino secretaries were notorious.[11] They tried first at Chanal, where the community asked that the INI cultural promoter also serve as the municipal secretary. This arrangement did not last long, however; sources claim that the indigenous did not respect him in his role as secretary.[12]

The INI and the state's Department of Indigenous Affairs tried again to replace a ladino secretary with an indigenous in Zinacantán following the disastrous alcohol monopoly raid in 1954. The man whom they chose, Antonio López Pérez, seemed qualified; he was a cultural promoter who had spent time in boarding schools in central Mexico during the Cárdenas years. He had also worked in Zinacantán's consumer cooperative.[13] But his appointment came at the height of the posh war, and he soon found himself investigating murders perpetrated by rival aguardiente producers. López Pérez soon ran afoul of Zinacantán's caciques and was replaced. INI records allude to Zinacantán's "internal divisions," but they also suggest that López Pérez lacked the appropriate preparation for the job. In 1955, the Coordinating Center offered an intensive course for aspiring municipal secretaries at its boarding school. The students took classes in accounts management, statistics, arbitration, Mexican law, and the preparation of birth, death, and marriage certificates. The CCI discontinued the program, however, in part because of the students' lack of formal educational training and in part because it was so difficult to dislodge and replace ladino secretaries.[14]

When Zinacantecos accused López Pérez's ladino replacement of extortion and other abuses of authority in 1956, Villa Rojas and Castellanos Cancino replaced him with an old hand—ladino Belisario Liévano.[15] Liévano's résumé was typical for the position—he had worked as a mounted policeman for Erasto Urbina, directed the Department of Indigenous Affairs, and been a labor contractor for the STI and a fiscal for Aguardientes de Chiapas.[16] Liévano ended up serving several years as Zinacantán's municipal secretary; the INI even added 200 pesos a month to his salary to promote INI projects.[17] The fact that the INI and the state's director of indigenous affairs agreed to fill the position with a man who had worked for enganchadores and the Pedreros shows that indigenismo in Chiapas ultimately rested on the shoulders of some rough customers.

The Liévano appointment also served as tacit recognition that the plan to replace ladino municipal secretaries with indigenous secretaries had been premature. The indigenistas had also learned that naming indigenous secretaries to municipalities that contained sizeable ladino populations (like Larráinzar or Oxchuc) was an invitation to disaster, or at least a riot, since the minority ladinos would panic if the sole ladino authority were replaced by an indigenous. But the Coordinating Center still sought a way to protect the indigenous from abusive ladino secretaries, like the one in Oxchuc who in 1959 charged 330 military conscripts thirty pesos each for their birth certificate, when the law allowed him to charge only three pesos. When Fidencio Montes learned of this case, he reminded the Coordinating Center of "the urgent need to prepare our best students so that they can serve as municipal secretaries in the future."[18]

But the CCI chose another path. Believing that young, literate bilinguals could rein in the ladino secretaries, the indigenistas encouraged promising bilingual promoters to become municipal presidents. By 1958, ten promoters had been elected to serve; during 1962–1964, INI promoters served as municipal presidents in six of the twelve municipalities in the INI's initial area of operations. In Chamula, INI promoters served as municipal president almost continuously during 1951–1964 and then again during 1968–1976. Beginning in 1977, former promoters and SEP teachers headed seven highland municipalities, and in 1980 they headed eight.[19] Although Romano claimed that "the CCI never tried to manipulate the elections of indigenous municipal presidents," it did pay salaries to INI promoters who won elections at a time when the posts were unpaid, as they were until the late 1960s.[20] This arrangement obviously gave the INI a certain amount of influence over municipal politics.

Growing Inequalities

While the INI provided direct support to an emerging indigenous leadership in highland Chiapas, it also provided them with access to INI resources, which, over time, were among the factors that led to growing divisions and tensions within indigenous municipalities. Although the INI claimed to seek collective rather than individual advancement, too often its programs relied on and favored INI cultural promoters and other members of an emerging indigenous middle class. Indigenistas in Chiapas celebrated the prosperity of

TABLE 9.1. Municipal presidents, 1968–1979 (former INI promoters and SEP bilingual teachers in bold).

	1968–1970	1971–1973	1974–1976	1977–1979
CHALCHIHUITÁN	Martín Domínguez Pérez	**Miguel Pérez Orozco**	Santiago Pérez Gómez	Martín Gómez Girón
CHAMULA	Juan Gómez Osob	Mariano Gómez López	Agustín Hernández López	Domingo Pérez Segundo
CHANAL	Miguel Hernández Jiménez	Pánfilo López Gómez	Ramiro Hernández Jiménez	Manuel Etzin Gómez
CHENALHÓ	Antonio Pérez Hernández	Manuel Gómez Cruz	**Enrique Ruíz Arias**	**Victorio Arias Pérez**
HUIXTÁN	Alfonso Santis Martín	Pedro Huet Pale	Pedro Huacash Méndez	Alonso Vázquez Huet
LARRÁINZAR	Manuel López López	Diego Díaz Hernández	Nicolás Hernández López	**Vicente Díaz Pérez**
MITONTIC	Vicente López Méndez	**Felipe Erasto López Vázquez**	Vicente Rodríguez López	**Vicente Pérez Pérez**
OXCHUC	**Marcelo Santis López**	Manuel Gómez López	**Antonio Morales Santis**	**Antonio Gómez López**
PANTELHÓ	Liborio Luna Flores	Julio Ballinas Urbina	Adán Morales Monterrosa	Alejandro Ramos Ramírez
TENEJAPA	**Antonio Jiménez Girón**	**Alonso Méndez Girón**	**Alonso Guzmán Méndez**	**Diego Méndez Girón**
ZINACANTÁN[1]	Pedro Pérez Pérez	Marcos Pérez González	Mariano Pérez Gil	Domingo Pérez Pérez
TOTALS	4	3	6	7

Sources: Pineda, Caciques culturales, 175; Montes Sánchez and Castro, Educación, lingüística y ayudasvisuales; and ICCITT, 1959, "Informe del mes de mayo de 1959," by Dir. de Ed. Fidencio Montes Sánchez.

1. Pineda speculates that, given Zinacantán's tradition of commerce, its "strongmen" were merchants, not promoters or teachers. Pineda, Caciques culturales, 155.

FIGURE 9.1. Oxchuc's transportation cooperative, created in 1953 by education promoters. Photographer unknown. Fototeca Nacho López, Comisión Nacional para el Desarrollo de los Pueblos Indígenas. 1963.

their charges, whom they regarded as apostles of the modernization process.[21] But they also turned a blind eye to the internal class differentiation that was observed in all indigenous communities and chose not to consider the clearly negative consequences of a privileged few emerging in spite of (or at the expense of) the many.[22]

Back in 1957, one of the CCI's most sensitive observers, Fidencio Montes, shared a conversation that he had had with Salvador Gómez Osob and Tuxum that revealed as much about the promoters as it did about the INI's blind spot. Gómez Osob was working as a nurse at the INI's Chamula clinic and had served a third stint as municipal president in 1953, while Tuxum was deeply involved in Chamula's consumer and transportation cooperatives. Both men had also served in Chamula's traditional religious cargo system. Standing in a room on the second floor of Tuxum's new house in Chamula's ceremonial center, Montes observed that the number of houses with tile roofs had been multiplying. Tuxum noted that Chamulas had been reluctant to use tile roofs because they feared the criticism of others. When Gómez Osob asked for his help in building a house with a tile roof in Ichintón, Tuxum agreed and decided to build one for himself in Chamula. "We overcame the criticism," he said triumphantly. Gómez Osob's house doubled as a store, while Tuxum's two-story house had a vaulted tile roof, large windows, tile floors, and a porch "so that our people know that we also have the right to live like everyone else. Those that can should make better houses. If it weren't for the INI," he continued, while serving sodas to Montes and his assistant on a brand-new metal desk, "we would never have dared to improve our houses."[23] Not coincidentally, Tuxum and his sons had just been invited by ladino businessmen to be the first exclusive distributors of the ubiquitous Coca-Cola (as well as Pepsi and, eventually, beer) in the indigenous highlands.[24]

Rus uses the term "scribes-principales" to remind us that internal differentiation in the highlands predates the INI. The young men who were trained as scribes by Erasto Urbina in the late 1930s were then coached to accept religious cargos and become principales in the early 1940s. They became INI promoters in the early 1950s. Rus claims that highland ladinos (like Hernán Pedrero) turned scribes-principales and INI promoters (usually one and the same) into business associates. At the height of the posh war, in 1954, Pedrero helped Tuxum purchase his first truck. Other well-heeled ladinos partnered with INI promoters throughout the highlands; by the 1960s, indigenous leaders and their closest relatives "held all the best government jobs, owned most of the stores and trucks, and possessed a disproportionate share of community land."[25]

Ironically, as INI promoters and former promoters became politically and economically integrated with the outside world and clearly profited from these relationships, they bolstered their moral authority inside their communities through public displays of their "Indianness." And they accused anyone who challenged the economic or political status quo of violating "tradition." In Chamula, where internal unity in the face of ladino interference had been a survival strategy, this was a grave offense; angry ancestral gods could send drought, crop failures, or epidemics.[26] The INI, the state government, and the PRI supported this self-serving use of "tradition" because all had an interest in maintaining political control over highland municipalities and ensuring that the indigenous leadership turned out the PRI vote during elections.

The renewed interest in "tradition" and "unity" in municipalities like Chamula, Huixtán, Tenejapa, and Zinacantán was in response to the situation on the ground—income inequality and other internal divisions were becoming widespread across the Chiapas highlands. Beginning in the late 1950s, Oxchuc entered a period of what Villa Rojas called "social disorganization due to the various forces that are acting upon its inhabitants," which included Catholics,

Protestants (*evangelistas*), INI employees, members of various political factions, and "a new generation that clashes with the conservatism of the old men who govern the municipality."²⁷ In the small Tseltal town of Amatenango, June Nash told of thirty murders in the period 1960–1965; the victims were young entrepreneurs who had ignored traditional government while pursuing their business interests. To explain rising tensions and the phenomenon of "envy" homicide in the municipality, Nash cites George Foster's work on the "limited good," which was the belief in traditional societies that the accumulation of wealth was a zero-sum game; one person's prosperity came at the expense of another, not as a result of increasing opportunities.²⁸ In Zinacantán, Frank Cancian found rising inequality and remarked that economic life was "monetized" during this period; George Collier also noted a rise in "class-based politics"; and Robert Wasserstrom noted that modernization in Chiapas "accelerated the differences between rich and poor campesinos."²⁹ In yet another sign of growing inequality and tension within indigenous municipalities, the director of the state's DGAI, Manuel Castellanos Cancino, was increasingly called on to deal with the abuses of indigenous moneylenders who charged interest rates ranging from 10 to 25 percent *a month*. Debtors who could not pay were thrown in jail or had their land taken. During the first eight months of 1968 alone, Castellanos Cancino intervened in fifty-two such cases.³⁰

By the late 1960s, many young people who had completed primary school (through grade six) sought a way out of this mounting economic and demographic crisis by pursuing entry-level positions as SEP bilingual cultural promoters. Those fortunate enough to land a position earned between three and four times the daily minimum wage in municipalities where most indigenous people did not earn *one* daily minimum wage. Applicants "beg us to give them a job as a cultural promoter; they say that they are willing to go wherever they are sent," wrote the Coordinating Center's subdirector of education, Ignacio León Pacheco. Students who had studied through the sixth grade or lived in a boarding school "had different life expectations. They have new needs, and they are looking for a way to sustain their new expectations." León recommended building a school of arts and crafts or a technical secondary school, or finding some way to channel students away from teaching. He then ended his report with a rather shocking admission. "The problem becomes worse every day," he wrote. "With the increase of teachers and schools that offer the full primary cycle, the number of graduates consequently increases." The "problem" now, according to the Coordinating Center's assistant director of education, was no longer mass illiteracy, monolingualism, and absenteeism. Rather, too many students were completing the sixth grade and expecting a better life.³¹

Bishop Samuel Ruiz and Misión Chamula

During the 1960s, while the Coordinating Center in Chiapas struggled to remain relevant, the diocese of Chiapas was revitalized by Bishop Samuel Ruiz. Born into a conservative family in the state of Guanajuato, the cradle of Sinarquismo, Ruiz studied in Rome in the late 1940s and early 1950s under the fiercely anticommunist Pope Pius XII. He was only thirty-five years of age when in 1959 Pope John XXIII appointed him bishop of Chiapas. On the heels of Fidel Castro's overthrow of the Batista dictatorship in Cuba, Mexican bishops and clerics were staunch Cold Warriors and defenders of the status quo. Ruiz was no exception—his first pastoral letter in 1961 condemned communism's "iniquities and countless crimes . . . and the BLACK background of its true doctrine."³² That same year, writer Fernando Benítez spent several weeks in the Chiapas highlands and interviewed the young bishop. Their exchange might surprise readers who are more familiar with Ruiz's later career, when his work with indigenous populations earned him death threats from enemies who called him the "Red Bishop."

Benítez wrote that Ruiz seemed agreeable enough, but "behind that appearance hides a fanatic."

> The young prelate spreads his hatred equally for a communism that he needs to invent daily . . . and a Protestantism against which he cannot fight, but which daily subtracts some sheep from his flock. His supporters in this fight are the Indians' exploiters, and their enemies, as one might guess, are none other than the members of the INI, the only ones that defend them and attempt to break the feudal structure of Chiapas.³³

Benítez was highly critical of coleto society and the smear campaign that targeted the INI at that time. He suspected that Ruiz at least tolerated this campaign. "Why not collaborate with the Institute instead of combating it?" Benítez asked the bishop. "Why not stop this denigrating campaign that is poisoning relations?" After some evasion, the bishop responded, "The functionaries at La Cabaña and the promoters speak in support of communism and General [Lázaro] Cárdenas." When Ruiz admitted that he had never been to an INI school and didn't know any promoters, Benítez cornered him. "I know the promoters, *señor Obispo*. None has even the slightest idea of what communism is." Ruiz responded that "some functionaries at La Cabaña speak against the church and we need to adopt a defensive attitude." The interview went downhill from there. Later, even the freewheeling Benítez felt that he "had gone too far." In his concluding remarks, he wrote:

> I wanted to talk to him about Father Las Casas, of the rocks that the encomenderos threw at him, of the anachronism of that old, rotten world of alcohol vendors, enganchadores, and gross superstitions. . . . But convincing the bishop that he should follow the example of his predecessor Fray Bartolomé de Las Casas would be like convincing the silly and sleepy governor that he should do something transcendent, something noble and revolutionary for the Indians of Chiapas.[34]

Shortly after this encounter, Ruiz would embark on a dramatic personal and spiritual transformation (he himself called it a "conversion") that would alter the history of modern Chiapas. In 1962, Pope John XXIII convened the Second Vatican Council, which consisted of four sessions lasting through 1965. Vatican II was intended to modernize certain church positions and practices. Bishop Ruiz participated in all four sessions. When he wasn't in Rome, he crisscrossed his diocese and witnessed the misery and injustice firsthand.[35] From 1962 to 1968, he helped lead the movement that trained six hundred indigenous lay catechists to spread the Gospel in their mother tongues.[36] These catechists helped Ruiz counter the inroads of Protestant missionaries. By the late 1960s, Ruiz was part of a continent-wide movement of progressive-minded Catholic bishops who embraced some variant of what became known as liberation theology. In 1968, he addressed the Second General Conference of Latin American Bishops in Medellín on the need to support the weak and the oppressed in their struggle against marginalization and dependency. The bishops agreed that the church should take a "preferential option for the poor" and oppose the "institutional violence" of poverty. This position eventually drew the wrath of some of the church hierarchy, especially Cardinal Joseph Ratzinger, who served as prefect of the Congregation for the Doctrine of the Faith, the Vatican office charged with policing orthodoxy, from 1981 to 2005. (Ratzinger then served as Pope Benedict XVI from 2005 to 2013.) Bishop Ruiz's transformation was complete; the conservative anticommunist from Guanajuato would soon become a threat to the status quo in highland Chiapas and a thorn in the side of the Vatican.[37]

As Bishop Ruiz became acquainted with his diocese, he became convinced that many communities were Catholic in name only; 450 years after the Spanish conquest of Mexico, he proposed establishing "missions" to "reevangelize" certain areas. Densely populated Chamula, located just a few kilometers from the diocesan seat of San Cristóbal, was the obvious place to start.[38] Ruiz founded Misión Chamula in 1966 and established it in Chamula's cabecera. Its director or "promoter" was Father Leopoldo Hernández, also known as Padre Polo. Christine Kovic describes this priest as "a complex character who at times made ethnocentric judgments," a man who nonetheless "had a genuine desire to better the lives of Chamulas."[39] He began by trying to reclaim the main church in Chamula from the native practitioners who used it for their traditional forms of worship.

In several ways, Misión Chamula functioned like a miniature INI Coordinating Center, complete with a health clinic, a crafts workshop, a brick factory, a tailor's shop, and a night school that taught home economics and Spanish classes. It raised purebred pigs, chickens, and other animals in the garden area inside of the church's walls.[40] The mission also trained native promoters and catechists, many of whom were drawn from the ranks of restless young people who had studied at INI schools. This mission's work was intentionally subversive, for, as Kovic notes, Padre Polo "worked to remove caciques from power and to replace them with younger Catholic leaders."[41] Moreover, most Chamulas believed that the church was on consecrated ground; building a pig shed and chicken coops in the church gardens was a senseless provocation that served as a rallying point for the mission's expulsion. As Kovic notes, Chamulas did not ask for the pig shed, since they rarely ate pork, and they certainly objected to its location. Undaunted, Padre Polo argued that Christian Chamulas *do* eat pork; to drive home the point, he sent piglets home with catechists.[42]

Like the INI fifteen years before it, the mission had to negotiate its way into Chamula. The former INI promoters who now functioned as Chamula's traditional elders imposed certain conditions on Padre Polo. Among them: he had to remain in the town center; he could not encourage the construction of Catholic buildings or shrines; and he could not interfere with the traditional rites practiced in Chamula.[43] Chamula's caciques accurately perceived the mission to be a threat to their interests. As more disaffected Chamulas were drawn to the mission and its activities, the more threatening it became. Finally, in 1969, Chamula's caciques struck back with cunning efficiency.

Chamula's *Cacicazgo* Defends Its Turf

By the late 1960s, Chamula's scribes-principales were at the height of their political and economic power. Tuxum, for example, had bought a finca, opened stores, owned several trucks, and lent money at usurious rates. A willing accomplice to highland ladino enganchadores and lowland planters, he had served for many years as the *secretario de trabajo y conflictos* (secretary of labor and conflicts) of the toothless STI. He was arguably the wealthiest and most powerful man in the Tsotsil highlands.[44]

Not surprisingly, a vigorous, diverse, democratic movement rose in opposition to Tuxum and the rest of Chamula's caciques. In the early 1960s, opposition came first from Protestants (mostly Presbyterians) who refused to pay municipal taxes to support the fiesta cycle, which they equated with paganism. They also refused to buy and consume the alcohol that was an integral part of Chamula's traditional religious practices and a key source of income for traditional leaders.[45] Later in the 1960s, merchants opened stores and challenged the caciques' economic grip on the municipality. Chamula's promoter-caciques responded to their challengers by intimidating them, forcing them to take on expensive religious cargos, and ordering attacks on the stores that they owned.[46]

To ensure their continued domination, some former promoters attempted to limit access to highly coveted teaching jobs. They made it difficult for nonrelatives to attend the *albergue* (boarding school) in the municipal center, finish the sixth grade, and become a promoter. Restricting the number of eligible candidates allowed them to reserve positions for their family members and keep local power in relatively few hands. As Rus notes, 80 percent of Chamula's promoters and teachers in 1975 were related to former promoters. (In neighboring Mitontic, this number rose to 100 percent.) This set the stage for a generational clash between the INI's privileged former charges and a rising generation of literate, educated Chamulas who saw their career aspirations blocked.[47]

The trigger came in 1965, when Chamulas from several outlying hamlets opposed a nine-peso tax that authorities in the cabecera intended to use to build two classrooms, a house for the municipal secretary, and a traditional church. The dissidents also alleged that the municipal president—a former INI promoter—kept a warehouse of Hernán Pedrero's aguardiente "and was requiring the officials to consume said aguardiente; those that did not were fined 100 pesos." The Coordinating Center and the DGAI investigated the matter and called a meeting of the parties in dispute. They convinced the authorities to reduce the tax to six pesos after it was agreed that the INI and the Chiapas state government would cover the difference between the amount collected and the actual cost of construction. As far as the aguardiente warehouse was concerned, the INI seemed happy to let the director of the DGAI resolve the matter.[48]

Three years later, in 1968, the INI once again backed its former promoters in a larger dispute. Chamula's Board of Moral, Civic, and Material Improvement levied a more onerous thirty-peso tax on all men, women, and children to pay for the construction of a new municipal seat.[49] Dissident groups of mostly young people in outlying hamlets refused to contribute; their leaders—two bilingual teachers—claimed that the new municipal building would be built with federal funds and that Chamula's powerful families were likely pocketing most of the collected revenues. In February, dissidents from the Chamulan hamlet La Candelaria wrote to the governor to complain that they had been "vilely exploited by the municipal presidents of Chamula for more than twenty years." Padre Polo's Misión Chamula had been active in La Candelaria, and it's likely that his catechists had a hand in crafting the daring letter. The dissidents complained of arbitrary taxes and forced "voluntary" contributions to support fiestas. They asked for their money back and for the dismissal of Chamula's municipal authorities. Most surprisingly, perhaps, they proposed that their community become part of the municipality of San Cristóbal de Las Casas. That Chamulas were willing to become part of the region's ladino center gives some indication of their level of frustration with the authorities in Chamula's cabecera.[50]

In April of that year, between two and three thousand Chamulas from twenty-six hamlets congregated on Guadalupe Hill in San Cristóbal. The dissidents were led by Domingo López Panela and Domingo Hernández Hernández, a bilingual teacher and an INI education promoter, respectively. They demanded the dismissal of Chamula's municipal president, former INI promoter Juan Gómez Osob (brother of Salvador and Domingo Gómez Osob). The director of the DGAI, Manuel Castellanos Cancino, talked them out of marching to Chamula and deposing Gómez Osob once and for all. But when the dissidents returned to Chamula, they were met with a hail of gunfire, and one person was wounded.[51]

Castellanos continued to back the authorities. "The work of the bilingual teacher and the education promoter has been negative in every sense," he wrote. He suggested that they were being "guided or directed by outsiders who have nothing to do with this matter," a clear allusion to Misión Chamula.[52] The

INI, the governor, and other state agencies also rallied around Gómez Osob and his allies. To avoid further trouble in the restive municipality, the Chiapas state government and the INI agreed to reimburse Chamulas who had contributed to the project. Chamula's strongmen had gotten away with another act of corruption. Fearing additional trouble, Castellanos met with several education promoters in other Tsotsil municipalities like Mitontic and Larráinzar, where teachers were leading similar movements, and extracted solemn pledges that they would respect the authorities.[53]

In early 1969, Chamula's leaders made yet another attempt to collect money to finish the project. When many Chamulas refused to collaborate, municipal president Gómez Osob wrote to the governor blaming "unpatriotic" people who "sowed hatred and discontent" and opposed the "unification of our people."[54] He also blamed Misión Chamula, which by now was holding meetings in several Chamulan hamlets. Gómez Osob still expected the state authorities (and the INI) to reflexively support him, even after the INI and the state government had already stepped in twice to preserve the peace. His faith in the authorities was well placed. Even the Teatro Petul was used to convince Chamulas from various hamlets that they should again contribute so that the municipal building could be finished. The troupe's long-standing director, Teodoro Sánchez Sánchez, condemned Chamula's dissidents, who "opposed the progress of their own pueblo" with the same vehemence that he used to combat poor hygiene, lice, and truancy.[55]

But the trouble in Chamula kept coming because its caciques knew that they were still indispensable to the INI and the state DGAI, and because Padre Polo was relentless. In early October 1969, some three hundred Chamulas, following orders from their religious leaders, demanded that Gómez Osob expel Padre Polo from the municipality. They threatened to kill him if he was not immediately sacked, alleging that the presence of pigs, chickens, and other animals near Chamula's sixteenth-century church constituted a threat to Mexico's national heritage. CCI director Maurilio Muñoz, Manuel Castellanos Cancino, the INI's subdirector of education, and a representative of the federal police traveled to Chamula to meet roughly one thousand angry Chamulas. Several of Chamula's religious and civil leaders spoke on behalf of the riotous crowd. They made several accusations: that Padre Polo did not respect San Juan, the patron saint of Chamula, allegedly saying that he "was made of wood, did not have a soul, and was therefore worthless"; that Misión Chamula's pigs and chickens produced bad odors inside the Temple of San Juan; that Padre Polo did not allow them to burn incense inside the church or perform traditional baptismal rites; and that he had invited several outsiders to join him in the parish, and that these people had defecated behind the church.[56] The priest also built temples in Chamula's hamlets, in violation of his initial agreement with the caciques.[57]

After these allegations had been aired, Tuxum finally spoke. His damning testimony against Padre Polo showcased his political acumen. He claimed that several Chamulas had seen the friar's car parked on the road that connects San Cristóbal to Chamula. As they approached the car, they saw three children playing in the trunk. Suddenly, they allegedly spotted the priest coming down from the woods in the company of a Chamula woman, adjusting his zipper. After dropping this libelous bombshell, Tuxum disingenuously backtracked. He told the priest's accusers that the priest was a man "and as such has his needs" and claimed that he was neither for nor against the priest. But before concluding his testimony, Tuxum let drop another bombshell: that he had heard that Padre Polo had been involved in a similar incident in Mitzitón, east of San Cristóbal. This concluded Tuxum's masterful performance, in which he displayed his ability to manipulate an angry mob and eliminate a powerful competing force in Chamula.[58]

Having collected these explosive allegations, CCI director Muñoz, Castellanos, and the two other men held one last meeting and invited the participation of Bishop Samuel Ruiz. After several hours and following direct consultation with the governor, the decision was made to remove the priest. In his report to INI director Alfonso Caso, Muñoz reported optimistically (and mistakenly) that "this concludes the conflict that arose in Chamula."[59]

Bishop Ruiz was understandably furious. That night, he wrote a hasty letter to the district attorney's office in San Cristóbal to vent his ire and explain his difficult decision to remove Padre Polo. "We do not know the true motives behind the allegations," he wrote. "Everything that has been shared with me personally is either completely false, is based on distorted information and in any case does not constitute crimes that should be expiated by a clandestine murder." He added that on the very day in 1966 that Padre Polo inaugurated Misión Chamula, "he received a very clear threat in front of me." He feared for the several hundred Chamulan Catholic converts who had just been left in an extremely vulnerable position. The bishop flatly stated that the expulsion was "an act of a cacicazgo." In a rambling concluding paragraph, he noted the following:

Given that this situation cannot be adequately controlled by the authorities

... I find myself obliged to order the Priest to leave Chamula, not because I believe the charges are true because many (?) believe them, nor because we are afraid to carry out our duties, but to spare the community the incontrollable opprobrium that such a crime would generate.... Our consciences could never justify the sacrifice of one person, under these circumstances.[60]

For its part, the CCI had once again backed caciques of its own creation. Muñoz held three meetngs in the restive municipality but did not once consult Chamulas who supported Padre Polo and defied Chamulan religious tradition. The need to politically control Chamula was greater than the need to protect the rights of hundreds of Chamulas. The Mexican Constitution, which the SIL's missionary linguists had painstakingly translated into Tseltal and Tsotsil in the early 1950s, guarantees freedom of religion, and the INI did in fact defend the concept of religious pluralism in some Tseltal municipalities. But in Chamula, this right was sacrificed at the altar of political expediency. Unfortunately for dissidents in Chamula and other Tsotsil municipalities, the troubles in the late 1960s merely constituted the opening act of a long, painful play that saw dozens killed and tens of thousands expelled in subsequent years.

Conclusion

So, to what extent was the INI to blame for the cacicazgos that emerged in the late 1960s in Chamula and elsewhere? By their own admission, the indigenistas encouraged literate bilinguals to lead their communities and promote the directed, integral changes that the INI wanted to see. They identified promising leaders, offered them training, and supplemented their salaries. The INI also offered economic opportunities to its protégés. The result was often internal stratification and tension. Blinded by a combination of naïveté, hubris, and paternalism, the indigenistas apparently never considered that their former charges might slip out of their control and leverage their privilege into brutal cacicazgos. What's clear is that by the late 1960s, as the INI's presence in the highlands withered, it could not or would not control or even contain its former protégés.

After 1970, the CCI no longer trained education promoters and teachers. But it still had supervisory control over roughly six hundred educators. To what extent could the INI prevent its promoters and teachers from dominating those they had been trained to serve? In 1971, the Coordinating Center's outgoing director, Carlos Felipe Verduzco, spoke with Alfonso Villa Rojas about the INI's crises in education and leadership.[61] His assessment of the problem was not particularly novel; due to some "imbalances" in the acculturative process, some promoters were "committing arbitrary acts and becoming caciques"; others were "becoming bureaucratized and behaving like the federal teachers"; and many did not live in the communities where they worked. But his proposed solution was unique, and it suggests the degree to which the initiative had passed from the INI to the catechist movement, which was now the driving force for change in the indigenous highlands.

> We need to orient the promoter ideologically; we need an ideology that fits the work that they are doing, so that they understand the social, economic, and historical context of their work environment. We are trying to elaborate that *mística*. . . . I realized this after observing the system that the [Jesuit] priests of Bachajón have established, which has some 500 catechists who, in reality, are our promoters. And what they do is a replica of what we are doing. . . . The catechists who are working in that region don't earn a salary [but] are ideologically motivated to do a job, which to me seems very orderly, very systematic.[62]

But how likely was it that the INI could rekindle the *mística* of the early 1950s, when Mexico's brightest young social scientists tried to bring the Mexican Revolution to Chiapas and dreamed of major economic transformations? It is also important to note that Bishop Ruiz fostered a very local, "Indianized" theology, turned important theological matters over to indigenous catechists, and gave them opportunities to assume leadership roles.[63] Was the INI also willing to relinquish partial control of its programs to the indigenous? Alexander Dawson writes that indigenistas relished their role as interlocutors "between the silent Indian and the revolutionary state," and Emiko Saldívar notes that the INI's paternalistic rhetoric about helping and protecting defenseless Indians helped indigenistas legitimize themselves.[64] Were the INI to empower the indigenous, they might find themselves out of work.

As a final reflection, we return to those INI promoters who *did* become caciques. Alan Knight reminds us that caciques are (ideally) "flexible" and at least somewhat "consensual." They usually mediate between competing factions. In the classic *pan o palo* (bread or the club) formulation of Mexican political culture, the best caciques "do not and cannot rule solely on the basis of *palo* [coercion]."[65] Based on these criteria, Chamula's cacicazgo falls short of the mark. By the late 1960s, when Misión Chamula was training converts to undermine the traditional leadership, the caciques could no longer forge consensus in an increasingly divided municipality. They were even less likely to mediate disputes with dissident Chamulas, who had their own hierarchies and vision. With little "pan" to offer their rivals in a resource-scarce environment, they came to rely increasingly on "palo" in the 1970s, when electoral disputes eventually led to multiple rounds of expulsions.

Part 3 Crisis, Rekindled Populism, and the Fate of Mexican Indigenismo

CHAPTER 10

The Generation of 1968, the Critique of Mexican Anthropology, and the INI's Response

⊚⊚⊚ ON OCTOBER 2, 1968, just ten days before Mexico would host the summer Olympic games, Mexican army and police personnel killed at least two hundred people attending a rally at the Tlatelolco public housing project in Mexico City.[1] The massacre at the Plaza of the Three Cultures brought a bloody end to more than two months of activism. Students had convened three huge marches, each one drawing hundreds of thousands of fellow students, faculty, parents, and even administrators, and they had begun to make overtures to peasants and workers who resided outside of Mexico City. Although the students' formal demands were quite modest, the movement called attention to the shortcomings of the Mexican Revolution and issued broad calls for democratization and social justice. This activism naturally threatened President Gustavo Díaz Ordaz's plan to use the Olympics to showcase the "Mexican Miracle." Nineteen sixty-eight marked the first time that a Spanish-speaking, "developing" country played host to the Olympics, and he was not about to let restless students ruin Mexico's coming-out party. Blame for the October 2 massacre has tended to fall on the president, his secretary of defense, General Marcelino García Barragán, and his interior minister, Luis Echeverría.[2]

At first blush, the events of 1968 would seem to have nothing to do with indigenismo. But Tlatelolco was a watershed moment in Mexican history, and its impact was felt far beyond the Plaza of the Three Cultures, which celebrated the supposed fusion of Mexico's indigenous, Spanish, and mestizo cultures. This was a generational rebellion that caught fire just as the Mexican Miracle was running out of steam.[3] Tlatelolco served as a requiem for the Mexican Miracle and the Mexican Revolution. It was "the starting point of a new crisis in Mexico," according to Héctor Aguilar Camín and Lorenzo Meyer:

On that date, an interval began during which the country lost confidence in its present, ceased celebrating and consolidating its achievements and miracles, and began to confront . . . its own previously ignored insufficiencies, failures, and miseries. The crisis of 1968 was not a structural crisis that would place at risk the very survival of the nation; it was, above all, a political, moral, and psychological crisis, a crisis of values and principles, which shook up the triumphant schemes of the governing elite; it was the bloody announcement that the times had changed.[4]

The Tlatelolco massacre and the "dirty war" that followed drove much of Mexico's political opposition underground. Some students joined urban guerrilla groups; others took up arms and headed for the hills. Those who did not join the armed struggle searched for alternative ways to manifest their frustration with the one-party state. Mexican indigenismo became an inviting target. It had become "that jewel on the crown of the Mexican Revolution," according to Claudio Lomnitz. "By 1968 the identification of Mexican anthropology and official nationalism was at its summit."[5] Four years earlier, on Independence Day (September 16), 1964, President Adolfo López Mateos had inaugurated the world-renowned National Museum of Anthropology. Octavio Paz called the museum the "womb of the patria." Mexican anthropology had even inspired a new, modern aesthetics, as seen in the design of the new museum and several buildings at the National University of Mexico.[6]

In 1970, five talented young anthropology professors declared open season on indigenista anthropology. Early that year they published a book that carried a derisive title—*De eso que llaman antropología mexicana* (What They Call Mexican Anthropology). The five contributors to this volume—Arturo Warman, Guillermo Bonfil Batalla, Margarita Nolasco Armas, Mercedes Olivera Bustamante, and Enrique Valencia—had participated in the student protests and had either been forced to resign their teaching posts at the National School of Anthropology and History or had chosen to do so voluntarily.[7] They were part of a slightly larger group of anthropologists dubbed the Siete Magníficos, the Magnificent Seven, by the national press.[8] Their manifesto lambasted Mexican anthropology for placing itself at the service of the state, accused the state of internal colonialism, and eviscerated the INI's assimilationist project.

Later that year, Luis Echeverría—one of the likely architects of the Tlatelolco massacre—became president of Mexico. To deal with Mexico's multiple crises, Echeverría tried to tap into the populist tradition of Lázaro Cárdenas.

When he began campaigning in October 1969, he crisscrossed the country and traveled to its most remote corners, as Cárdenas had done. Tata Lázaro died on October 19, 1970, about six weeks before Echeverría took office. His death and burial at the Monument to the Revolution in Mexico City provoked a tremendous outpouring of grief from peasants and the National Campesino Confederation (Confederación Nacional Campesina, or CNC). This greatly impressed Echeverría. Indeed, as Amelia Kiddle and Joseph Lenti suggest, "he appears to have seen the death of Cárdenas as a political opportunity."[9]

As president, Echeverría tried to win back public support for the PRI by offering a strong, interventionist state, a renewed commitment to cultural and economic nationalism, and a political opening (*apertura democrática*). He used anti-imperialist language and warmly embraced Chile's Marxist president Salvador Allende. He had the presidential residence decorated with Mexican furniture and handicrafts, and his wife, María Esther Zuno de Echeverría, wore traditional indigenous clothes. Ironically, the man who had ordered the military takeover of the UNAM in September 1968 made several overtures to students by lowering the voting age and investing heavily in public higher education. This investment did not translate into the kind of middle-class support that Echeverría courted, however.[10] Since the middle class and business elite opposed his economic agenda, it was imperative that he win the support of rural Mexico. But the countryside had been in upheaval for some time. Several armed insurgencies, drawing from peasant organizations and teachers' unions, prowled rural Chihuahua and Guerrero.[11] And now, to further complicate matters, Mexican indigenismo was in crisis.

The publication of *De eso que llaman antropología mexicana* opened the floodgates of criticism in the broader Mexican academic community and helped sever, once and for all, the relationship that had subordinated Mexican anthropology to the needs of the state. It also led to a period of reflection and self-critique at the INI. In the end, the prescription for the ills of Mexican indigenismo was to do much more of the same. For the INI, this translated into a robust budget and fifty-eight additional Coordinating Centers. But little was done to address the theoretical and programmatic crises that had afflicted Mexican indigenismo during the preceding two decades.

The "Magnificent Seven" Lead the Charge

De eso que llaman antropología mexicana was not the first book to criticize anthropological practice in Mexico, but it made the biggest splash because it benefited from spectacular timing. It came at the tail end of the aggressively anti-intellectual presidency of Gustavo Díaz Ordaz and was published less than two years after Tlatelolco. INI founder and director Alfonso Caso passed away within months of its publication, which opened a period of critique and reflection at the INI, and incoming president Luis Echeverría had just concluded his neo-Cardenista campaign that promised a revival of Mexican indigenismo.[12]

Arturo Warman's biting lead essay set the tone by taking broad swipes at anthropology as a discipline, noting its roots in the Victorian era, when Western imperialism was at its height. Anthropology was "a scientific tool of white expansion" that helped imperialist powers understand their colonial subjects. This critique gained traction in Mexico and elsewhere in the developing world, especially after Eric Wolf revealed that US anthropologists had offered their services as part of US counterinsurgency policy in Latin America and Southeast Asia from the mid-1950s through the late 1960s.[13]

Warman's critique of Mexican anthropology, and indigenismo in particular, was not far behind. Ever since Manuel Gamio proposed in the 1910s and early 1920s that anthropology serve as a tool of scientific government, "anthropology has voluntarily linked itself to the service of power," wrote the man who would later become director of the INI (1988–1991) and minister of agrarian reform (1994–1999). The relationship had become one of "concubinage. And now we're paying the price."[14] Warman argued that contemporary anthropology had lost its critical function because "its hands are tied by its bureaucratic function." Indigenista theory had become dogma. What's more, it was dated and just flat wrong. "The old arguments are repeated and the myth of patriotic integration—so often prophesized and never achieved—lives on," he wrote.[15]

Guillermo Bonfil continued in this vein, writing that the objectives of indigenismo had remained the same for decades. "Stated brutally, it consists in disappearing Indians. Yes, there is talk of preserving indigenous values, without ever explaining clearly how this is to be achieved." Education programs were used "to 'educate' the Indian so that he will abandon his 'bad habits' and change his attitude and mentality, so that he will produce and consume more."[16] The indigenista's job, Bonfil concluded, was to introduce change in the communities "so that the goals of the dominant society are achieved with the least amount of conflict and tension. Stated less elegantly, the anthropologist is a specialist at manipulating Indians."[17]

Mercedes Olivera trained her sights on the sorry state of anthropological research at both the INAH and the INI. "After the theoretical contributions of Aguirre Beltrán and the accumulation of information about the regions that interested the INI during the first fifteen years, research work has been substituted by simple experience," she wrote. "That is to say, anthropological research is no longer done within the INI." The solutions to indigenous problems were therefore "arbitrary and do not take into account the characteristics of the societies in which they are applied." Olivera's argument carried her to a damning conclusion. "If indigenista institutions no longer do research, the obvious reason is that research is not indispensable to their work."[18]

Margarita Nolasco, for her part, accused the INI of focusing on the symptoms of the indigenous condition, not the causes. The Coordinating Centers "were planned to carry out integral development among both the indigenous and mestizo populations, but in reality they work exclusively among the indigenous."[19] Like many of the INI's external critics, Nolasco overlooked the INI's early, utopian attempts to work with mestizos and carry out integral, regional development, and seemed unaware that ferocious local opposition had forced the INI into several strategic retreats.

One of the volume's more devastating common critiques concerned the end result of the INI's timeworn commitment to national integration. Nolasco, who later headed the research component of a progressive regional development agency in Oaxaca, wrote that Mexican indigenismo gave the indigenous only one unattractive option. "To survive, they need to change, but the class structure of global capitalism has them immobilized," she wrote. Their only hope would be to "leave their region of refuge and become proletarianized, that is, they can trade colonial exploitation for class exploitation."[20] Bonfil also believed that the INI's goal of integration on an equal plane with other Mexicans was an empty promise, since Mexican society was plagued with grave inequalities and the indigenous would almost certainly enter the mainstream at the bottom.[21] On the other hand, as Bonfil wryly noted, indigenista institutions—and indigenous communities—were perhaps more integrated into national life than was usually presumed.

> It is not surprising that, in spite of indigenismo's noble intentions and motivations, the vices that form part of public life in Mexico, like corruption, improvisation, sinecures, favoritism, and many others have not been absent in its history. This should not be attributed solely to indigenismo—and even less so to the Indians ... but if these vices are present in the life of the indigenous communities, it is proof of their national integration.[22]

One measure of the impact of *De eso que llaman antropología mexicana* was the response of INI director Alfonso Caso. The critiques clearly got under the skin of the world-renowned archaeologist and indigenista, the man who had founded both the INAH and the INI. Interviewed just a few days before he died, as it turned out, Caso jokingly called the young anthropologists "worms," impugned their writing ability, and compared them unfavorably to *pepenadores*, people who sift through trash in search of something useful, the difference being that the critical anthropologists "scatter the trash that they produce."[23] Caso was seventy-four years old at the time. He died of a heart attack on November 30, 1970, the night before Luis Echeverría took office as president of Mexico. He had just learned, to his dismay, that he would not continue at the helm of the INI and was furious that Echeverría's team had not even solicited his input concerning his replacement. Anthropologist Andrés Medina has remarked that Caso died a "symbolic death." For the ambitious Caso, the news "was a blow for him politically, a coup de grace." Medina also called Caso an "authoritarian caudillo" and a "dictator" and suggested that his passing created an opening for a new generation to reshape an institute that had changed little in two decades.[24]

The Critique Deepens

The magníficos focused most of their critiques on the INI's long-standing theoretical underpinnings, especially its insistence on integration and cultural assimilation. This critique took on a hemispheric dimension in January 1971, when Guillermo Bonfil joined ten other high-profile Latin American social scientists at a symposium in Barbados to indict the allegedly colonial and classist nature of indigenista policies and accuse national states of direct or indirect responsibility for "many crimes of genocide and ethnocide." The Barbados Declaration I called for the creation of truly multiethnic states "where each ethnicity has the right to manage its own affairs" and where all indigenous populations have "the right to be and remain themselves." The scholars then trained their sights on anthropology, which "rationalized and justified in academic terms . . . the situation whereby some pueblos dominate others, and has offered knowledge and techniques that maintain, reinforce, or mask colonial relationships."[25] For many, this emphatic statement represented a watershed marking the end of classic indigenismo. Bonfil, who became director of the INAH in 1972, later asked: "Are we willing to accept that ours is and should continue to be an ethnically and linguistically plural society? . . . Or will we continue to obstinately insist on the ideal of the Napoleonic nation-state, anxious to homogenize and apply middle-class norms to everyone's lives?"[26]

Not only was INI theory stale and misguided, critics argued, but it had failed to deliver on its stated goal of assimilation. When he established the INI in 1948, Alfonso Caso predicted that the "indigenous problem" would disappear in twenty years. In 1968, however, there were more Indians in Mexico—based on the most common linguistic criteria—than there had been when the institute was founded.[27] Just days before his death in 1970, Caso made another prediction—that if incoming president Echeverría dedicated sufficient funds, he was sure that "in not more than twenty-five years we could finish resolving the [indigenous] problem."[28] For the INI's critics, not only was Caso's goal of assimilation highly questionable, apparently it was also a moving target. What Caso still insisted on calling the "indigenous problem" would not be "resolved" by 1995, either. On the heels of the Zapatista uprising in Chiapas, what risked disappearing were not the indigenous but the INI.

Internal Critiques

The critique of Mexican applied anthropology and the death of the INI's founder and longtime director initially caught the INI flat-footed. By late 1971, however, the indigenistas had inaugurated a remarkably public process of self-critique. In September of that year, President Echeverría presided over an extraordinary session of the INI Council. Three of the men who had directed the INI's pilot CCI in the 1950s were present at this meeting: Gonzalo Aguirre Beltrán, who now directed the INI and also served as the SEP's undersecretary for popular culture and extracurricular education; Alfonso Villa Rojas, who was now the INI's assistant director; and Agustín Romano. Other old Chiapas hands present at this meeting were anthropologists Fernando Cámara Barbachano and Carlos Incháustegui and economist Alejandro Marroquín. The plural nature of this meeting was underscored by the presence and participation of invited guests, including three of the seven magníficos (Guillermo Bonfil Batalla, Margarita Nolasco Armas, and Ángel Palerm), writers Fernando Benítez and Juan Rulfo, photographer Gertrude Duby, UNAM rector and sociologist Pablo González Casanova, and two functionaries from the Summer Institute of Linguistics.[29] The regime still had the capacity to repress, as it had demonstrated as recently as June 10, 1971, when a known paramilitary group attacked student demonstrators at the Monument to the Revolution in Mexico City. An estimated fifty students were killed in what became known as the

FIGURE 10.1. President Luis Echeverría (at the head of the table) listening to INI director Gonzalo Aguirre Beltrán (speaking into the microphone) at an extraordinary meeting of the INI's Council of Directors, September 13, 1971. Photographer unknown. Fototeca Nacho López, Comisión Nacional para el Desarrollo de los Pueblos Indígenas. 1971.

Corpus Christi massacre.[30] Three months later, however, the president still sought to maintain the appearance of plurality and dialogue, and his populist agenda required a revival of indigenismo.

The INI's new director, Gonzalo Aguirre Beltrán, set the tone for the meeting (and established its limits) with his opening remarks. He summarized and defended the INI's work and forcefully rebutted comments made by Bishop Samuel Ruiz to the newspaper *Excélsior* accusing the INI of ethnocide.[31] Most of the other scheduled presenters directed the various state ministries that constituted the INI Council. Not surprisingly, they stuck to their scripts, flattered President Echeverría, and refrained from critiquing the INI. A handful of more independent presenters gently criticized the previous administration and suggested that the INI's theoretical approach was outdated. Pablo González Casanova, author of the influential book *La democracia en México*, implied a critique when he called for a national indigenous conference where "for the first time the indigenous man will appear as a political man, who will present his problems, and to whom we must listen closely, respectfully."[32]

President Echeverría responded that the INI had already contemplated such a meeting. He promised to attend the event and provide it with a budget sufficient to guarantee its success. He also agreed to open a school of applied anthropology in San Cristóbal de Las Casas to train promoters and social scientists from all over Latin America.

What livened this rather stodgy meeting was an exchange involving writer Fernando Benítez, author of an exhaustive, four-volume study titled *Los indios de México*. In his prepared remarks, Benítez called for more land reform and a purge of landowners, moneylenders, and corrupt functionaries who enriched themselves at the expense of the indigenous. He even suggested that some of the most ruthless exploiters were members of the PRI. When the director of the Department of Agrarian Affairs and Colonization (Departamento de Asuntos Agrarios y Colonización), the minister of agriculture and livestock, and the general secretary of the CNC rose to defend their work in front of the president, Benítez rebutted their arguments and reminded them of his personal friendship with Echeverría.[33]

If the Benítez exchange (and the controversy that followed) enlivened an otherwise predictable affair, the proceedings of this historic meeting contained an additional surprise. Titled *¿Ha fracasado el indigenismo?* (Has Indigenismo Failed?), the book included transcripts of the reports delivered by the INI Council, newspaper articles written by the various reporters in attendance, and—most remarkably—a devastatingly critical essay written by former INI economist Alejandro Marroquín. In his prepared remarks at the meeting, Marroquín—who was serving as director of the Department of Anthropology at the Instituto Indigenista Interamericano—pulled his punches. But he was preparing a book manuscript on behalf of the III titled *Balance del indigenismo* that spared nothing. His chapter on Mexican indigenista policy was included as the penultimate chapter of *¿Ha fracasado el indigenismo?* Although the editors of the volume added a footnote explaining that Marroquín's analysis only covered the period up to November 1970—in other words, it did not apply to the Echeverría administration—the chapter's inclusion in a book published and financed by the SEP is nothing short of shocking. If anything, it suggests that Echeverría's commitment to dialogue and *apertura* was real, at least when it came to indigenista policy at that particular moment.

Marroquín's critique of Mexican indigenismo packed a powerful one-two punch. On the one hand, the man who had tried in vain to transform the regional economy of highland Chiapas lamented that "structural changes have not been made in the regions of refuge, and as a result, the ladino-indigenous equation—which involves the exploitation and oppression of the Indians—has not been modified. All changes that benefit the indigenous threaten the privileged situation of the ladinos; that is the root cause of their resistance."[34] The INI's impotence had simply made matters worse. "The INI does not have the power to make the distinct state and federal agencies comply with its decisions. Its authority is merely moral." This led to Marroquín's second important claim. Unable to bring about fundamental, much-needed changes, some INI functionaries had been "bureaucratized," preferring "the daily routine, free of problems, over fighting with very powerful functionaries who could easily eliminate them from their posts." High-level INI employees became petty bureaucrats, and the INI became just another step on their career ladder. As if there could be any doubt, Marroquín concluded that "the *mística indigenista* has been lost."[35]

And the bureaucracy had certainly grown. Marroquín reported that in 1970, 51 percent of the INI's total budget went to cover salaries, leaving relatively little to promote development.[36] In other words, indigenismo may have "failed" the indigenous, but not the indigenistas. Moreover, the administration had become "excessively centralized." INI technicians and directors were found not in the indigenous countryside but in Mexico City, and indigenista programs "were slowly devoured by bureaucratic rust."[37]

As office work and paper pushing took precedence over applied anthropology, the INI's scientific work went into a sharp decline, as Olivera had noted. In the 1950s, Coordinating Centers were opened only after anthropologists had conducted exhaustive preliminary studies of the target populations, which then allowed the INI to tailor its development programs to local needs. This tradition of top-notch research was lost in the 1960s. "The preliminary studies have declined notably" and generally confused description with analysis, noted Marroquín. Indigenista programs developed in Mexico City were applied in various indigenous settings irrespective of regional differences or idiosyncrasies. "Without these preliminary studies, many indigenistas do not even have a functional concept of the region where they are operating, and, therefore, their horizons are limited to the community," Marroquín wrote, although limited horizons might have become a survival tactic once major structural change had been taken off the table.[38] "Unfortunately the INI arrived at a period in which the authority of the anthropologist was disregarded and their advisory role practically became a dead letter," he added. During the recently concluded sexenio of Gustavo Díaz Ordaz (1964–1970), the INI entered a period of "frank decline," symbolized by the exodus of families from Chamula and other municipalities in highland Chiapas to the Lacandón rainforest "after living for more than twenty years under the INI's protection." Marroquín concluded his devastating postmortem with the observation that "the INI's best years are behind it," a remarkable admission to be printed in a SEP volume at a time when President Echeverría had assigned an important political role to the INI.[39]

Another former INI insider, Ricardo Pozas, deepened the critique when he published a controversial fifty-page pamphlet a few years later, in 1976. *La antropología y la burocracia indigenista* was broader, more ideological, and more acid than Marroquín's analysis. Whereas Marroquín attributed the INI's expanding bureaucracy to its impotence, Pozas saw more sinister motives—he believed that the bureaucracy was intentionally designed to frustrate the work of socially committed anthropologists (like himself) who identified with the indigenous and included them in the planning and execution of development programs. Pozas held special contempt for INI founder Alfonso Caso, who had been dead for six years. Pozas called him the "Central Figure" who "accommodated himself to all the oscillations of four presidential administrations. The [indigenista] bureaucrats won the trust of the Central Figure by means of subservience and adulation."[40] Since the "Central Figure" was more interested in bureaucracy than he was in anthropological practice, he and his sons could import expensive cars from Europe, go on hunting safaris in Africa, and have luxurious vacation homes in Acapulco. Pozas also accused "an anthropologist" who directed the CCI in Chiapas (surely he meant Alfonso Villa Rojas) of "hiding from the Indians when they came to the offices of the Coordinating Center to do paperwork; on the other hand, he attended very well to North American researchers or tourists, giving them free lodging, even if this meant that sometimes CCI employees had to give up their own rooms."[41]

According to Pozas, when the indigenista bureaucracy was not frustrating socially committed anthropologists, it was trying "to control the Indian and nullify his attempts to fight and liberate himself." He believed that the INI's expansion during the Echeverría administration was a political decision meant "to extend its influence to all indigenous zones, in order to monopolize the decisions and maintain control of the population."[42] Pozas and others also accused the INI of applying practices that politically isolated indigenous Mexicans, a curious stance for a nationalist institute with integrationist aims. When indigenistas taught the indigenous to distrust ladinos and mestizos, Pozas wrote, they "strengthened the reality of one's Indian identity, and in practical terms fostered useless antagonism" between the groups.[43]

Pozas's pamphlet provoked a predictably bitter rebuke from INI director Aguirre Beltrán. He defended the Echeverría administration, which had invested so much in the INI, and impugned Pozas's writing skills and his contradictory theoretical positions.[44] In many ways, Aguirre was right—the pamphlet is at times tendentious and poorly written. Pozas partially undermined his own credibility by making a few reckless claims, arguing—for example—that the INI taught the indigenous to read and write in their native tongue "to favor the cultural penetration of the North Americans and the religious sects that want to save their souls."[45] Wild accusations notwithstanding, Pozas's critique showcased the convictions of a talented social scientist who broke with the INI in 1956 and was still angry enough about the INI's trajectory that he felt compelled to denounce it twenty years later.

Salomón Nahmad Sittón's incisive critique of the INI's bureaucracy echoes that of Pozas in many ways. Nahmad entered the INI in 1961 and learned early lessons about the institute's subculture under Alfonso Caso. Shortly after the young anthropologist had been commissioned to research and write on the condition of the Mixe of Oaxaca, he returned to Mexico City and urged immediate action. But his findings were neither analyzed nor discussed because Caso had other priorities—he was constructing a new building for the INI's central offices. "The luxurious building absorbed all the resources, and the programs and projects of the various CCIs were paralyzed," noted Nahmad.[46] He also observed that the INI's central administration was divided between people like Julio de la Fuente, who understood the problems of the countryside but had no decision-making authority, and the bureaucrats who served in don Alfonso's "court." When Caso arrived to work every morning, "the bureaucratic courtesans waited at the door of the institution, and when he left his office the court accompanied him to his automobile. The ritual was daily and everything else was put on hold." Nahmad denounced "the elegant cars, the uniformed chauffeurs . . . the mansions built in Pedregal . . . the honorary doctorates, the homages and the recognition of elite international academics."[47] In an interview, Nahmad suggested that Caso himself had perhaps lost interest in the indigenista cause; he spent his mornings tending to the indigenista bureaucracy and spent his afternoons reading and publishing pre-Columbian codices.[48]

Nahmad eventually held several different posts at the INI. He became convinced "that the enemies of the indigenous were both inside and outside of the INI."[49] The institute had been saddled with outdated integrationist theory, stifled by Caso and the indigenista bureaucracy, and corrupted by Mexico's

FIGURE 10.2. INI director Aguirre Beltrán (center); in the left of the picture is Salomón Nahmad Sittón, who was assistant director of the INI from 1972 to 1978. Photographer unknown. Fototeca Nacho López, Comisión Nacional para el Desarrollo de los Pueblos Indígenas. 1974[?].

political culture. Nahmad concluded that the only way to accomplish real change was to organize the indigenous politically and put indigenismo in their hands, positions that would cost him dearly when he became INI director in 1982.

In Defense of the INI

How did the indigenistas respond to these external and internal critiques? Several voices rose to defend the INI, including three of the CCI's first directors: Aguirre Beltrán, Romano, and Villa Rojas. (De la Fuente died in 1970; Pozas, as noted above, had become one of the INI's most implacable critics.) In fact, Aguirre Beltrán spent much of his six-year stint as INI director defending the institute's record. One of his many books, titled *Obra polémica*, was a collection of his most vigorous, searing public defenses.

Following Tlatelolco, critics of the Mexican government understandably accused dependencies of the federal government—like the INI—of being part of "the system," part of an authoritarian, repressive apparatus. Villa Rojas,

Romano, and others countered that the INI's meager budget prevented it from sponsoring the Machiavellian, ethnocidal schemes envisioned by its critics. Nobody knew this better than Villa Rojas, who directed the CCI in San Cristóbal as it sank into its permanent budget crisis. In 1976, he noted that "the lack of an adequate budget and the existence of vested interests that oppose its mission" were the two greatest obstacles to the Coordinating Center in San Cristóbal. "The environment in which we work is always dangerous and under surveillance, to the point where directing a Coordinating Center is like being in the eye of a tropical storm."[50]

Romano elaborated on this latter point. If the INI supported the maintenance of the status quo, why did regional elites and state governments so often oppose and obstruct INI programs? And why was the INI not more generously funded by the federal government? "The truth is that indigenista programs do not enthuse the governing elite," he wrote. "Indigenismo is tolerated but not encouraged; it is maintained through inertia." The reason, according to Romano, was abundantly clear. The INI "fights to break the status quo and liquidate the vested interests of certain powerful groups. It is therefore wrong to affirm that indigenismo today favors the perpetuity of the 'system.'"[51]

If the INI's inadequate budget served as proof that it was not part of "the system," the INI's defenders believed that it was also too small to be solely or even partly responsible for the emergence of exploiters from among the ranks of the indigenous. Pozas, who believed that the INI had accomplished next to nothing in its first quarter century, believed that the penetration of capitalism had been so effective that it, rather than the INI, was responsible for creating a class of parasitic exploiters. Even Aguirre Beltrán conceded that "society at large" had a greater impact on indigenous society than the INI could ever hope to have.[52]

In 1970, when the wave of critiques threatened to become a tsunami, Fernando Benítez rose to the INI's defense. "What could the INI do against the innumerable mafias that plague Mexico?" he asked. "Very little, in fact, when the *acaparadores*, the land invaders, and the thieves pay for the complicity of the judge, the municipal president, and the little politicians."

> When people bitterly and unjustifiably attacked the work of the INI in three different states, they attacked the only organization that was doing something for the indigenous. [Before the INI,] nobody said a word about the gigantic logging companies and those who enjoy usufruct of indigenous forests, nor the monopolists in Tehuacán [Puebla] and Córdoba that

enriched themselves on the misery of the Mazatecs, Mixtecs, and Zapotecs; nobody accused the racists of Tlaxiaco [Oaxaca] or of San Cristóbal de Las Casas, inveterate thieves of Indians, nor the finqueros or the aguardiente producers that always bought the protection of the old ruling class.[53]

Benítez offered a somewhat premature postmortem of national indigenismo that could have also described the history of the INI in highland Chiapas.

Without a doubt the INI lost more battles than it won. . . . It spent an excessive amount of time combating—almost always without success—the monopolies, the latifundistas, and the minor regional politicians, allies of the exploiters. A radical structural change . . . was beyond its reach.[54]

Still, for Benítez, it was better to have a weak INI than to have no INI at all. "The INI made hundreds of thousands of indigenous people conscious of their true worth, gave them schools, and defended their interests." Although the INI was generally outflanked, outgunned, and outspent, and was unable to build a new economic system, "it won that one irreversible victory."[55]

Another renowned Mexican writer, Juan Rulfo, offered a similar defense of the INI's record. Author of *El llano en llamas* (1953) and *Pedro Páramo* (1955), Rulfo became the INI's director of dissemination and publications (*difusión y publicaciones*) in 1962 and held the position for more than fifteen years. "It is strange that the INI is attacked," he wrote. "Formed when the Cardenista ejido was destroyed . . . the INI, in spite of its scarce resources, fought for Indians' lands, combated the caciques and the monopolists, founded schools and clinics, established experimental farms, and snatched some forests from the greed of the clear-cutters." Perhaps most importantly, Rulfo wrote, the INI "gave thousands of human beings a consciousness of their rights. It taught them how to defend themselves."[56]

Some INI veterans went further, defending the INI's much-maligned policy of cultural assimilation. Three old Chiapas hands were among the INI's most ardent defenders on this point. Romano wrote: "If it is not advisable to integrate the indigenous into our national society, to what other kind of society can we integrate him? Should we wait until a new, more just society is created?"

To delay action until time itself or the ideologues of total change, or the armed struggle, or any other circumstance manages to modify the present state of things is to fall into the comfortable and pleasant laissez-faire liberalism of nineteenth-century indigenista policy that proclaimed the theoretical equality of all Mexicans, mestizos and indigenous, in order to justify doing nothing for them.[57]

Alfonso Villa Rojas wrote a more scathing rebuttal of those who criticized the INI's campaign to modernize indigenous communities. Responding directly to Gilberto López y Rivas, who had accused the INI of ethnocide, Villa Rojas justified the disappearance of "obsolete" ways of life.

> It's true that the rain gods lose their charm where irrigation systems are introduced . . . and that traditional healing rites and the other resources of witches and herb doctors are lost with the introduction of antibiotics, but this does not necessarily lead to the degeneration of the indigenous, nor their automatic entry into "the most exploited sectors of the dominant nationality." It would be worse to deny the indigenous and other marginalized groups the same opportunities and benefits that modern technology offers other Mexicans.[58]

Villa Rojas took his argument one step further when he decried the cultural relativism that inspired the critiques of cultural assimilation. "This belief is based on the myth of attributing equal validity to all cultures, from those that exist in the Amazon where head-hunting is considered sporting to those that apply the advances of Science and Technology."[59] Villa Rojas closed his impassioned defense by noting that ethnocide was much more likely to occur when the INI was *not* involved and when change came abruptly to groups that had not benefited from anthropological management and assistance.

Former indigenista Ricardo Pozas was even less apologetic about the cultural loss that some indigenous groups experienced as a result of the modernization process. He believed that ethnicity prevented the indigenous from developing a class identity and joining the class struggle. "We know that ethnic identity . . . is negative and was developed by the Indians as a reaction to the exploitation and social stigma that they suffered during the Colony." He issued an unapologetic call for indigenous self-determination and the class struggle, even if it meant the possible disappearance of indigenous cultures.

> We know that the Indians themselves will take charge of their own liberation and that the road to that liberation is the class struggle[,] . . . that in this struggle we do not need to defend the conservation and reproduction of the

TABLE 10.1. The proliferation of INI Coordinating Centers.

SEXENIO	PRESIDENT	NEW CCIS
1946–1952	Miguel Alemán	2
1952–1958	Adolfo Ruiz Cortines	3
1958–1964	Adolfo López Mateos	5
1964–1970	Gustavo Díaz Ordaz	2
1970–1976	Luis Echeverría	58

indigenous, nor *lamentar en lloriqueos* [tearfully mourn] the death of this culture; nor will we protest the process of "ethnocide" to which indigenous languages, traditional dress, handicrafts, and folk religions are exposed. . . . The Indians and history will decide if they survive or disappear.[60]

Conclusions

The crisis in Mexican anthropology and indigenismo came at the worst possible moment for the Mexican government. At a time when the distressed and increasingly crowded Mexican countryside was becoming restless, indigenismo was supposed to be a core part of President Echeverría's populist rural strategy. But the national and international critique of anthropology at large and the INI in particular forced a public and sometimes painful reckoning.

Given the gravity of the critique, the federal response might be considered surprising. The Echeverría administration forged ahead as planned and increased the INI's budget dramatically, from 26 million pesos in 1970 to 450 million pesos in 1976. Instead of charting a new course and hammering out a new indigenista theory and practice, the INI soldiered on with only slight modifications, using Echeverría's largesse to create fifty-eight additional Coordinating Centers.

As Andrés Fábregas has noted, this growth was "artificial" because "there was no longer a theoretical base to sustain it. It was, rather, a very pragmatic state policy." The proliferation of Coordinating Centers tended to multiply existing problems and add new ones. An institute that had trouble finding qualified staff for twelve CCIs now had to staff seventy, and some of the newly created centers were directed not by anthropologists but by economists and accountants.[61]

Ironically, this dramatic increase in spending did not revive the INI's pilot Coordinating Center in Chiapas. As the next chapter details, the INI found itself outflanked by a populist governor who invested in his own indigenista project and made the Coordinating Center redundant. The CCI in San Cristóbal was closed to make way for the INI's answer to its critics—an experimental school of rural development. Chiapas would get one last chance to shape the trajectory of Mexican indigenismo, but as the Mexican state grappled with the unfolding crisis in the countryside, its own institutional decay, and the mobilization of peasants and the indigenous throughout the country, there were limits to what the INI and the federal government could accept.

CHAPTER 11
Indigenismo and the Populist Resurgence (1970–1976)

●●● AT FIRST BLUSH, the election of Chiapas governor Manuel Velasco Suárez in 1970 could have signaled a reprieve for the INI's beleaguered Coordinating Center in highland Chiapas. To stave off Chiapas's looming economic and social crises, the governor—like President Echeverría—opted for populist strategies and spent handsome sums on rural programs. During the ensuing six years, when public sector spending in Mexico more than doubled, federal and state expenditures in Chiapas grew almost tenfold.[1] Yet the CCI in San Cristóbal did not benefit from this largesse. Governor Velasco Suárez had been born in San Cristóbal. Like many coletos, he resented and mistrusted the INI, which, after twenty years of work in the region, was still regarded as a federal intruder. Velasco Suárez planned to make the INI obsolete by creating a much better funded state-based indigenista project called the Program of Social and Economic Development of Highland Chiapas (Programa de Desarrollo Socio-Económico de Los Altos de Chiapas, or PRODESCH). So while the INI benefited overall from Echeverría's populist priorities, its most emblematic Coordinating Center actually closed in 1972 to make way for the School of Regional Development (Escuela de Desarrollo Regional, or EDR).

PRODESCH Eclipses the INI

In fall 1970, shortly before Velasco Suárez took office as governor, he commissioned a fact-finding report on the condition of the indigenous in the highlands and in the Lacandón rainforest. The report pulled no punches and indirectly indicted the INI's failure to eradicate many timeworn forms of exploitation. Acaparadores still descended on indigenous sellers every morning as they entered San Cristóbal, commandeering their cabbage, cauliflower, squash, beans, oranges, apples, flowers, poultry, and even sheep and "throwing them a few coins, generally about 85 percent less than the normal price for the product." The ladino administrator at the municipal market charged the indigenous between two and four times the authorized fee to sell their goods. Indigenous caciques controlled transportation to and from San Cristóbal; passengers traveled "like animals, with as many as forty people standing in the back of a pickup with their packages." In San Cristóbal, indigenous passengers who took the "Lacandonia" bus line often received the kind of treatment that was meted out to African American passengers in the Jim Crow South. If they did not get onto the bus quickly, they were verbally abused and occasionally hit, and they were forced to give up their seats for "better-dressed" ladino passengers. Three organizations "appear to protect indigenous workers, but in fact exploit them": the STI (directed by Chamula caciques Agustín Méndez Gómez and Tuxum), the DGAI, and the state's Labor Arbitration Board (Junta Central de Conciliación y Arbitraje). The thirty-five clauses of the STI's collective bargaining contract were mostly ignored. Finally, the report noted that Chamula municipal president Juan Gómez Osob had indeed pocketed the money that had been collected to build the town hall a few years earlier. The report ended with a clarion call for the incoming governor to "urgently address" these matters.[2]

If conditions for the indigenous in and around San Cristóbal were deplorable, they might have been even worse in rural areas north, south, and east of the highlands. Peasants—both indigenous and ladino—had lost hope in the agrarian reform process and, one by one, broke with the official CNC and sought independent, collective, and democratic solutions to their problems. East of the highlands, in Ocosingo, catechists and Maoists helped organize ejido unions beginning in 1971; three years later, in a foreshadowing of future conflicts, the Mexican army would liquidate a cell of the Forces of National Liberation (Fuerzas de Liberación Nacional, or FLN) in the same large municipality. This guerrilla organization would ultimately spawn the EZLN. South of the highlands, in Venustiano Carranza, peasants invaded ranches belonging to local caciques, triggering a violent repression. North of San Cristóbal, in Simojovel, Tsotsil and Ch'ol resident debt peons invaded a number of private coffee plantations in 1971, then broke with the CNC and clashed with ranchers who were turning their land over to livestock.[3] Rural Chiapas was about to explode, and Governor Velasco Suárez knew it.

The governor launched PRODESCH in late 1971, claiming support from five UN entities, including the Food and Agriculture Organization (FAO), the

Educational, Scientific, and Cultural Organization (UNESCO), the International Children's Emergency Fund (UNICEF), the Department of Economic and Social Affairs (UNDESA), and the World Health Organization (WHO).[4] PRODESCH would usurp the CCI's role as a "coordinator" of thirteen federal government ministries. When announcing this initiative, the governor ignored the INI's Coordinating Center and made no mention of its historical role, although he warned darkly of "many obstacles, some detractors, and not a few enemies even among those who called themselves indigenistas and have made themselves immobile 'owners' of the matter that so deeply concerns us."[5]

PRODESCH's budget allowed it to work in more than two dozen Tsotsil, Tseltal, Tojolabal, and Ch'ol municipalities in central and northern Chiapas. On paper, its investment in agriculture, communications, education, and health from 1972 to 1976 was impressive. A PRODESCH report claimed that corn farmers who received technical assistance saw yields increase by 292 percent; the road network more than doubled (and more than tripled in the highlands); the number of students enrolled in schools in its area of operations increased from 39,712 to 64,811; the number of people receiving immunizations grew by 800 percent; and seventy-one communities received electricity. This latter improvement allowed some farmers to pump water to irrigate their fields. Communities with electricity also installed electric corn grinders, which freed women to do other types of work.[6]

Because PRODESCH focused most of its projects in the Tsotsil and Tseltal highlands, Aguirre Beltrán decided to close the Coordinating Center in San Cristóbal in late 1971 and redirect its budget to open two new centers on the fringes of the INI's traditional area of influence: Bochil, west of the highlands, and Ocosingo, to the east, where the INI planned to work with the local Tseltal population and other indigenous groups that were settling in the Lacandón rainforest.[7]

The year 1972 was a fateful one for the CCI in San Cristóbal. Starting in January, its new director, Ricardo Ferré d'Amaré, was charged with handing over all of its remaining development projects—except education—to PRODESCH. Most of the INI's commitments to local indigenous populations fell by the wayside. Ferré responded to requests for piped water, roads, and clinics with the rather shocking admission that "since this center no longer has funds to help indigenous communities, it cannot grant the aid requested."[8] The fate of the medical clinic at La Libertad is a case in point. Here, where the INI promoted land reform in the 1950s and enjoyed some of its greatest successes, the Tseltal authorities felt betrayed. As they wrote in June 1972, "we've wasted a lot of time waiting for the Director to come to La Libertad and formally hand the clinic over to a new nurse.... We need to know who will tend to us, because as you know, for us, illness doesn't take a vacation. If you cannot grant us our wishes, we will immediately send a telegram to Mexico City so that they can resolve this matter."[9]

True to their word, one month later, they took their case all the way up to Aguirre Beltrán in Mexico City. "Why does the INI abandon us now?" they asked, "especially since we now understand that medicine cures the illnesses that afflict us."

> We knew the founders of the INI, back in 1951. They were caring and very friendly toward the parents and children when they visited our communities. We especially remember Prof. Fidencio Montes Sánchez, Director of Education, and Prof. Salvatierra, Education Inspector.... We think that the indigenistas in the 1950s really worked for the indigenous. They never treated us like this Mister Ricardo Ferré. We accomplished many things with them. We were baldíos and resident debt peons, and they helped us get our land, "La Libertad," where we grow our crops and live.... We can prove that with our efforts, we laid out the streets of our town, we built our school, our clinic, a monument to the Mexican flag, and the municipal building. We built all of this ourselves. Men, women, and students worked Saturdays and Sundays carrying rocks, sand, lime, and wood on our backs.

The people of La Libertad felt that their sweat-equity entitled them to basic services, and two decades of work with the INI had given them the self-confidence necessary to work the system and make their needs known. "We ask that the INI continue working with us. When the state government arrives, the INI can leave, but no sooner."[10]

But CCI director Ferré had already shuttered the Coordinating Center and sent most of its employees and equipment to either Bochil or Ocosingo. By July 1, Ferré had left Chiapas to become director of the new Coordinating Center in La Huasteca (in Huijutla, Hidalgo), and all that remained at La Cabaña was the fledgling School of Regional Development.[11]

The School of Regional Development

Viewed in retrospect, the EDR was perhaps the INI's last great opportunity to reclaim its bragging rights as the Western Hemisphere's leader in indigenista policy. Planning for the school began in June 1971 as part of the INI's attempt to respond to its critics and support the populist politics of the Echeverría administration. Aguirre Beltrán proposed a national center to train regional development specialists like bilingual cultural promoters, nurses, social workers, and other professionals who would work in indigenous areas. Aguirre's center would also provide one year of university-level training for anthropologists, doctors, agronomists, veterinarians, lawyers, and others—presumably employees and future employees of INI Coordinating Centers—who were about to direct regional development programs of their own.[12]

In September 1971, Aguirre called a meeting of some of the INI's most seasoned hands (Alejandro Marroquín, Agustín Romano, and Alfonso Villa Rojas) as well as several of Mexico's brightest critical anthropologists, a few of whom had recently accepted posts in the federal government: Guillermo Bonfil Batalla, Salomón Nahmad Sittón, Ángel Palerm, and Arturo Warman. Together, they modified and radicalized Aguirre's proposal and created what became known as the School of Regional Development, which would operate on the grounds of the Coordinating Center in San Cristóbal. Villa Rojas opened the school in late 1971 but was unable to hire teachers for the School of Anthropology, leaving important gaps in the curriculum. Villa Rojas was no radical, and so his remarks concerning these gaps suggest the degree to which the critical anthropologists had reshaped Aguirre's initial proposal. "We would have liked to hear something about 'The democratic opening and the appeasement of students'; 'The national bourgeoisie and internal colonialism'; 'Class conflict and underdevelopment'; 'Marxist analysis and the indigenous problem'; and other themes of great social relevance," Villa Rojas wrote. "For now we can only hope that these grave deficiencies can be corrected in the future, when the School is better consolidated and has hired the necessary number of teachers."[13]

In July 1972, Villa Rojas returned to Mexico City, and Mercedes Olivera Bustamante became director of the school. The appointment of Olivera, one of the magníficos, might be considered a surprise move. Her chapter in *De eso que llaman antropología mexicana* accused both the INAH and the INI of abandoning their commitment to research. As director of the EDR, Olivera would get her opportunity to support research and train the next generation of Mexican indigenistas.

Olivera and her team immediately began searching for indigenous collaborators in Chiapas's Ch'ol municipalities in the north of the state, like Sabanilla, Tila, and Tumbalá, where the INI had never worked. As she wrote to a teacher in Tila, "we are trying to improve upon the old promoters, turning them into agents of politicization (in addition to literacy and Spanish instructors, etc.)." She added, "to avoid the problem of corruption and ensure that the promoters are truly linked to their communities, we have agreed that the community members should choose their representatives."[14] Olivera also changed the curriculum at the School for the Formation of Promoters to nurture ethnic and class consciousness among the students, to train them as researchers of indigenous history and culture, to help them become community organizers, and to train them to teach in both Spanish and their mother tongue.[15] Among the school's other goals:

1. Make the indigenous conscious of their historical and social reality and the possibilities of their own development.
2. Disconnect them from the dominant culture and orient them toward the revaluation of their own culture.
3. Make them aware of the problem of their marginalization and encourage them to react and find channels for the solution of their problems.
4. Inspire them to feel the possibility of change and improvement through collective effort.
5. Form truly indigenous institutions that will help them emerge from their marginalization and take their own place in the nation.[16]

On a theoretical level, Olivera knew exactly what she wanted to do. But the practice of training bilingual promoters was more complicated than she expected. "Some communities selected young women to be promotoras and sent them to La Cabaña for training," she said in a 2009 interview. "We soon realized that many of them, eight or ten, did not know how to read or write. They were functional illiterates with one year of schooling; some were monolingual [in Ch'ol]. They weren't ready yet to become promotoras. We agreed to teach literacy in their communities so that the following year they'd be eligible to begin training. So we sent them back to their communities with letters explaining our commitment." But the response of the young women's parents caught Olivera by surprise. "They would not accept their daughters back into their communities because they had been away for a week, in San Cristóbal." Olivera explained that the girls could not have their stipends until they first learned to read and write. "But the parents said, 'Now you have to decide what to do with them. Put them to work in the houses, because we are not going to receive them.'" Eventually, Olivera convinced some parents to take their daughters back, but four young women were not allowed to return. Two ended up staying with Olivera for several months. Olivera remarked that "the experience had a great impact on me."[17]

In the course of the interview, Olivera related another "very powerful learning experience" with the young indigenous men and women who were training to become promoters. "We had just spent three months discussing the recuperation of their cultures. One day their stipend money arrived. Three months' worth." So the students went into town to spend some of their money. When they returned to La Cabaña, "some of the young women had cut off their braids, some got perms or wore miniskirts. The men bought dark sunglasses, loud radios, and cowboy boots." After the shock subsided, Olivera realized that "we cannot throw up a wall and block out Western cultural forms," that in Mexican society, the markings of prestige are very Western. Teaching to value one's culture was simply not enough; teaching and recovering forms of community organization and collective identity were equally important. Taken together, these experiences "taught us how difficult it was to implement a different kind of project."[18]

Olivera's plan to reshape Mexican indigenismo was even most clearly manifested in the School of Anthropology. She quickly hired additional professors and announced that, starting in January 1973, the school would offer a one-year program for advanced undergraduates and a two-year master's program in social anthropology with an emphasis on indigenismo. The curriculum for both programs included coursework on ethnohistory and ecology in Tseltal zones, colonialism, dependency and underdevelopment in Latin America, regional planning, Tseltal language training, and months of fieldwork in Tseltal communities in Ocosingo. Both programs involved Tseltals in the collection of data as well as the diagnosis of problems and the search for solutions. As Olivera noted, "this kind of participation was aimed at creating an ethnic and class consciousness in the indigenous and, fundamentally, putting research at the service of the community."[19]

In short, the EDR presented itself as an antidote to the INI's more paternalistic policies and offered itself as a tool to help indigenous people "find their own paths to liberate themselves from dependency and domination" so that "the indigenous communities are the ones that benefit directly from the research and manage their own economic, social, and cultural development."[20] This experiment in "participatory indigenismo" represented a clear departure from the INI's development strategy of the previous two decades.

Was INI director Aguirre Beltrán on board with the EDR's ideological

FIGURE 11.1. The short-lived School of Regional Development. Director Mercedes Olivera Bustamante is in the second row, center, leaning to her right. Photographer unknown. Fototeca Nacho López, Comisión Nacional para el Desarrollo de los Pueblos Indígenas. 1972.

orientation? It would appear that he was. After all, he was the one who had invited anthropologists—some of them quite radical—to discuss and refine his proposal for the school in September 1971. He had approved its Marxist content, and he surely had a hand in selecting a magnífico to run the school. However, in late 1972, Aguirre suddenly decided to withdraw his support of the school and its ambitious director, Mercedes Olivera.

The detonator came in November 1972, when the EDR hosted a three-day meeting of the directors, assistant directors, and anthropologists of the twelve existing Coordinating Centers. Some of Mexico's most renowned anthropologists presented or commented on the proposal to change Mexican indigenismo, including magníficos Guillermo Bonfil, Enrique Valencia, and Arturo Warman.[21] Anthropologist Carlos Incháustegui clearly welcomed this opportunity to discuss the INI's problems. "We have always engaged in self-criticism in our institution, we have always evaluated our activities, but almost always in private," he wrote. "Unfortunately, there was a time when internal critique was considered a sign of disloyalty to the Institute or its principles. Now that we are being asked for our opinions and participation, years of silence weigh heavily."[22]

The INI was at a theoretical and practical crossroads. Some indigenistas argued that the INI should continue to strive to integrate indigenous peoples into the dominant Mexican nationality, while others believed that it should further the cause of ethnic revindication and pluralism. Still others felt that the INI should help the indigenous liberate themselves through the class struggle. A satirical bulletin distributed at the time of this meeting captures the spirit of the times and points to the intense debate over the INI's role. In the excerpt below, a bartender is interviewing one of the seven dwarves. (In this satire, Mercedes Olivera is almost certainly Snow White.)

"Look," the dwarf said,

we are worried by countless problems: pollution, the war in Vietnam, the demographic explosion, traffic issues, the reelection of Fidel Velázquez,[23] juvenile delinquency, the Chinese-Japanese rapprochement, the diminishing infallibility of the Pope, the return of Perón to Argentina.... And now you come along with the brilliant idea of asking me what is indigenismo.
[...]
You see, before, the situation was simple; only three letters—I. N. I.— and we all knew very well what it meant, from Guachochi to Tehuacán.[24]
But now there are so many doubts that a cousin of ours in Valladolid got ill upon learning what the INI has become. Thanks to interviewers like you, mister bartender, it should be called INDIA or Nationalist Institute of Denunciation of Injustices and Abuses. The dwarf from the southern Isla Negra (now in Paris)[25] says that "the history of poetry is the history of accusations," but here we aren't writing poems. We're mining copper with pick and shovel.[26]

The future trajectory of Mexican indigenismo seemed to hang in the balance at this high-stakes meeting. According to one observer, "a good number of theologians, anarchists, and young anthropologists attended, all in support of the new ideas that Olivera endorsed."[27] They were countered by Aguirre Beltrán and the directors of the Coordinating Centers, who continued to support the thesis of assimilation and national integration. Aguirre eventually accused the young radicals of proposing "a regional, exclusively indigenous structure based on ethnic consciousness. This leads to the creation of a caste structure and represents, in my judgment, a regression." To illustrate his point, he drew parallels with the Black Power, Native American, and Chicano movements in the United States. "These movements emerged as a response to the tremendous discrimination and exploitation that their members experience, but this is not the model that we should follow. They are desperate racist responses to the discrimination that exploits them."[28]

Olivera, for her part, claimed in an interview that the meeting proceeded as planned until Chiapas governor Velasco Suárez entered the meeting hall, uninvited.[29] According to Olivera, Aguirre was furious. Olivera may have fanned the flames when she distributed a document at the meeting that reflected months of collective consultation over how to reorient the indigenista project. She hoped to discuss the document with all of the CCI's directors. "Perhaps we were naïve to think that Aguirre agreed with our program," she noted, because her proposal "cayó como una bomba" (fell like a bomb).[30]

The impact of the November meeting was not immediately felt. Days later, the EDR's assistant director, Manuel Esparza, continued to plan for upcoming courses. He sent invitations to guest lecturers including Guillermo Bonfil, Friedrich Katz, Alejandro Marroquín, Andrés Medina, and Margarita Nolasco. School director Olivera, for her part, penned a fascinating mea culpa to Aguirre Beltrán that stressed her desire to continue within the INI to reshape indigenista policy. Aguirre later allowed part of the letter to be published. "I have received from you, now, the greatest lesson that a disciple could ever receive," she wrote. "I realize that I have much to learn from you and from the CCI directors, especially those that have dedicated a good part of their lives and their daily effort to indigenista practice." Then, she appeared to apologize on behalf of an entire generation of critical anthropologists.

> Our research has allowed us to shield ourselves with theory instead of bravely confronting practice. . . . This made it easy to critique indigenismo. . . . Our presence in the INI forms part of a contradiction . . . that is part of a complex historical process. If we know how to take advantage of this experience, if we work with the humility and perseverance that you have taught us and ask of us, if our position continues to be open to critique and self-criticism, it is probable that a positive theoretical breakthrough will emerge.[31]

Weeks later, however, it became clear that the EDR in its current form was doomed and that Olivera's job was in jeopardy. First, the EDR lost control over the stipends that it had promised students. Then, the INI cancelled the master's program in social anthropology. The EDR retracted the invitations that it had sent to guest lecturers just one month earlier.[32] The future of the school was already in doubt when Olivera left for the Christmas holiday. When she returned to San Cristóbal, "they didn't let me enter La Cabaña. The administrator had his orders. And they had already sacked my office." The director's house, where Olivera resided, "had also been cleaned out."³³ The INI directors in Mexico City had forced her hand. Olivera had no choice but to resign. She and some of the EDR's former teachers and students later joined rural theater brigades linked to the National Company of Popular Subsistence (Compañía Nacional de Subsistencias Populares, or CONASUPO). The troupes toured the indigenous countryside presenting plays that depicted scenes of class and/or ethnic exploitation until they too were deemed a threat and the brigades were disbanded.³⁴

Several years later, when Aguirre Beltrán was no longer INI director, Olivera wrote about her experience at the helm of the EDR in an official INI publication. "We recognize our lack of tact and our political inexperience," she wrote. "We placed ourselves at complete odds with the political line of official indigenismo, our boss. While we had planned to work to instill ethnic and class consciousness in the indigenous . . . and to encourage them to participate in the transformation of society, for the INI the object of the school was limited to development and Spanish language training." Olivera wrote that the INI "considered it unpatriotic to formulate special programs for the indigenous population because it threatened national unity."³⁵ If Aguirre only meant for the EDR to train bilingual promoters, anthropologists, and others to facilitate government programs and assimilate ethnic groups, as Olivera claimed, why did he allow the project to radicalize in 1971? And why did he name a critical anthropologist to direct the school?

Asked in 2009 why she had agreed to work for the INI, Olivera replied that she accepted the offer to direct the EDR because she saw it "as a challenge and as an opportunity to renew indigenista policy." Olivera admits that she and her cohort may have misread Aguirre when he named several magníficos to key posts in the SEP and the INI. "I thought Dr. Aguirre Beltrán was giving us the opportunity to put our ideas to practice," she said. In retrospect, she came to think that "the opposite was the case. He wanted to prove that integrationist indigenismo was correct."³⁶ Or, perhaps Aguirre was simply trying to co-opt them.

After Mercedes Olivera tendered her resignation, the School of Regional Development underwent a major reorientation. It had no director for the first eight months of 1973 but was administered—from a distance—by the Centro Coordinador Indigenista Tzotzil,³⁷ which reopened in early 1973 with a skeletal crew. The school continued to train bilingual cultural promoters, including now Tojolabals who had at least a fifth- or sixth-grade education. But none of the courses featured Marxist content or covered politically sensitive topics like colonialism or underdevelopment. Instead, the school offered seminars like "The Supernatural World of the Indigenous," delivered by Harvard Project director Evon Vogt, his student Jane Collier, and others; and "Crafts and Indigenous Art," by graphic artist Alberto Beltrán.[38]

By 1976, as the Echeverría presidency drew to a close, the School of Regional Development was a shadow of its former self, a crippled institution that bore no resemblance to the school that had caused such a stir just four years earlier. Its activities were exceedingly modest. Aspiring cultural promoters wrote biographies of local heroes, toured schools, and administered questionnaires. The school also provided satisfactory lodging for the indigenous who stayed the night at La Cabaña. As assistant director Manuel Arias Pérez modestly concluded in one biannual report, "some of the work that we have accomplished will probably be useful for the young indigenous people in the municipalities."[39]

Caciquismo and Democracy in Chamula, Round 2

The School of Regional Development was a quixotic attempt to forge a new kind of indigenismo that might extirpate many of the "sins" of the INI's assimilationist model. While the school rose and quickly fell at La Cabaña, some of the negative outcomes of old-school indigenismo, like caciquismo and inequality, continued to feed tensions in the indigenous municipalities located just a few kilometers away. The expulsion of Padre Polo and the withdrawal of Misión Chamula from Chamula proper, detailed in chapter 9, ended the first round of conflict in the municipality. But more was to come. After a brief flirtation with democracy in indigenous municipalities, Governor Velasco Suárez and PRODESCH acquiesced to Chamula's "traditional" caciques. In the dramatic events that followed, the INI was a mere bystander, although not an entirely indifferent one, since the protagonists on both sides were former INI promoters.

Jan Rus suggests that while state and federal agencies had agreed to bail out the caciques—twice—in the late 1960s, nobody was satisfied with Chamula's leadership. Certainly the INI could not have been pleased, since the caciques' repression usually targeted other people educated and trained by the INI. The caciques had become a liability—they seemed too greedy, repressive, and incompetent. Bishop Samuel Ruiz helped convince Governor Velasco Suárez that he should ease out the "gangsters" via free elections in which dissidents would participate.[40] In fall 1970, following the governor's election, Chamula's dissidents ran an opposition candidate for the first time in the history of the municipality. The candidate, a former INI education promoter and SEP zone inspector named Mariano Gómez López, had the backing of Padre Polo and Misión Chamula, now based in San Cristóbal. The state government recognized Gómez López's victory, allowed a democratic election for municipal judge, and approved a new municipal secretary and scribes.[41] In 1971, state indigenistas (and PRI commissars) Ángel Robles and Pablo Ramírez intervened on behalf of poor Chamulas who had been forced by the caciques to take on expensive religious cargos. They also cracked down on moneylenders throughout the Chiapas highlands who routinely charged interest rates well above the 2 percent monthly allowed by law and who incarcerated debtors, their spouses, and even their siblings until debts were paid.[42] The reform effort continued into 1972, when PRODESCH investigated allegations that Tuxum and fourteen members of his clique of scribes-principales were responsible for arson, armed attacks, fraud, the suppression of religious freedom, and a 1965 murder. That year, Tuxum and four subordinates spent seven months in jail awaiting trial.[43]

But Chamula's imprisoned caciques still had plenty of allies in the municipality. The remaining elders and the municipal council essentially went on strike and threatened to withhold votes from the PRI in upcoming elections. Sensing the ground shifting under his feet, the new municipal president backed away from his original supporters and from Padre Polo. The state government soon determined that Chamula was ungovernable without its caciques. Tuxum and his associates were released, their accusers were jailed, and Padre Polo and the dissidents were warned that they would be killed if they ever set foot in Chamula again.[44]

Undaunted, Misión Chamula began to prepare for the 1973 municipal elections. It offered leadership training courses that familiarized young Chamulas with agrarian law, the legal code, and the rights and obligations enshrined in the Mexican Constitution. These Chamulas, much like the INI's original promoters, were taught to promote integral community development. But they were also being equipped to take back their communities; one of the stated goals of the courses was to give people the tools to resist the power of the caciques. Padre Polo also started a Tsotsil credit union, which gave Chamulas an alternative to usurious moneylenders like Tuxum. For the upcoming elections, dissidents chose as their candidate Domingo Díaz Gómez, a young merchant who had received leadership and catechist training from Misión Chamula. He was only twenty-three years old.[45]

The dissidents' hopes were soon dashed, however, because Governor

Velasco Suárez and PRODESCH were no longer interested in experiments with democracy in Chamula or anywhere else in the highlands. On primary election day, Díaz Gómez appeared to have more support than his opponent, a former INI promoter and SEP teacher named Agustín López Hernández. But PRODESCH secretary Pablo Ramírez began disqualifying opposition voters on spurious grounds—"the young, the married women, and the short, just because he felt like it," according to the dissidents—and then engaged in some electoral alchemy. When the final tally was announced, the cacique's candidate, López Hernández, was declared the winner. Chamula's dissidents wrote an impassioned letter of protest to the governor. "As you will understand, *Señor Gobernador*, 'we can't swallow this ox whole.' We might be indigenous, but we are not STUPID."[46]

When the general election was held in November, Díaz Gómez again ran against López Hernández. In the official nomination papers that he submitted to the PRI's state committee, the caciques' candidate pledged to oversee "traditional" fiestas and—in a submissive gesture—promised to "be close to all the authorities of the Government, so that they can help us to think better and resolve the problems that we have."[47] When it looked like Díaz Gómez would again win, PRODESCH director Ángel Robles announced that the votes would be tallied in the state capital, Tuxtla Gutiérrez. Ten days later, the "traditional" candidate, López Hernández, was declared the winner. Dissidents demanded another election, to take place on December 31, but they were foiled when the cacique puppet took office on December 30 backed by Ángel Robles, Pablo Ramírez, and army troops.[48] Díaz Gómez and his supporters—"liberationist" Catholics, Adventists, and Presbyterians—were jailed. Months later, when Chamulan dissidents tried to speak with President Echeverría during his visit to Chiapas, Governor Velasco Suárez cut them off, saying that "these people are well-known agitators."[49]

At this point, Padre Polo encouraged the dissidents to ally themselves with the opposition center-right Party of National Action (PAN). In June 1974, three PAN congressmen came to Chamula to open an office and issue direct challenges to the cacique clique, calling out by name Tuxum, Salvador Gómez Osob, Juan Gómez Osob, municipal president Agustín López Hernández, and others, along with PRODESCH officials Ángel Robles and Pablo Ramírez.[50] Meanwhile, the caciques' harassment of dissidents reached a new, more ominous level. By fall 1974, many dissidents felt that all legal and electoral avenues had been closed off to them, and they opted to seize Chamula's municipal palace by force. They chose a propitious moment to do so.[51]

The Congreso Indígena: Indigenous Protest at Two Levels

In 1973, Governor Velasco Suárez made plans to hold an Indigenous Congress (Congreso Indígena) in San Cristóbal the following year to commemorate the five-hundred-year anniversary of the birth of Chiapas's first resident bishop, Bartolomé de Las Casas.[52] In recognition of Bishop Samuel Ruiz's work with the indigenous (and, perhaps, of the PRI's negligible influence in the settler communities of eastern Chiapas), the governor asked for the bishop's organizational assistance. Thomas Benjamin writes that the Velasco Suárez administration envisioned a "colorful gathering . . . of politicians, academics, and Indian artisans and musicians who would promote tourism and confine questions of human rights to tedious discussions of history."[53] And if complaints did arise, Rus writes that PRODESCH and the governor "assumed most of the complaints would be directed at the 'old,' 'paternalistic' politics of the INI."[54]

But Bishop Ruiz was determined to turn the governor's populist ploy into a meaningful event where indigenous people set the agenda, spoke their own languages, shared common grievances, and explored common solutions. For years, Ruiz and his team of over one thousand indigenous catechists and diocesan workers had been encouraging indigenous communities to reflect on their social condition (*tomar conciencia*) and organize themselves collectively.[55] They would spend nearly a year preparing communities for the congress. Lawyers and former teachers and students of the EDR offered courses in history, agrarian law, and economics. Neil Harvey claims that "it was through such courses that community leaders gained a political education."[56]

During the congress—which ran from October 14 to 17, 1974—1,230 delegates (587 Tseltals, 330 Tsotsils, 152 Tojolabals, and 161 Ch'ols) denounced abuses and made demands on the state. Beginning with agrarian issues, they complained that their claims had languished in inefficient, corrupt bureaucracies for decades and demanded that the local agrarian reform offices hire indigenous employees. Ladino land invaders had turned workable land into pasture for livestock, which resulted in hunger and mass migration into the forest in search of land.[57] Commerce was controlled by ladinos and indigenous caciques; merchants and monopolists constituted "A GREAT PLAGUE."[58] As if channeling Alejandro Marroquín, they declared their intent to combat acaparadores by organizing themselves in cooperatives. On the topic of health, delegates demanded bilingual medical pluralism and a network of clinics and nurses "that know the two medicines, that of pills and that of plants."[59] On education, delegates denounced absentee teachers who refused to provide bilingual education. After finishing the sixth grade, students knew nothing but "become exploiters, following the example of their teachers."[60] The delegates also requested an indigenous newspaper in the four indigenous languages "by and for the indigenous to facilitate our own communication" and vowed to continue organizing their communities and linking their struggles with those of other indigenous groups in Mexico.[61]

It's hard to overstate the importance of the Congreso Indígena. For the first time in Chiapas, four distinct ethnic groups were invited to share grievances and lay the groundwork for future, collective action.[62] One of the conference organizers, Jesús Morales Bermúdez, observed at the time that the congress's dynamic and content "were more than the State could tolerate." Indigenous mobilization "would be difficult to control in the future." But for the time being, the state would have to turn its immediate attention—again—to Chamula.[63]

Just as the congreso was about to begin, 150 Chamulan dissidents tried to call national attention to their plight by taking their municipal seat by force. They were backed by Misión Chamula and two busloads of radical students from the state teachers college in Tuxtla.[64] This action greatly embarrassed the governor and PRODESCH's directors, who had hoped to use the congreso to showcase their supposedly more participatory, democratic approach to indigenismo. Hours later, soldiers regained control of the building; PRODESCH director Ángel Robles supervised the operation.[65] When congreso delegates denounced the situation to Governor Velasco Suárez, he became so angry that he withdrew from the congress and refused to attend the closing ceremonies.[66]

The state government's unconditional support for the caciques had become starkly clear. A week later, the caciques jailed roughly two dozen of their principal political rivals under the watchful supervision of PRODESCH officials Robles and Ramírez. The caciques also announced that the "evangelists"—as they now labeled the liberationist Catholics as well as the Protestants—represented a permanent offense to San Juan, Chamula's patron saint; they were blamed for several years of bad harvests. The only way to appease the saint and prevent an even more catastrophic harvest was to expel the dissidents.[67] Once the attacks began, desperate Adventists at Majomut hamlet went so far as to ask the general of the Thirty-First Military Zone (the state's highest-ranking army officer) to send a battalion to their community. "We can provide lodging and everything that your troops need during the time that you remain in our community, so that we are protected," they wrote. The help never arrived. A few days later, on November 2, the caciques unleashed more violence in two dozen Chamula hamlets. More than 250 dissidents were rounded up, beaten, and incarcerated. Many of their homes were sacked and burned.[68] Pablo Iribarrén writes that some of the victims were not even political dissidents; rather, they were economic rivals of Chamula's caciques.[69]

The caciques also targeted religious shrines that had sprung up in Chamula's dissident hamlets and had become important symbols of local autonomy. Liberationist Catholic shrines were destroyed in the presence of (former seminarian) Ángel Robles and Chamula's municipal president. The Adventists' church in Majomut was razed to the ground, and residents were tied up, beaten, and taken to Chamula's cabecera. The Adventists claimed that the attackers stole "some thirty Bibles that we were studying at the moment of our detention, twenty hymnals, chickens, turkeys, medicine, hatchets, machetes, and our harvest of corn and beans."[70] The caciques then turned their attention to the PAN. On November 4, they used megaphones to encourage people to destroy the PAN's office in Chamula and everything inside of it; the man who ran the office was beaten and incarcerated.[71] Tuxum's trucks ferried the victims down to San Cristóbal, where they were transferred to PRODESCH trucks and taken to Hernán Pedrero's Pujiltic sugarcane plantation with orders not to return for three months.[72] Two years later, Chamula's caciques unleashed a fresh round of violence against Chamula's Protestant population.[73] Rus characterizes these abuses as "even worse than in 1974, with scores of severe beatings and several rapes."[74] Estimates of the number of expelled range from six hundred to two thousand. Ultimately, this scenario was repeated (albeit with less violence) in other highland municipalities like Cancuc, Chalchihuitán, Chenalhó, Larráinzar, Mitontic, Tenejapa, and Zinacantán, where young, educated, reform-minded entrepreneurs and religious dissidents (often one and the same) also clashed with older, entrenched caciques.[75]

Thus began the pattern of violent expulsions that reached its maximum expression in the 1980s. Expulsion became the preferred way of ridding densely populated municipalities of anyone who challenged the political and economic authority of "traditional" caciques. Waves of expulsions continued into the 1990s and early twenty-first century. As Henri Favre notes, Chamula became recognized de facto as a kind of indigenous reservation that governed itself according to its own customs, clearly outside the law of the land.[76]

In fall 1974, when the first expulsions took place, the CCI's director in San Cristóbal was once again Agustín Romano. This steady, reliable indigenista, who had directed the center during its heyday in 1954–1956 and presided over its bureaucratic phase in the mid-1960s, must have wondered how the INI could have become so irrelevant. In a letter to Aguirre, he seems disconnected and uninformed, or, at least, unable to keep a handle on the events that swirled around him. "I have not intervened in these kinds of affairs. We believe that they fall under the jurisdiction of the state government and PRODESCH," he wrote, with apparent relief. "Nevertheless, these problems are a concern to the indigenous communities, and they affect our work."[77]

Conclusions

The early to mid-1970s were highly tumultuous in Chiapas, and PRODESCH was an institutional response to the growing restlessness of indigenous communities. Dizzy with success at the end of his six-year term of office, governor Velasco Suárez claimed that PRODESCH "had become the most positive reality that had ever been offered to the indigenous."[78] But its unflinching support for authoritarian caciques after 1972 may be its most enduring legacy.[79] State indigenistas worked with the promoter-caciques whom they inherited from the INI, and their manipulation of local politics was unprecedented. PRODESCH was also deeply corrupt. As June Nash notes, PRODESCH funds "often promoted private expenditures by local officials, with the new caciques of Zinacantán, Amatenango, and Tenejapa investing in consumer durables such as cement-block houses and television sets, as well as trucks used for personal profit."[80] Caciques also obtained and retained soft drink and liquor monopolies. And when they ran into political trouble, they could count on PRODESCH, the state PRI, and the governor to back them up.

PRODESCH also carried out no new land reform and created very few permanent jobs, and its transportation cooperatives served mainly to create a class of ruthless intermediaries.[81] Its critics point to an astonishing lack of coordination between the various state agencies that it supervised. PRODESCH built roads, dug wells, installed electricity, and built health centers, but often the net result was less than the sum of its parts. Critics also note that PRODESCH embarked on development projects without first studying the target community, and its projects tended to facilitate individual capital accumulation rather than collective advancement, which accelerated community polarization and ethnic and community disintegration.[82] If these critiques sound familiar, it is because they also described many INI development programs. Like other populist projects, PRODESCH barely outlasted its progenitor, Governor Velasco Suárez. Funding for PRODESCH programs declined; the program was renamed and subsequently disappeared in 1982.

For its part, the INI pivoted to respond to its critics at the national level. When it created the School of Regional Development, the INI demonstrated that it was sensitive to accusations that it was a paternalistic institution of cultural assimilation. It tried, briefly, to embrace pluralism and participatory indigenismo. The INI chose one of its sharpest critics to direct this school, a bold move that indicated an initial openness to change. However, there were limits to the INI's tolerance for participatory indigenismo. Following the 1968 student movement, and in the midst of a deepening economic crisis, the Mexican state was worried about its very survival and had little room to maneuver. Needless to say, the INI, as an instrument of this corporatist state, could hardly allow the School of Regional Development to "empower" indigenous people to seek their own solutions to their problems.

If the fate of the EDR pointed to the INI's inability to reform itself from within, the 1974 Congreso Indígena demonstrated that the Mexican state was losing its grip on the indigenous. Delegates from Chiapas's four largest ethnic groups vowed to work together to recover and obtain land, form cooperatives, eliminate intermediaries and usurers, combat caciquismo, and communicate via a newspaper printed in four languages. Their plans were foiled by a concerted PRI counterattack that involved co-optation and repression. The Congreso Indígena held its last meeting in March 1977. But participants and observers alike believe that the congress set an important precedent. Indigenous delegates set aside their differences, discussed common problems, and plotted common solutions. A class identity was beginning to emerge, alongside a pan-indigenous identity. Communities became politically active, and leaders stepped forward.[83] Even if the movement's momentum was temporarily lost, the next generation of indigenous leaders would build on the congress's success. In fact, as Antonio García de León writes, many illiterate congreso participants brought along their literate sons as "secretaries." Among those who attended the meetings in this capacity was Zapatista leader Tacho, who was just thirteen years of age at the time of the congreso. In a 1996 interview, Comandante Tacho referred to the Zapatista uprising as "the rebellion of the secretaries."[84]

Conclusion

It is difficult to draw hard and fast conclusions about Mexican indigenismo between 1951 and 1976 because the INI evolved along with national priorities, its budget, and the strength of local opposition. The indigenistas themselves had diverse objectives. In the early 1950s, those of Cardenista extraction embarked on a utopian nation-building mission, believing that they were finally bringing the Mexican Revolution to Chiapas. Indigenismo at that time was an explicitly antiracist, aspirational program of development and national integration, arguably the last great project of social engineering undertaken by Mexico's postrevolutionary government.

By the early 1960s, idealists had given way to pragmatists who had a more institutional, careerist vision. According to Salomón Nahmad, those who visited the INI's central offices in Mexico City had to discern whether employees were affiliated "with the utopians and the leftists or with the refined administrators."[1] For Mexico's federal government, which increasingly focused on the burgeoning, industrializing cities, indigenismo became part of a political project, a way to keep the countryside at bay while providing urban dwellers with cheap food and energy.

Assessing Mexican indigenismo is further complicated by the fact that its programs often pursued contradictory objectives and produced contradictory outcomes. In the 1950s, some indigenistas in Chiapas sought to implement collectivist strategies to improve the indigenous economy. But by the early 1960s, after most indigenistas had resigned themselves to their limitations, the consumer cooperatives had folded and the Teatro Petul appeared to sanction the inequalities that were becoming increasingly hard to ignore. INI Literacy Centers and schools taught students about their constitutional rights, but in the late 1960s the INI looked the other way when promoter-caciques violated those rights. In 1972, when the INI chose a critical anthropologist to run the School of Regional Development, it fired her less than a year later after she rather predictably charted a new course for Mexican indigenismo.

Viewed in hindsight, it's clear that the odds were always stacked against the INI. When the Centro Coordinador Indigenista Tzeltal-Tzotzil opened in 1951, there was little evidence of a state or federal presence in the region. Unable to "coordinate" nonexistent institutions, the INI began to offer the basic services that the federal and/or state government should have been providing all along. The indigenistas' most important allies were the hastily trained Tseltals and Tsotsils who served as bilingual cultural promoters in their home communities. They used negotiation and persuasion to open dozens of Literacy Centers and promote the INI's economic development and infrastructure programs. In eastern Chiapas, indigenistas facilitated land reform in several Tseltal communities, and INI education programs were warmly embraced.

The CCI in Chiapas may have reached its apogee in 1955. In that year, Alfonso Villa Rojas published an article in *América Indígena* that touted the spirit of "constant self-criticism" at the CCI. "At no time is there an attempt to hide failures, because it is understood that this is the work of pioneers." Imbued with the mística of the times, Villa Rojas remarked that ENAH's indigenista training program would be relocated to La Cabaña because the CCI "constitutes Mexico's most important center of managed social transformation.... The region represents a true anthropological laboratory where the student has the opportunity to observe in vivo the most varied cultural forms as well as their diverse reactions to the penetration of Western civilization."[2]

That same year, the INI's heroic struggle with the Chiapas state government and the Pedrero alcohol monopoly ended in compromise. Negotiations with governor Efraín Aranda Osorio reined in the worst abuses of the monopoly, but it is no coincidence that the INI simultaneously suspended Alejandro Marroquín's ambitious survey of the highlands. The INI also shelved its utopian plans to industrialize the region and work with ladino populations, with serious implications for the national indigenista blueprint.

After 1955, the indigenistas soft-pedaled their economic development programs and focused increasingly on the indigenous themselves. The fortuitous emergence of the Teatro Petul helped support the INI's education, vaccination, hygiene, and clean water campaigns. CCI doctors took steps to accommodate the medically plural environment in which they operated. As demand for schooling slowly grew, budget limitations forced the INI to outsource its education program to the SEP, and the indigenistas gradually lost control over the bilingual cultural promoters, their most important agents of change.

During the "long sixties," the INI faced strong political headwinds locally and in Mexico City. Even if the federal government had wanted a strong INI—which was doubtful, especially during the Díaz Ordaz years (1964–1970)—it is perfectly clear that state governments and powerful local interests favored just the opposite.[3] The CCI's agriculture and livestock programs remained necessarily modest. Shifting national priorities and local opposition took land and labor reform off the table, and the indigenistas struggled to provide Tseltal and Tsotsil farmers with the credit they needed. Many of the CCI's most creative collaborators resigned from their posts, and the INI struggled to attract high-caliber replacements. Late in the decade, the CCI's Forestry Department suffered stinging defeats at the hands of ladino logging companies, and the indigenistas found themselves tending to the collateral damage of the federal government's hydroelectric projects.

Meanwhile, INI promoters-turned-caciques tightened their political and economic grip on their municipalities. The INI has rightly been blamed for aiding and abetting caciquismo in Chiapas and elsewhere, but this outcome is hardly surprising in the context of a profoundly undemocratic corporatist state and a political culture based on patronage and repression.

By the time presidential candidate Luis Echeverría made indigenismo one of the pillars of his populist platform, Mexican anthropology and the INI were in deep crisis. The anthropological critique came at a pivotal time, forever severing the five-decades-long relationship that had bound Mexican anthropology to the needs of the Mexican state. In Chiapas, the INI's historic Coordinating Center made way for the state government's better-funded PRODESCH. La Cabaña played host to the ephemeral School of Regional Development, the INI's daring, desperate attempt to answer its critics.

The Coordinating Center in San Cristóbal reopened in 1973 at a time when the INI was finally enjoying robust budgets. It largely served as a training center for those who would staff the dozens of new Coordinating Centers that the INI was opening throughout rural Mexico. But INI theory and practice had become anachronistic, unable to keep pace with autonomous indigenous organization and mobilization. The INI's star indigenous puppeteer, Teodoro Sánchez, led a team that trained three people from each CCI in the art of puppetry. Given the success of the Teatro Petul in the Chiapas highlands in the 1950s and early 1960s, perhaps the INI cannot be blamed for trying to recapture the magic of days gone by. But the indigenistas would learn, to their great dismay, that the puppets could not replicate their success in other regions of Mexico where the indigenous had already been exposed to radio and television.[4] As the INI whiled away its time training puppeteers, indigenous people began to join independent unions and political movements. This became abundantly clear at the 1974 Congreso Indígena in San Cristóbal.

The Echeverría administration, meanwhile, came to selectively embrace "participatory indigenismo" as a means of responding to and channeling indigenous political mobilization. President Echeverría set in motion at least sixty-five regional indigenous conferences, and the CNC urged each indigenous ethnic group in Mexico to form a Supreme Council (Consejo Supremo) and send delegates to the First National Congress of Indigenous Peoples.[5] Luz Olivia Pineda argues that in Chiapas, the selection of delegates to the councils was hardly democratic; the CNC and the state government chose them—mostly bilingual teachers—with no input from the communities.[6] But María Muñoz has recently argued that "the organization of the first National Congress of Indigenous Peoples and the regional indigenous congresses of 1975 that preceded it [was] neither wholly independent nor completely state controlled. Instead, negotiation was constant" and provided indigenous people with the opportunity to shape official indigenismo and press their demands on a sympathetic federal government.[7]

During the administration of president José López Portillo (1976–1982), the INI officially disavowed its long-standing commitment to cultural assimilation. Its new director, Ignacio Ovalle Fernández, stated that indigenous communities had an "indisputable right" to preserve their ethnic identity, which was "a special part of the personality of a plural nation like ours." Ovalle pledged to end policies "that aimed at homogenization and cultural mestizaje, as well as paternalistic measures that supplanted the initiative of the communities themselves."[8] But the INI also lost its autonomy; it was folded into the National Plan for Depressed Zones and Marginalized Groups (Coordinación General del Plan Nacional para Zonas Deprimidas y Grupos Marginados, or COPLAMAR) and became merely the executor of presidential social and economic policy in indigenous regions. No longer guided by anthropologists or anthropological principles, the INI forever relinquished its place at the vanguard of hemispheric indigenismo.[9]

Indigenismo's Legacy in Chiapas and Mexico

In the end, what sort of impact did indigenismo have on the intended targets of indigenista policy—the indigenous—and the practitioners of this policy—the indigenistas? And did indigenismo deliver the kind of political, economic, and cultural results that the Mexican state wanted to see?

THE INDIGENOUS

Indigenistas proclaimed that INI projects would develop entire communities. In the Chiapas highlands, however, the evidence overwhelmingly suggests otherwise. Ulrich Köhler noted in 1963 that the INI's economic development programs were given less importance than the education and public health programs and "had barely passed the experimental phase."[10] In summer 1967, sixteen years after the CCI first opened its doors, the CCI's director had to ask Alfonso Caso for a loan in order to buy ten tons of corn each week to alleviate hunger in parts of Oxchuc, Chenalhó, and Pantelhó. The indigenous could not feed themselves, much less export to a regional or national market. Like Fidencio Montes eleven years earlier, and in spite of the CCI's attempts to stimulate agricultural production, education subdirector Ignacio León Pacheco declared that hunger was still the single most important factor undermining education programs.[11]

Much has changed in the ensuing decades, but grinding poverty, malnutrition, and marginalization persist in the Coordinating Center's original zone of operations. In 2011, sixty years after the CCI opened its doors, Daniel Villafuerte published work showing that Chiapas was still Mexico's poorest state; 78.5 percent of Chiapanecos lived in moderate or extreme poverty.[12] More to the point, the twelve indigenous municipalities in the Coordinating Center's original zone of operations ranked among the state's poorest, as shown in table C.1.[13]

If the INI failed to lift entire communities and municipalities out of poverty and extreme poverty, how did indigenous individuals fare? As discussed in chapter 9, INI development programs fostered a small indigenous bourgeoisie. Some promoters and former promoters ended up controlling stores, transportation cooperatives, and even municipalities. Ricardo Pozas stated in an interview that Aguirre Beltrán, Romano, and others promoted an individualistic indigenismo that taught the promoters to look out for themselves. He was not surprised that many of them had become caciques. "They were never taught to take interest in their own pueblo; there was no effort to prepare them so that the whole community would benefit," he said. "They began to distinguish themselves from the rest of the population."[14]

These self-serving beneficiaries of Mexican indigenismo have attracted perhaps a disproportionate amount of scholarly attention in recent years. Often overlooked is the fact that indigenista policy also empowered thousands of

TABLE C.1. Chiapas's poorest municipalities (out of a total of 119) (2011).

		PERCENTAGE OF TOTAL POPULATION IN POVERTY (COMBINES EXTREME AND MODERATE POVERTY)	PERCENTAGE OF TOTAL POPULATION IN EXTREME POVERTY
1.	Cancuc (not a municipality in 1951)	94.7	80.5
3.	Chalchihuitán	96.8	79.8
7.	Larráinzar	96.3	73
8.	Chanal	96.1	69.1
11.	Mitontic	95.9	71.8
14.	Tenejapa	95.7	65.2
15.	Chenalhó	95.6	72.3
16.	Chilón	95.3	70.6
20.	Zinacantán	94.9	64.8
21.	Chamula	94.8	69.7
29.	Oxchuc	93.5	62
34.	Huixtán	92.9	60.5

Source: Villafuerte Solís, "La catástrofe neoliberal en Chiapas," 316–19.

indigenous to work toward the improvement of their communities as cultural promoters and as teachers, nurses, mechanics, and agronomists. Other beneficiaries of INI programs include the tens of thousands of indigenous children and adults who were educated in INI schools and countless others who benefited from the INI's infrastructure programs, its public health and hygiene campaigns, and its numerous modest innovations to stimulate local economic development.

The INI also instructed the indigenous about their rights as Mexican citizens. Mercedes Olivera recalls that in 2001, the INI held a simple ceremony in San Cristóbal to commemorate the fiftieth anniversary of the

FIGURE C.1. Girls at an INI school. Photographer unknown. Fototeca Nacho López, Comisión Nacional para el Desarrollo de los Pueblos Indígenas. 1968.

founding of the Coordinating Center. Among those in attendance were Olivera and five elderly indigenous leaders who had been part of the first generation of cultural promoters. During his presentation, one of the indigenous men directed his comments at Olivera. His remarks, she wrote, "moved me profoundly." He said:

> You were not in agreement with the INI; you thought everything had to be criticized. But look, there is something about the INI that I hold in my heart. It showed us how to recognize our enemies; the wealthy farmers and large landowners. And we struggled against them until the government gave us their lands.

"Despite what was questionable about the integrationist policies," Olivera notes in a recent reflection, "[the INI] had produced a transformation in the lives, consciousness, and hopes of indigenous peoples—changes that in many cases were the foundation for further struggles. But this can only be appreciated with the distance that time provides us."[15]

THE INDIGENISTAS

When Alejandro Marroquín implied in 1971 that the indigenistas had fared better than the indigenous, he was only partly right. While it's true that many bureaucrats carved out comfortable careers in the INI's central offices, for most INI employees, indigenismo was not an easy, comfortable, or well-remunerated career. During the "long sixties," in fact, salaries were so low that the Coordinating Center could not attract quality teachers or anthropologists. Indigenismo could also be a political minefield. The CCI's second director, Ricardo Pozas, left the INI due to irreconcilable professional and personal differences with Alfonso Caso; nearly twenty years later, Mercedes Olivera paid a high price for testing the limits of INI theory and practice. So did Salomón Nahmad. As director of the INI in 1982, he tried to implement a policy of indigenous development (*etnodesarrollo*) that gave indigenous groups administrative control of indigenismo. In October of that year, he was apprehended, held incommunicado for three days, and then sent to jail, where he spent more than five months. After Mexican and foreign intellectuals and indigenous groups lobbied the Mexican government on his behalf, he was released and the charges dropped. He had been formally accused of fraud, but it appears that he committed his real "crime" when he placed Yaquis in charge of their Coordinating Center in Sonora.[16]

Indeed, directing the INI might have been one of Mexico's most complicated jobs, and it may have even disqualified aspirants for other posts. For the politically ambitious Alfonso Caso, the INI was a dead end. A precandidate for the presidency himself in 1951, Caso backed the wrong candidate in the 1964 presidential election; six years later, after learning that his tenure at the helm of the INI had ended, he suddenly died. His successor, Gonzalo Aguirre Beltrán, wanted to become governor of his native Veracruz after directing the INI but instead retreated back to academia.[17] So while it may be the case that the INI served as a step on the bureaucratic ladder for some, an indigenista career may have disqualified others who aspired to the highest offices in the land.

For their part, indigenous indigenistas often took great personal risks when they agreed to work for the INI and promote its policies of modernization and assimilation. Indigenismo was certainly their ticket to a more comfortable, prosperous life for themselves and their families, but most of them also truly believed in the indigenista cause. Among the indigenous indigenistas profiled in this book, Zapotec educator Fidencio Montes spent his entire career with the INI, establishing and supervising education programs in a variety of indigenous regions. Tsotsil puppeteer Teodoro Sánchez worked for the CCI for twenty-five years, promoting modern medicine, hygiene, clean water campaigns, and education. Agapito Núñez Tom, who helped Tseltal baldíos create La Libertad, inspired more than fifty of his students to become teachers or cultural promoters.[18] Otomí anthropologist Maurilio Muñoz Basilio helped open three INI Coordinating Centers and served as the first indigenous director of the CCI in San Cristóbal (1969–1970 and 1977).[19] These indigenous men and many, many others personified the mística indigenista and, over the years, became some of the INI's staunchest supporters.

THE MEXICAN STATE

Mexican indigenismo failed to develop the Chiapas highlands in a transformative, meaningful way and never accomplished Caso's goal of eradicating what he called the "Indian problem." In this respect, the INI failed the Mexican state. Yet one may argue just as persuasively that the Mexican state failed the INI by denying it the resources and the political backing needed to achieve its goals.

In other respects, however, Mexico's INI carried out successful public policy. The INI was the first governmental institution in Latin America to apply the social sciences to indigenous development. In the 1950s, it was ahead of its time in its approach to language instruction and its use of indigenous agents of change. After a period of trial and error, its approach to preventive medicine was decades ahead of what other Latin American countries were doing. The INI also promoted Mexico's official mestizo nationalism until critical anthropologists challenged and then overturned that paradigm in the 1970s. The INI was a nationalist project, so much so that Aguirre Beltrán told renowned anthropologist Ángel Palerm that his Spanish (Catalan) origins disqualified him from ever directing a Coordinating Center.[20]

The INI also lent prestige to Mexico on the international stage. Beginning in 1959, Mexico's ENAH began hosting a two-year program on the applied social sciences for the Organization of American States (OAS). For Juan Comas, writing in 1964, the INI was still at the vanguard of hemispheric indigenismo. "The fact that the project is based in Mexico . . . shows that our country can offer the rest of the continent's Indo-mestizo nations a valued experience using applied social anthropology to solve the problems of incorporation and integration of aboriginal groups and communities to their respective nationality."[21] That same year, the Mexican government, the Pan-American Union, and the OAS agreed to a joint program to train personnel to promote the modernization of indigenous communities. Students spent the first year (1965) at the INI's Coordinating Center in San Cristóbal and the second year (1966) in Peto, Yucatán; INI personnel provided the instruction. This program was open to students from all member states and offered instruction in applied anthropology, cultural assimilation, and the theory behind the CCIs.[22]

Still, the inescapable fact is that Mexican indigenismo fell far short of its goals. Indigenistas overestimated their ability to induce and manage change in the countryside and oversold their ability to resolve the Indian "problem." To quote Köhler, "the INI certainly did not practice the kind of systematic cultural engineering that one might expect" from an institute that devoted itself to managed cultural change.[23] And while it's true that INI programs in Chiapas and elsewhere resulted in reduced infant mortality rates, increased life expectancy, enhanced educational opportunities, increased crop output, and improved infrastructure, these outcomes were observed throughout rural Mexico, including in places where the INI was *not* involved.[24]

The INI's much-maligned programs of cultural assimilation and integration are similarly hard to assess because it is difficult to separate out the INI's efforts and results from the secular, modernizing trends that have influenced Mexico since the 1950s. It is difficult to ascertain whether the gradual diminution of the most outrageous racist practices in the Chiapas highlands can be attributed to the INI's efforts—which included conferences, legal action, puppet shows, and parades through San Cristóbal on national holidays—or to other factors, including the strength of indigenous organizations and the growing awareness of human rights issues. Tseltals and Tsotsils may have taken on identities as Mexicans, but they also became *more* conscious of their ethnic identities, not less. Some municipalities have even undergone a process of "reindianization." After Tsotsils in Larráinzar began expelling ladinos from their municipality in 1974, the percentage of nonindigenous speakers dropped notably in other nearby municipalities, including Chalchihuitán, Venustiano Carranza, Chenalhó, Huixtán, Mitontic, Simojovel, Tenejapa, and Teopisca.[25] In numerical terms, today there are more self-identifying Tseltals and Tsotsils than ever before in history. Manuel Gamio and Alfonso Caso, who so often predicted the resolution and disappearance of the "Indian problem," would be shocked by the sheer number and the cultural vitality of Tseltals and Tsotsils residing in the hamlets, towns, and cities of Chiapas today.

Last of all, we consider whether the INI advanced the Mexican state's political agenda. As some critics have noted, indigenismo became a hegemonic tool used for state building. It stabilized and institutionalized the difference between indigenous and ladino/mestizo populations in the countryside. Once a given population was determined to be sufficiently backward, monolingual, and isolated from the political, economic, and social life of the country, it could be labeled "indigenous," "othered" by a dominant society that traced most of its roots back to Europe. These "indigenous" became susceptible, vulnerable even, to a host of state interventions, including hydroelectric projects.[26]

In a more directly political sense, the INI tried to advance the state's political agenda at the local, regional, and national levels. In the municipalities, the indigenistas sought to diminish the number of functionaries, secularize power, and strengthen the authority of the municipal presidents. They hoped to marginalize curanderos and elders and promote young bilinguals who embodied the kind of modernization that the INI desired. What often resulted was a generational split, as seen in Oxchuc, and the emergence of promoter-caciques who, ironically, used "tradition" to cement their power. At the regional level, Caso and Aguirre both sought to use federal power to weaken local nonindigenous elites, but in the case of Chiapas, this initiative was quickly neutralized.[27] Nationally, the INI insinuated indigenous communities more completely into Mexico's corporatist, one-party state. In Chiapas, the state's director of indigenous affairs was a PRI delegate and a member of the PRI's National Executive Committee (Comité Ejecutivo Nacional) charged with "advising" the indigenous municipalities at election time. The Coordinating Center sent cultural promoters to regional party conventions and was expected to provide vehicles to shuttle Tsotsils and Tseltals to the PRI's political rallies.[28] INI promoters and former promoters and teachers helped turn the highlands into a reserve of pro-PRI votes that, until recently, was used to offset PRI losses in the cities and in northern Mexico.

Final Reflections

The most ironic, unintended consequence of Mexican indigenismo may be that it prepared the indigenous for a future of independent, often radical advocacy that fell well outside the corporatist institutions of the Mexican state. Young people who attended INI schools were empowered by their literacy skills and their civics lessons. By the 1970s, a few thousand young Tsotsils and Tseltals had completed the sixth grade, and hundreds had finished secondary school. INI Literacy Centers and schools helped create a more participatory citizenry that began contesting local elections. Jan Rus notes that the violent expulsions that began in Chamula in 1974 have been cited as proof that the Chamulas (and other Tsotsils) are antidemocratic and easily beholden to "traditional" caciques. But the opposite argument can also be made "if we focus less on the expellers than the expelled." Rus continues:

> How many others have fought so persistently, and at such cost, against corporatism, the PRI and *caciquismo*, as the thousands of Chamula *expulsados*? Rather than monolithic, repressive supporters of the one-party state, the indigenous people of Chamula, viewed through their religious dissidents, could just as well be seen as heroes of the national struggle for a more pluralistic, open society.[29]

Viewed in this light, Chamulas and others who have fought to democratize their municipalities are not as exotic as some might imagine them to be. Like university students and middle-class activists in Mexico's largest cities, like indigenous youth in Oaxaca,[30] many young indigenous in Chiapas fought cacicazgos and the corrupt practices of Mexico's authoritarian one-party state. Some of them joined opposition parties. Those who were expelled ended up either in colonias surrounding San Cristóbal or in jungle communities in eastern Chiapas, where they tended to engage in more egalitarian democratic practices. They often joined one of a number of independent organizations that broke away from the corporatist CNC and the PRI.[31] Perhaps these young Tsotsils and Tseltals who had attended INI schools in the 1950s and 1960s were more "integrated" into mainstream Mexican life than some realized.

Some scholars have taken this argument a step further. They suggest that Mexican indigenismo may have inadvertently led to *indianismo*, which may be defined as the ideology of independent and democratic indigenous organizations operating outside of official state institutions. Xóchitl Leyva Solano notes that following the Zapatista rebellion in 1994, indigenismo "formed an organic part of neo-Zapatista networks, which gave Zapatismo strength and depth at the national and international levels."[32] In 1995, before the Zapatistas entered into extended negotiations with the federal government, they even invited Gonzalo Aguirre Beltrán to serve as one of their advisers.[33] And Shannan Mattiace notes that in the months and years following the uprising, the INI itself was perceived as being "one of the more progressive federal agencies," its officials and employees "sympathetic to indigenous 'causes.'"[34] During the first round of negotiations between the Mexican government and the rebels, the government invited current and former INI officials to serve as advisers to its team. But the government disinvited the INI for the second and third rounds, perhaps believing that INI officials had "gone native" and were openly supportive of many EZLN demands.[35]

Ironically, even the emergence of Subcomandante Marcos as the EZLN's chief ideologue and spokesman can be considered one of Mexican indigenismo's legacies. Rafael Sebastián Guillén Vicente was a mestizo who had majored in philosophy at the UNAM. He taught design at the Autonomous Metropolitan University (UAM) at Xochimilco until 1984, when he left his job to join a handful of fellow mestizo revolutionaries in the Lacandón rainforest.[36] He reemerged as "Marcos" ten years later, on January 1, 1994, and led the Zapatista uprising. From that date until 2014, when Marcos was retired, many indigenous and nonindigenous people in Mexico and beyond accepted this mestizo poet-philosopher from the northern state of Tamaulipas to be the authentic spokesman of the indigenous movement in Chiapas and beyond. Pedro Pitarch proposes that Marcos flourished in a Mexican setting because the postrevolutionary Mexican state "has dominated representation of the indigenous population through various types of corporative organizations [like the INI] whose leadership is historically non-indigenous."

> There is therefore a long tradition of accepting (and considering quite normal) that non-indigenous representation speaks for the indigenous peoples and of supposing that indigenous people have some basic difficulty expressing themselves. . . . Perhaps only in Mexico could a personality like Subcommander Marcos have emerged who speaks not only for the indigenous in his organization but also for the indigenous of Chiapas and Mexico in general without any serious question of his legitimacy.[37]

From this perspective, the well-educated, cosmopolitan Marcos might be considered simply one more enlightened mestizo who spoke for the indigenous, albeit from an autonomous position well outside the institutional framework of the Mexican state. A Marcos-type figure would be completely out of the question in Guatemala or in an Andean setting, where indigenismo never enjoyed as much sustained state support—modest though it was—as in postrevolutionary Mexico.

This book was premised on the notion that the time has come to reassess

Mexican indigenismo, for so long a target of often bitter critiques born of disappointment and frustration. Using historical documents to interrogate timeworn assumptions, it has exposed an often remarkable journey from utopian dreams and innovation to a period of stagnation and neglect, followed by an undeniable trend toward bureaucratization and careerism. Even some of the INI's fiercest critics like Mercedes Olivera and Margarita Nolasco have conceded that its legacy is neither black nor white; rather, it is mostly gray, with many complicated, ambivalent outcomes, just as there are with other postrevolutionary Mexican institutions like the SEP, the CNC, and the Ministry of Agrarian Reform (Secretaría de Reforma Agraria, or SRA). We may well question why some Mexicans expected so much more out of the INI than they did from the SEP, the CNC, the SRA, and other federal ministries that enjoyed budgets that were exponentially larger than the INI's, and why they held the INI to a higher, more democratic standard than the federal system of which is was a part. There may be some truth to Fernando Benítez's observation that the INI served to "ease our guilty conscience." When it failed to achieve all of its objectives, it became "the scapegoat on which we try to unload the regret that we feel toward an unjust situation, a wound that has been open since the times of the conquest."[38]

Notes

Introduction

1. The communiqué was signed by representatives of the following groups: COLPUMALI, COCICH, FIPI, MUKTAVINIK, OIMI, Promejoramiento de la Raza, ORIACH, CIPC, OMIECH, MODECH, Tres Nudos, Grupo Maya, CIOAC, ARIC Democrática, ORCOA, Maya Shan, Oxi'm Ch'ui Vitz, and four other groups (illegible). My thanks to Ángel Baltazar Caballero for sharing this document with me.

2. In 1999, the Centro de Lengua, Arte, y Literatura Indígena (CELALI) proposed that the letter *z* be removed from written Tzotzil. Today, indigenous and bilingual writers use *ts* in place of *tz*. This book will conform to current practice and will use the *tz* spelling of "Tzotzil" and "Tzeltal" only when referring to the INI's Coordinating Center, which naturally features the *tz* spelling that was common decades ago.

3. Carlos Montemayor, "Adiós al INI," *La Jornada*, May 25, 2003; and Saldívar Tanaka, *Prácticas cotidianas del estado*, 60, 115.

4. Giraudo, "Neither 'Scientific' nor 'Colonialist,'" 13; and Departamento de Asuntos Indígenas, *Primer Congreso Indigenista Interamericano*.

5. Sáenz, *México íntegro*.

6. Giraudo, "Un campo indigenista transnacional," 82–87.

7. Giraudo and Lewis, "Pan-American *Indigenismo*," 5; and Rus, "Rereading Tzotzil Ethnography," 203–4.

8. Nash, *Mayan Visions*, 13.

9. Tarica, *The Inner Life of Mestizo Nationalism*, xiv, xxiii.

10. López, *Crafting Mexico*, 7, 9.

11. Lomnitz, "Bordering on Anthropology," 168.

12. Gamio, "Heterogeneidad de la población," 27–28; see also de la Peña, "Nacionales y extranjeros," 62.

13. Lomnitz, "Bordering on Anthropology," 184–85; see also Gamio, *Antología*; and Gamio, *Forjando patria*.

14. Dawson, *Indian and Nation*, xiv–xv.

15. López, *Crafting Mexico*, 11.
16. Archivo Histórico de la Secretaría de Educación Pública (hereafter AHSEP), Dirección de Educación Federal, Informes, 1652 (4763), Exp. 1778/1, Fo. 100, from Dir. de Ed. Fed. Eduardo Zarza to Jefe del Departamento de Educación Rural, SEP, Mexico City, dated from Tuxtla, July 26, 1928.
17. Dawson, *Indian and Nation*, 73.
18. López, *Crafting Mexico*, 149–50; and Vaughan, *Cultural Politics in Revolution*, 150–51.
19. The conference was known in Spanish as the Primer Congreso Indigenista Interamericano.
20. Dawson, *Indian and Nation*, 83–85; de la Peña, "La antropología, el indigenismo," 77; and Departamento de Asuntos Indígenas, *Primer Congreso Indigenista Interamericano*.
21. Gamio, *Antología*, 28–29.
22. Archivo General de la Nación (hereafter AGN), Ávila Camacho, 709/4, Departamento de Asuntos Indígenas, various; Dawson, *Indian and Nation*, 139–41; and de la Peña, "La antropología, el indigenismo," 76–77.
23. Dawson, *Indian and Nation*, 142; and Greaves Laine, "Entre el discurso y la acción," 256–63.
24. "Ley que crea el Instituto Nacional Indigenista," in *INI, 30 años después*, 359–60; on the parliamentary debate, see 339–58.
25. *Acción Indigenista*, various issues from 1953; Caso, "Definición del indio y lo indio," 338; and Malinowski and de la Fuente, *Malinowski in Mexico*, 6–10.
26. Alfonso Caso, "La nación mexicana," *Acción Indigenista*, no. 3 (September 1953).
27. Caso, "Un experimento de antropología social," 86 (emphasis mine).
28. Caso, "La nación mexicana."
29. Alfonso Caso, "El Instituto Nacional Indigenista," *Acción Indigenista*, no. 1 (July 1953).
30. Comas, *La antropología social aplicada*, 76; see also "Conclusiones sobre indigenismo," *Acción Indigenista*, no. 29, November 1955.
31. Bonfil Batalla, "Del indigenismo de la revolución a la antropología crítica," 44.
32. Benjamin, "A Time of Reconquest," 432.
33. Comisión Nacional para el Desarrollo de los Pueblos Indígenas (hereafter CDI), Biblioteca Juan Rulfo (hereafter BJR), Alfonso Caso, Informe de Actividades presentados por el Dir. Gen. Dr. Alfonso Caso, 1949–1970, from Caso to Presidente, January 10, 1950.
34. CDI, BJR, Alfonso Caso, Informe de Actividades presentados por el Dir. Gen. Dr. Alfonso Caso, 1949–1970, esp. Caso's reports to Alemán dated July 30, 1949, January 10, 1950, and "Resúmen de actividades desarrolladas durante el año de 1950 en el INI."
35. Romano Delgado, "Veinticinco años del Centro Coordinador Indigenista Tzeltal-Tzotzil," 44–45.

36. López Caballero, "Las políticas indigenistas," 71–72.
37. Ibid., 92–96.
38. The best-known critique is a collection of essays by Arturo Warman, Guillermo Bonfil Batalla, Margarita Nolasco Armas, Mercedes Olivera Bustamante, and Enrique Valencia titled *De eso que llaman antropología mexicana*; see also Medina Hernández and García Mora, *La quiebra política*, vol. 2.
39. Saldívar Tanaka, *Prácticas cotidianas del estado*, 60, 136; Taylor, *Indigeneity in the Mexican Cultural Imagination*; and Tarica, *The Inner Life of Mestizo Nationalism*, 1.

Chapter 1

1. Gossen, *Four Creations*; and Laughlin and Sna Jtz'ibajom, *Monkey Business Theatre*.
2. Rus, "Rereading Tzotzil Ethnography," 203; and Aguirre Beltrán, *Formas de gobierno indígena*, 140–49.
3. Viqueira, *Encrucijadas chiapanecas*, 17.
4. Instituto Nacional de Estadística y Geografía, *Censo de Población y Vivienda 2010*; and Viqueira, *Encrucijadas chiapanecas*, 262.
5. Vogt, *Fieldwork Among the Maya*, 209; and Vogt, *Zinacantán*, 588–610.
6. Palacios, "The Social Sciences, Revolutionary Nationalism, and Interacademic Relations," 61.
7. Vogt, *Fieldwork Among the Maya*, 352.
8. Vogt, *Zinacantán*, 588.
9. Viqueira, *Encrucijadas chiapanecas*, 311–12; and Favre, "El cambio sociocultural," 162.
10. Rus, "Rereading Tzotzil Ethnography," 204–6.
11. Vogt, *Fieldwork Among the Maya*, 352 (emphasis mine).
12. Rus, "Rereading Tzotzil Ethnography," 205.
13. Viqueira, *Encrucijadas chiapanecas*, 315–18.
14. Aguirre Beltrán, *Formas de gobierno indígena*, 99; Viqueira, "Las causas de una rebelión india," 106–9, 115; and Siverts, *Oxchuc*, 27.
15. Viqueira, *Encrucijadas chiapanecas*, 22, 88, 277, 336.
16. Ibid., 315; see also Wasserstrom, *Class and Society*, 6.
17. Benjamin, "A Time of Reconquest," 429–33; and Clayton, *Bartolomé de Las Casas*, 314–18, 325–29.
18. Wasserstrom, *Class and Society*, 12–13, 32–68, 96–106.
19. Viqueira, *Encrucijadas chiapanecas*, 342.
20. Ibid., 338; and Wasserstrom, *Class and Society*, 18, 20–28.
21. Benjamin, "A Time of Reconquest," 425.
22. Benjamin, *A Rich Land, a Poor People*, 13–14; and Wasserstrom, *Class and Society*, 110.
23. Rus, "Whose Caste War?," 132.

24. Viqueira, *Encrucijadas chiapanecas*, 68; and Wasserstrom, *Class and Society*, 27–31, 102.

25. Bonfil Batalla, "Del indigenismo de la revolución," 50, 52; Collier, *Fields of the Tzotzil*, 17; Viqueira, *Encrucijadas chiapanecas*, 61, 89, 341–42; and Wasserstrom, *Class and Society*, 250–51.

26. Washbrook, "El estado porfiriano en Chiapas," 262–63.

27. Ibid., 258.

28. Guzmán López, Rus, and Socios de la Unión "Tierra Tzotzil," *Kipaltik*; Rus and Collier, "A Generation of Crisis," 36; and Washbrook, "Una Esclavitud Simulada," 395–401.

29. Rus, "Coffee and the Recolonization of Highland Chiapas," 258, 283–85.

30. Rus, "Repensar la Revolución mexicana en Chiapas," 495.

31. Benjamin, *A Rich Land, a Poor People*, 99–143; and Rus, "Revoluciones contenidas," 68–71.

32. Archivo Histórico del Municipio de San Cristóbal de Las Casas (hereafter AHMSCLC), 1917, Tomo 2, Borrador de Circulares, 1917, signed by J. A. Castro, General de Brigada, Gobernador y Comandante Militar del Estado de Chiapas, October 30, 1914.

33. Legorreta Díaz, "La contrarrevolución en Ocosingo," 203–4; and Rus, "Revoluciones contenidas," 74.

34. For more on the Mexican Revolution in Chiapas, see Benjamin, *A Rich Land, a Poor People*; Lewis, *The Ambivalent Revolution*; and Rus, "Revoluciones contenidas."

35. AHSEP, Dir. de Misiones Culturales, Institutos Sociales, Caja 29, Exp. 7, de Judith Mangino, Trabajadora Social al Prof. Rafael Ramírez, Dir. de Misiones Culturales, SEP, dated from San Cristóbal de Las Casas, October 13, 1927.

36. Personal communication from two reliable sources, August 2009.

37. De la Fuente, "Relaciones étnicas en Mesoamérica," 287.

38. AHMSCLC, various from 1920s and 1930s, including 1929, Tomo 2, "Correspondencia de fuera del distrito, Mayo de 1929," from Carmen Hernández to Gobernador del Estado, dated from San Cristóbal de Las Casas, April 25, 1929; and Favre, "El cambio socio-cultural," 164.

39. Colby and van den Berghe, "Ethnic Relations in Southeastern Mexico," 779; Siverts, *Oxchuc*, 39; and de la Fuente, "Relaciones étnicas en Mesoamérica," 272–73.

40. Siverts, *Oxchuc*, 38.

41. Castellanos, *Ciudad Real*.

42. See, for example, AHMSCLC, 1936–1937, from Pres. Muni. Ciudad Las Casas Evaristo Bonifaz to all municipal presidents in his district, dated from Ciudad Las Casas, September 30, 1936.

43. Chiapas's Department of Indigenous Social Action, Culture, and Protection has undergone several name changes over the years:

> 1934–1948: Departamento de Acción Social, Cultura y Protección Indígena

1948–1951: Departamento de Protección Indígena
1952–1982: Dirección General de Asuntos Indígenas
1983: Subsecretaría de Asuntos Indígenas
1984–1988: Subsecretaría de Asuntos Indígenas
1988–1991: Coordinación de Asuntos Indígenas
1992–1994: Dirección de Asuntos Indígenas

44. AHSEP, Dirección General de Educación Primaria en los Estados y Territorios, Caja 5324 (304), Exp. 18, Fo. 11, from Inspector Andrés Cancúa Neri to Jefe del DER Celso Flores Zamora in Mexico City, dated from Motozintla, January 1936.

45. AHMSCLC, 1937/5, from el Pres. Mpal. Salbador [sic] Gómez to Señor Presidente Municipal de Ciudad Las Casas, January 1, 1937; see also AGN, Cárdenas, Elecciones Chiapas, Municipales, 544.5/1038, from Cárdenas to Secretario de Gobernación, dated from Palacio Nacional, Mexico City, December 13, 1937; and Rus, "The 'Comunidad Revolucionaria Institucional,'" 275.

46. Secretaría de Pueblos Indios, Archivo Histórico (hereafter SEPI, AH), Dirección General de Asuntos Indígenas (hereafter DGAI), 1950, Box 2, Exp. 77.5, "Contrato colectivo de trabajo celebrado por el 'Sindicato de Trabajadores Indígenas del Estado de Chiapas,' representado por su Secretario General ——, y de otra por el propietario de la Finca Cafetera ——."

47. Rus, Rus, and Hernández, *Abtel ta pinka*, 32; see also Aguirre Beltrán, *Formas de gobierno indígena*, 141–42.

48. Sna Jtz'ibajom, *¡Vámanos al paraíso!*, 77–118. An English translation can be found in Laughlin and Sna Jtz'ibajom, *Monkey Business Theatre*, 121–48.

49. Rus, "The Struggle Against Indigenous Caciques," 174.

50. Rus, "The 'Comunidad Revolucionaria Institucional,'" 267.

51. Aguirre Beltrán, *Formas de gobierno indígena*, 142; Rus, "The 'Comunidad Revolucionaria Institucional,'" 281–82; and Wasserstrom, *Class and Society*, 167–69.

52. SEPI, AH, DGAI, 1950, Caja 1, from Agentes Montados José Humberto Molina and Rafael López to the Jefe del Departamento de Acción Social y Protección Indígena del Estado, August 10, 1950.

53. SEPI, AH, DGAI, 1950, Caja 3, Exp. 77.29, from Jefe de la Agencia Gratuita de Colocaciones to Delegado de Tránsito Federal in Tuxtla, July 7, 1947.

54. SEPI, AH, DGAI, 1951, 2, Exp. 77.27, from Blas J. Cancino, Severo Villafuerte, Arturo Zúñiga, and seven others to Jefe del DPI in San Cristóbal, April 23, 1951; and from Jefe del DPI Guillermo Zozaya to Jefe de la Agencia Gratuita de Colocaciones in San Cristóbal, April 27, 1951 (emphasis mine).

55. Köhler, *Cambio cultural dirigido*, 314.

56. Teratol and Péres, *Travelers to the Other World*, 45–46.

57. Legorreta Díaz, "La contrarrevolución en Ocosingo," 223.

58. Aguirre Beltrán, *Formas de gobierno indígena*, 109.

59. Saldívar Tanaka, *Prácticas cotidianas del estado*, 66.

60. Ibid., 66–67; see also Aguirre Beltrán, *Regiones de refugio*.
61. "Cursos de especialización para antropólogos," *Acción Indigenista*, no. 7 (January 1954).
62. Krauze, *Caudillos culturales*.
63. León Portilla, "Alfonso Caso," 877–85; and López, *Crafting Mexico*, 179–80.
64. Téllez Girón López and Vázquez León, *Palerm en sus propias palabras*, 294–96; see also Medina, "Diez años decisivos," 39.
65. Aguirre Beltrán, "Formación de una teoría," 11–40; and de la Peña, "Gonzalo Aguirre Beltrán," 355–82. See also Aguirre Beltrán, *Obra polémica*; and Aguirre Beltrán, "Entrevista a Gonzalo Aguirre Beltrán," 203–26.
66. Báez Jorge, introduction to *Pensamiento antropológico*, 9–17; see also Romano Delgado, "Julio de la Fuente."
67. Pozas, *La antropología y la burocracia indigenista*, 1; see also Pozas, *Chamula*.
68. Bricker and Vogt, "Alfonso Villa Rojas," 994–98; and Andrés Medina Hernández, personal communication, August 2, 2006.
69. Ángel Baltazar Caballero, personal communication, November 19, 2004.
70. Vogt, *Fieldwork Among the Maya*, 77.
71. Archivo Histórico del Centro Coordinador Indigenista Tzeltal-Tzotzil (hereafter AHCCITT), 1951, Serie Dirección, 42–1951/2, 17–1951/2, 53–1951–3, 74–1951–3.
72. Wasserstrom, *Class and Society*, 104.
73. Agustín Romano Delgado, interview, Mexico City, January 16, 1995.
74. Andrés Medina Hernández, interview, Mexico City, August 2, 2006. For more information on the Casa del Estudiante Indígena, see Dawson, "Wild Indians"; and Lewis, *The Ambivalent Revolution*, 60–63.
75. AGN, Cárdenas, Leyes, Proyectos diversos, 545.3/147, "Al margen de las afirmaciones presidenciales sobre el problema social de la incorporación indígena a la vida nacional," by Rafael Molina Betancourt, sent to Sec. Particular, Presidencia de la República, June 30, 1936.
76. Guiteras-Holmes, *Perils of the Soul*, 10, 15–17. On the role of Manuel Arias Sojob and Tomás Pérez Arias in Chenalhó's schooling tradition, see Arias Pérez, "Movimientos indígenas contemporáneos," 383, 388; and Eber, "*Buscando una nueva vida*," 138.
77. Arias Pérez, "Movimientos indígenas contemporáneos," 385, 388; and Köhler, *Cambio cultural dirigido*, 241.
78. Slocum and Watkins, *The Good Seed*, 43, 103, 117.
79. Nash, *Mayan Visions*, 57. On the abuses of Oxchuc's lineage heads and curers, see Slocum and Watkins, *The Good Seed*, 47–53; and Villa Rojas, *Etnografía tzeltal de Chiapas*.
80. Siverts, *Oxchuc*, 184; and Slocum and Watkins, *The Good Seed*, 112–13.
81. SEPI, AH, Departamento de Acción Social, Cultura y Protección Indígena (hereafter DPI), 1951, 1, Exp. 77.11, from Pres. Municipal of Oxchuc to Jefe del DPI Guillermo Zozaya, July 1950.

82. SEPI, AH, DPI, from Jefe del DPI Guillermo Zozoya to Sec. Gen. de Gobierno in Tuxtla, July 19, 1950.
83. Slocum and Watkins, *The Good Seed*, 120, 125; Siverts, *Oxchuc*, 181–82; and "Una mujer los civilizó," *Tiempo: Seminario de la Vida y la Verdad* 32, no. 814 (December 9, 1957): 50–55.
84. Slocum and Watkins, *The Good Seed*, 181.
85. Romano Delgado, "Problemas fundamentales," 20–21.
86. CDI, BJR, Francisco Alarcón, "El programa de salud del Centro Coordinador."
87. AHCCITT, 1951, Serie Dirección, from Manuel Castellanos to Director of CCITT, dated from San Cristóbal, December 14, 1951; see also Romano Delgado, *Historia evaluativa*, 1:317.
88. CDI, BJR, Informe del Centro Coordinador Indigenista Tzeltal-Tzotzil (hereafter ICCITT), 1952, from Julio de la Fuente, "Programa de Trabajo para 1952."
89. AHCCITT, 1951, various; and Romano Delgado, *Historia evaluativa*, 1:317–18.

Chapter 2

1. AHSEP, Dirección de Educación Federal, Chiapas, Caja 5581 (3530), Exp. 4482/29, Fo. 69, from Castellanos to Téllez in Tuxtla, Ciudad Las Casas, October 1, 1942; see also Escuelas Rurales Federales, Chiapas, 6050, Exp. 7222/19, "Supervisión Escolar," by Castellanos, Sibactel, Tenejapa, April 7, 1943.
2. AHSEP, 5655 (1848); Dir. Gral. de Ed. Primaria en los Edos. y Territorios, Exp. 23, Fos. 41–44, from Dir. Gen. de Ed. Prim. en los Edos. y Terrs. Lucas Ortiz B., January 23, 1945.
3. Swadesh, a Yale-trained linguist, returned to the United States in 1941 to help the army write language primers in Chinese and Russian. In 1949, he lost his post at the City College of New York after an FBI informant accused him of being a communist. He returned to Mexico in the 1950s to work at the Instituto Politécnico Nacional, ENAH, and the INI. See Price, *Threatening Anthropology*, 97–106.
4. De la Peña, "La antropología, el indigenismo," 78.
5. SEPI, AH, DPI, 1951, Caja 2, Exp. 77.1, Acta signed by Florence Gerdel and Marianna Slocum, February 20, 1951.
6. Slocum and Watkins, *The Good Seed*, 148–49.
7. CDI, BJR, ICCITT, 1951, from Aguirre Beltrán to Caso, "Informe del mes de marzo de 1951," April 2, 1951; and Romano Delgado, *Historia evaluativa*, 1:322–23.
8. CDI, BJR, ICCITT, 1952, from Julio de la Fuente, "Programa de Trabajo para 1952."
9. The initial Chamulan promoters were Pascual Patixtán Likanchitom, Salvador Sánchez Gómez, Domingo Santis Diezmo, Pascual López Calixto, Mariano Jiménez Taquibeket, Agustín López Ventana, Domingo Gómez Osob, Domingo Santis Bulemó, and Juan López Tuxum (brother of Salvador López Castellanos, alias Tuxum).
10. The initial promoters from Chenalhó were Pedro Arias Pérez, Dionisio Arias

Gutiérrez, Mariano Pérez Gutiérrez, Antonio Arias Pérez, Juan Mendez Santis, Mariano Ruiz Arias, Miguel Pérez Moreno, Manuel Pérez Pérez, and Hilario Pérez Sánchez.

11. Romano Delgado, *Historia evaluativa*, 1:321–22; Saldívar Tanaka, *Prácticas cotidianas del estado*, 65; and Onofre Montes Ríos, interview, February 10, 1995, Mexico City.

12. Romano Delgado, *Historia evaluativa*, 1:325.

13. AHCCITT, 1951, Serie Dirección, 90–1951–5, "Mis impresiones de los promotores del Centro Tzeltal-Tzotzil," by Kenneth Weathers, December 1951.

14. Ibid.

15. Weathers was right—López Calixto served as Chamula's municipal president from 1959 to 1961. A gentle, patient man, he taught kindergarten and first grade for thirty years and encouraged girls to attend. López Calixto and Rus, "Cómo perdí a mi hermanito."

16. CDI, BJR, ICCITT, 1952, from de la Fuente to Caso, April 16, 1952.

17. Ibid., "Informe de labores realizadas durante el tiempo comprendido del 15 de octubre a la fecha," by Fidencio Montes Sánchez, November 14, 1952.

18. Ibid., 1952, "Informe de las labores realizadas, en el ramo educativo, comprendido del 15 de agosto a la fecha," probably Fidencio Montes Sánchez.

19. Ibid., 1957, "Informe de junio de 1957," by Dir. de Ed. Fidencio Montes Sánchez.

20. Ibid., 1958, "Informe de junio de 1957," by Dir. de Ed. Fidencio Montes Sánchez.

21. Ibid., 1957, "Informe de junio de 1957," by Dir. de Ed. Fidencio Montes Sánchez.

22. De la Fuente, *Yalalag*.

23. Benítez, *Los indios de México*, 1:219–27; and CDI, BJR, undated document written by Dr. Olga J. Montes García, Montes's niece.

24. From 1964 to 1966, Montes directed the Coordinating Center at Jamiltepec, Oaxaca; from 1967 to 1970, he directed the CCI at Huautla de Jiménez. He retired in 1970 but continued serving as an adviser to the INI. Years after his death in 1980, President Carlos Salinas de Gortari awarded him the Manuel Gamio medal for his contributions to Mexican indigenismo. CDI, BJR, undated document written by Dr. Olga J. Montes García, Montes's niece.

25. CDI, BJR, ICCITT, 1953, from Pozas to Dir. del INI Alfonso Caso, dated from Las Casas, March 23, 1953.

26. Horcasitas de Pozas and Pozas, "Del monolingüismo en lengua indígena," 153, 155–59; see also Scanlon and Lezama Morfín, *México pluricultural*, 326–29.

27. Romano Delgado, *Historia evaluativa*, 1:331–32.

28. CDI, BJR, ICCITT, 1952, various; and Romano Delgado, "Veinticinco años del Centro Coordinador Indigenista Tzeltal-Tzotzil," 45–46.

29. CDI, BJR, ICCITT, 1953, from Dir. de Ed. Fidencio Montes Sánchez, February 20, 1953; CDI, BJR, ICCITT, 1953, "Informe de actividades realizades del 15 de marzo al 15 de abril," from Dir. de Ed. Fidencio Montes Sánchez, April 18, 1953; and Modiano and Pérez Hernández, "Educación," 57.

30. Romano Delgado, "Veinticinco años del Centro Coordinador Indigenista Tzeltal-Tzotzil," 40, 45–46.

31. CDI, BJR, ICCITT, 1952, "Informe de julio," by Fidencio Montes Sánchez.

32. One such critique reads as follows: "The INI, as with all the institutions that preceded it, never thought to include women among its promoters." Garza Caligaris and Hernández Castillo, "Encounters and Conflicts of the Tzotzil People," 42.

33. CDI, BJR, ICCITT, 1953, from Pozas to Caso, September 1, 1953, taken from "Informe del mes de Julio de 1953," by Dir. de Ed. Fidencio Montes Sánchez.

34. CDI, BJR, ICCITT, 1953, "Informe de labores del mes de agosto de 1953," by Fidencio Montes Sánchez, and "Informe de Lingüística," by Evangelina Arana Osnaya, June–September 1953.

35. Romano Delgado, "Problemas fundamentales."

36. Romano Delgado, *Historia evaluativa*, 2:75.

37. CDI, BJR, ICCITT, 1955, "Informe de los trabajos realizados por los alumnos del internado del INI, durante los meses de diciembre de 1954 y enero de 1955," by Andrés Santiago Montes, February 17, 1955.

38. Ibid., 1956, "Informe de noviembre de 1956," by Dir. de Ed. Fidencio Montes Sánchez, and "Informe de las diferentes actividades llevadas a cabo en el presente mes de septiembre," by Prof. Onofre Montes Ríos, October 5, 1956.

39. Ibid., 1957, "Informe de junio de 1957," by Dir. de Ed. Fidencio Montes Sánchez.

40. Ibid., 1957, "Informe de junio de 1957," by Dir. de Ed. Fidencio Montes Sánchez; Romano Delgado, *Historia evaluativa*, 2:74; and Instituto Nacional Indigenista, *Realidades y proyectos*, 38.

41. CDI, BJR, ICCITT, 1954, from Romano to Caso, June 17, 1954, and Romano to Caso, September 21, 1954.

42. Ibid., 1955, "Informe de abril de 1955," from Dir. de Ed. Fidencio Montes Sánchez to Agustín Romano Delgado, and "Informe de mayo," from Romano to Caso, May 31, 1955.

43. Ibid., 1956, "Informe de julio de 1956," from Dir. de Ed. Fidencio Montes Sánchez.

44. Ibid., 1958. In 1967, the director of the Coordinating Center reported eight Tsotsil promotoras (four from Chamula, three from Chenalhó, and one from Chalchihuitán) and nine Tseltals; see AHCCITT, 1967/3, Dir., from Alberto Jiménez Rodríguez to Lynda L. Jones in Provo, Utah, July 31, 1967.

45. CDI, BJR, ICCITT, 1957, "Informe de agosto de 1956," from Dir. de Ed. Fidencio Montes Sánchez, and "Informe," from Onofre Montes Ríos, February 28, 1957.

46. Romano Delgado, "Problemas fundamentales," 20, 22.

47. AHCCITT, 1954, Sección Dirección, Serie Dirección, Exp. 49-1954/2, from Prof. Ramón Hernández López.

48. CDI, BJR, ICCITT, 1956, "Informe de labores correspondiente al mes de agosto," by Dir. del Centro Alfonso Villa Rojas.

49. Ibid., 1956, from Subdirector Gonzalo Aguirre Beltrán, October 23, 1956.

50. Ibid., 1953, "Informe del mes de noviembre de 1953," by Prof. Fidencio Montes Sánchez.

51. Ibid., various; 1956, "Informes" from Prof. Fidencio Montes Sánchez, July 1956 and August 1956; 1957, "Informe de junio de 1957," from Prof. Fidencio Montes Sánchez.
52. Modiano and Pérez Hernández, "Educación," 56; and Saldívar Tanaka, *Prácticas cotidianas del estado*, 70.
53. Aguirre Beltrán, *Formas de gobierno indígena*, 139.

Chapter 3

1. Dawson, *Indian and Nation*, 142.
2. Rus, "Rereading Tzotzil Ethnography," 203.
3. CDI, BJR, Alfonso Caso, "Informe de Actividades presentado por el Dir. Gen. Dr. Alfonso Caso, 1949–1970," from Caso to Presidente, January 10, 1950.
4. Aguirre Beltrán, *Formas de gobierno indígena*, 143.
5. Ibid., 143–44.
6. CDI, BJR, Alfonso Villa Rojas, "Sugerencias para un programa de investigación social en los Altos de Chiapas," January 31, 1954, found in folder titled "Investigaciones de Chiapas," by Alejandro Marroquín.
7. The Sinarquistas were a nationalist, proto-fascist Catholic lay organization founded in 1937 to oppose the administration of Lázaro Cárdenas and the ruling party.
8. CDI, BJR, found in a folder titled "Investigaciones de Chiapas," by Alejandro Marroquín.
9. Ibid., market observation on March 14, 1955, Alejandro Marroquín, "Investigaciones de Chiapas."
10. Ibid., Alejandro Marroquín, "Investigaciones de Chiapas."
11. Ibid.
12. "Conclusiones sobre indigenismo," *Acción Indigenista*, no. 29 (November 1955): 1; and Romano Delgado, *Historia evaluativa*, 1:345.
13. "Caminos de penetración," *Acción Indigenista*, no. 9 (March 1954); and CDI, BJR, ICCITT, 1951, from Gonzalo Aguirre Beltrán to INI director Dr. Alfonso Caso, dated from San Cristóbal de Las Casas, April 7, 1951.
14. Aguirre Beltrán, *Formas de gobierno indígena*, 145.
15. Pozas, *Chamula*, 193; and Holland, *Medicina maya*, 125–27.
16. Romano Delgado, "Problemas fundamentales," 20–21.
17. Romano Delgado, *Historia evaluativa*, 1:347.
18. CDI, BJR, ICCITT, 1951, from Gonzalo Aguirre Beltrán to Alfonso Caso, dated from Las Casas, November 15, 1951.
19. It appears that this rape case was never tried in court.
20. AHCCITT, Ser. Dirección, 16-1951/1, from Gonzalo Aguirre Beltrán to Alfonso Caso; CDI, BJR, ICCITT, 1951, from Gonzalo Aguirre Beltrán to Alfonso Caso, dated from Las Casas, September 1, 1951; Köhler, *Cambio cultural dirigido*, 180–81; and Romano Delgado, *Historia evaluativa*, 2:312.
21. Favre, *Cambio y continuidad*, 365.

22. Romano Delgado, *Historia evaluativa*, 2:314.
23. CDI, BJR, ICCITT, 1956, "Informe de noviembre de 1956," from Dir. de Ed. Prof. Fidencio Montes Sánchez.
24. Ibid., 1953, "Informe del mes de noviembre de 1953," from Dir. de Ed. Fidencio Montes Sánchez, and 1960, "Informe de abril de 1960," from Fidencio Montes Sánchez.
25. Ibid., 1953, "Informe de la visita realizada a los parajes de Oxchuc, Huixtán, y Chanal durante los días comprendidos del 11 al 15 de mayo de 1953," by Fidencio Montes Sánchez.
26. Lewis and Sosa Suárez, *Monopolio de aguardiente*, annex 26, "Entrevistas con evangélicos de Oxchuc."
27. CDI, BJR, ICCITT, 1953, from Dir. of CCI Ricardo Pozas to Alfonso Caso, September 1, 1953.
28. Ibid., Ricardo Pozas to Alfonso Caso, July 7, 1953.
29. Ibid., "Informe de la visita realizada a los parajes de Oxchuc, Huixtán, y Chanal durante los días comprendidos del 11 al 15 de mayo de 1953," by Fidencio Montes Sánchez, and "Informe de la visita realizada en la región tzeltal en compañía del Director del CCITT y del Asuntos Indígenas del Estado durante los días comprendidos del 8 de juio de 1953," by Reynaldo Salvatierra, June 19, 1953.
30. Ibid., 1953, Ricardo Pozas to Alfonso Caso, July 7, 1953, and October 7, 1953; see also Aguirre Beltrán, Villa Rojas, Romano Delgado, et al., *El indigenismo en acción*, 128–30.
31. CDI, BJR, ICCITT, 1953, "Informe de la visita realizada en la región tzeltal," from Reynaldo Salvatierra, October 15, 1953; and Onofre Montes Ríos, interview, February 10, 1995, Mexico City.
32. CDI, BJR, ICCITT, 1955, "Informe de la revisión de las tareas encomendadas a las alumnas del internado durante las vacaciones en sus parajes correspondientes," by Lucía Morales Quiroz, January 28, 1955.
33. Ibid., from Dir. de Ed. Fidencio Montes Sánchez to Agustín Romano Delgado, June 21, 1955.
34. Ibid., 1954, from Agustín Romano Delgado to Alfonso Caso, February 9, 1954.
35. Ibid., 1956, "Informe de las actividades desarrolladas durante el mes de septiembre de 1956," from Librado Mendoza Jarquín, October 5, 1956; and Slocum and Watkins, *The Good Seed*, 15.
36. CDI, BJR, ICCITT, 1956, "Informe de septiembre de 1956," by Dir. de Ed. Fidencio Montes Sánchez.
37. Collier, "Peasant Politics and the Mexican State," 83.
38. *Acción Indigenista*, no. 4 (October 1953); "Petul, cooperativista," *Acción Indigenista*, no. 31 (January 1956); and Marroquín, "Consideraciones sobre las cooperativas organizadas," 6–7.
39. CDI, BJR, ICCITT, 1953, from Ricardo Pozas to Alfonso Caso, Las Casas, March 23, 1953, from Pozas to Caso, April 23, 1953, and from Pozas to Caso, June 3, 1953; and Romano Delgado, *Historia evaluativa*, 2:277–79.

40. CDI, BJR, ICCITT, 1953, "Informe que rinde a la Dirección del CCITT Raúl Rodríguez acerca de la labor realizada en la cooperativa de consumo de Chamula, Chis., del 20 de abril al 19 de mayo de 1953."
41. Incháustegui, "Reconocimiento a la Cooperativa de Oxchuc," 3.
42. Ibid., 2.
43. Marroquín, "Consideraciones sobre las cooperativas organizadas."
44. CDI, BJR, ICCITT, 1954, "Informe del mes de marzo," from Agustín Romano Delgado to Alfonso Caso, April 23, 1954.
45. Ibid., 1953, "Informe del mes de julio de 1953" from Dir. de Ed. Fidencio Montes Sánchez.
46. *Acción Indigenista*, no. 31 (January 1956); and Marroquín, "Consideraciones sobre las cooperativas organizadas."
47. "Acción integral en salubridad," *Acción Indigenista*, no. 7 (January 1954).
48. Romano Delgado, *Historia evaluativa*, 2:145.
49. Aguirre Beltrán, "Estructura y función," 39.
50. Aguirre Beltrán, *Formas de gobierno indígena*, 146; see also Robles Garnica, "Programa de salud."
51. Romano Delgado, *Historia evaluativa*, 2:121; see also Holland, *Medicina maya*, 211–12.
52. Robles Garnica, "Tres años en los Altos," 466.
53. Ibid., 466–68.
54. CDI, BJR, ICCITT, 1951, from Dir. del CCITT Gonzalo Aguirre Beltrán to Dir. del INI Alfonso Caso, December 12, 1951; Holland, *Medicina maya*, 213–14; and Köhler, *Cambio cultural dirigido*, 264–65.
55. Roberto Robles Garnica, "El programa de salud," *Acción Indigenista*, no. 68 (February 1959).
56. CDI, BJR, ICCITT, 1951, "Informe sobre el estudio epidemiológico de un brote de tifo en Chichihuistán y parajes cercanos en el municipio de Teopisca, Chis.," by Jefe del Servicio Médico Dr. Ángel Torres F.
57. Ibid.
58. CDI, BJR, ICCITT, 1951, from Gonzalo Aguirre Beltrán to Alfonso Caso, Las Casas, December 12, 1951; see also Holland, *Medicina maya*, 215–17.
59. CDI, BJR, ICCITT, 1951, "Informe sobre el estudio epidemiológico de un brote de tifo en Chichihuistán y parajes cercanos en el municipio de Teopisca, Chis.," by Jefe del Servicio Médico Dr. Ángel Torres F. Drawing from interviews taken several years after the events took place, William Holland tells a more dramatic version in his book *Medicina maya*. According to Holland, the elderly couple was tied together, the curandero was extremely drunk, and the inhabitants of Chichihuistán had sharpened stones, prepared "to perform a very ancient and very effective social sanction" against the couple. Holland also wrote that a terrified INI nurse was required to join the curandero in his prayers. She allegedly got on her knees and said the rosary. Holland, *Medicina maya*, 216–17.

60. Holland, *Medicina maya*, 214.
61. CDI, BJR, ICCITT, 1953, from Dr. Roberto Robles Garnica to Prof. Ricardo Pozas, Las Casas, October 30, 1953.
62. Ibid.
63. CDI, BJR, ICCITT, 1953, from Dr. Julio Palacios Ruíz to Dir. Ricardo Pozas, May 1953.
64. "Actividades del Centro Coordinador Tzeltal-Tzotzil," *Acción Indigenista*, no. 7 (January 1954).
65. AHCCITT, 1954, Sección Dirección, Serie Dirección, Exp. 49-1954/2, from Prof. Ramón Hernández López.
66. Navarrete Cáceres, *Rosario Castellanos*, 19.
67. CDI, BJR, ICCITT, 1952, from Ricardo Pozas to Alfonso Caso, March 23, 1953.
68. Robles Garnica, "Tres años en los Altos."

Chapter 4

1. CDI, BJR, "Expediente Julio de la Fuente," interview with Rebeca Ortega Cano.
2. Lewis and Sosa Suárez, *Monopolio de aguardiente*.
3. Ibid., 180–94; see also Eber, *Women and Alcohol*; and Vogt, *Zinacantán*, 195–212, 218–20, 233–35.
4. Collier, *Fields of the Tzotzil*, 174.
5. Lewis and Sosa Suárez, *Monopolio de aguardiente*, 188.
6. Ibid., 190–94.
7. Denatured alcohol, or methylated spirit, is ethyl alcohol that is unfit for drinking but is still useful for industrial purposes.
8. Lewis and Sosa Suárez, *Monopolio de aguardiente*, 80–83, 320–21, 368.
9. Ibid., 183–85.
10. Bobrow-Strain, *Intimate Enemies*, 69; see also Siverts, *Oxchuc*, 39.
11. Guzmán López and Rus, *Lo'il sventa k'ucha'al la jmankutik jpinkakutik Kipaltik*, 3.
12. Lewis and Sosa Suárez, *Monopolio de aguardiente*, 359. For background on the aguardiente industry in Chiapas, see Blasco López, "La industria aguardentera chiapaneca," 455–79.
13. CDI, BJR, Ricardo Pozas Arciniega, "Chamula, notas de campo," 1945–1946; and Lewis and Sosa Suárez, *Monopolio de aguardiente*, 141–44.
14. De la Fuente's commission claimed that Moctezuma won the lottery; Evon Vogt claimed that the winner was his brother, Hernán. Still others speculate that neither won the lottery but used it as a way to explain their sudden wealth. See Vogt, *Fieldwork Among the Maya*, 77; and Lewis and Sosa Suárez, *Monopolio de aguardiente*, annex 12.
15. A garrafón is a heavy glass jug that contains seventeen to twenty liters.
16. Lewis and Sosa Suárez, *Monopolio de aguardiente*, 172–77.
17. *Diario Oficial*, January 26, 1949; *Informe rendido por el C. Gobernador del*

Estado Francisco J. Grajales en 1949, 54–55; and Lewis and Sosa Suárez, *Monopolio de aguardiente*, 141–44.

18. Lewis and Sosa Suárez, *Monopolio de aguardiente*, 64–72, 145–77, 358–63.

19. Ibid., 357; "25,000 agricultores bajo una infamante y odiosa explotación," *La Prensa*, May 12, 1950; and AGN, Alemán, monopolies, 523.1/53, various.

20. Collier, *Fields of the Tzotzil*, 175.

21. Lewis and Sosa Suárez, *Monopolio de aguardiente*, 108, 213, annex 12, "Entrevista con el Sr. Moctezuma Pedrero."

22. Ibid., 180.

23. CDI, BJR, ICCITT, 1957, "Informe de agosto de 1957," by Dir. de Ed. Fidencio Montes Sánchez.

24. Lewis and Sosa Suárez, *Monopolio de aguardiente*, 371–72.

25. "Balacera entre fiscales y fabricantes clandestinos," *La Opinión*, November 13, 1951; and Lewis and Sosa Suárez, *Monopolio de aguardiente*, annex 13, "Asalto en Las Ollas."

26. Aguirre Beltrán, "Formación de una teoría," 18.

27. AHCCITT, 1951,1, from Gonzalo Aguirre Beltrán to Gobernador del Estado, Las Casas, November 15, 1951.

28. CDI, BJR, ICCITT, 1951, from Gonzalo Aguirre Beltrán to Alfonso Caso, November 15, 1951.

29. Lewis and Sosa Suárez, *Monopolio de aguardiente*, annex 13, "Asalto en Las Ollas."

30. CDI, BJR, ICCITT, 1951, from Gonzalo Aguirre Beltrán to Alfonso Caso, Las Casas, November 15, 1951.

31. Ibid., from Alfonso Caso to Gonzalo Aguirre Beltrán, dated from Mexico City, December 7, 1951, and from Alfonso Caso to Governor Francisco Grajales, n.d.

32. Ibid., 1952, from Consejero Técnico Aguirre Beltrán to Dir. Julio de la Fuente, January 31, 1952; and Lewis and Sosa Suárez, *Monopolio de aguardiente*, annex 22, "Intervención de funcionarios y empleados de hacienda ante la Procuraduría de Asuntos Indígenas y el Centro Coordinador."

33. AHCCITT, 1953, Serie Dir., Sección Dir., 1953, 22–1953/1 from INI Secretario Salas Ortega to Ricardo Pozas, Mexico City, June 13, 1953; AHCCITT, 1953, 4–1953/1, from Ricardo Pozas to Alfonso Caso, Las Casas, June 30, 1953; and CDI, BJR, ICCITT, 1953, from Reynaldo Salvatierra C., "Informe de las visitas realizadas en las escuelas de Yaltem del Municipio de Chamula, Tres Puentes y Tibo del Municipio de Larráinzar en los días 11, 12, 13, y 14 de agosto de 1953."

34. AGN, Ruiz Cortines, Las Ollas, 542.1/400, from Dominga Jiménez Banco, Domingo Jiménez Conde, Manuel Ruiz Escandón, Pedro de la Cruz, to Pres. Adolfo Ruiz Cortinez [sic], October 23, 1953.

35. "El alcoholismo," *Acción Indigenista*, no. 6 (December 1953).

36. Lewis and Sosa Suárez, *Monopolio de aguardiente*, annex 24, "Casos de decomisos y atropellos a indígenas: Homicidio de Mariano Pérez Hacienda"; see also

SEPI, AH, DGAI, 1954, from Pres. Muni. Martín Pérez Gil to Jefe del Departamento, 1954.

37. *El Universal*, January 24, 1954; cited in Lewis and Sosa Suárez, *Monopolio de aguardiente*, annex 24, "Casos de decomisos y atropellos a indígenas: Homicidio de Mariano Pérez Hacienda."

38. Lewis and Sosa Suárez, *Monopolio de aguardiente*, annex 24, "Casos de decomisos y atropellos a indígenas: Homicidio de Mariano Pérez Hacienda."

39. CDI, BJR, ICCITT, 1954, from Agustín Romano Delgado to Alfonso Caso, February 9, 1954.

40. Lewis and Sosa Suárez, *Monopolio de aguardiente*, annex 24, "Casos de decomisos y atropellos a indígenas: Homicidio de Mariano Pérez Hacienda."

41. Archivo Histórico del Estado de Chiapas (AHECh), Tuxtla Gutiérrez, Sec. 2, Caja 39, Serie 273, Exp. 3, "Asuntos relacionados con el Consejo Nacional Indigenista," from Efraín Aranda Osorio to Alfonso Caso, Tuxtla Gutiérrez, February 23, 1954; and Lewis and Sosa Suárez, *Monopolio de aguardiente*, 355.

42. Lewis and Sosa Suárez, *Monopolio de aguardiente*, 355, "Informe de la Comisión al Dr. Alfonso Caso, Director General del Instituto Nacional Indigenista."

43. Ibid., 247.

44. Ibid., 140–41, 161–66, 326.

45. Ibid., 362–68.

46. Ibid., 101, 199–206, 361–67.

47. Ibid., 92, 111, 325; and Rus, "The 'Comunidad Revolucionaria Institucional,'" 284.

48. Lewis and Sosa Suárez, *Monopolio de aguardiente*, annex 7, "Copias de documentos conocidos durante la gira Ocosingo-Yajalón."

49. Ibid., annex 12, "Entrevista con el Sr. Moctezuma Pedrero."

50. Aguirre Beltrán, "Formación de una teoría," 18.

51. *La Voz de Chiapas*, May 16, 1954; and Martínez, *La prensa maniatada*, 335–36.

52. "Enérgica batida contra el clandestinaje aguardentero," *El Heraldo* (Tuxtla Gutiérrez), March 1, 1953; and "Otro magnífico golpe de los fiscales a los contrabandistas de alcoholes," *Diario del Sur* (Tapachula), July 7, 1953; both cited in Lewis and Sosa Suárez, *Monopolio de aguardiente*, annex 25.

53. Pedro Alvarado Lang, "Muertes colectivas por alcohol," *El Heraldo* (Tuxtla Gutiérrez), July 8, 9, 13, 14, 1954; and Moctezuma Pedrero, "Los mortales efectos del alcohol desnaturalizado," *El Heraldo* (Tuxtla Gutiérrez), July 28, 1954; both cited in Lewis and Sosa Suárez, *Monopolio de aguardiente*, annex 12.

54. "Los expendios de aguardiente explotan a la clase indígena," *El Demócrata* (San Cristóbal de Las Casas), June 14, 1953.

55. "San Cristóbal en manos de los capitalistas de Teopisca," *El Demócrata* (San Cristóbal de Las Casas), July 12, 1953.

56. "Comentarios breves," *El Coleto* (San Cristóbal de Las Casas), August 5, 1954.

57. "Descubiertas dos fábricas clandestinas," *El Coleto* (San Cristóbal de Las Casas),

July 27, 1954; "Robaron en una bodega de don Hernán Pedrero," *El Coleto*, August 5, 1954; "Decubrieron tres fábricas clandestinas," *El Coleto*, August 6, 1954; "Otra fábrica clandestina de aguardiente que es descubierta," *El Coleto*, August 15, 1954; "Por elaboración clandestina están detenidos," *El Coleto*, August 17, 1954; "Comentando," *El Coleto*, August 19, 1954; and "La tragedia de Teopisca," *Más Allá* (San Cristóbal de Las Casas), August 30, 1954.

58. *El Coleto* (San Cristóbal de Las Casas), September 9, 1954.
59. "Comentando," *El Coleto* (San Cristóbal de Las Casas), October 16, 1954.
60. Héctor Guisa V., "Don Moctezuma Pedrero Argüello no tiene autoridad moral para autonombrarse enemigo del alcoholismo en Chiapas," *La Voz del Sureste*, June 12, 1955.
61. "D. Moctezuma Pedrero declara no consumir productos alcohólicos que elabora, ni menos permitir que sus empleados los ingieran," *La Voz del Sureste*, June 27, 1955.
62. "El INI cooperará con 25 mil pesos para el Sumidero," *La Voz de San Cristóbal*, December 11, 1954; and "Odiosa indiferencia oficial ante la desgracia colectiva," *Más Allá*, August 21, 1955.
63. AHCCITT, 1953, Ser. Dirección, Sec. Educación, 14–1953/1, "Lingüística," "Propaganda en Chamula con motivo de la fiesta de Santa Rosa."
64. CDI, BJR, ICCITT, 1953, from Ricardo Pozas to Alfonso Caso, October 7, 1953.
65. Lewis and Sosa Suárez, *Monopolio de aguardiente*, 372–74.
66. Agustín Romano Delgado, personal communication, July 15, 1998.
67. AHCCITT, 1955, Ser. Dirección, Sec: Dirección, 1955, 1–1955/1, from Sub-Dir. of INI Gonzalo Aguirre Beltrán to Dir. of CCITT Agustín Romano Delgado, Mexico City, May 27, 1955.
68. AGN, Ruiz Cortines, 523.1/81, Pedrero, from Gerente Hernán Pedrero Argüello and Comisario Moctezuma Pedrero Argüello, Plantaciones Agrícolas Intensivas, S. de R. L. de C. V., to Ruiz Cortines, Tuxtla, January 7, 1954. By October 1957, the Pedreros still had not received a positive response to their loan request.
69. Ibid., 544.2/1, various, López Mateos, Pedreros, 113.2/1.
70. CDI, BJR, ICCITT, 1958, "Informe de mayo de 1958," by Dir. de Ed. Fidencio Montes Sánchez; see also AGN, López Mateos, 542.8, from Macario Guzmán Estrada to Adolfo López Mateos, Yajalón, June 4, 1959; and Vogt, *Fieldwork Among the Maya*, 92–93.
71. Rus, "The Struggle Against Indigenous Caciques," 176.
72. Rus, "The 'Comunidad Revolucionaria Institucional,'" 289; and Pineda, *Caciques culturales*.

Chapter 5

1. CDI, BJR, Alejandro Marroquín, "Investigaciones de Chiapas, 1955."
2. Romano Delgado, *Historia evaluativa*, 2:284.

3. CDI, BJR, ICCITT, 1956, "Informe de labores correspondiente al mes de septiembre, 1956," by Alfonso Villa Rojas, October 13, 1956.

4. Ibid., 1958, from Dr. Francisco Alarcón to Alfonso Villa Rojas, May 12, 1958.

5. Ibid., 1958, "Informe de mayo de 1958," by Dir. of Ed. Fidencio Montes Sánchez.

6. Ibid., 1958, "Informe de marzo," by Dir. Alfonso Villa Rojas (emphasis in the original). See also CDI, BJR, César Tejeda Fonseca, "Experiencias en el cambio económico dirigido en la region tzeltal-tzotzil," unpublished manuscript, 1957.

7. Ricardo Pozas, interview by Jan Rus, December 4, 1975. My thanks to Jan Rus for sharing the interview transcript. See also Vázquez León, "Entrevista a Ricardo Pozas Arciniega," 152.

8. CDI, BJR, ICCITT, 1959, "Informe del movimiento de fondos habidos en el mes de diciembre de 1959, en las cooperativas de consumo y beneficio social que funcionan bajo la asesoría del CCTT," from Agustín Castellanos C., January 15, 1960.

9. Vogt, *Fieldwork Among the Maya*, 101.

10. Romano Delgado, *Historia evaluativa*, 2:196.

11. Ibid., 192; see also Collier, *Fields of the Tzotzil*, 110–15.

12. Wasserstrom, *Class and Society*, 201–12.

13. AHCCITT, 1966/2, Dir., "Programa de trabajo que presenta la Sección de Agricultura del CCTT, para desarrollar durante el año de 1966," December 14, 1965; and Romano Delgado, *Historia evaluativa*, 2:290–91.

14. Collier, *Fields of the Tzotzil*, 79–108; and Romano Delgado, *Historia evaluativa*, 2:198–200.

15. CDI, BJR, ICCITT, 1959, "Informe de 1959," by Alfonso Villa Rojas. For more on how the agrarian reform process frustrated indigenous petitioners, see Reyes Ramos, *El reparto de tierras*, esp. 84–106.

16. CDI, BJR, ICCITT, 1957, "Informe de labores correspondientes al mes de abril," by Alfonso Villa Rojas.

17. "Centro Tzeltal-Tzotzil: El problema del maíz," *Acción Indigenista*, no. 5 (November 1953); Romano Delgado, *Historia evaluativa*, 2:207–8; and Wasserstrom, *Class and Society*, 201.

18. Romano Delgado, *Historia evaluativa*, 2:209, 215–21.

19. Ibid., 240–46.

20. AHCCITT, 1966/2, Dir., "Plan de Trabajo para el año de 1966," by Dir. de Ganadería Narciso Castillejos Gómez, December 14, 1965; CDI, BJR, César Tejeda Fonseca, "Experiencias en el cambio económico dirigido en la region tzeltal-tzotzil," unpublished manuscript, 1957; and Romano Delgado, *Historia evaluativa*, 2:244–46.

21. CDI, BJR, ICCITT, 1952, from Consejero Técnico Gonzalo Aguirre Beltrán to Dir. Julio de la Fuente, January 31, 1952.

22. Aguirre Beltrán, "Estructura y función," 33.

23. Nolasco Armas, "La antropología aplicada," 85.

24. Nash, *Mayan Visions*, 67, 69.

25. CDI, BJR, ICCITT, 1956, "Informe de julio de 1956," from Dir. de Ed. Fidencio Montes Sánchez; see also Benítez, *Los indios de México*, 1:241–54.

26. CDI, BJR, ICCITT, 1957, "Informe de octubre de 1957," from Dir. de Ed. Fidencio Montes Sánchez; 1958, "Informe de abril," by Alfonso Villa Rojas; "Informe de julio de 1958," by Dir. de Ed. Fidencio Montes Sánchez; and Romano Delgado, *Historia evaluativa*, 2:75, 101.

27. Núñez Tom, "Tareas del promotor," 121–25; and CDI, BJR, ICCITT, 1958, "Informe de julio de 1958," by Dir. de Ed. Fidencio Montes Sánchez.

28. CDI, BJR, ICCITT, 1957, "Informe de octubre," by Dir. de Ed. Fidencio Montes Sánchez.

29. Ibid., 1956, "Informe de labores correspondiente al mes de octubre," by Alfonso Villa Rojas, November 14, 1956; 1957, "Informe del mes de julio, 1957," by Otilio Vázquez Olivera; and "Informe," from Ismael Sánchez Carrera, October 1959.

30. Ibid., 1957, "Informe de labores correspondiente al mes de mayo 1957," by Alfonso Villa Rojas.

31. Ibid.,1959, "Abril de 1959," by Alfonso Villa Rojas; and Köhler, *Cambio cultural dirigido*, 275–76.

32. CDI, BJR, ICCITT, 1957, "Informe de labores correspondiente al mes de febrero, 1957," by César Tejeda Fonseca.

33. Cancuc lost its municipal status in 1922 and became an agencia municipal of Ocosingo. It regained its municipal status in 1989.

34. Guiteras-Holmes, *Perils of the Soul*, 354.

35. CDI, BJR, ICCITT, 1957, "Informe de labores correspondientes al mes de mayo 1957," by Alfonso Villa Rojas; and Köhler, *Cambio cultural dirigido*, 322.

36. De la Peña, "Nacionales y extranjeros," 65–66; Stoll, *Fishers of Men*, 68–70; and Townsend, *Lázaro Cárdenas*.

37. Slocum and Watkins, *The Good Seed*, 166.

38. AHCCITT, 1955, Ser. Dirección, Sec. Dirección, 24–1955/1, from Dir. Agustín Romano Delgado to Srita. Marianna Slocum in Corralito, Chis., Las Casas, January 28, 1955.

39. CDI, BJR, ICCITT, 1955, "Informe sobre el caso especial del sector evangélico de la región de Oxchuc y del reclutamiento de las alumnas del Internado. Actividad realizada del 28 de enero al 3 de febrero," by Insp. Reynaldo Salvatierra, February 5, 1955.

40. AHCCITT, 1955, Ser. Dirección, Sec. Dirección, 24–1955/1, from Marianna Slocum to Dir. Agustín Romano Delgado, from Corralito, January 31, 1955.

41. Ibid., Ser. Dirección, Sec. Dirección, 1–1955/1, from Agustín Romano Delgado to Alfonso Caso, March 11, 1955.

42. Ibid., from Gonzalo Aguirre Beltrán to Agustín Romano Delgado, March 17, 1955.

43. Ibid., from Agustín Romano Delgado to Gonzalo Aguirre Beltrán, March 22, 1955.

44. Romano Delgado, *Historia evaluativa*, 2:50–51. One Tsotsil primer and one Tseltal primer were made in 1975. No longer did the INI make special cartillas for the variants of Tsotsil spoken in Chamula, Chenalhó, Huixtán, and Zinacantán.

45. CDI, BJR, ICCITT, 1956, "Informe de octubre de 1956," by Dir. de Ed. Fidencio Montes Sánchez; and "Fragmentos del informe del investigador Alfonso Fabila, referentes a la intervención de los misioneros protestantes norteamericanos en la zona de Oxchuc."

46. AHCCITT, 1957, Ser. Dirección, Sec. Dirección, 1–1957/1, from Alfonso Villa Rojas to Francisco Gómez Sánchez in Mesbiljá, Oxchuc, June 17, 1957; and CDI, BJR, ICCITT, 1957, "Informes de julio de 1957," from Dir. de Ed. Fidencio Montes Sánchez.

47. CDI, BJR, ICCITT, 1957, "Informe del mes de julio, 1957," by Prof. Otilio Vázquez Olivera.

48. Emphasis mine. The "unity" of indigenous people was typically more imagined than real, but Fabila was correct to imply that these particular religious divisions were new.

49. CDI, BJR, "Fragmentos del informe del investigador Alfonso Fabila, referentes a la intervención de los misioneros protestantes norteamericanos en la zona de Oxchuc."

50. "Una mujer los civilizó," *Tiempo* 32, no. 814 (December 9, 1957): 50–55; see also CDI, BJR, Julio de la Fuente, "Rectificaciones y aclaraciones al artículo sobre la señorita Slocum."

51. In 1950, only 2 percent of the population of Chiapas was Protestant. By 2000, that number had risen to 42 percent. Today, many specialists estimate that more than half of all Chiapanecos are Protestants, and most of the converts are indigenous. In eastern Chiapas, Protestantism is deeply rooted, especially in and around Oxchuc, where Marianna Slocum and Florence Gerdel are still fondly remembered; see Guzmán Arias, "Misioneros al servicio de Dios y del Estado"; Morales Bermúdez, *Entre ásperos caminos llanos*, 116; and Rivera Farfán et al., *Diversidad religiosa y conflicto en Chiapas*.

52. Lomnitz, "Bordering on Anthropology," 189.
53. Vogt, *Fieldwork Among the Maya*, 107–12; and Vogt, *Zinacantán*, x.
54. Rus, "Rereading Tzotzil Ethnography," 203–4.
55. Vogt, *Fieldwork Among the Maya*, 347.
56. Rus, "Rereading Tzotzil Ethnography," 205.
57. Vogt, *Fieldwork Among the Maya*, 209.
58. Ibid., 210 (emphasis in the original).
59. Wilson, "Serving Two Mistresses," 420.
60. Rus, "Rereading Tzotzil Ethnography," 206.
61. AHCCITT, 1955, Ser. Dirección, Sec. Dirección, 1–1955/1, from Gonzalo Aguirre Beltrán to Agustín Romano Delgado, dated from Mexico City, February 2, 1955; and Romano Delgado, "Problemas fundamentales," 1.
62. AHCCITT, 1955, Ser. Dirección, Sec. Dirección, 1–1955/1, various, from Alfonso

Villa Rojas to Sec. Tres. del INI Antonio Salas Ortega, February–March 1956 (emphasis in the original).

63. Ibid., 1956, Ser. Dirección, Sec. Lingüística, 1956, 1–1956/1, from Alfonso Villa Rojas to Antonio Salas Ortega, February 24, 1956.

64. Ibid., August 7, 1956.

65. *Acción Indigenista*, no. 26 (August 26, 1955).

66. Sol Tax, "El gran despertar del mundo indígena," *Acción Indigenista*, no. 42 (December 1956).

Chapter 6

1. "Los materiales audiovisuales," *Acción Indigenista*, no. 13 (July 1954).
2. Beezley, "Introduction," 307–8.
3. Jackson Albarrán, "*Comino Vence al Diablo*," 358–59, 362–65.
4. Sánchez claims that there were five original puppeteers: two mestizas, a man and a woman from Zinacantán, and himself (from Ixtapa). See Sánchez Sánchez, *Alma del teatro Guiñol Petul*, 48.
5. AHCCITT, 1953/1, Ser. Dirección, Sec. Educación, "Lingüística"; and Castro, "Las metas del Teatro Petul," 2.
6. Sánchez Sánchez, *Alma del teatro Guiñol Petul*, 57–58.
7. Ibid., 58–59.
8. CDI, BJR, ICCITT, 1954, "Informe de la actividades desarrolladas durante el mes de septiembre de 1954," by Andrés Santiago Montes, September 20, 1954, 400.
9. Ibid., "Informe de noviembre de 1954," by Dir. de Ed. Fidencio Montes Sánchez, 539.
10. Ibid., "Informe de los trabajos efectuados durante el mes de noviembre por el grupo de Teatro Guignol bajo de dirección de Marco Antonio Montero, en el CCITT del INI," December 6, 1954.
11. Ibid.
12. Ibid.
13. Ibid.
14. Ibid.
15. *Acción Indigenista*, no. 21 (March 1955).
16. *Acción Indigenista*, no. 24 (June 1955).
17. Ibid.; *Acción Indigenista*, no. 70 (April 1959); and Sánchez Sánchez, *Alma del teatro Guiñol Petul*, 7–48.
18. Montes Sánchez, "Apertura educativa en los Altos de Chiapas," 88. In Chamula today, a puppet troupe calls itself the Petul Xun Theater.
19. Navarrete Cáceres, *Rosario Castellanos*, 122; and Castellanos and Montero, *Teatro Petul*, 1:4.
20. Marco Antonio Montero, *Petul visita el INI*, in Castellanos and Montero, *Teatro Petul*, 1:9–23. On Grajales's campaign against the Catholic Church and religion in

general, see Lewis, *The Ambivalent Revolution*, 67–80; Lisbona Guillén, *Persecución religiosa en Chiapas*; and Ríos Figueroa, *Siglo XX*, 73–109.

21. CDI, BJR, ICCITT, 1956, "Informe de labores correspondiente al mes de noviembre de 1956," by César Tejeda Fonseca, dated from San Cristóbal de Las Casas, December 10, 1956; and Sánchez Sánchez, *Alma del teatro Guiñol Petul*, 85.

22. Ibid., 1957, Castellanos's report included in Alfonso Villa Rojas's "Informe de labores correspondiente al mes de mayo 1957."

23. Zepeda, "Palabras en la fiesta," 186.

24. Agustín Romano Delgado, interview, Mexico City, January 16, 1995.

25. CDI, BJR, ICCITT, 1962, Teodoro Sánchez Sánchez, "Informe," cited in "Informe de labores realizadas en el Departamento de Ayudas Visuales durante el mes de febrero de 1962," by Marcelino Jiménez, Jefe del Departamento de Ayudas Visuales, 222.

26. Castellanos, *Petul en la Escuela Abierta*, in Castellanos and Montero, *Teatro Petul*, 1:65.

27. CDI, BJR, ICCITT, 1956, "Informe general de las actividades de la Escuela Abierta, desarrolladas en Oxchuc, durante los días 8 y 22 de julio de 1956," by Prof. Librado Mendoza Jarquín, July 31, 1956.

28. Ibid., "Escuela abierta de Chamula," by Carlo Antonio Castro.

29. Castellanos, *Petul en la campaña anti-alcóhlica*, in Castellanos, *Teatro Petul*, 3:17–28.

30. Castellanos, *Petul y el diablo extranjero*, in Castellanos, *Teatro Petul*, vol. 2.

31. CDI, BJR, ICCITT, 1956, from Prof. Onofre Montes Ríos, October 5, 1956. Silz may have been mistaken for an aguardiente inspector; see Fernández-Galán Rodríguez, "La muerte de un alemán," 425–64.

32. Castellanos and Montero, *Teatro Petul*, 1:8.

33. CDI, BJR, ICCITT, 1962, enero-febrero, Teodoro Sánchez Sánchez, "Informe," cited in "Informe de labores realizadas en el Departamento de Ayudas Visuales durante el mes de febrero de 1962," by Marcelino Jiménez, Jefe del Departamento de Ayudas Visuales, San Cristóbal de Las Casas, 223.

34. Sánchez Sánchez, *Alma del teatro Guiñol Petul*, 72. For another case involving infertility, see Montes Sánchez and Castro, *Educación, lingüística y ayudas visuales*, 8.

35. CDI, BJR, ICCITT, 1962, Teodoro Sánchez Sánchez, "Informe," cited in "Informe de labores realizadas en el Departamento de Ayudas Visuales durante el mes de febrero de 1962," by Marcelino Jiménez, Jefe del Departamento de Ayudas Visuales, San Cristóbal de Las Casas, February 1962, 224; see also Sánchez Sánchez, *Alma del teatro Guiñol Petul*, 75–76.

36. Sánchez Sánchez, *Alma del teatro Guiñol Petul*, 71.

37. CDI, BJR, ICCITT, 1960: 2, "Informe del mes de mayo," from Teodoro Sánchez Sánchez, June 17, 1960, 69–70.

38. Castellanos and Montero, *Teatro Petul*, 1:3.

39. "Sección audiovisual en el Papaloapan," *Acción Indigenista*, no. 69 (March 1959).

40. CDI, BJR, ICCITT, 1963: 3, "Informe correspondiente al mes de junio de 1963," from Dir. of Departamento de Ayudas Visuales Marcelino Jiménez, quoting Teodoro Sánchez Sánchez, head of the Tseltal group.
41. AHCCITT, 1970/1, Ser. Dirección, Sec. Ayudas Visuales, from Jefe del Grupo Pedro Pérez to Marcelino Jiménez, May 11, 1967.
42. Ibid., "Informes originales, 1962–70," from Pedro Pérez to Marcelino Jiménez, April 18, 1967, and May 11, 1967.
43. Susan Cato, "La historia del teatro guiñol de Chiapas de Marco Antonio Montero y Rosario Castellanos," *Proceso*, no. 905 (March 7, 1994): 62.
44. "Incident at Yalentay," in Ahern, *A Rosario Castellanos Reader*, 221.

Chapter 7

1. On medical pluralism in contemporary Mayan settings, see, among others, Adams and Hawkins, *Health Care in Maya Guatemala*.
2. For traditional healing in the Tseltal municipality of Amatenango, see Nash, *In the Eyes of the Ancestors*, 209; for Oxchuc, see Villa Rojas, *Etnografía tzeltal de Chiapas*, 317–458. For a discussion of the soul and traditional healing in Cancuc, see Pitarch, *The Jaguar and the Priest*.
3. In Chenalhó, it was believed that the animal spirit companions resided in a nearby forest. See Köhler, *Cambio cultural dirigido*, 115.
4. Holland, *Medicina maya*, 99–103; and Vogt, *Zinacantán*, 369–72.
5. Holland, *Medicina maya*, 120, 133, 161, 172, 178.
6. Ibid., 122.
7. Vogt, *Zinacantán*, 373.
8. Villa Rojas, *Etnografía tzeltal de Chiapas*, 354.
9. Romano Delgado, *Historia evaluativa*, 2:138, 139.
10. Holland, *Medicina maya*, 228–30.
11. Ibid., 231–32.
12. Roberto Robles Garnica, "El programa de salud," *Acción Indigenista*, no. 68 (March 1959); and Romano Delgado, *Historia evaluativa*, 2:138.
13. CDI, BJR, ICCITT, 1956, "Informe de octubre de 1956," from Dir. de Ed. Fidencio Montes Sánchez; Romano Delgado, *Historia evaluativa*, 2:134, 139; and Holland, *Medicina maya*, 185.
14. After working for many years with the INI and the SSA, Dr. Robles created and then directed the Department of Preventive Medicine in his home state of Michoacán in the 1970s and collaborated closely with Cuauhtémoc Cárdenas when he was governor of Michoacán (1980–1986). Robles joined Cárdenas in forming the Democratic Current (Corriente Democrático) within the PRI, then broke away from the PRI in 1988 to cofound the National Democratic Front (Frente Democrático Nacional, or FDN), which supported Cárdenas's frustrated candidacy in the 1988 presidential elections. Dr. Robles served one term as senator for the FDN (1988–1994) and helped

Cárdenas create the center-left Party of the Democratic Revolution (PRD), eventually succeeding Cárdenas as PRD party secretary. He tried to become the PRD's candidate for governor of Michoacán in 1995 but felt he was victim of a fraud in the PRD's internal election. He renounced his PRD membership and served as minister of health in the administration of PRI governor Víctor Manuel Tinoco Rubí (1996–2002). Dr. Robles died in Morelia, Michoacán, in January 2012. See Silvio Maldonado, "Una estrella que se apaga," *Núcleo Informativo: Periódico Electrónico*, January 31, 2012.

15. Navarette Cáceres, *Rosario Castellanos*, 38; and Romano Delgado, *Historia evaluativa*, 2:138.

16. Sánchez Sánchez, *Alma del teatro Guiñol Petul*, 67.

17. Sherman, *The Power of Plagues*, 118–21, 127.

18. Souder, *On a Farther Shore*, 244–63.

19. Sánchez Sánchez, *Alma del teatro Guiñol Petul*, 73.

20. Roberto Robles Garnica, "El programa de salud," *Acción Indigenista*, no. 68 (February 1959).

21. Navarette Cáceres, *Rosario Castellanos*, 18.

22. *Acción Indigenista*, no. 24 (June 1955).

23. Ibid.

24. CDI, BJR, ICCITT, 1955, "Plan de campaña contra el tifo en la region tzeltal-tzotzil," by Dr. Roberto Robles; 1956, "Actividades desarrolladas en el periodo de julio 1955–julio '56," from Robles, August 1, 1956; and Alfonso Villa Rojas to Roberto Robles Garnica, November 30, 1956.

25. Ibid., 1956, "Informe de la gira realizada por el Teatro Guiñol, por el municipio de Oxchuc, durante el mes de noviembre," by Rosario Castellanos.

26. Cueto, *Cold War, Deadly Fevers*, 117, 131, 148–49.

27. CDI, BJR, ICCITT, 1957, "Informe de la supervisión a la sección de salubridad del CCTT efectuada del 12 al 26 de junio de 1957," by Dr. Roberto Robles, July 11, 1957.

28. Rosario Castellanos, *Petul, promotor sanitario*, in Castellanos, *Teatro Petul*, 3:5–14; and Sánchez Sánchez, *Alma del teatro Guiñol Petul*, 68.

29. CDI, BJR, ICCITT, 1958, from Dr. Francisco Alarcón to Alfonso Villa Rojas, May 12, 1958; and Romano Delgado, *Historia evaluativa*, 2:154.

30. CDI, BJR, ICCITT, 1959, "Septiembre de 1959," by Alfonso Villa Rojas.

31. Ibid., 1956, "Informe de labores correspondiente al mes de agosto," by Alfonso Villa Rojas; and Köhler, *Cambio cultural dirigido*, 276.

32. CDI, BJR, ICCITT, 1958, "Informe de abril," by Alfonso Villa Rojas.

33. Ibid., 1957, "Informe del mes de mayo," from Dir. de Salubridad Dr. Franciso Alarcón Navarro, May 31, 1957; and 1963, from Dir. del Departamento de Ayudas Visuales Marcelino Jiménez, citing Teodoro Sánchez.

34. Vogt, *Zinacantán*, 386–87, 447–54.

35. Robles Garnica, "Tres años en los Altos," 472.

36. CDI, BJR, ICCITT, 1957, "Informe de labores correspondiente al mes de abril, 1957," by Alfonso Villa Rojas.

37. Ibid., 1958, "Informe de labores, julio de 1958," by Alfonso Villa Rojas.
38. Ibid., "Informe de mayo," by Alfonso Villa Rojas.
39. Nash, *Mayan Visions*, 67. Nash attributes this particular accusation to Héctor Díaz-Polanco, "Lo nacional y lo étnico en México," 32–42.
40. Holland, *Medicina maya*, 211, 222.
41. Vogt, *Zinacantán*, 608.
42. Nash, *In the Eyes of the Ancestors*, 209; and Vogt, *Zinacantán*, 608.
43. Holland, *Medicina maya*, 222, 226, 234.
44. Ibid., 243–44.
45. Ibid., 224, 242.
46. Robles Garnica, "Tres años en los Altos," 472–73.
47. Holland, *Medicina maya*, 238.
48. Ibid., 227, 235–36.
49. Nash, *Mayan Visions*, 67.
50. Holland, *Medicina maya*, 239, 241–42.
51. CDI, BJR, ICCITT, 1956, "Informe de labores correspondiente al mes de septiembre, 1956," from Alfonso Villa Rojas, October 13, 1956; 1959, "Informe de abril," by Alfonso Villa Rojas; Favre, *Cambio y continuidad*, 363; Köhler, *Cambio cultural dirigido*, 268; and Romano Delgado, *Historia evaluativa*, 2:125.
52. Romano Delgado, *Historia evaluativa*, 2:128, 175.
53. Roberto Robles Garnica, "El programa de salud," *Acción Indigenista*, no. 68 (February 1959).

Chapter 8

1. Gillingham, "Sex, Death and Structuralism," 621.
2. Vogt, *Fieldwork Among the Maya*, 139.
3. CDI, BJR, ICCITT, 1959, "Marzo de 1959," by Alfonso Villa Rojas.
4. Ibid., "Febrero de 1959," "Marzo de 1959," and "Abril de 1959," by Alfonso Villa Rojas.
5. Benítez, *Los indios de México*, 1:211.
6. CDI, BJR, Carlos Incháustegui, "Cuatro puntos sobre política indigenista," unpublished manuscript, November 1972, 4, 7; see also Romano Delgado, "Problemas fundamentales," 2.
7. CDI, BJR, ICCITT, 1957, from Carlo Antonio Castro, "Informe correspondiente al mes de mayo de 1957 (Lingüística)."
8. Gómez Montero, "Alberto Beltrán recuerda," 190–91.
9. Rosario Castellanos, letter to Marco Antonio Montero, October 10, 1957, in Navarrete Cáceres, *Rosario Castellanos*, 26.
10. Navarrete Cáceres, *Rosario Castellanos*, 26.
11. In 1960, Castellanos took on San Cristóbal's ladinos in a collection of searingly critical short stories entitled *Ciudad Real*. She dedicated this book to the INI in

Chiapas, suggesting that the anger and frustration that motivated her resignation had subsided. See also Gastón García Cantú, "Rosario Castellanos: El vínculo con la tierra y sus dioses," *Excélsior*, August 11, 1974.

12. Köhler, *Cambio cultural dirigido*, 329.
13. CDI, BJR, ICCITT, 1958, from "Informe de mayo" by Alfonso Villa Rojas.
14. Köhler, *Cambio cultural dirigido*, 171.
15. AHCCITT, 1969, from Subdirector Técnico General Héctor Sánchez Calderón to Dir. del CCITT Maurilio Muñoz, dated from Mexico City, June 17, 1969.
16. Ibid., 1967, 1, Exp. 3, to Jefe de la Sección de Salubridad Dr. Ricardo Romero Flores from Enfra. Rosenda Cruz Morales, October 20, 1967.
17. Ibid., to Jefe de la Sec. de Salubridad Dr. Ricardo Romero Flores from Dr. Miguel Muñoz Pavón, October 28, 1967.
18. CDI, BJR, ICCITT, 1961, "Dirección," by Dir. Raúl Rodríguez Ramos, early 1961.
19. Ibid., 1960, "Informe anual que abarca del primero de septiembre de 1959 al treinta y uno de agosto de 1960," by Dir. de Ed. Fidencio Montes Sánchez.
20. Ibid., 1959, "Informe del mes de mayo de 1959," by Dir. de Ed. Fidencio Montes Sánchez.
21. Ibid., from Alfonso Villa Rojas, February 1959; and "9 jóvenes terminan los cursos de educación en el internado del INI," *Acción Indigenista*, no. 81 (March 1960).
22. Köhler, *Cambio cultural dirigido*, 240; and CDI, BJR, ICCITT, 1960, "Informe de marzo de 1960," from Alfonso Villa Rojas.
23. CDI, BJR, ICCITT, 1960, "Informe de marzo de 1960" and "Informe de abril de 1960," by Fidencio Montes Sánchez.
24. Ibid., "Informe de mayo de 1960," from Fidencio Montes Sánchez.
25. See Lewis, *The Ambivalent Revolution*.
26. CDI, BJR, ICCITT, 1954, "Informe de junio," from Dir. de Ed. Andrés Santiago Montes to Dir. del CCITT Prof. Alberto Jiménez Rodríguez, June 30, 1964; see also Greaves Laine, "De la cartilla al libro de texto gratuito," 192–95.
27. Greaves Laine, "De la cartilla al libro de texto gratuito," 193; Modiano and Pérez Hernández, "Educación," 64; and Pineda, *Caciques culturales*, 80, 110. In 1963, INI cultural promoters were paid 400 pesos monthly; federal teachers earned twice that amount. See Köhler, *Cambio cultural dirigido*, 173.
28. CDI, BJR, ICCITT, 1964, "Informe anual de labores," by Dir. de Ed. Andrés Santiago Montes to Dir. del CCITT Alberto Jiménez Rodríguez, December 10, 1964.
29. AHCCITT, 1969/4, Ser. Dir., "Programa de trabajo para el año 1969"; CDI, BJR, ICCITT, 1964, from Dir. de Ed. Andrés Santiago Montes to Dir. del CCITT Alberto Jiménez Rodríguez, August 31, 1964; and "Informe anual de labores," from Dir. de Ed. Andrés Santiago Montes to Dir. Alberto Jiménez Rodríguez, December 10, 1964.
30. CDI, BJR, ICCITT, 1965, from Supervisor Escolar J. Encarnación Hernández López, "Informe correspondiente al mes de abril de 1965."
31. Ibid., 1964, from Dir. de Ed. Andrés Santiago Montes to Dir. del CCITT Alberto Jiménez Rodríguez, September 30, 1964.

32. Romano Delgado, *Historia evaluativa*, 2:44–47.

33. Arana de Swadesh, "¿Cúal será el futuro de la educación indígena?," 242; and Greaves Laine, "De la cartilla al libro de texto gratuito," 193–95.

34. CDI, BJR, ICCITT, 1965, from Dir. de Ed. Andrés Santiago Montes, April 30, 1965, and from Supervisor Escolar J. Encarnación Hernández López, "Informe correspondiente al mes de abril de 1965."

35. Arias Pérez, "Movimientos indígenas contemporáneos," 389–91; CDI, BJR, ICCITT, 1964, from Dir. de Ed. Andrés Santiago Montes to Dir. del CCITT Alberto Jiménez Rodríguez, September 30, 1964; and Montes Sánchez, "Apertura educativa en los Altos de Chiapas," 92.

36. Pozas Arciniega, "El indigenismo y la ayuda mutua," 158.

37. Miranda hailed from Chilapa, Guerrero, where Caso wanted to open another Coordinating Center to work with the nearby Mixtec, Nahua, and Tlapanec populations.

38. Andrés Medina Hernández, interview, August 12, 2011; and Nahmad Sittón, "Una experiencia indigenista," 284, 290.

39. AHCCITT, 1967/1, Exp. 1, to Prof. Alberto Jiménez Rodríguez from Sub-Director Gen. Admin. Antonio Salas Ortega, dated from Mexico City, June 8, 1967.

40. Ibid., Exp. 3, from Dir. de la Sec. de Salubridad Dr. Ricardo Romero Flores to Prof. Alberto Jiménez Rodríguez, March 15, 1967.

41. Ibid., from Dir. de la Sec. de Salubridad Dr. Ricardo Romero Flores to Jefe del Departamento de Medicina Social Dr. José López Rodríguez, September 7, 1967.

42. Romano Delgado, *Historia evaluativa*, 2:130.

43. AHCCITT, 1968/2, Dirección, from Nicolás T. Zavala to Dir. del CCITT Maurilio Muñoz Basilio, November 1967–October 1968; and AHCCITT, 1968/1, Dirección, Exp. 1, from Dir. del CCITT Maurilio Muñoz Basilio to Asesor Técnico del INI Antonio Salas Ortega, 1968.

44. AHCCITT, 1967/1, Exp. 3, to Subdirector Gral. Administrativo del INI from Dir. del CCI Alberto Jiménez Rodríguez, August 25, 1967.

45. Ibid., 1970/4, Dirección, Exp. 84, from Jefe de la Sección de Salubridad Dr. Gregorio Alapisco González to Dir. of CCITT Maurilio Muñoz Basilio, November 28, 1970.

46. Ibid., December 2, 1970.

47. Marco Antonio Montero, *El sueño de Petul*, in Castellanos and Montero, *Teatro Petul*, 1:25–41.

48. Romano Delgado, *Historia evaluativa*, 2:169, 253.

49. CDI, BJR, ICCITT, 1960, "Informe de junio," by Alfonso Villa Rojas.

50. CDI, BJR, "Seminario Indigenista Latinoamericano," report by Técnico Forestal Eliseo Peraldo Porras, San Cristóbal de Las Casas, 1971.

51. CDI, BJR, ICCITT, 1960, "Junio de 1960," by Alfonso Villa Rojas.

52. Ibid. (emphasis in the original).

53. Ibid., 1961, "Junio de 1960," by Alfonso Villa Rojas.

54. Romano Delgado, *Historia evaluativa*, 2:254; and Luis Suárez, "Del México superviviente," *Acción Indigenista*, no. 84 (June 1960).
55. CDI, BJR, ICCITT, 1961, January–February, "Informe del mes de febrero de 1961," by Dir. de CCITT Raúl Rodríguez Ramos.
56. Ibid., by Dir. Raúl Rodríguez Ramos.
57. Ibid., "Informe mensual," from Jefe del Departamento Forestal Eliseo Peralta Porras to Dir. de Centro Raúl Rodríguez Ramos.
58. Ibid., 1964, from Ing. Eliseo Peralta Porras to Dir. Agustín Romano Delgado, January 15, 1964.
59. AHCCITT, 1968/1, Dirección, Exp. 1, from Dir. del CCITT Maurilio Muñoz Basilio to Asesor Técnico del INI Antonio Salas Ortega, July 9, 1968; 1969/5, "Informe annual, 1969; CDI, BJR, ICCITT, 1961, January–February, "Informe del mes de febrero de 1961," by Dir. de CCITT Raúl Rodríguez Ramos; 1964, from Ing. Eliseo Peralta Porras, February 18, 1964; and Romano Delgado, *Historia evaluativa*, 2:255.
60. AHCCITT, 1969/1, Dirección, from Jefe de la Sección de Agricultura Antonio Vera Mora to Prof. Maurilio Muñoz Basilio, August 25, 1969.
61. SEPI, AH, DGAI, 1969/1, Exp. 77.53.8, from Dir. of DGAI Manuel Castellanos Cancino to Governor and Pres. of the Comisión Forestal en el Edo. José Castillo Tielemans, June 26, 1969; and AHCCITT, 1969/4, Dirección, "Programa de trabajo para el año 1969," by Maurilio Muñoz Basilio.
62. AHCCITT, 1969/1, Dirección, from Jefe de la Sección de Agricultura Antonio Vera Mora to Prof. Maurilio Muñoz Basilio, August 25, 1969.
63. CDI, BJR, ICCITT, 1971, "Informe anual de actividades desarrolladas por el CCI durante el año de 1971," from Dir. del Centro Carlos Felipe Verduzco to Gonzalo Aguirre Beltrán, December 13, 1971.
64. Sariego, *El indigenismo en Chihuahua*, 146.
65. Barabas and Bartolomé, "Desarrollo hidráulico y etnocidio," 2:356–57.
66. Rosario Castellanos, letter to Janet Marren and Marcey Jacobsen, dated from Nuevo Paso Nacional, November 27, 1957, from the collection of Helga Lobell. My thanks to Carter Wilson and Jan Rus for sharing this letter.
67. Instituto Nacional Indigenista, *Realidades y proyectos*, 124–27.
68. Partridge, Brown, and Nugent, "The Papaloapan Dam and Resettlement Project," 258.
69. The accusation was levied by Barabas and Bartolomé; see "Desarrollo hidráulico y etnocidio," 2:353–67. Aguirre's scathing response can be found in the same volume; see "Etnocidio en México," 369–83.
70. AHCCITT, 1969/3, Dirección, "Informe sobre el estudio de la localidades de Vega del Paso y San Francisco, ambas del municipio de Venustiano Carranza, Chiapas, relativo al reacomodo de la poblacion que traerá consigo la construcción de la presa La Angostura," by Jefe del Departamento Legal, Moisés Flores Rocha; and 1970/3, Dirección, "Informe sobre la situación que guardan actualmente los indígenas de Vega del Paso," by Prof. Ignacio León Pacheco, March 15, 1970.

71. AHCCITT, 1969/4, Dirección, to Alfonso Torres, Coord. General de las Obras del Alto Grijalva, from Presidente del Comité de Bienes Comunales Bartolomé Martínez Vásquez and others, dated from Venustiano Carranza, April 7, 1969.
72. Ibid., 1970/3, Dirección, from Bartolomé Gómez Mendoza and fifty-two others to Maurilio Muñoz Basilio, June 25, 1970.
73. Ibid., from Bartolomé Gómez Mendoza and thirty-eight others to Dir. del CCITT, September 10, 1970.
74. Nahmad Sittón, "Estudio introductorio," 34.
75. ACCITT, 1970/3, Dirección, from Dir. del CCITT Maurilio Muñoz Basilio to Luis Torres Ordoñez, Dir. de Promoción Económica, INI, September 30, 1970.
76. Ibid., 1970/1, Dirección, "Informe de labores realizadas por el CCITT, correspondiente del 1 de diciembre de 1969 al 15 de septiembre de 1970," by Dir. del CCITT Maurilio Muñoz Basilio.
77. Secretaría de Industria y Comercio, *VIII Censo general de población, 1960*; and Secretaría de Industria y Comercio, *IX Censo general de población, 1970*.
78. Rus, "The 'Comunidad Revolucionaria Institucional,'" 292.
79. SEPI, AH, DGAI, 1968/2, "Informe de las actividades desarrolladas en la Dir. Gral. de Asuntos Indígenas del 1 de noviembre de 1967 al 15 de septiembre de 1968"; and SEPI, AH, DGAI, 1970, Exp. 76.54.12, from Pres. of Asociación Agrícola Local de Cafeticultores de Huixtla Jaime Fernández Artendariz.
80. SEPI, AH, DGAI, 1973, Box 3, Exp. 77, from Delegado de Asuntos Indígenas Ramiro Aranda Osorio to Dir. Gral. de Asuntos Indígenas, SCLC, dated from Motozintla, January 4, 1971.
81. Ibid., 1971/3, from Delegado Ramiro Aranda Osorio to Dir. de Asuntos Indígenas Ángel Robles, SCLC, dated from Motozintla, August 26, 1971.
82. Ibid., "Plan de Trabajo," from Delegado de Asuntos Indígenas Ramiro Aranda Osorio, dated from Motozintla, May 22, 1971.
83. Ibid., 1969/3, Exp. 77.53.10, from Sec. Gen. del STI Agustín Méndez Gómez to Gerente de la Asociación Agrícola Local de Cafeticultores de Soconusco Fernando Acosta Ruiz, August 26, 1969; and from Agustín Méndez Gómez to Manuel Castellanos Cancino, October 20, 1969.
84. Viqueira, *Encrucijadas chiapanecas*, 80; see also Benjamin, *A Rich Land, a Poor People*, 223; and García de León, *Fronteras interiores*, 119.
85. Reyes Ramos, *El reparto de tierras*, 91–92.
86. CDI, BJR, ICCITT, 1967, to Dir. del CCITT Prof. Alberto Jiménez Rodríguez, from Jefe de la Sección de Agricultura Ing. Antonio Vera Mora, March 26, 1968.
87. CDI, BJR, "Seminaro Indigenista Latinoamericano," San Cristóbal de Las Casas, report by Jefe de la Sección Jurídica Moisés Flores Rocha, March 1971.
88. Mariátegui, *Seven Interpretive Essays*, 22.
89. CDI, BJR, ICCITT, 1967, "Proyecto de reacomodo de los excedentes de la población indígena de los Altos de Chiapas," signed by Subdirector General Administrativo Antonio Salas Ortega, Contadora Irma García Zamora, and Controlador General Ernesto Sentíes Hoyos, October 5, 1967.

90. Marroquín, "La política indigenista en México," 225.
91. AHCCITT, 1969/5, "Informe annual, 1969."

Chapter 9

1. See, among others, Vázquez León, "Entrevista a Ricardo Pozas Arciniega," 164–65; García de León, "Chamula: Una larga historia de resistencia," 13–18; Instituto Nacional Indigenista, ¿Ha fracasado el indigenismo?; Pineda, Caciques culturales; and Rus, "The Struggle Against Indigenous Caciques," 169–200.
2. Knight, "Caciquismo in Twentieth-Century Mexico," 11–14.
3. Pineda, Caciques culturales; Rus, "The 'Comunidad Revolucionaria Institucional'"; and Rus, "The Struggle Against Indigenous Caciques."
4. Rus, "The Struggle Against Indigenous Caciques," 174.
5. Ibid., 174–75.
6. Pitarch, The Jaguar and the Priest, 96. Guiteras-Holmes conducted fieldwork in Cancuc in 1944 as a student at Mexico's Escuela Nacional de Antropología e Historia but was refused entry into the municipality in 1953 on suspicions that she was a Protestant. See Guiteras-Holmes, Perils of the Soul.
7. Pitarch, The Jaguar and the Priest, 95.
8. Ibid., 116; and CDI, BJR, ICCITT, 1959, "Marzo de 1959," by Alfonso Villa Rojas.
9. Romano Delgado, Historia evaluativa, 1:268.
10. Aguirre Beltrán, Formas de gobierno indígena, 149.
11. CDI, BJR, INI, Libro de Actas, de septiembre de 1950 a diciembre de 1951, 38–39.
12. Köhler, Cambio cultural dirigido, 315.
13. López Pérez, Cómo defenderse del ladino, 49.
14. CDI, BJR, ICCITT, 1955, from Director del Internado Profr. Librado Mendoza Jarquín's "Informe de las actividades realizadas en el internado dependiente del Instituto Nacional Indigenista, durante el tiempo comprendido del 10 al 20 de junio de 1955."
15. Ibid., 1956, "Informe de labores correspondiente al mes de octubre," by Alfonso Villa Rojas.
16. Francisco Liévano, interview by Jan Rus, San Cristóbal de Las Casas, October 28, 1975, and January 14, 1976. My thanks to Jan Rus for sharing his transcribed notes.
17. Vogt, Fieldwork Among the Maya, 99.
18. CDI, BJR, ICCITT, 1959, "Informe de septiembre," by Dir. Fidencio Montes Sánchez.
19. Pineda, "Maestros bilingües," 292.
20. Romano Delgado, Historia evaluativa, 3:337; and Jan Rus, personal communication, January 2016.
21. Acción Indigenista, no. 2 (August 1953).
22. Collier, "Peasant Politics and the Mexican State," 72, 80, 83.
23. CDI, BJR, ICCITT, 1957, "Informe de agosto de 1957," by Dir. de Ed. Fidencio Montes Sánchez.

24. Rus, "The Struggle Against Indigenous Caciques," 175.
25. Rus, "The 'Comunidad Revolucionaria Institutional,'" 292, 293.
26. Ibid., 294.
27. CDI, BJR, ICCITT, 1958, from "Informe de mayo" by Alfonso Villa Rojas.
28. Nash, *In the Eyes of the Ancestors*, 244–47, 279; see also Foster, "Peasant Society," 293–315.
29. Cancian, *The Decline of Community in Zinacantán*, 78–79; Collier and Quaratiello, *Basta! Land and the Zapatista Rebellion*, 107–24; Wasserstrom, *Class and Society*, 212; and Favre, "El cambio socio-cultural," 177–80.
30. SEPI, AH, DGAI, 1968/2, "Informe de las actividades desarrolladas en la Dirección General de Asuntos Indígenas del 1 de noviembre al 15 de septiembre de 1968," by Manuel Castellanos Cancino.
31. CDI, BJR, ICCITT, 1968, from Subdirector Técnico de Educación Prof. Ignacio León Pacheco to Dir. del CCI Maurilio Muñoz Basilio, August 31, 1968.
32. Fazio, *Samuel Ruiz*, 62–63 (emphasis in the original).
33. Benítez, *Los indios de México*, 1:151.
34. Ibid., 1:152–54. The governor at the time was Samuel León Brindis.
35. In 1958, the diocese of Tapachula was created by Ruiz's predecessor; in 1965, Ruiz oversaw the creation of the diocese of Tuxtla Gutiérrez. See Morales Bermúdez, *Entre ásperos caminos llanos*, 140.
36. Fazio, *Samuel Ruiz*, 78.
37. Ibid., 93–95; Kovic, *Mayan Voices for Human Rights*, 47–53; MacEóin, *The People's Church*, 24–27; and Morales Bermúdez, *Entre ásperos caminos llanos*, 117–59.
38. Rus, "The Struggle Against Indigenous Caciques," 182.
39. Kovic, *Mayan Voices for Human Rights*, 77.
40. Iribarrén, *Misión Chamula*, 3–6.
41. Kovic, *Mayan Voices for Human Rights*, 77.
42. Ibid., 79, 81.
43. Iribarrén, *Misión Chamula*, 4; and Kovic, *Mayan Voices for Human Rights*, 77.
44. Iribarrén, *Misión Chamula*, 21–22; and Rus, "The Struggle Against Indigenous Caciques," 175.
45. Gossen, *Telling Maya Tales*, 217.
46. Rus, "The 'Comunidad Revolucionaria Institucional,'" 298; see also Cantón Delgado, "Las expulsiones indígenas," 153–55.
47. AHCCITT, 1968/2, Dirección, "Síntesis de las labores desarrolladas por el Centro Coordinador Tzeltal-Tzotzil," September 1, 1967–August 31, 1968; and Rus, "The Struggle Against Indigenous Caciques," 177–78.
48. CDI, BJR, ICCITT, 1965, from Dir. de Ed. Andrés Santiago Montes, May 31, 1965.
49. The daily minimum wage in 1968 was three pesos, but since most Chamulas earned far short of the minimum wage the tax amount was quite onerous. Cash advances ranged from thirty-three to seventy-two pesos.

50. SEPI, AH, DGAI, 1968, from Manuel López Ich, Miguel Díaz Teltuc, Martín de la Cruz Zuron, Nicolás Santis, Domingo Pérez Vicente and others from Las Ollas hamlet, La Candelaria colonia, to Gov. del Estado, February 22, 1968.

51. Ibid., 1968/2, from Manuel Castellanos Cancino, "Informe de las actividades desarrolladas en la Dirección General de Asuntos Indígenas del 1 de noviembre de 1967 al 15 de septiembre de 1968"; and AHCCITT, 1967/1 Subdirección.

52. SEPI, AH, DGAI, 1968/3, Exp. 77.52.8, from Manuel Castellanos Cancino to Dir. Gral. de Asuntos Indígenas Luis Felipe Obregón, September 18, 1968.

53. Ibid., 1968/2, from Manuel Castellanos Cancino, "Informe de las actividades desarrolladas en la Dirección General de Asuntos Indígenas del 1 de noviembre de 1967 al 15 de septiembre de 1968"; Favre, "El cambio socio-cultural," 187; and Rus, "The Struggle Against Indigenous Caciques," 181.

54. AHCCITT, 1969/3, from Pres. Municipal Juan Gómez Osob, Síndico Municipal Juan Patishtán Gómez, and several others to Gov. José Castillo Tielemans, dated from Chamula, February 12, 1969.

55. Ibid., 1970/4, Ser.: Dirección, from Teodoro Sánchez Sánchez, "Informe de las actividades desarrolladas por el suscrito maestro 'B' de G.P.N.U.T.F., comisionado en el departamento audiovisual del CCITT, durante el primer trimestre correspondiente a los meses de diciembre de 1968, enero y febrero de 1969," January 28, 1970. Note how Sánchez now refers to himself as a "maestro."

56. Ibid., 1970/1, Departamento Legal, from Dir. de Asuntos Indígenas Manuel Castellanos Cancino, Dir. del CCI Maurilio Muñoz Basilio, and Agente del Ministerio Público Ledín Ruiz to Subsecretario General del Gobierno del Estado Francisco Pineda Aguilar, San Cristóbal, October 12, 1969.

57. Kovic, *Mayan Voices for Human Rights*, 79, 81.

58. AHCCITT, 1970/1, Departamento Legal, from Dir. de Asuntos Indígenas Manuel Castellanos Cancino, Dir. del CCI Maurilio Muñoz Basilio, and Agente del Ministerio Público Ledín Ruiz to Subsecretario General del Gobierno del Estado Francisco Pineda Aguilar, San Cristóbal, October 12, 1969.

59. Ibid., 1969/3, from Dir. of CCI Maurilio Muñoz Basilio to Dir. of INI Alfonso Caso, October 9, 13, 1969.

60. Ibid., 1971/1, Departamento Legal, Exp. 1, to Agente del Ministerio Público from Obispo de San Cristóbal de Las Casas Samuel Ruiz, October 12, 1969.

61. Verduzco was about to become director of the INI's new Selva Lacandona Coordinating Center in Ocosingo, in eastern Chiapas.

62. CDI, BJR, ICCITT, 1971, "Información del Señor Carlos Felipe Verduzco, Director del Centro de Chiapas," interview by Alfonso Villa Rojas, September 2, 1971, Mexico City.

63. García de León, *Fronteras interiores*, 122; and Fazio, *Samuel Ruiz*, 102, 117.

64. Dawson, *Indian and Nation*, 98; and Saldívar Tanaka, *Prácticas cotidianas del estado*, 60, 136.

65. Knight, "Caciquismo in Twentieth-Century Mexico," 14, 17, 33, 37, 43.

Chapter 10

1. The actual death toll is disputed. The official count stands at 49, international journalists reported upward of 325 dead, and other estimates range as high as 750.
2. Carey, *Plaza of Sacrifices*; and Poniatowska, *La noche de Tlatelolco*.
3. Zolov, *Refried Elvis*.
4. Aguilar Camín and Meyer, *In the Shadow of the Mexican Revolution*, 201.
5. Lomnitz, "Bordering on Anthropology," 168–69.
6. Coffey, *How a Revolutionary Art Became Official Culture*, 127–29.
7. De la Peña, "La antropología y la política indigenista en México."
8. Ángel Palerm and Rodolfo Stavenhagen rounded out the Magnificent Seven but did not contribute chapters to *De eso que llaman antropología mexicana*.
9. Kiddle and Lenti, "Co-opting Cardenismo," 180–81.
10. Basurto, "The Late Populism of Luis Echeverría," 97–105; Knight, "Cárdenas and Echeverría," 28, 32; and Walker, *Waking from the Dream*, 26.
11. Aviña, *Specters of Revolution*; and Rodríguez Kuri, "Challenges, Political Opposition, Economic Disaster," 497.
12. Medina Hernández, "Diez años decisivos," 63–64.
13. Ibid., 49–53; and Price, *Weaponizing Anthropology*, 25–26.
14. Warman, "Todos santos y todos difuntos," 28–29.
15. Ibid., 34–35.
16. Bonfil Batalla, "Del indigenismo de la revolución," 43.
17. Ibid., 55, 59.
18. Olivera Bustamante, "Algunos problemas de la investigación antropológica actual," 110–11.
19. Nolasco Armas, "La antropología aplicada," 82–84; see also Saldívar Tanaka, *Prácticas cotidianas del estado*, 67.
20. Nolasco Armas, "La antropología aplicada," 81.
21. Bonfil Batalla, "Del indigenismo de la revolución," 43; see also Esteva, "Lo indígena y lo campesino," 264; and Olivera Bustamante, "Una incursion en el campo indigenista," 246.
22. Bonfil Batalla, "Del indigenismo de la revolución," 45.
23. Sodi M., "Algunas ideas de Alfonso Caso," 198.
24. Andrés Medina Hernández, interview, Mexico City, August 2, 2006.
25. "Declaración de Barbados: Por la liberación del indígena," in Medina Hernández and García Mora, *La quiebra política*, 2:520, 523–24.
26. Bonfil Batalla, "Admitamos que los indios no nacieron equivocados," 150.
27. Campbell, "El indigenismo necesita una nueva teoría," 133.
28. Sodi M., "Algunas ideas de Alfonso Caso," 198.
29. Instituto Nacional Indigenista, *¿Ha fracasado el indigenismo?*, 9–13.
30. Responsibility for the Corpus Christi massacre remains a subject of debate. Those who argue that Echeverría himself ordered the attack include Elaine Carey

(*Plaza of Sacrifices*, 164–68) and Enrique Krauze (*La presidencia imperial*, 403–18). See also Paula Carrizosa, "Echeverría se encargó de operar personalmente el 'halconazo,' reveló Herrera Burquetas," *La Jornada de Oriente*, July 24, 2011; and "Alfonso Martínez Domínguez: 'La matanza fue preparada por Luis Echeverría,'" *Proceso*, November 7, 2002. Recently, Louise Walker has argued that Echeverría's old-guard rivals—including Mexico City mayor Alonso Martínez Domínguez—tried to use the attack to embarrass the president. An infuriated Echeverría sacked Martínez Domínguez and the police chief in the days following the attack; see Walker, *Waking from the Dream*, 27–30.

31. Aguirre Beltrán, *Obra polémica*, 172.
32. Instituto Nacional Indigenista, *¿Ha fracasado el indigenismo?*, 90–91.
33. Ibid., 159.
34. Marroquín, "La política indigenista en México," 218.
35. Ibid., 220–21.
36. Ibid., 208–9.
37. Ibid., 221–22, 225.
38. Ibid., 218–19; see also Horcasitas de Pozas and Pozas, "Del monolingüismo en lengua indígena," 148.
39. Marroquín, "La política indigenista en México," 219, 225; and Pozas Arciniega, "El indigenismo y la ayuda mutua," 157.
40. Pozas, *La antropología y la burocracia indigenista*, 33–34.
41. Ibid., 35, 36.
42. Ibid., 38.
43. Ibid., 16.
44. Aguirre Beltrán, "Sobre 'La antropología y la burocracia indigenista,'" 449–57. A more serious critique of Pozas's pamphlet can be found in the same volume; see Albores Z., "*Antropología y burocracia indigenista*, nota crítica," 459–69.
45. Pozas, *La antropología y la burocracia indigenista*, 32.
46. Nahmad Sittón, "Una experiencia indigenista," 284, 290.
47. Ibid., 285–86.
48. Salomón Nahmad Sittón, interview, Oaxaca City, August 6, 2011.
49. Nahmad Sittón, "Una experiencia indigenista," 294.
50. Villa Rojas, Introduction to *El indigenismo en acción*, 19.
51. Romano Delgado, "La política indigenista en México," 1069.
52. Pozas Arciniega, "El indigenismo y la ayuda mutua," 160; and Campbell, "Aguirre Beltrán," 105.
53. Secretaría de Educación Pública, *Alfonso Caso*, 14.
54. Instituto Nacional Indigenista, *¿Ha fracasado el indigenismo?*, 161.
55. Secretaría de Educación Pública, *Alfonso Caso*, 15–16.
56. Rulfo, "Juan Rulfo y Fernando Benítez hablan sobre los indios," 126.
57. Romano Delgado, "La política indigenista en México," 1072.
58. Villa Rojas, "Integración y etnocidio," 145.
59. Ibid., 147.

60. Pozas Arciniega, "El indigenismo y la ayuda mutua," 161.

61. Campbell, "El indigenismo necesita una nueva teoría," 132; Herrasti, "Instituto Nacional Indigenista," 256; and Saldívar Tanaka, *Prácticas cotidianas del estado*, 45–46.

Chapter 11

1. Cancian, *The Decline of Community in Zinacantán*, 30–31.

2. Archivo General del Estado (hereafter AGE), "Problemas sociales, de urgente resolución al grupo indígena Chamula y Lacandón, Chiapas," by I. P. S., November 1970.

3. On Simojovel, see Toledo Tello, *Historia del movimiento indígena en Simojovel*, 101–40. On the FLN, see García de León, *Fronteras interiores*, 151–56, 163–66, 176; and Tello Díaz, *Chiapas: La rebelión de las Cañadas*, 61–66. On Ocosingo and Venustiano Carranza, see Harvey, *The Chiapas Rebellion*, 79–80, 99–101.

4. CDI, BJR, "Guión Informe PRODESCH, San Cristóbal," n.d.

5. AGE, "PRODESCH: Sumario de un esfuerzo promocional que se transforma en acciones para la superación del hombre," 1976.

6. Romano Delgado, *Historia evaluativa*, 3:328–31.

7. Ibid., 3:323.

8. AHCCITT, 1972/1, Dirección, from Dir. del Centro Ricardo Ferré d'Amaré to Pres. Municipal of Chamula Prof. Mariano Gómez López, April 7, 1972.

9. Ibid., Sec.: Dirección, Subser.: Correspondencia, Exp. 1, from Agente Municipal of La Libertad, Huixtán Vicente Sántiz and four others, to Administrador del CCITT Eloy Romero Herrera, June 25, 1972.

10. Ibid., Exp. 13, from Agente Auxiliar Municipal Vicente López Sántiz and sixty-six others from nearby colonias to Dir. of INI Gonzalo Aguirre Beltrán, dated from La Libertad, Huixtán, July 17, 1972.

11. Ibid., Dirección, from Dir. del Centro Ricardo Ferré d'Amaré to Jefe de la Sección de Zootencia Ángel Gaona Rivera, June 26, 1972.

12. Ibid., 1971/5, Dirección, Exp. 111, "Centro Nacional para la formación de promotores en desarrollo regional," by Gonzalo Aguirre Beltrán, June 8, 1971.

13. Ibid., 1972/1, EDR, Sec. Dirección EDR; Subser. Correspondencia, Exp. 7, "Breve informe sobre el Departamento de Antropología de la Escuela de Desarrollo Regional de enero 5 a junio 30 de 1972," by Alfonso Villa Rojas.

14. Ibid., 1972, from Dir. de EDR Mercedes Olivera Bustamante to Prof. Manuel Coello, Tila, Chis., dated from San Cristóbal de Las Casas, August 16, 1972.

15. Olivera Bustamante, "Una incursion en el campo indigenista," 250.

16. AHCCITT, 1972/1, Sec. Dir. EDR, Subser. Correspondencia, Exp. 6, "Sección de Antropología," November 1972.

17. Mercedes Olivera Bustamante, interview, San Cristóbal de Las Casas, August 20, 2009.

18. Ibid.

19. AHCCITT, 1972/1, Sec. Dir. EDR, Subser. Correspondencia, Exp. 5, "Estudios

de Antropología Social en la Escuela de Desarrollo Regional del Instituto Nacional Indigenista," dated from San Cristóbal, October 1972; Exp. 6, "Sección de Antropología," 1972; and Olivera Bustamante, "Una incursion en el campo indigenista," 250.

20. AHCCITT, 1972/1, Sec. Dir. EDR, Subser. Correspondencia, Exp. 5, "Estudios de Antropología Social en la Escuela de Desarrollo Regional del Instituto Nacional Indigenista," dated from San Cristóbal, October 1972.

21. Ibid., "Invitación a los Directores, Subdirectores y Antropólogos de los Centros Coordinadores del INI," October 25, 1972. The following sessions were programmed at the meeting:

> Nov. 3. Situación del indígena dentro de la sociedad nacional
> Exposición: Escuela de Desarrollo Regional
> Comentaristas: Dr. Alejandro Marroquín y Dr. Roger Bartra
>
> La política indigenista oficial del INI
> Exposición: Dr. Gonzalo Aguirre Beltrán
> Comentaristas: Lic. Raul Benítez Zenteno y Prof. Arturo Warman
>
> Nov. 4. Evalución de los conceptos teóricos de la política indigenista
> Exposición: Dr. Guillermo Bonfil
> Comentaristas: Prof. Enrique Valencia y Dr. Ángel Palerm
>
> Realización de la política indigenista en un Centro Coordinador
> Exposición: Prof. Carlos Incháustegui
> Comentaristas: Prof. Salomón Nahmad Sittón y Dr. Ricardo Ferré d'Amaré
>
> Nov. 5. Conclusiones
> Coordinador: Roberto Varela

22. CDI BJR, Carlos Incháustegui, "Cuatro puntos."

23. Fidel Velázquez directed the Confederation of Mexican Workers (Confederación de Trabajadores Mexicanos, CTM), Mexico's most important official labor confederation, from 1941 until his death in 1997.

24. Guachochi, in the Sierra Tarahumara, was the site of the INI's second Coordinating Center. It opened in 1952. The CCI in Tehuacán, Puebla, opened in July 1972, just four months before the meeting.

25. A reference to Chile's Nobel laureate, poet Pablo Neruda, who served as President Salvador Allende's ambassador to Paris.

26. CDI, BJR, Carlos Incháustegui, "Cuatro puntos." This satirical "bulletin" was found in Incháustegui's file; he may well have been the author; "Boletín Único de la Reunión sobre 'política indigenista,'" by Cantinero.

27. Salvatierra, "Realización de 'una aventura del pensamiento,'" 99; see also

Aguirre Beltrán's address, "Teoría y práctica de la educación indígena: La ordenación," in SEPI, AH, DGAI, 1972/7.

28. Salvatierra, "Realización de 'una aventura del pensamiento,'"101; see also Hernández Castillo, *Histories and Stories from Chiapas*, 103–4.

29. Mercedes Olivera Bustamante, interview, San Cristóbal de Las Casas, August 17, 2009.

30. Mercedes Olivera Bustamante, comments made at the INTERINDI panel at the International Conference of Americanists, Mexico City, July 21, 2009.

31. Salvatierra, "Realización de 'una aventura del pensamiento,'" 101–2.

32. AHCCITT, 1972/1, Sec. Dir. EDR, Subser. Correspondencia, from Assistant Dir. Manuel Esparza to Dir. Adjunto del INI Salomón Nahmad Sittón, December 13, 1972; and to Scott Rubinson, Universidad Iberoamericana, Mexico City, from Manuel Esparza, Subdir. de la EDR, December 14, 1972.

33. Mercedes Olivera Bustamante, interview, San Cristóbal de Las Casas, August 17, 2009.

34. Pérez Castro, "Bajo el símbolo de la ceiba," 311; and Mattiace, *To See with Two Eyes*, 72.

35. Olivera Bustamante, "Una incursion en el campo indigenista," 252–53.

36. Mercedes Olivera Bustamante, interview, San Cristóbal de Las Casas, August 20, 2009.

37. With the creation of the Coordinating Center in Ocosingo in October 1971, the CCI in San Cristóbal no longer served Tseltal communities.

38. AHCCITT, 1973, Sec. Dir., Ser. Dir., EDR, from Assistant Dir. of the CCI and acting manager of the Escuela de Desarrollo Regional Vicente Villanueva Rosales to Ángel Palerm, April 16, 1973; and from Dir. de la Escuela Gladys Villavicencio R., various.

39. Ibid., "Informe de labores," by Auxiliar de la Escuela de Desarrollo Regional Prof. Manuel Arias Pérez and Directora Nancy Modiano, June 30, 1976.

40. Rus, "The Struggle Against Indigenous Caciques," 184.

41. SEPI, AH, DGAI, 1971/5, Presidencia Municipal, Chamula, various; Favre, "El cambio socio-cultural," 187–88; and Iribarrén, *Misión Chamula*, 25.

42. SEPI, AH, DGAI, 1971, various, from Dir. Gral. de Asuntos Indígenas Ángel Robles Ramírez to Pres. Muni. Chamula, 1971; and 1972/1, from Secretario Pablo Ramírez Suárez to Presidente Municipal, Chamula, February 28, 1972.

43. Ibid., 1972/1, from Dir. Gral. de Asuntos Indígenas Ángel Robles Ramírez to Municipal President and Judge, Chamula, March 16, 1972; and Rus, "The Struggle Against Indigenous Caciques," 185.

44. SEPI, AH, DGAI, 1972/1, from Pres. Muni. Mariano Gómez López to Dir. de Asuntos Indígenas Ángel Robles Ramírez, dated from Chamula, March 29, 1972; Iribarrén, *Misión Chamula*, 25; and Rus, "The Struggle Against Indigenous Caciques," 184–86.

45. AGE, 1973, "Municipio de Chamula"; Iribarrén, *Misión Chamula*, 16–17, 24, 28; and Kovic, *Mayan Voices for Human Rights*, 82–83.

46. SEPI, AH, DGAI, 1974/3, Exp. 72, from La Comisión (Domingo Gómez López, Domingo López Ángel, Domingo de la Cruz Conejo, Domingo Hernández Mechij, Juan Hernández Shilón, Manuel Gómez Conejo, Miguel Santis Santis, Domingo Santis Santis, Mariano Pérez Lustre, Manuel Hernández Lunes, Sebastián Patishtán Hernández, Nicolás Hernández Gómez), to Governor Manuel Velasco Suárez, dated from San Juan Chamula, September 17, 1973 (emphasis in the original).

47. AGE, 1973, "Municipio de Chamula," to Pres. del Comité Directivo Estatal del PRI in Tuxtla, from Chamula, August 19, 1973.

48. SEPI, AH, DGAI, 1974, from Domingo Hernández Aguilar, Domingo Hernández Hernández, Manuel Gómez de la Cruz, and Rafael Hernández López, to Srio. de Gobernación Mario Moya Palencia, dated from Mexico City, February 22, 1974.

49. Favre, "El cambio socio-cultural," 188–89; Iribarrén, *Misión Chamula*, 28–29, 31; and Rus, "The Struggle Against Indigenous Caciques," 187–89.

50. SEPI, AH, DGAI, 1974/3, Exp. 72, "Investigaciones políticas y sociales del estado de Chiapas," by Dip. Fed. José Ángel Conchello Dávila, Dip. Fed. Álvaro Fernández de Ceballos, and Dip. Fed. Gerardo Medina Valdez, Chamula, June 9, 1974.

51. Ibid.,1974/1, to Procurador General de Justicia in Tuxtla, July 1, 1974. For more on the 1973 elections and subsequent expulsions, see Rivera Farfán et al., *Diversidad religiosa y conflicto en Chiapas*, 165–99; and Morquecho Escamilla, "Expulsiones en los Altos de Chiapas," 61.

52. In the 1970s, researchers working in the Archivo de Indias in Seville discovered that Las Casas was probably born in November 1484, a decade later than had been supposed.

53. Benjamin, "A Time of Reconquest," 426.

54. Rus, "The Struggle Against Indigenous Caciques," 190.

55. According to Andrés Medina, who was conducting fieldwork in Chanal at the time, many of Ruiz's catequistas had trained to become promotores but had been unable to find work. Andrés Medina Hernández, interview, Mexico City, August 12, 2011.

56. Harvey, *The Chiapas Rebellion*, 77; see also Morales Bermúdez, "El Congreso Indígena de Chiapas," 307–8, 312.

57. Archivo Histórico Diocesano de San Cristóbal de Las Casas (hereafter AHDSC), Chiapas, "Acuerdos del I Congreso Indígena 'Fray Bartolomé de Las Casas.'"

58. Womack, *Rebellion in Chiapas*, 156 (emphasis in the original).

59. AHDSC, "Acuerdos del I Congreso Indígena 'Fray Bartolomé de Las Casas.'"

60. See also Womack, *Rebellion in Chiapas*, 157–58.

61. AHDSC, "Acuerdos del I Congreso Indígena 'Fray Bartolomé de Las Casas.'"

62. García de León, *Fronteras interiores*, 168–69; Harvey, *The Chiapas Rebellion*, 77–78; Kovic, *Mayan Voices for Human Rights*, 54–57; and Morales Bermúdez, "El Congreso Indígena de Chiapas," 313–15.

63. Morales Bermúdez, "El Congreso Indígena de Chiapas," 317.

64. Favre described the latter as "Communists, Trotskyites, and Maoists of every stripe"; see Favre, "El cambio socio-cultural," 189.

65. Rus, "The Struggle Against Indigenous Caciques," 190.
66. Arias Pérez, "Movimientos indígenas contemporáneos," 391.
67. SEPI, AH, DGAI, 1974/1, from Dir. Gen. de Ed. Extraescolar en el Medio Indígena, Departamento de Procuradores to Gob. Manuel Velasco Suárez, November 21, 1974; and Favre, "El cambio socio-cultural," 189–90.
68. SEPI, AH, DGAI, 1974/1, from La Comisión de San Juan Chamula to Pres. de la Suprema Corte de Justicia Lic. Eugenio Guerrero López, Mexico City.
69. Iribarrén, *Misión Chamula*, 32–35.
70. SEPI, AH, DGAI, 1974/1, various, including to C. Agente del Ministerio Público, Oficinas del PRODESCH, dated from Chamula, November 9, 1974; and from Unión Mexicana de Adventistas del Séptimo Día Sr. Francisco Flores Chablé and Pastor Pedro Arano Molina to Sec. of Gobernación Mario Moya Palencia, Mexico City, December 16, 1974.
71. Ibid., from various to General de la 31a Zona Militar, late October; and from Dominga Gómez Saltillo and Verónica Díaz Gómez to Pres. de la Suprema Corte de Justicia Eugenio Guerrero López, Mexico City.
72. Fazio, *Samuel Ruiz*, 143; and Rus, "The Struggle Against Indigenous Caciques," 191.
73. "Continúa la protesta de un grupo chamula aquí," *Avante*, November 2, 1976. For a pro-PRODESCH view, see "El problema indígena de Chamula, religioso," *La voz de sureste*, November 2, 1976; and for a sneering treatment of the protesters, see "Los chamulas fueron con su manifestación de protesta a Tuxtla Gutiérrez," *Avante*, November 5, 1976.
74. Rus, "The Struggle Against Indigenous Caciques," 195.
75. Ibid., 179.
76. Favre, "El cambio socio-cultural," 190.
77. AHCCITT, 1974/1, Sec. Dir.; Subser. Correspondencia, Exp. 14, from Dir. del CCITT Agustín Romano Delgado to Gonzalo Aguirre Beltrán, November 6, 1974.
78. AGE, "PRODESCH: Sumario de un esfuerzo promocional que se transforma en acciones para la superación del hombre," 1976.
79. Favre, "El cambio socio-cultural," 186.
80. Nash, *Mayan Visions*, 93.
81. Pineda, *Caciques culturales*, 102–3.
82. CDI, BJR, "Guión Informe PRODESCH San Cristóbal," 1979. See also AHCCITT, 1973, Sec. Dir.; Ser. Dir. EDR, Exp. 12, "La coordinación como factor fundamental para el desarrollo de las regiones de refugio indígenas," by Salomón Nahmad Sittón, delivered at Tercer Seminario de Educación Indígena, Oaxtepec, Morelos, July 1972.
83. García de León, *Fronteras interiores*, 171–73; Morales Bermúdez, "El Congreso Indígena de Chiapas," 314, 318–36; Stephen, *¡Zapata Lives!*, 115–19; and Womack, *Rebellion in Chiapas*, 148–58.
84. García de León, *Fronteras interiores*, 170.

Conclusion

1. Nahmad Sittón, "Una experiencia indigenista," 285.
2. Villa Rojas, "Adiestramiento de personal," 217.
3. AHCCITT, 1973, Sec. Dir., Ser. Dir. E.D.R., Exp. 12, from Salomón Nahmad Sittón, "La coordinación como factor fundamental para el desarrollo de las regiones de refugio indígenas," delivered at Tercer Seminario de Educación Indígenas, Oaxtepec, Morelos, July 1972, 9.
4. AHCCITT, Ser. Dir., Sec. Dir., 1974, 81-1974/4, from Antrop. Raúl Rodríguez Ramos to Agustín Romano Delgado, December 23, 1974; CDIFD, "Teatro Guiñol," by Marcelino Jiménez, July 9, 1982; and Navarrete Cáceres, *Rosario Castellanos*, 20.
5. Muñoz, *Stand Up and Fight*, 10-13, 113, 147-48.
6. Pineda, *Caciques culturales*, 120-26.
7. Muñoz, *Stand Up and Fight*, 6, 11; see also Dillingham, "Indigenismo Occupied," 550.
8. Ovalle Fernández, "Bases programáticas de la política indigenista," 12, 20.
9. Andrés Medina Hernández, interview, Mexico City, August 2, 2006; and Saldívar Tanaka, *Prácticas cotidianas del estado*, 98-101.
10. Köhler, *Cambio cultural dirigido*, 309.
11. AHCCITT, 1967/3, Dir., to Prof. Alberto Jiménez Rodríguez from Subdirector Técnico de Educación Ignacio León Pacheco, August 31, 1967.
12. Extreme poverty is defined as the condition of those who do not have the means to provide for their most basic needs, like food.
13. The next poorest state is strife-ridden Guerrero, with 67.4 percent of the population living in moderate or extreme poverty, followed by Oaxaca with 67.2 percent; see Villafuerte Solís, "La catástrofe neoliberal en Chiapas," 316-19. Villafuerte's information comes from the Consejo Nacional para la Evaluación de la Política de Desarrollo Social, 2011, Pobreza en México y en las entidades federativas, 2008-2010.
14. Vázquez León, "Entrevista a Ricardo Pozas Arciniega," 164-65.
15. Olivera Bustamante, "From Integrationist Indigenismo to Neoliberal De-Ethnification," 101.
16. Nahmad also claims that he was targeted politically by SEP director Jesús Reyes Heroles; see Dalton, "Encierro intelectual," 170-76; Nahmad Sittón, "Una experiencia indigenista," 301-4; and Saldívar Tanaka, *Prácticas cotidianas del estado*, 109.
17. Nahmad Sittón, "Una experiencia indigenista," 295.
18. Onofre Montes Ríos, interview, Mexico City, February 10, 1995; and Aguirre Beltrán, Villa Rojas, Romano Delgado, et al., *El indigenismo en acción*, 121-26.
19. Muñoz developed a personal friendship with President Echeverría in the 1970s and served one term as congressman in his home state of Hidalgo. He also founded the Consejo Supremo Otomí, now Consejo Supremo Hñahñu. See Nahmad Sittón, "Estudio introductorio," 34.
20. Téllez Girón López and Vázquez León, *Palerm en sus propias palabras*, xxxix-xl.

21. Comas, *La antropología social aplicada*, 63.
22. AHCCITT, 1966/2, Dir., "Convenio entre el gobierno de los Estados Unidos Mexicanos y la Unión Panamericana, Secretaría General de la Organización de los Estados Americanos, para el Establecimiento del proyecto 208, Programa interamericano de adiestramiento de personal en Desarrollo de Comunidades Indígenas del programa de cooperación técnica en los Estados Unidos Mexicanos"; and Comas, *La antropología social aplicada*, 63–64.
23. Köhler, *Cambio cultural dirigido*, 173–74.
24. Nahmad Sittón, "Compromiso y subjetividad," 81.
25. Nash, *Mayan Visions*, 99.
26. De la Peña, "La antropología y la política indigenista en México"; López Caballero, "Las políticas indigenistas," 71, 80–85; Saldívar Tanaka, *Prácticas cotidianas del estado*, 17, 95; and Teófilo da Silva, "Indigenismo como ideologia y prática de dominação," 23–24.
27. Nahmad Sittón, "Compromiso y subjetividad," 102.
28. CDI, BJR, ICCITT, 1961, various; 1963, "Informe mensual correspondiente al mes de junio de 1963" by Dir. del Centro Agustín Romano Delgado; and SEPI, AH, DGAI, 1968/2, "Informe de las actividades desarrolladas en la Dirección General de Asuntos Indígenas del 1 de noviembre de 1967 al 15 de septiembre de 1968."
29. Rus, "The Struggle Against Indigenous Caciques," 171.
30. Dillingham, "Indigenismo Occupied," 549–82.
31. Harvey, *The Chiapas Rebellion*; Leyva Solano, "Indigenismo, Indianismo and 'Ethnic Citizenship,'" 571; and Rus, "Local Adaptation to Global Change," 85.
32. Leyva Solano, "Indigenismo, Indianismo and 'Ethnic Citizenship,'" 570.
33. Aguirre was too frail to accept the invitation. Vázquez León, *Historia de la etnología*, 211.
34. Mattiace, "From Indigenismo to Indigenous Movements," 201; see also Henck, *Subcommander Marcos*, 297–98, 306.
35. Mattiace, *To See with Two Eyes*, 120.
36. Henck, *Subcommander Marcos*, 29–37, 43.
37. Pitarch, "The Political Uses of Maya Medicine," 203; see also Mattiace, "From Indigenismo to Indigenous Movements," 196–208.
38. Secretaría de Educación Pública, *Alfonso Caso*, 14–15.

References

Archival Sources

Archivo General del Estado (AGE), Tuxtla Gutiérrez, Chiapas
Archivo General de la Nación (AGN), Mexico City
Archivo Histórico del Centro Coordinador Indigenista Tzeltal-Tzotzil (AHCCITT), San Cristóbal de Las Casas, Chiapas
Archivo Histórico del Estado de Chiapas (AHECh), Tuxtla Gutiérrez, Chiapas
Archivo Histórico Diocesano de San Cristóbal de Las Casas, Chiapas (AHDSC)
Archivo Histórico de la Secretaría de Educación Pública (AHSEP), Mexico City
Archivo Histórico del Municipio de San Cristóbal de Las Casas (AHMSCLC), San Cristóbal de Las Casas, Chiapas
Comisión Nacional para el Desarrollo de los Pueblos Indígenas, Biblioteca Juan Rulfo (CDI, BJR), Mexico City
Secretaría de Pueblos Indios, Archivo Histórico (SEPI, AH), San Cristóbal de Las Casas, Chiapas

Interviews

Andrés Medina Hernández, 2006 and 2011, Mexico City.
Onofre Montes Ríos, February 10, 1995, Mexico City.
Salomón Nahmad Sittón, August 4, 6, 2011, Oaxaca City.
Mercedes Olivera Bustamante, August 17, 20, 2009, San Cristóbal de Las Casas.
Agustín Romano Delgado, January 16, 1995, and July 15, 1998, Mexico City.
Jorge Santiago, August 1, 2011, San Cristóbal de Las Casas.

Periodicals

Acción Indigenista, 1951–1964.
Avante, San Cristóbal de Las Casas, Chis., 1976.

El Coleto, San Cristóbal de Las Casas, Chis., 1954.
El Demócrata, San Cristóbal de Las Casas, Chis., 1953.
Diario del Sur, Tapachula, Chis., 1953.
Diario Oficial, Tuxtla Gutiérrez, Chis., 1949.
Excélsior, Mexico City, 1974.
El Heraldo, Tuxtla Gutiérrez, Chis., 1954.
La Jornada, Mexico City, 2003, 2012.
Más Allá, San Cristóbal de Las Casas, Chis., 1954, 1955.
La Opinión, San Cristóbal de Las Casas, Chis., 1951.
La Prensa, Mexico City, 1950.
Proceso, Mexico City, 1994, 2002.
Tiempo: Seminario de la Vida y la Verdad, Mexico City, 1957.
El Universal, Mexico City, 1954.
Uno Más Uno, Mexico City, 1979.
La Voz de Chiapas, 1954, 1976.
La Voz de San Cristóbal, San Cristóbal de Las Casas, Chis., 1954.
La Voz del Sureste, Mexico City, 1955.

Primary and Secondary Sources

Adams, Walter Randolph, and John P. Hawkins, eds. *Health Care in Maya Guatemala: Confronting Medical Pluralism in a Developing Country*. Norman: University of Oklahoma Press, 2007.

Aguilar Camín, Héctor, and Lorenzo Meyer. *In the Shadow of the Mexican Revolution: Contemporary Mexican History, 1910–1989*. 1993. Translated by Luis Alberto Fierro. Austin: University of Texas Press, 1996.

Aguirre Beltrán, Gonzalo. "Entrevista a Gonzalo Aguirre Beltrán." In *Caminos de la antropología: Entrevistas a cinco antropólogos*, edited by Jorge Durand and Luis Vázquez León. Mexico City: Consejo Nacional para la Cultura y las Artes/Instituto Nacional Indigenista, 1990.

———. "Estructura y función de los Centros Coordinadores." In *El indigenismo en acción: XXV aniversario del Centro Coordinador Indigenista Tzeltal-Tzotzil, Chiapas*, edited by Gonzalo Aguirre Beltrán, Alfonso Villa Rojas, Agustín Romano Delgado, et al. Mexico City: Instituto Nacional Indigenista/Secretaría de Educación Pública: 1976.

———. "Etnocidio en México: Una denuncia irresponsable." In *La quiebra política de la antropología social en México*, vol. 2, *La polarización (1971–1976)*, edited by Andrés Medina Hernández and Carlos García Mora, 369–83. Mexico City: Universidad Nacional Autónoma de México, 1986.

———. "Formación de una teoría y una práctica indigenistas." In Instituto Nacional Indigenista, *INI 40 años*. Mexico City: Instituto Nacional Indigenista, 1988.

———. *Formas de gobierno indígena*. Mexico City: Imprenta Universitaria, 1953.

———. *Obra polémica.* 1976. Mexico City: Instituto Nacional Indigenista/Universidad Veracruzana, 1992.
———. *Regiones de refugio: El desarrollo de la comunidad y el proceso dominical en mestizo América.* Mexico City: Instituto Indigenista Interamericano, 1967.
———. "Sobre 'La antropología y la burocracia indigenista.'" In *La quiebra política de la antropología social en México,* vol. 2, *La polarización (1971–1976),* edited by Andrés Medina Hernández and Carlos García Mora. Mexico City: Universidad Nacional Autónoma de México, 1986.
Aguirre Beltrán, Gonzalo, Alfonso Villa Rojas, Agustín Romano Delgado, et al. *El indigenismo en acción: XXV aniversario del Centro Coordinador Indigenista Tzeltal-Tzotzil, Chiapas.* Mexico City: Instituto Nacional Indigenista/Secretaría de Educación Pública, 1976.
Aguirre Beltrán, Gonzalo, et al. *Pensamiento antropológico e indigenista de Julio de la Fuente.* Mexico City: Instituto Nacional Indigenista, 1980.
Ahern, Maureen, ed. *A Rosario Castellanos Reader.* 1988. Austin: University of Texas Press, 1996.
Alarcón, Francisco. "El programa de salud del Centro Coordinador." Unpublished manuscript, 1955.
Albores Z., Beatriz. "*Antropología y burocracia indigenista*, nota crítica." In *La quiebra política de la antropología social en México,* vol. 2, *La polarización (1971–1976),* edited by Andrés Medina Hernández and Carlos García Mora. Mexico City: Universidad Nacional Autónoma de México, 1986.
Arana de Swadesh, Evangelina. "¿Cúal será el futuro de la educación indígena?" In Instituto Nacional Indigenista, *INI, 30 años después: revisión crítica.* Mexico City: Instituto Nacional Indigenista, 1978.
Arias Pérez, Jacinto. "Movimientos indígenas contemporáneos del estado de Chiapas." In *El arreglo de los pueblos indios: La incansable tarea de reconstitución,* edited by Jacinto Arias Pérez. Mexico City: Secretaría de Educación Pública/Gobierno del Estado de Chiapas/Instituto Chiapaneco de Cultura, 1994.
Aviña, Alexander. *Specters of Revolution: Peasant Guerrillas in the Cold War Mexican Countryside.* New York: Oxford University Press, 2014.
Báez Jorge, Félix. Introduction to *Pensamiento antropológico e indigenista de Julio de la Fuente,* by Gonzalo Aguirre Beltrán et al. Mexico City: Instituto Nacional Indigenista, 1980
Barabas, Alicia, and Miguel Bartolomé. "Desarrollo hidráulico y etnocidio: Los pueblos mazateco y chinanteco de Oaxaca." In *La quiebra política de la antropología social en México,* vol. 2, *La polarización (1971–1976),* edited by Andrés Medina Hernández and Carlos García Mora. Mexico City: Universidad Nacional Autónoma de México, 1986.
Basurto, Jorge. "The Late Populism of Luis Echeverría." In *Latin American Populism in Comparative Perspective,* edited by Michael L. Conniff. Albuquerque: University of New Mexico Press, 1982.

Beezley, William H. "Introduction." *The Americas* 67, no. 3 (January 2011): 307–14.
Benítez, Fernando. *Los indios de México*. 4 vols. Mexico City: Ediciones Era, 1968.
Benjamin, Thomas. *A Rich Land, A Poor People: Politics and Society in Modern Chiapas*. Albuquerque: University of New Mexico Press, 1989.
———. "A Time of Reconquest: History, the Maya Revival, and the Zapatista Rebellion in Chiapas." *American Historical Review* 105, no. 2 (April 2000): 417–50.
Blasco López, Juan Miguel. "La industria aguardentera chiapaneca antes, durante y después del periodo revolucionario, 1890–1930." In *La Revolución mexicana en Chiapas un siglo después*, edited by Justus Fenner and Miguel Lisbona Guillén. Mexico City: Universidad Nacional Autónoma de México/Instituto de Investigaciones Antropológicas/Programa de Investigaciones Multidisciplinarias sobre Mesoamérica y el Sureste, 2010.
Bobrow-Strain, Aaron. *Intimate Enemies: Landowners, Power, and Violence in Chiapas*. Durham, NC: Duke University Press, 2007.
Bonfil Batalla, Guillermo. "Admitamos que los indios no nacieron equivocados." In Instituto Nacional Indigenista, *INI, 30 años después: revisión crítica*. Mexico City: Instituto Nacional Indigenista, 1978.
———. "Del indigenismo de la revolución a la antropología crítica." In *De eso quellaman antropología mexicana*, by Arturo Warman, Margarita Nolasco Armas, Guillermo Bonfil Batalla, Mercedes Olivera Bustamante, and Enrique Valencia. Mexico City: Editorial Nuestro Tiempo, 1970.
Bricker, Victoria R., and Evon Z. Vogt. "Alfonso Villa Rojas (1906–1998)." *American Anthropologist* 100, no. 4 (December 1998): 994–98.
Campbell, Federico. "Aguirre Beltrán: Las regiones de refugio están a punto de desaparecer." In Instituto Nacional Indigenista, *INI, 30 años después: revisión crítica*. Mexico City: Instituto Nacional Indigenista, 1978.
———. "El indigenismo necesita una nueva teoría y, sobre ella, reelaborar una nueva praxis: Andrés Fábregas." In Instituto Nacional Indigenista, *INI, 30 años después: revisión crítica*. Mexico City: Instituto Nacional Indigenista, 1978.
Cancian, Frank. *The Decline of Community in Zinacantán: Economy, Public Life, and Social Stratification, 1960–1987*. Stanford, CA: Stanford University Press, 1992.
Cantón Delgado, Manuela. "Las expulsiones indígenas en los Altos de Chiapas: Algo más que un problema de cambio religioso." *Mesoamérica* 33 (June 1997): 147–69.
Carey, Elaine. *Plaza of Sacrifices: Gender, Power, and Terror in 1968 Mexico*. Albuquerque: University of New Mexico Press, 2005.
Caso, Alfonso. "Definición del indio y lo indio." In *Homenaje a Alfonso Caso: Obras escogidas*. Mexico City: Patronato para el Fomento de Actividades Culturales y de Asistencia Social a las Comunidades Indígenas, 1996.
———. "Un experimento de antropología social en México." In Instituto Nacional Indigenista, *INI, 30 años después: revisión crítica*. Mexico City: Instituto Nacional Indigenista, 1978.

Castellanos, Rosario. *Balún Canán*. Mexico City: Fondo de Cultura Económica, 1957.
———. *Ciudad Real*. Xalapa: Universidad Veracruzana, 1960.
———. *Teatro Petul*. Vols. 2–3. Mexico City: Instituto Nacional Indigenista, 1962.
Castellanos, Rosario, and Marco Antonio Montero. *Teatro Petul*. Vol. 1. Mexico City: Instituto Nacional Indigenista, 1958.
Castro, Carlo Antonio. "Las metas del Teatro Petul." In *Educación, lingüística y ayudas visuales del Centro Coordinador Tzeltal Tzotzil*, edited by Fidencio Montes Sánchez, Onofre Montes Ríos, and Andrés Santiago Montes. Mexico City: Instituto Nacional Indigenista, 1955.
Clayton, Lawrence A. *Bartolomé de Las Casas: A Biography*. New York: Cambridge University Press, 2012.
Coffey, Mary K. *How a Revolutionary Art Became Official Culture: Murals, Museums, and the Mexican State*. Durham, NC: Duke University Press, 2012.
Colby, Benjamin N., and Pierre L. van den Berghe. "Ethnic Relations in Southeastern Mexico." *American Anthropologist* 63, no. 4 (1961): 772–92.
Collier, George A. *Fields of the Tzotzil: The Ecological Bases of Tradition in Highland Chiapas*. Austin: University of Texas Press, 1975.
———. "Peasant Politics and the Mexican State: Indigenous Compliance in Highland Chiapas." *Mexican Studies/Estudios Mexicanos* 3, no. 1 (Winter 1987): 71–98.
Collier, George A., with Elizabeth Lowery Quaratiello. *Basta! Land and the Zapatista Rebellion in Chiapas*. Oakland: Institute for Food and Development Policy, 1994.
Comas, Juan, ed. *La antropología social aplicada en México: Trayectoria y antología*. Mexico City: Instituto Indigenista Interamericano, 1964.
Cueto, Marcos. *Cold War, Deadly Fevers: Malaria Eradication in Mexico, 1955–1975*. Washington, DC: Woodrow Wilson Center Press, 2007.
Dalton, Margarita. "Encierro intelectual: Entrevista con Salomón Nahmad." *Desacatos* 9 (Spring–Summer 2002): 163–76.
Dawson, Alexander S. *Indian and Nation in Revolutionary Mexico*. Tucson: University of Arizona Press, 2004.
———. "'Wild Indians,' 'Mexican Gentlemen,' and the Lessons Learned in the Casa del Estudiante Indígena, 1926–1932." *The Americas* 57, no. 3 (2001): 329–61.
De la Fuente, Julio. "Relaciones étnicas en Mesoamérica." In *La antropología social aplicada en México: Trayectoria y antología*, edited by Juan Comas. Mexico City: Instituto Indigenista Interamericano, 1964.
———. *Yalalag: Una villa zapoteca serrana*. Mexico City: Museo Nacional de Antropología, 1949.
De la Peña, Guillermo. "La antropología, el indigenismo y la diversificación del patrimonio cultural mexicano." In *La antropología y el patrimonio cultural de México*, edited by Guillermo de la Peña. Mexico City: Consejo Nacional para la Cultura y las Artes, 2011.
———. "La antropología y la política indigenista en México." In *Las ciencias sociales y*

su papel en la construcción de Estado nacional, edited by Enrique Florescano, Cristina Puga, and Óscar Contreras. Mexico City: Consejo Nacional para la Cultura y las Artes/Fondo de Cultura Económica, forthcoming.

———. "Gonzalo Aguirre Beltrán." In Instituto Nacional Indigenista, *INI 40 años*. Mexico City: Instituto Nacional Indigenista, 1988.

———. "Nacionales y extranjeros en la historia de la antropología mexicana." In *La historia de la antropología en México: Fuentes y transmisión*, edited by Mechthild Rutsch. Mexico City: Plaza y Valdés/Universidad Iberoamericana/Instituto Nacional Indigenista, 1996.

Departamento de Asuntos Indígenas. *Primer Congreso Indigenista Interamericano.* Mexico City: Departamento de Asuntos Indígenas, 1940.

Díaz-Polanco, Héctor. "Lo nacional y lo étnico en México." *Cuadernos Políticos* 52 (October–December 1987): 32–42.

Dillingham, A. S. "Indigenismo Occupied: Indigenous Youth and Mexico's Democratic Opening (1968–1975)." *The Americas* 72, no. 4 (October 2015): 549–82.

Durand, Jorge, and Luis Vásquez, eds. *Caminos de la antropología: Entrevistas a cinco antropólogos*. Mexico City: Consejo Nacional para la Cultura y las Artes/Instituto Nacional Indigenista, 1990.

Eber, Christine. "*Buscando una nueva vida*: Liberation Through Autonomy in San Pedro Chenalhó, 1970–1998." In *Mayan Lives, Mayan Utopias: The Indigenous Peoples of Chiapas and the Zapatista Rebellion*, edited by Jan Rus, Rosalva Aída Hernández Castillo, and Shannan L. Mattiace. Lanham, MD: Rowman and Littlefield, 2003.

———. *Women and Alcohol in a Highland Town*. Austin: University of Texas Press, 1995.

Esteva, Gustavo. "Lo indígena y lo campesino: Supervivencia del pasado o simiente de proyecto futuro." In Instituto Nacional Indigenista, *INI, 30 años después: revisión crítica*. Mexico City: Instituto Nacional Indigenista, 1978.

Favre, Henri. "El cambio socio-cultural y el nuevo indigenismo en Chiapas." *Revista Mexicana de Sociología* 47, no. 3 (July–September 1985): 161–96.

———. *Cambio y continuidad entre los Mayas de México*. 1971. Mexico City: Instituto Nacional Indigenista, 1984.

Fazio, Carlos. *Samuel Ruiz: El caminante*. Mexico City: Espasa Calpe Mexicana, 1994.

Fernández-Galán Rodríguez, María Elena. "La muerte de un alemán." In *Anuario 1994 del Centro de Estudios Superiores de México y Centroamérica*. Tuxtla Gutiérrez, Chis.: Universidad de Ciencias y Artes de Chiapas/Centro de Estudios Superiores de México y Centroamérica, 1995.

Foster, George M. "Peasant Society and the Image of Limited Good." *American Anthropologist* 67, no. 2 (April 1965): 293–315.

Gamio, Manuel. *Antología*. 1975. Mexico City: Universidad Nacional Autónoma de México, 1993.

———. *Forjando patria*. 1916. Mexico City: Editorial Porrúa, 1960.

———. "Heterogeneidad de la población." In Instituto Nacional Indigenista, *INI, 30*

años después: revisión crítica. Mexico City: Instituto Nacional Indigenista, 1978.
García de León, Antonio. "Chamula: Una larga historia de resistencia." In *La violencia en Chamula*, edited by Juan Jaime Manguen Escobar, Antonio García de León, and Oliverio Ichín Santiesteban. San Cristóbal de Las Casas, Chis.: Universidad Autónoma de Chiapas, 1977.
———. *Fronteras interiores: Chiapas, una modernidad particular*. Mexico City: Océano, 2002.
Garza Caligaris, Anna María, and Rosalva Aída Hernández Castillo. "Encounters and Conflicts of the Tzotzil People with the Mexican State." In *The Other Word: Women and Violence in Chiapas Before and After Acteal*, edited by Rosalva Aída Hernández Castillo. Copenhagen: International Work Group for Indigenous Affairs, 2001.
Gillingham, Paul. "Sex, Death and Structuralism: Alternative Views of the Twentieth Century." In *A Companion to Mexican History and Culture*, edited by William H. Beezley. Malden, MA: Wiley-Blackwell, 2011.
Giraudo, Laura. "Neither 'Scientific' nor 'Colonialist': The Ambiguous Course of Inter-American Indigenismo in the 1940s." *Latin American Perspectives* 39, no. 5 (September 2012): 12–32.
———. "Un campo indigenista transnacional y 'casi profesional': La apertura en Pátzcuaro (1940) de un espacio por y para los indigenistas." In *La ambivalente historia del indigenismo: Campo interamericano y trayectorias nacionales 1940–1970*, edited by Laura Giraudo and Juan-Martín Sánchez. Lima: Instituto de Estudios Peruanos, 2011.
Giraudo, Laura, and Stephen E. Lewis. "Pan-American *Indigenismo* (1940–1970): New Approaches to an Ongoing Debate." *Latin American Perspectives* 39, no. 5 (September 2012): 1–11.
Gómez Montero, Sergio. "Alberto Beltrán recuerda cuando se ilustraba la acción educativa, 'quitando la venda de la ignorancia a los indios.'" In Instituto Nacional Indigenista, *INI, 30 años después: revisión crítica*. Mexico City: Instituto Nacional Indigenista, 1978.
González Casanova, Pablo. *La democracia en México*. Mexico City: Ediciones Era, 1965.
Gossen, Gary. *Four Creations: An Epic Story of the Chiapas Mayas*. Norman: University of Oklahoma Press, 2002.
———. *Telling Maya Tales: Tzotzil Identities in Modern Mexico*. New York: Routledge, 1999.
Greaves Laine, Celicia. "De la cartilla al libro de texto gratuito: Una experiencia en los Altos de Chiapas." In *Cincuenta años de historia en México*, vol. 2, edited by Alicia Hernández Chávez and Manuel Miño Grijalva. Mexico City: El Colegio de México, 1991.
———. "Entre el discurso y la acción: Una polémica en torno al Departamento de Asuntos Indígenas." In *México: historia y alteridad: Perspectivas*

multidisciplinarias sobre la cuestión indígena, edited by Yael Bitrán. Mexico City: Universidad Iberoamericana, 2001.

Guiteras-Holmes, Calixta. *Perils of the Soul: The World View of a Tzotzil Indian*. New York: Free Press of Glencoe, 1961.

Guzmán Arias, Isaac. "Misioneros al servicio de Dios y del Estado: Presencia del ILV en Oxchuc, Chiapas." Master's thesis, Centro de Investigaciones y Estudios Superiores en Antropología Social–Sureste, 2012.

Guzmán López, Salvador, and Jan Rus, eds. *Lo'il sventa k'ucha'al la jmankutik jpinkakutik Kipaltik: La historia de cómo compramos nuestra finca*. San Cristóbal de Las Casas, Chis.: El Taller Tzotzil, 1990.

Guzmán López, Salvador, Jan Rus, and Socios de la Unión "Tierra Tzotzil." *Kipaltik*. San Cristóbal de Las Casas, Chis.: El Taller Tzotzil, 1999.

Hartch, Todd. *Missionaries of the State: The Summer Institute of Linguistics, State Formation, and Indigenous Mexico, 1935–1985*. Tuscaloosa: University of Alabama Press, 2006.

Harvey, Neil. *The Chiapas Rebellion: The Struggle for Land and Democracy*. Durham, NC: Duke University Press, 1998.

Henck, Nick. *Subcommander Marcos: The Man and the Mask*. Durham, NC: Duke University Press, 2007.

Hernández Castillo, R. Aída. *Histories and Stories from Chiapas: Border Identities in Southern Mexico*. Austin: University of Texas Press, 2001.

Herrasti, Lourdes. "Instituto Nacional Indigenista." In *La antropología en México: Panorama histórico 7, Las instituciones*, coordinated by Carlos García Mora. Mexico City: Instituto Nacional de Antropología e Historia, 1988.

Holland, William R. *Medicina maya en los Altos de Chiapas*. Mexico City: Instituto Nacional Indigenista, 1963.

Horcasitas de Pozas, Isabel, and Ricardo Pozas. "Del monolingüismo en lengua indígena al bilingüismo en lengua indígena y nacional." In *Pensamiento indigenista y antropológico de Julio de la Fuente*, by Gonzalo Aguirre Beltrán et al. Mexico City: Instituto Nacional Indigenista, 1980.

Incháustegui, Carlos. "Reconocimiento a la Cooperativa de Oxchuc." In Agustín Romano Delgado, "Problemas fundamentales del Centro Tzeltal Tzotzil." Unpublished manuscript, 1955.

Instituto Nacional de Estadística y Geografía. *Censo de Población y Vivienda 2010: Panorama sociodemográfico de México*. Mexico City: Instituto Nacional de Estadística y Geografía, 2011.

Instituto Nacional Indigenista, ed. *¿Ha fracasado el indigenismo? Reportaje de una controversia (13 de septiembre de 1971)*. Mexico City: Secretaría de Educación Pública, 1971.

———. *INI, 30 años después: revisión crítica*. Mexico City: Instituto Nacional Indigenista, 1978.

———. *INI 40 años*. Mexico City: Instituto Nacional Indigenista, 1988.

———. *Realidades y proyectos: 16 años de trabajo*. Mexico City: Instituto Nacional Indigenista, 1964.
Iribarrén, Pablo. *Misión Chamula: Experiencia de trabajo pastoral de los años 1966–1977 en Chamula*. San Cristóbal de Las Casas, Chis.: Ediciones Pirata, 2002.
Jackson Albarrán, Elena. "*Comino Vence al Diablo* and Other Terrifying Episodes: Teatro Guiñol's Itinerant Puppet Theater in 1930s Mexico." *The Americas* 67, no. 3 (January 2011): 355–74.
Kiddle, Amelia M., and Joseph U. Lenti. "Co-opting Cardenismo: Luis Echeverría and the Funeral of Lázaro Cárdenas." In *Populism in Twentieth-Century Mexico: The Presidencies of Lázaro Cárdenas and Luis Echeverría*, edited by Amelia M. Kiddle and María L. O. Muñoz. Tucson: University of Arizona Press, 2010.
Knight, Alan. "Caciquismo in Twentieth-Century Mexico." In *Caciquismo in Twentieth-Century Mexico*, edited by Alan Knight and Wil Pansters. London: Institute for the Study of the Americas, 2005.
———. "Cárdenas and Echeverría: Two 'Populist' Presidents Compared." In *Populism in Twentieth-Century Mexico: The Presidencies of Lázaro Cárdenas and Luis Echeverría*, edited by Amelia M. Kiddle and María L. O. Muñoz. Tucson: University of Arizona Press, 2010.
Köhler, Ulrich. *Cambio cultural dirigido en los Altos de Chiapas: Un estudio sobre la antropología social aplicada. 1969*. Mexico City: Instituto Nacional Indigenista/Secretaría de Educación Pública, 1975.
Kovic, Christine. *Mayan Voices for Human Rights: Displaced Catholics in Highland Chiapas*. Austin: University of Texas Press, 2005.
Krauze, Enrique. *Caudillos culturales en la revolución mexicana*. Mexico City: Siglo Veintiuno Editores, 1976.
———. *La presidencia imperial: Asenso y caída del sistema politico mexicano (1940–1996)*. Mexico City: Tusquets Editores, 2002.
Laughlin, Robert, and Sna Jtz'ibajom. *Monkey Business Theatre*. Austin: University of Texas Press, 2008.
Legoretta Díaz, María del Carmen. "La contrarrevolución en Ocosingo y su impronta en la sociedad regional." In *La Revolución mexicana en Chiapas un siglo después*, edited by Justus Fenner and Miguel Lisbona Guillén. Mexico City: Universidad Nacional Autónoma de México/Instituto de Investigaciones Antropológicas/Programa de Investigaciones Multidisciplinarias sobre Mesoamérica y el Sureste, 2010.
León Portilla, Miguel. "Alfonso Caso, 1896–1970." *American Anthropologist* 75, no. 3 (June 1973): 877–85.
Lewis, Stephen E. *The Ambivalent Revolution: Forging State and Nation in Chiapas, 1910–1945*. Albuquerque: University of New Mexico Press, 2005.
Lewis, Stephen E., and Margarita Sosa Suárez, eds. *Monopolio de aguardiente y alcoholismo en los Altos de Chiapas: Un estudio "incómodo" de Julio de la Fuente*.

Mexico City: Comisión Nacional para el Desarrollo de los Pueblos Indígenas, 2009.
Leyva Solano, Xóchitl. "Indigenismo, Indianismo and 'Ethnic Citizenship' in Chiapas." *Journal of Peasant Studies* 32, nos. 3-4 (July-October 2005): 555-83.
Lisbona Guillén, Miguel. *Persecución religiosa en Chiapas (1910-1940)*. Mexico City: Universidad Nacional Autónoma de México/Programa de Investigaciones Multidisciplinarias sobre Mesoamérica y el Sureste/Instituto de Investigaciones Antropológicas, 2009.
Lomnitz, Claudio. "Bordering on Anthropology: Dialects of a National Tradition in Mexico." In *Empires, Nations, and Natives: Anthropology and State-Making*, edited by Benoît de L'Estoile, Federico Neiburg, and Lygia Sigaud. Durham, NC: Duke University Press, 2005.
López, Rick A. *Crafting Mexico: Intellectuals, Artisans, and the State after the Revolution*. Durham, NC: Duke University Press, 2010.
López Caballero, Paula. "Las políticas indigenistas y la 'fabrica' de su sujeto de intervención en la creación del primer Centro Coordinador del Instituto Nacional Indigenista." In *Nación y alteridad: Mestizos, indígenas y extranjeros en el proceso de formación nacional*, edited by Daniela Gleizer and Paula López Caballero. Mexico City: Universidad Autónoma Metropolitana Cuajimalpa/Ediciones de Educación y Cultura, 2015.
López Calixto, Pascual, with Jan Rus. "Cómo perdí a mi hermanito: Una historia oral de Chamula, ca. 1928-29." In *Anuario*. Tuxtla Gutiérrez: Universidad Autónoma de Chiapas, 2010.
López Pérez, Antonio. *Cómo defenderse del ladino*. 1985. Translated by José González Hernández and Jan Rus. San Cristóbal de Las Casas, Chis.: Ediciones Pirata, 2008.
MacEóin, Gary. *The People's Church: Bishop Samuel Ruiz of Mexico and Why He Matters*. New York: Crossroad Publishing Company, 1996.
Malinowski, Bronislaw, and Julio de la Fuente. *Malinowski in Mexico: The Economics of a Mexican Market System*. Boston: Routledge and Kegan Paul, 1982.
Mariátegui, José Carlos. *Seven Interpretive Essays on Peruvian Reality*. Austin: University of Texas Press, 1971.
Marroquín, Alejandro. "Consideraciones sobre las cooperativas organizadas por el Centro Coordinador Indigenista Tzeltal-Tzotzil." In "Problemas fundamentales del Centro Tzeltal Tzotzil," edited by Agustín Romano Delgado. Unpublished manuscript, 1955.
———. "La política indigenista en México." In *¿Ha fracasado el indigenismo? Reportaje de una controversia (13 de septiembre de 1971)*, edited by the Instituto Nacional Indigenista. Mexico City: Secretaría de Educación Pública, 1971.
Martínez, Sarelly. *La prensa maniatada: El periodismo en Chiapas de 1827 a 1958*. Mexico City: Fundación Manuel Buendía, 2004.
Mattiace, Shannan L. "From Indigenismo to Indigenous Movements in Ecuador and

Mexico." In *Highland Indians and the State in Modern Ecuador*, edited by A. Kim Clark and Marc Becker. Pittsburgh: University of Pittsburgh Press, 2007.
———. *To See with Two Eyes: Peasant Activism and Indian Autonomy in Chiapas, Mexico*. Albuquerque: University of New Mexico Press, 2003.
Medina Hernández, Andrés. "Diez años decisivos." In *La quiebra política de la antropología social en México*, vol. 1, *La impugnación*, edited by Andrés Medina Hernández and Carlos García Mora. Mexico City: Universidad Nacional Autónoma de México, 1983.
Medina Hernández, Andrés, and Carlos García Mora, eds. *La quiebra política de la antropología social en México*. Vol. 1, *La impugnación*. Mexico City: Universidad Nacional Autónoma de México, 1983.
———. *La quiebra política en la antropología social en México*. Vol. 2, *La polarización (1971–1976)*. Mexico City: Universidad Nacional Autónoma de México, 1986.
Modiano, Nancy, and Antonio Pérez Hernández. "Educación." In *El indigenismo en acción: XXV aniversario del Centro Coordinador Indigenista Tzeltal-Tzotzil, Chiapas*, edited by Gonzalo Aguirre Beltrán, Alfonso Villa Rojas, Agustín Romano Delgado, et al. Mexico City: Instituto Nacional Indigenista/Secretaría de Educación Pública, 1976.
Montes Sánchez, Fidencio. "Apertura educativa en los Altos de Chiapas." In *El indigenismo en acción: XXV aniversario del Centro Coordinador Indigenista Tzeltal-Tzotzil, Chiapas*, edited by Gonzalo Aguirre Beltrán, Alfonso Villa Rojas, Agustín Romano Delgado, et al. Mexico City: Instituto Nacional Indigenista/Secretaría de Educación Pública, 1976.
Montes Sánchez, Fidencio, Carlo Antonio Castro, et al. *Educación, lingüística y ayudas visuales del Centro Coordinador Tzeltal Tzotzil*. Serie Mimeográfica, no. 11. Mexico City: Instituto Nacional Indigenista, 1955.
Morales Bermúdez, Jesús. "El Congreso Indígena de Chiapas: Un testimonio." *Anuario Indigenista*, nos. 1–2 (1995): 305–40.
———. *Entre ásperos caminos llanos: La diócesis de San Cristóbal de Las Casas, 1950–1995*. Mexico City: Casa Juan Pablos, Universidad de Ciencias y Artes de Chiapas, Universidad Intercultural de Chiapas, Consejo de Ciencia y Tecnología del Estado de Chiapas, 2005.
Moreno-Brid, Juan Carlos, and Jaime Ros. *Development and Growth in the Mexican Economy: A Historical Perspective*. New York: Oxford University Press, 2009.
Morquecho Escamilla, Gaspar. "Expulsiones en los Altos de Chiapas." In *Movimiento campesino en Chiapas: Expulsiones, ideología y luchas por la tierra*. San Cristóbal de Las Casas, Chis.: Desarrollo Económico y Social de los Mexicanos Indígenas, 1994.
Muñoz, María L. O. *Stand Up and Fight: Participatory Indigenismo, Populism, and Mobilization in Mexico, 1970–1984*. Tucson: University of Arizona Press, 2016.
Nahmad Sittón, Salomón. "Compromiso y subjetividad en la experiencia de un

antropólogo mexicano." *Revista de Dialectología y Tradiciones Populares* 63, no. 1 (January–June 2008): 75–119.

———. "Estudio introductorio." In *Fuentes para la historia del indigenismo en México: Diarios de campo de Maurilio Muñoz en la Cuenca del Papaloapan (1957–1959)*, edited by José Martín González Solano and Margarita Sosa Suárez. Mexico City: Comisión Nacional para el Desarrollo de los Pueblos Indígenas, 2009.

———. "Una experiencia indigenista: 20 años de lucha desde investigador hasta la cárcel en defensa de los indios de México." *Anales de Antropología* 27 (1990): 269–305.

Nash, June. *In the Eyes of the Ancestors: Belief and Behavior in a Mayan Community*. New Haven, CT: Yale University Press, 1970.

———. *Mayan Visions: The Quest for Autonomy in an Age of Globalization*. New York: Routledge, 2001.

Navarrete Cáceres, Carlos. *Rosario Castellanos, su presencia en la antropología mexicana*. Mexico City: Universidad Nacional Autónoma de México/Programa de Investigaciones Multidisciplinarias sobre Mesoamérica y el Sureste, 2007.

Nolan-Ferrell, Catherine. *Constructing Citizenship: Transnational Workers and Revolution on the Mexico-Guatemala Border, 1880–1950*. Tucson: University of Arizona Press, 2012.

Nolasco Armas, Margarita. "La antropología aplicada en México y su destino final: El indigenismo." In *De eso que llaman antropología mexicana*, by Arturo Warman, Margarita Nolasco Armas, Guillermo Bonfil Batalla, Mercedes Olivera Bustamante, and Enrique Valencia. Mexico City: Editorial Nuestro Tiempo, 1970.

Núñez Tom, Agapito. "Tareas del promotor al fundarse el Centro Coordinador." In *El indigenismo en acción: XXV aniversario del Centro Coordinador Indigenista Tzeltal-Tzotzil, Chiapas*, edited by Gonzalo Aguirre Beltrán, Alfonso Villa Rojas, Agustín Romano Delgado, et al. Mexico City: Instituto Nacional Indigenista/Secretaría de Educación Pública: 1976.

Olivera Bustamante, Mercedes. "Algunos problemas de la investigación antropológica actual." In *De eso que llaman antropología mexicana*, by Arturo Warman, Margarita Nolasco Armas, Guillermo Bonfil Batalla, Mercedes Olivera Bustamante, and Enrique Valencia. Mexico City: Editorial Nuestro Tiempo, 1970.

———. "From Integrationist Indigenismo to Neoliberal De-Ethnification in Chiapas: Reminiscences." *Latin American Perspectives* 39, no. 5 (September 2012): 100–110.

———. "Una incursion en el campo indigenista: La Escuela de Desarrollo." In *Instituto Nacional Indigenista, INI, 30 años después: revisión crítica*. Mexico City: Instituto Nacional Indigenista, 1978.

Ovalle Fernández, Ignacio. "Bases programáticas de la política indigenista." In Instituto

Nacional Indigenista, *INI, 30 años después: revisión crítica*. Mexico City: Instituto Nacional Indigenista, 1978.

Palacios, Guillermo. "The Social Sciences, Revolutionary Nationalism, and Interacademic Relations: Mexico and the United States, 1930–1940." In *Populism in Twentieth-Century Mexico: The Presidencies of Lázaro Cárdenas and Luis Echeverría*, edited by Amelia M. Kiddle and María L. O. Muñoz. Tucson: University of Arizona Press, 2010.

Partridge, William L., Antoinette B. Brown, and Jeffrey B. Nugent. "The Papaloapan Dam and Resettlement Project: Human Ecology and Health Impacts." In *Involuntary Migration and Resettlement: The Problems and Responses of Dislocated People*, edited by Art Hansen and Anthony Oliver-Smith. Boulder, CO: Westview Press, 1982.

Pérez Castro, Ana Bella. "Bajo el símbolo de la ceiba: La lucha de los indígenas cafeticultores de las tierras de Simojovel." In *Chiapas: Los rumbos de otra historia*, edited by Juan Pedro Viqueira and Mario Humberto Ruz. Mexico City: Universidad Nacional Autónoma de México, 1995.

Pineda, Luz Olivia. *Caciques culturales: El caso de los maestros bilingües de los Altos de Chiapas*. Puebla: Altres Costa-Amic, 1993.

———. "Maestros bilingües, burocracia y poder político en Los Altos de Chiapas." In *Chiapas: Los rumbos de otra historia*, edited by Juan Pedro Viqueira and Mario Humberto Ruz. Mexico City: Universidad Nacional Autónoma de México, 1995.

Pitarch, Pedro. *The Jaguar and the Priest: An Ethnography of Tzeltal Souls*. Austin: University of Texas Press, 2010.

———. "The Political Uses of Maya Medicine: Civil Organization in Chiapas and the Ventriloquism Effect." *Social Analysis* 51, no. 2 (Summer 2007): 185–206.

Poniatowska, Elena. *La noche de Tlatelolco: Testimonios de historia oral*. Mexico City: Ediciones Era, 1971.

Pozas, Ricardo. *La antropología y la burocracia indigenista*. Mexico City: Editorial Tlacuilco, 1976.

———. *Chamula: Un pueblo indio en los Altos de Chiapas*. Mexico City: Instituto Nacional Indigenista, 1959.

Pozas Arciniega, Ricardo. "El indigenismo y la ayuda mutua en la comunidad indígena." In Instituto Nacional Indigenista, *INI, 30 años después: revisión crítica*. Mexico City: Instituto Nacional Indigenista, 1978.

Price, David H. *Threatening Anthropology: McCarthyism and the FBI's Surveillance of Activist Anthropologists*. Durham, NC: Duke University Press, 2004.

———. *Weaponizing Anthropology: Social Science in Service of the Militarized State*. Oakland: AK Press, 2011.

Reyes Ramos, María Eugenia. *El reparto de tierras y la política agraria en Chiapas, 1914–1988*. Mexico City: Universidad Nacional Autónoma de México, 1992.

Ríos Figueroa, Julio. *Siglo XX: Muerte y resurrección de la Iglesia Católica en Chiapas*.

Mexico City: Universidad Nacional Autónoma de México/Programa de Investigaciones Multidisciplinarias sobre Mesoamérica y el Sureste, 2002.

Rivera Farfán, Carolina, María del Carmen García Aguilar, Miguel Lisbona Guillén, Irene Sánchez Franco, and Salvador Meza Díaz. *Diversidad religiosa y conflicto en Chiapas: Intereses, utopías y realidades.* Mexico City: Universidad Nacional Autónoma de México/Centro de Investigaciones y Estudios Superiores en Antropología Social/Consejo de Ciencia y Tecnología del Estado de Chiapas, 2005.

Robles Garnica, Roberto. "Programa de salud para una zona indígena." Unpublished manuscript.

——. "Tres años en los Altos de Chiapas." *América Indígena* 37, no. 2 (April–June 1977).

Rodríguez Kuri, Ariel. "Challenges, Political Opposition, Economic Disaster, Natural Disaster and Democratization, 1968 to 2000." In *A Companion to Mexican History and Culture,* edited by William H. Beezley. Malden, MA: Wiley-Blackwell, 2011.

Romano Delgado, Agustín. *Historia evaluativa del Centro Coordinador Indigenista Tzeltal-Tzotzil.* 3 vols. Mexico City: Instituto Nacional Indigenista/Comisión Nacional para el Desarrollo de los Pueblos Indígenas, 2002–2004.

——. "Julio de la Fuente, el hombre y el antropólogo." In *Pensamiento antropológico e indigenista de Julio de la Fuente,* by Gonzalo Aguirre Beltrán et al. Mexico City: Instituto Nacional Indigenista, 1980.

——. "La política indigenista en México y la antropología aplicada." *América Indígena* 29, no. 4 (October 1969).

——, ed. "Problemas fundamentales del Centro Tzeltal Tzotzil." Unpublished manuscript, Biblioteca Juan Rulfo, 1955.

——. "Veinticinco años del Centro Coordinador Indigenista Tzeltal-Tzotzil." In *El indigenismo en acción: XXV aniversario del Centro Coordinador Indigenista Tzeltal-Tzotzil, Chiapas,* edited by Gonzalo Aguirre Beltrán, Alfonso Villa Rojas, Agustín Romano Delgado, et al. Mexico City: Instituto Nacional Indigenista/Secretaría de Educación Pública, 1976.

Rulfo, Juan. "Juan Rulfo y Fernando Benítez hablan sobre los indios." In Instituto Nacional Indigenista, *INI, 30 años después: revisión crítica.* Mexico City: Instituto Nacional Indigenista, 1978.

Rus, Jan. "Coffee and the Recolonization of Highland Chiapas, Mexico: Indian Communities and Plantation Labor, 1892–1912." In *The Global Coffee Economy in Africa, Asia, and Latin America, 1500–1989,* edited by William Gervase Clarence-Smith and Steven Topik. Cambridge: Cambridge University Press, 2003.

——. "The 'Comunidad Revolucionaria Institucional': The Subversion of Native Government in Highland Chiapas, 1936–1968." In *Everyday Forms of State Formation: Revolution and the Negotiation of Rule in Modern Mexico,* edited by Gilbert M. Joseph and Daniel Nugent. Durham, NC: Duke University Press, 1994.

———. "Local Adaptation to Global Change: The Reordering of Native Society in Highland Chiapas, Mexico, 1974–1994." *European Review of Latin American and Caribbean Studies* 58 (June 1995): 71–89.

———. "Repensar la Revolución mexicana en Chiapas: ¿Fue la Revolución el fenómeno social más trascendental para el siglo XX en Chiapas?" In *La Revolución mexicana en Chiapas un siglo después*, edited by Justus Fenner and Miguel Lisbona Guillén. Mexico City: Universidad Nacional Autónoma de México/Instituto de Investigaciones Antropológicas/Programa de Investigaciones Multidisciplinarias sobre Mesoamérica y el Sureste, 2010.

———. "Rereading Tzotzil Ethnography: Recent Scholarship from Chiapas, Mexico." In *Pluralizing Ethnography: Comparison and Representation in Maya Cultures, Histories, and Identities*, edited by John M. Watanabe and Edward F. Fischer. Santa Fe: School of American Research Press, 2004.

———. "Revoluciones contenidas: los indígenas y la lucha por Los Altos de Chiapas, 1910–1925." *Mesoamérica* 46 (2004): 57–85.

———. "The Struggle Against Indigenous Caciques in Highland Chiapas: Dissent, Religion and Exile in Chamula, 1965–1977." In *Caciquismo in Twentieth-Century Mexico*, edited by Alan Knight and Wil Pansters. London: Institute for the Study of the Americas, 2005.

———. "Whose Caste War? Indians, Ladinos, and the Chiapas 'Caste War' of 1869." In *Spaniards and Indians in Southeastern Mesoamerica: Essays on the History of Ethnic Relations*, edited by Murdo J. MacLeod and Robert Wasserstrom, 127–68. Lincoln: University of Nebraska Press, 1983,.

Rus, Jan, and George A. Collier. "A Generation of Crisis in the Central Highlands of Chiapas: The Cases of Chamula and Zinacantán, 1974–2000." In *Mayan Lives, Mayan Utopias: The Indigenous Peoples of Chiapas and the Zapatista Rebellion*, edited by Jan Rus, Rosalva Aída Hernández Castillo, and Shannan L. Mattiace. Lanham, MD: Rowman and Littlefield, 2003.

Rus, Jan, Diana Rus, and José Hernández, eds. *Abtel ta pinka/Trabajo en la finca*. San Cristóbal de Las Casas, Chis.: Instituto de Asesoría Antropológica para la Región Maya, 1986.

Rus, Jan, Rosalva Aída Hernández Castillo, and Shannan L. Mattiace, eds. *Mayan Lives, Mayan Utopias: The Indigenous Peoples of Chiapas and the Zapatista Rebellion*. Lanham, MD: Rowman and Littlefield, 2003.

Sáenz, Moisés. *México íntegro*. Lima: Imprenta Torres Aguirre, 1939.

Saldívar Tanaka, Emiko. *Prácticas cotidianas del estado: Una etnografía del indigenismo*. Mexico City: Universidad Iberoamericana/Plaza y Valdés, 2008.

Salvatierra, Reynaldo. "Realización de 'una aventura del pensamiento.'" In *El indigenismo en acción: XXV aniversario del Centro Coordinador Indigenista Tzeltal-Tzotzil, Chiapas*, edited by Gonzalo Aguirre Beltrán, Alfonso Villa Rojas,

Agustín Romano Delgado, et al. Mexico City: Instituto Nacional Indigenista/Secretaría de Educación Pública: 1976.
Sánchez Sánchez, Teodoro. *Alma del teatro Guiñol Petul: Autobiografía de Teodoro Sánchez*. Tuxtla Gutiérrez, Chis.: Talleres Gráficos del Estado, 1993.
Sariego, Juan Luis, ed. *El indigenismo en Chihuahua*. Chihuahua: Escuela Nacional de Antropología e Historia, Unidad Chihuahua, 1998.
Scanlon, Arlene Patricia, and Juan Lezama Morfín. *México pluricultural: de la castellanización a la educación indígena bilingüe y bicultural*. Mexico City: Secretaría de Educación Pública, 1982.
Secretaría de Educación Pública. *Alfonso Caso*. Mexico City: Secretaría de Educación Pública, 1975.
Secretaría de Industria y Comercio. *VIII Censo general de población, 1960: Estado de Chiapas*. Mexico City: Secretaría de Industria y Comercio, 1963.
———. *IX Censo general de población, 1970: Estado de Chiapas*. Mexico City: Secretaría de Industria y Comercio, 1971.
Sherman, Irwin W. *The Power of Plagues*. Washington, DC: ASM Press, 2006.
Siverts, Henning. *Oxchuc: Una tribu maya de México*. Mexico City: Instituto Nacional Indigenista, 1969.
Slocum, Marianna, with Grace Watkins. *The Good Seed*. Orange, CA: Promise Publishing Company, 1988.
Sna Jtz'ibajom. *¡Vámanos al paraíso!* In *Xcha'kuxesel ak'ob elav ta slumal batz'i viniketik ta Chyapa II/Renacimiento del teatro maya en Chiapas II*. Obra colectiva de Sna Jtz'ibajom. Mexico City: Imprenta Andina/Instituto Nacional Indigenista, 1996.
Sodi M., Demetrio. "Algunas ideas de Alfonso Caso." In Instituto Nacional Indigenista, *INI, 30 años después: revisión crítica*. Mexico City: Instituto Nacional Indigenista, 1978.
Souder, William. *On a Farther Shore: The Life and Legacy of Rachel Carson*. New York: Crown Publishers, 2012.
Stephen, Lynn. *¡Zapata Lives!* Berkeley: University of California Press, 2002.
Stoll, David. *Fishers of Men or Founders of Empire? The Wycliffe Bible Translators in Latin America*. London: Zed Press, 1982.
Tarica, Estelle. *The Inner Life of Mestizo Nationalism*. Minneapolis: University of Minnesota Press, 2008.
Taylor, Analisa. *Indigeneity in the Mexican Cultural Imagination: Thresholds of Belonging*. Tucson: University of Arizona Press, 2009.
Téllez Girón López, Ricardo, and Luis Vázquez León, eds. *Palerm en sus propias palabras: Las entrevistas al Dr. Ángel Palerm Vich realizadas por Marisol Alonso en 1979*. Puebla: Benemérita Universidad Autónoma de Puebla/Centro de Investigaciones y Estudios Superiores en Antropología Social, 2013.
Tello Díaz, Carlos. *Chiapas: La rebelión de las Cañadas*. Madrid: Acento Editorial, 1995.
Teófilo da Silva, Cristhian. "Indigenismo como ideología y prática de dominação:

Apontamentos teóricos para urna etnografía do indigenismolatino-americano em perspectiva comparada." *Latin American Research Review* 47, no. 1 (2012): 16–34.

Teratol, Romin, and Antzelmo Péres, with Robert Laughlin. *Travelers to the Other World: A Maya View of North America*. Albuquerque: University of New Mexico Press, 2010.

Toledo Tello, Sonia. *Historia del movimiento indígena en Simojovel, 1970–1989*. Tuxtla Gutiérrez: Universidad Autónoma de Chiapas, 1996.

Townsend, William. *Lázaro Cárdenas: Mexican Democrat*. Ann Arbor, MI: George Wahr, 1952.

Valencia, Enrique. "Colonialism o capitalismo en la situación indígena." In Instituto Nacional Indigenista, *INI, 30 años después: revisión crítica*. Mexico City: Instituto Nacional Indigenista, 1978.

Vaughan, Mary Kay. *Cultural Politics in Revolution: Teachers, Peasants, and Schools in Mexico, 1930–1940*. Tucson: University of Arizona Press, 1997.

Vázquez León, Luis. "Entrevista a Ricardo Pozas Arciniega." In *Caminos de la antropología: Entrevistas a cinco antropólogos*, edited by Jorge Durand and Luis Vázquez León. Mexico City: Consejo Nacional para la Cultura y las Artes/ Instituto Nacional Indigenista, 1990.

———. *Historia de la etnología: La antropología sociocultural mexicana*. Mexico City: Primer Círculo, 2014.

Villafuerte Solís, Daniel. "La catástrofe neoliberal en Chiapas: Pobreza, precarización laboral y migraciones." In *Viejas y nuevas migraciones forzadas en el sur de México, Centroamérica y el Caribe*, edited by Enrique Baltar Rodríguez, María da Gloria Marroni, and Daniel Villafuerte Solís. Mexico City: Universidad de Quintana Roo, 2013.

Villa Rojas, Alfonso. "Adiestramiento de personal." In *La antropología social aplicada en México: Trayectoria y antología*, edited by Juan Comas. Mexico City: Instituto Indigenista Interamericano, 1964.

———. *Etnografía tzeltal de Chiapas: Modalidades de una cosmovisión prehispánica*. Tuxtla Gutiérrez, Chis: Gobierno del Estado de Chiapas, 1990.

———. "Integración y etnocidio." In Instituto Nacional Indigenista, *INI, 30 años después: revisión crítica*. Mexico City: Instituto Nacional Indigenista, 1978.

———. Introduction to *El indigenismo en acción: XXV aniversario del Centro Coordinador Indigenista Tzeltal-Tzotzil, Chiapas*, edited by Gonzalo Aguirre Beltrán, Alfonso Villa Rojas, Agustín Romano Delgado, et al. Mexico City: Instituto Nacional Indigenista/Secretaría de Educación Pública: 1976.

Viqueira, Juan Pedro. "Las causas de una rebelión india: Chiapas, 1712." In *Chiapas: Los rumbos de otra historia*, edited by Juan Pedro Viqueira and Mario Humberto Ruz. Mexico City: Universidad Nacional Autónoma de México, 1995.

———. *Encrucijadas chiapanecas: Historia, economía, religión e identidades*. Mexico City: Tusquets Editores, 2002.

Vogt, Evon Z. *Fieldwork Among the Maya: Reflections on the Harvard Chiapas Project*. Albuquerque: University of New Mexico Press, 1994.

———. *Zinacantán: A Maya Community in the Highlands of Chiapas*. Cambridge, MA: Belknap Press of Harvard University Press, 1969.

Walker, Louise E. *Waking from the Dream: Mexico's Middle Class after 1968*. Stanford, CA: Stanford University Press, 2013.

Warman, Arturo. "Todos santos y todos difuntos." In *De eso que llaman antropología mexicana*, by Arturo Warman, Margarita Nolasco Armas, Guillermo Bonfil Batalla, Mercedes Olivera Bustamante, and Enrique Valencia. Mexico City: Editorial Nuestro Tiempo, 1970.

Warman, Arturo, Margarita Nolasco Armas, Guillermo Bonfil Batalla, Mercedes Olivera Bustamante, and Enrique Valencia. *De eso que llaman antropología mexicana*. Mexico City: Editorial Nuestro Tiempo, 1970.

Washbrook, Sarah. "El estado porfiriano en Chiapas en vísperas de la Revolución: consolidación, modernización y oposición hasta 1911." In *La Revolución mexicana en Chiapas un siglo después*, edited by Justus Fenner and Miguel Lisbona Guillén. Mexico City: Universidad Nacional Autónoma de México/Instituto de Investigaciones Antropológicas/Programa de Investigaciones Multidisciplinarias sobre Mesoamérica y el Sureste, 2010.

———. *Producing Modernity in Mexico: Labour, Race and the State in Chiapas, 1876-1914*. New York: Oxford University Press, 2012.

———. "'Una Esclavitud Simulada': Debt Peonage in the State of Chiapas, Mexico, 1876-1911." *Journal of Peasant Studies* 33, no. 3 (July 2006): 367-412.

Wasserstrom, Robert. *Class and Society in Central Chiapas*. Berkeley: University of California Press, 1983.

Wilson, Carter. "Serving Two Mistresses: María Escandón's Life with Rosario Castellanos and Trudi Blom." *Southwest Review* 96, no. 3 (2011): 414-31.

Womack, John, Jr., ed. *Rebellion in Chiapas: An Historical Reader*. New York: New Press, 1999.

Zepeda, Eraclio. "Palabras en la fiesta." In Instituto Nacional Indigenista, *INI, 30 años después: revisión crítica*. Mexico City: Instituto Nacional Indigenista, 1978.

Zolov, Eric. *Refried Elvis: The Rise of the Mexican Counterculture*. Berkeley: University of California Press, 1999.

Index

Page numbers in italic text indicate illustrations.

Abasolo, Ocosingo, 72–74, 123, 173
acaparadores, 64, 140, 240, 245, 259; definition, 26
Acción Indigenista, 8, 85, 101, 131–32, 134, 137, 150, 172, 193
acculturation, 4–6, 153; Aguirre Beltrán and, 31, 62–64, 68. *See also* assimilation
agrarian reform, 7, 24–25, 37, 41, 70, 116–17, 120, 130, 121, 203, 235, 247, 262, 266
agricultural programs (of the CCI), 42, 44, 49, 58, 61, 113, 198, 267, 269; budget woes and, 176, 181, 202–3, 115–21
aguardiente, 25, 67, 76, 83–84, 134, 139, 146, 148, 158, 217–18; definition, 92; uses of, 92–94. *See also* Aguardientes de Chiapas
Aguardientes de Chiapas, 95–112, 208
Aguirre Beltrán, Gonzalo, 11, 17, 29–31, 34, 42–43, 60, 64, 67–69, 106, 111, 126, 199, 207–8; biography, 30–31; as director of CCI, 42–43, 50, 69, 80, 98–99, 120–21; as director of INI, 233, 234, 238–39, 239, 240, 247–49; EDR and, 249–55, 269,

272–73, 275–76; traditional medicine and, 80–84
alcohol, 5, 10, 23, 39, 41, 48, 61, 67, 75, 134, 140, 207, 215; alcoholism, 38, 51, 196; monopoly, 91–112; Protestants and, 127, 217. *See also* aguardiente; Aguardientes de Chiapas
Alemán, President Miguel, 6, 12, 31, 63, 107, 243
Amatenango del Valle, 58, 78, 85, 114, 130, 168, 171, 173, 203, 213, 262
anthropology, 18, 128, 130, 230, 232; applied, 52, 132, 155, 179, 235–37, 266; Mexican, 2–6, 13, 18, 30–34, 64–65, 86–87, 93, 97–98, 128–29, 172, 179, 198, 228. *See also* critical anthropologists
antibiotics, 37, 83, 157, 165, 169, 171, 173, 242. *See also* medicine, Western
Aranda Osorio, Governor Efraín, 100, 102–3, 110–12
Aranda Osorio, Ramiro, 201
assimilation, 3, 6, 13, 31, 33, 40, 55, 58, 182–83, 228, 232–33. *See also* acculturation

baldíos, INI work with, 70, 72, 74, 86,

337

baldíos (*continued*)
121–23, 200, 248, 273. See also *terrenos baldíos*
Belisario Domínguez hamlet, in Chenalhó, 56–57, 136, *151*, 181
Beltrán, Alberto, 177, 256
Benítez, Fernando, 51, 176, 233, 235, 240–41, 278; Bishop Samuel Ruiz interview, 214–15
bilingual method (of teaching literacy), 8, 12, 31, 42, 51–52, 188, 204
boarding school (at La Cabaña), 47, 56–60, 72–73, 122, 125, 153, 181, 183–84, *184*
Bonfil Batalla, Guillermo, 228, 230–33, 249, 252, 254. See also critical anthropologists; *los magníficos*
budget crisis, 12, 115–16, 121, 130, 159, 175–89, 199, 202, 239–40

cacicazgo, 36, 206; in Chamula, 217–22, 276. See also caciquismo
caciquismo, 13, 43, 62, 205–23, 256, 263, 267, 276; definition, 10
Cancuc, 68–70, 123–24, 142, 147, 152, 206–7, 261, 270
Cárdenas, President Lázaro, 5–8, 26, 36, 124, 140, 208, 214, 228–29
cargo system, 28, 36–37, 70, 93, 95, 157, 211–12, 217, 257; definition, 21–22
cartillas, 45, 70, 182; definition, 22
cattle ranching, 202–4, 118–19, 199
Caso, Alfonso, 7–8, 10–13, 63, 71, 86, 91, 99, 103, 123, 127–30, 189, 272–75; biography, 30–31; critique of, 237–38; death of, 230–33; logging and, 193–95, 204
Castellanos, Rosario, 26, 176, 178, 198; as director of Teatro Petul, 139–47, 150–54, 163
Castellanos Cancino, Manuel, 69, 86, 98, 102, 195, 208, 213, 218–20

Castellanos Castellanos, Manuel, 41–43
caste system, 63–67
Castro, Carlo Antonio, 146, 178
Catholic Church, 19–20, 22, 37–39, 106. See also Ruiz, Bishop Samuel; Catholics; liberation theology; Misión Chamula
Catholics, 39, 71, 73, 85, 125, 152, 177, 205, 212; in Chamula, 216–220, 258, 261. See also Catholic Church
CDI (National Commission for the Development of Indigenous Peoples) 3, 92, 113
CFE (Federal Electricity Commission), 196, 199–200
Chamula, San Juan, 18, 21, 26–27, 32, 34–40, 237, 270, 276; clinic in, 80–84, 130; cooperatives in, 76–78, 115; first promoters from, 43–47, 52; land shortage in, 117–18; Literacy Centers in, 57–63; posh war in, 92–110; roads in, 68–70; Teatro Petul in, 135–38, 142–46, 149. See also caciquismo; *cacicazgo*; Misión Chamula; Tuxum
Chanal, 47, 68, 84, 173, 180, 195, 203, 208, 210, 270
Chenalhó, San Pedro, 35–40, 43–44, 47–48, 56–57, 68–69
CNC (National Campesino Confederation), 229, 235, 246, 268, 276, 278
coleto, 109, 176, 214, 245; definition, 65
Commission to Study the Problem of Alcohol in Chiapas, 91, 103–11
Congreso Indígena, 259–60, 263, 268
Constitution of 1917, 24–25, 140, 221, 257, 265
cooperatives: consumer, 47, 64, 67, 71, 75–79, 87, 98, 101, 113–15, 140, 159, 195, 208, 211, 259, 263, 265; transportation, 69, 87, 114, *211*, 262, 269
critical anthropologists, 63, 121, 199,

228–33, 249, 252. *See also* Olivera Bustamante, Mercedes
critical anthropology. *See* critical anthropologists
cultural promoters: definition, 12; training of, 39–62. *See also* caciquismo; Literacy Centers
curanderos, 155–72, 275; definition, 38. *See also* medicine, traditional

Dawson, Alexander, 5, 63, 222
DDT, 58, 75, 81–85, 140; campaign to eradicate typhus, 159–66, 172, 176
De eso que llaman antropología mexicana, 228–29, 232, 249
deforestation, 76, 196
De la Fuente, Julio, 11, 26, 60, 75, 120, 139, 144, 238–39; biography, 31–32, 32; as CCI director, 34, 38, 50, 50–54, 60; director of alcohol study, 103
democracy, 17, 246, 268; in Chamula, 217, 256–60, 276; Echeverría and, 228–29
DGAI (Department of Indigenous Affairs; state office), 102, 114, 195, 200–2, 213, 217–19, 246
Díaz Ordaz, President Gustavo, 189, 204, 227, 230, 236, 243, 267
DPI (Department of Indigenous Social Action, Culture, and Protection), 35, 39, 43–44; definition, 26–29

Echeverría, President Luis, 13, 196, 227–38, 243, 245, 249, 258, 267–68
EDR (School of Regional Development), 245, 248–55, 259, 263
education. *See* boarding school; *cartillas*; cultural promoters; *grado preparatorio*; Literacy Centers; SEP
El Corralito, 37, 39, 71–73, 123; problems at, 126–127. *See also* Slocum, Marianna

ENAH (National School of Anthropology and History), 6, 10, 266, 273
enganchadores, 25–29, 41, 61, 64, 95, 116, 200–201, 207–8, 215, 217; definition, 23. *See also enganche*
enganche, 17, 23–25, 55, 93, 114, 201; definition, 5. *See also enganchadores*
erosion, 116, 118, 191, 196
ethnocide, accusations of, 13, 168, 199, 232, 234, 242–43
EZLN (Zapatista Army of National Liberation), 1, 246, 277. *See also* Zapatistas

Fabila, Alfonso, 127
female students, 52, 54–60, 73–74, 125, 181–85, 184. *See also promotoras*

Gamio, Manuel, 4–6, 31, 64, 230, 274
Gerdel, Florence, 37–39, 85, 127, 173
Gómez Osob, Juan, 210, 218–19, 246, 258
Gómez Osob, Salvador, 36, 46, 80, 110, 115, 205, 211–12, 218, 258
González Casanova, Pablo, 233–34
grado preparatorio, 47, 123, 181–82, 186–87. *See also* bilingual method; cultural promoters; Literacy Centers
Grajales, Governor Francisco, 95, 98–99
Guiteras-Holmes, Calixta, 206

¿Ha fracasado el indigenismo? 235–37. *See also* Marroquín, Alejandro
Harvard Chiapas Project, 18–19, 33, 37, 176, 256; relationship with INI, 128–30. *See also* Vogt, Evon; Rus, Jan
health promoters, indigenous, 80, 85, 157, 170–71
Hernández López, Ramón, 60, 85
Holland, William, 68, 157–58; conclusions of, 169–73
Huachochi, Sonora (INI CCI), 31, 34, 191

Huajam Yalcuc, 142; forest ejido in, 193, 196–97; medical outpost in, 172–73, 180
Huixtán, 40, 43, 105, 166, 193, 203, 210, 212, 270; *baldíos* in, 121–22; INI clinic in, 80, *82*, 172

Ichintón, 36, 46–47, 68, 135, 211
IFCM (Federal Institute of Teacher Training), 181, 187–88
INAH (National Institute of Anthropology and History), 6, 30, 231–32, 249
Incháustegui, Carlos, 76–77, 176, 233, 252
indianismo, 276–77
indirect method (of teaching literacy), 42, 49, 51–52. *See also* bilingual method
industrialization, 8, 63–64, 67, 86, 113, 121, 175, 189, 265–66
INI Council of Directors, 7, 10–11, 50, 63, 233–34
integral development, 62–63, 120–22, 182, 231
integration, national, 3–6, 7–8, 64, 67, 75, 127, 140–42, 230–33. *See also* acculturation; assimilation

Jímenez Rodríguez, Alberto, 180, 189–90
Juárez, President Benito, 46, 74–75, 140, 142, 145
Jurado, Carlos, 177

Knight, Alan, 205, 222
Köhler, Ulrich, 166, 178–79, 182–83, 269, 274

La Independencia, Oxchuc, 122, 181, 189
La Libertad, Oxchuc, 54, *122*, 173, 181, 247–48, 273
land reform. *See* agrarian reform
Larráinzar, San Andrés: general, 21, 26, 57–58, 68–69, 100, 137, 163, 203, 210, 261, 270, 274; medicine in, 169–73
Las Casas, Bartolomé de, 17, 20–21, 215, 259
Las Margaritas (colonization of), 203–204
liberation theology, 94, 214–16. *See also* Ruiz, Bishop Samuel; Misión Chamula
Liévano, Abraham, 70
Liévano, Belisario, 208–9
Literacy Centers, 42–49, 53–57, 72, 87, 110, 181, 265–66, 275
Lobato, Rodofo, 192–93
Lomnitz, Claudio, 4–5, 228
López Castellanos, Salvador. *See* Tuxum
López Mateos, President Adolfo, 111, 189, 228, 243
los magníficos (also "siete magníficos"), 228, 232–33, 249, 252, 255. *See also* critical anthropologists

Marroquín, Alejandro: critique of INI, 204, 233–37, 272; support for cooperatives, 75–78, 114, 259; survey of highlands, 65–67, 86–87, 113, 266
Mazatecs, 10, 51, 150, 197–200, 241
medical pluralism, 12, 155–73, 259
medicine, traditional, 38, 79–86, 199, 147, 155–58, 166, 169–73, 242. *See also curanderos*
medicine, Western, 79–86, 93, 124, 147, 155–73. *See also* antibiotics; Holland, William; preventive medicine
Medina, Andrés, 232, 254
Mesbiljá, Oxchuc, 71–72, 74, 126
mestizaje, 30, 34, 64, 268
Mexican Revolution, 4–5, 8–11, 23–26, 86, 175, 222, 227–28, 265

Miguel Alemán dam, 10, 150, 197
Misión Chamula, 206, 214–23, 256–57, 260. *See also* Ruiz, Bishop Samuel; Padre Polo
mística indigenista, 8, 12, 63, 87, 113, 139, 222, 236, 266, 273
Mitontic, 44, 57, 68, 203, 210, 217, 219, 261, 270, 274
modernization: general, 1, 3, 5, 12, 18, 64, 72, 124, 128, 242; inequality and, 211, 213; Teatro Petul and, 133–154. *See also* integral development
monopoly, alcohol. *See* aguardiente; Aguardientes de Chiapas; Pedrero, Hernán; Pedrero, Moctezuma
Montero, Marco Antonio, 135–37, 151, 153, 178
Montes Ríos, Onofre, 50, 59
Montes Sánchez, Fidencio, 47–50, 50, 54, 57, 59–61; 78, 153–54, 160, 181, 183, 209, 211–12, 248, 269, 272; in Oxchuc and Ocosingo, 70–75, 114, 122
Muñoz Basilio, Maurilo, 190, 195, 204, 273; conflict in Chamula, 219–21; comuneros at Venustiano Carranza, 199–200

Nahmad Sittón, Salomón, 238, *239*, 249, 265, 272
Nash, June, 38, 121, 168–69, 171, 173, 213, 262
nationalism, 4, 7, 51–52, 74–75, 104, 108, 128, 176, 201–2. *See also* integration, national
Nolasco, Margarita, 121, 228, 231, 254, 278
Núñez Tom, Agapito, *54*, 121–23, *122*, 273

OAS (Organization of American States), 273
Ocosingo, 29, 71–73, 121–23, 126, 130, 206, 246–48, 251

Olivera Bustamante, Mercedes, 228, 230–31, 236, 270–71; as director of EDR, 249–55, 252, 272
Ordóñez, Miguel, 206–7
Oxchuc, 26, 33–40, 203, 210–12, 270; cooperative in, 114–15; Literacy Centers in, 52–54; medicine in, 157, 161, 163, 169, 173; religious division in, 85, 125–27; success in, 70–77, 114, 122, 130, 187; Teatro Petul in, 135, 145, 147, 152

Padre Polo (Father Leopoldo Hernández), 216–21
Palerm, Ángel, 30–31, 233, 249, 273
PAN (National Action Party), 258, 261
Papaloapan River Basin, 10; INI CCI at, 31, 33–34, 51, 150, 178, 197–200
participatory indigenismo, 251, 263, 268
paternalism, 6–7, 97, 221–22, 251, 259, 263, 268
patriotism. *See* nationalism
Pedrero, Hernán, 12, 70, 87, 212, 261; alcohol monopoly and, 91–112, 132, 217, 266
Pedrero, Moctezuma, 12, 87; alcohol monopoly and, 91–112
Pohló, Chenalhó, 47–49
posh war, 91–111, 208, 212. *See also* aguardiente; Aguardientes de Chiapas
Pozas, Ricardo: biography, 31–32; as CCI director, 34, 51–52, 55–56, 68, 72, 86, 100; cooperatives and, *71*, 76, 114–15; critiques INI, 188, 237–42, 269, 272
preventive medicine, 12, 81, 85–86, 141, 159–72, 273
PRI (Institutional Revolutionary Party), 30, 65–66, 175, 212, 229, 235, 257–59, 262–63, 275–76
PRODESCH (Program of Social and Economic Development of

PRODESCH (*continued*)
  Highland Chiapas), 245–47, 256–62, 267
promoters, cultural: *baldío* liberation and, 121–24; caciquismo and, 112, 115, 205–22, 255–62, 265; cooperatives and, 76–80; definition, 12; at EDR, 249–51; first generation of, 35, 37, 39–61, 69–75, 87, 100, 118; legacy of, 266–73, 275; Protestantism and, 125–27; subsequent training of, 181, *183*, 186–88. *See also* Literacy Centers
promotoras, 42, 55–59, *185*, 250–51. *See also* female students
Protestantism, 37–39, 51, 94, 214; Bishop Samuel Ruiz and, 214–15; in Chamula, 217, 260–61; in Oxchuc, 52, 71–74, 124–27. *See also* SIL; Slocum, Marianna

Redfield, Robert, 18, 31–33, 129
region of refuge, 22, 30
road construction, 10–11, 36, 46–47, 67–70, 87, 96, 109, 116, *117*, 141, 150, 204; logging and, 191–92; PRODESCH and, 247, 262
Robles Garnica, Dr. Roberto, 81–82, *82*, 85–87, 155, 158–61, 167, 170. *See also* preventive medicine
Rodríguez Ramos, Raúl, 76, 181, 193
Romano Delgado, Agustín, 10, *33*, 34, 36, 40, 44, 54, 68–69, 114, 116, 209; as CCI director, 56, 58–59, 85, 130, 261–62; conflict with Slocum, 125–26; critique of, 269; defense of INI, 233, 239–41
Ruiz, Bishop Samuel, 206, 214–16, 220, 222, 234, 256, 259
Ruiz Cortines, President Adolfo, 100, 107, 111, 243
Rulfo, Juan, 233, 241

Rus, Jan, 21, 23, 63; on caciques in Chamula, 205, 212, 217, 256, 259, 261, 275–76; on Harvard Chiapas Project, 128–30

Sáenz, Moisés, 3, 6, 51
Saldívar, Emiko, 30, 222
Salvatierra, Reynaldo, 50, 72–73, 125, 248
Sánchez Sánchez, Teodoro, 135, 138–39, 142–43, 147–51, 159, 219, 267, 272
Santiago Montes, Andrés, 135, 187
school attendance, 42, 49, 52–53, 59–60, 87, 93, 118, 123, 140, 181–82, 188
SEP (Ministry of Public Education), 5, 25, 73–74, 181–83, 235, 237, 278; before INI, 36, 40, 41–44; caciquismo and SEP teachers, 205, 209–10, 257–58; collaboration with, 186–90, 204; puppets and, 134; training INI promoters, 53, 61, 70. *See also* cultural promoters
SIL (Summer Institute of Linguistics), 37–39, 43–44, 51, 71, 124–28, 221. *See also* Slocum, Marianna
Slocum, Marianna, 37, *38*, 39, 43–44, 61–62, 70, 74, 85; clash with Romano, 124–30, 173. *See also* SIL
SSA (Ministry of Public Health), 80, 189–90
STI (Indigenous Workers' Union), 27–28, 78, 114, 200–202, 208, 217
Subcomandante Marcos (Rafael Sebastián Guillén Vicente), 277

Tax, Sol, 10, 18, 31–33, 123, 129, 132
Teatro Petul: general, 12, 57, 78, 133–54, 191, 219, 265–67, *138*, *144*, *149*, *151*; promoting health campaigns, 155, 159–68, *161*, 172; promoting schools, 188
Tenejapa, 26, 58, 61, 70, 143, 187, 191, 210, 261–62, 270, 274

terrenos baldíos, 21. See also *baldíos*
Tlatelolco massacre, 227–28, 230, 239
Tlaxiaco, Oaxaca (INI CCI), 31, 186, 241
Townsend, William, 124, 127
Tuxum (Salvador López Castellanos): as cacique, 207, 212, 217, 220, 257–58, 261; INI programs and, 115, 211; as Urbina scribe, 36, 206
typhoid eradication, 82–84, 140, 142, 165–66, 172
typhus eradication, 75, 79, 82–83, 140, 146, 155, 159–65, 171, 190

Urbina, Erasto, 26–28, 36–37, 43, 45, 61, 69–70, 81, 98, 206, 212

vaccination campaigns: for animals, 119, 140–41; for humans, 41, 69, 81–82, 84–87, 140, 142, 155, 160, 163–66, 172–73, 190, 266. *See also* preventive medicine; Teatro Petul
Valencia, Enrique, 228–29, 252. See also *los magníficos*
Velasco Suárez, Governor Manuel, 112, 254, 259; PRODESCH and, 245–46, 256–58, 262
Venustiano Carranza (municipality), 197, 200, 246, 274
Vera Mora, Antonio, 195, 202
Villa Rojas, Alfonso, 10, 64–65; biography, 32–34; budget crisis and, 130–31, 175–76; as CCI director, 114–18, 123–24, 179, 191–93, 208, 266; defense of INI, 239–42; EDR and, 249; Harvard Chiapas Project and, 128–29; and health campaigns, 164, 166, 168, 172
Viqueira, Juan Pedro, 18, 20, 202
Vogt, Evon, 18–20, 33–34, 37, 128–29, 132, 157, 169, 256. *See also* Harvard Chiapas Project

Warman, Arturo, 228, 230, 249, 252. See also *los magníficos*
water, piped, 79, 85–86, 122, 130, 140, 165, 167, 167–68, 190, 247, 266
Weathers, Dr. Ken, 44–46
witchcraft. *See* medicine, traditional

Xun (puppet), 139, 144–46, 163

Yashtinin, San Cristóbal de Las Casas, forest ejido at, 192–94, *194*, 196–97
Yochib, Oxchuc: general, 33, 37; medicine in, 80, 85, 161, 173

Zapatistas, 1–3, 94. *See also* EZLN
Zinacantán, 26, 34–37, 40, 43, 60, 68, 117, 203, 270; caciques in, 208, 212–13, 261–62; cooperative in, 114; Harvard Chiapas Project in, 18–20, 128–29; health campaigns in, 157–66; posh war in, 101–2; Teatro Petul in, 135–36, 142

www.ingramcontent.com/pod-product-compliance
Lightning Source LLC
Chambersburg PA
CBHW030519230426
43665CB00010B/688